MW01041700

WOMEN IN NEWFOUNDLAND
AND LABRADOR

weather's edge

A COMPENDIUM

WOMEN IN NEWFOUNDLAND
AND LABRADOR

weather's edge

A COMPENDIUM

Linda Cullum, Carmelita McGrath, Marilyn Porter, editors

killick press
an imprint of Creative Publishers

St. John's, Newfoundland and Labrador
2006

© 2006

Canada Council for the Arts   **Conseil des Arts du Canada**

We acknowledge the support of The Canada Council for the Arts for our publishing program.

We acknowledge the financial support of the Government of Newfoundland and Labrador through the Department of Tourism Culture and Recreation for our publishing program.

We acknowledge the financial support of the Government of Canada through the Book Publishing Industry Development Program (BPIDP) for our publishing program.

The editors gratefully acknowledge the contribution of the Cultural Economic Development Program (CEDP), Department of Tourism, Culture and Recreation, Government of Newfoundland and Labrador.

Printed on acid-free paper

Published by
KILLICK PRESS
an imprint of CREATIVE BOOK PUBLISHING
a Transcontinental associated company
P.O. Box 1815, Stn. C, St. John's, NL A1C 5P9

First Edition
Cover Design: Beth Oberholtzer
Layout: Joanne Snook-Hann

Printed in Canada by:
TRANSCONTINENTAL

Library and Archives Canada Cataloguing in Publication

Weather's edge : a compendium / Linda Cullum, Carmelita McGrath, Marilyn Porter, editors.

Includes bibliographical references.
ISBN 1-894294-95-5

1. Women--Newfoundland – Literary collections. 2. Canadian literature (English) – Newfoundland and Labrador. 3. Canadian literature (English) – Women authors. 4. Canadian literature (English) – 20th century. 5. Canadian literature (English) – 21st century. 6. Newfoundland and Labrador – Literary collections. I. Cullum, Linda K. (Linda Kathleen), 1949- II. McGrath, Carmelita III. Porter, Marilyn, 1942-

PS8255.N4W42 2005   C810'.809718   C2005-906880-9

TABLE OF CONTENTS

Woman in Newfoundland and Labrador
Weather's Edge: A Compendium

Introduction

This compendium sets out to capture the richness and diversity of women's lives in Newfoundland and Labrador. It includes contributions from short story writers, scholars, poets and community activists and policy makers as well as extracts from letters, diaries and short biographical pieces.

Ten years ago, Marilyn Porter and Carmelita McGrath, together with Barbara Neis, decided to put together a collection of writings that would, in some way, capture the growing body of work on and by women — both academic and creative — that had flourished since the second wave women's movement in the 1970s. We saw this as a useful gathering together of pieces that had appeared in widely scattered publications, but also as an important act of recognition of the richness and specificity of work focusing on women's lives in this province; the particularity of women's experience in a specific place. This volume, *Their Lives and Times: Women in Newfoundland and Labrador: A Collage* (Killick, 1995), while partial and incomplete, is still useful and still in print.

In 2004, joined by Linda Cullum, Marilyn and Carmelita decided that it was high time to prepare another volume, this time concentrating on work on and about Newfoundland and Labrador women carried out since 1995. This has proved a more difficult task, in part because of the growing number of writers and scholars who are addressing women's issues. Most of the items in this book are written by young women or new scholars. Unlike most anthologies, many of the contributions to this book are previously unpublished. Others have been published in specialised outlets or academic journals. One of the goals of this book is to present as much writing by and about women as possible to the widest audience possible.

Weather's Edge builds directly on the success of *Their Lives and Times: Women in Newfoundland and Labrador: A Collage*, responding to the demands of a new reading public and taking advantage of the innovations in thinking and writing that have taken place in the last decade. Ten years ago, women and girls searching for accounts of their own lives could find little that was relevant. Newfoundland men's lives were documented and discussed, especially in the locally produced social sciences and in the published literature, but women were largely invisible. Much has changed since then. Writers, such as Bernice Morgan, have ensured that women's history is widely known and there are few young Newfoundland and Labrador girls today who do not know something of *Random Passage* and what it says of the founding mothers of this society. Scholars now routinely integrate gender into their research and publications, and many, not just women, have found the experiences of women a rich focus for their work.

When we searched for contributions to this anthology we found a much greater variety of topics and approaches than when we worked on *Their Lives and Times*. Some writers are continuing to document women's experiences in a time of change and crisis. The cod moratorium and its effects has been a particular concern for writers of all kinds. Others are opening up new areas for our consideration. The short story writers and poets, in particular, reflect a change in tone, one that has a certain edginess in it, and a willingness to engage with difficult topics. This, in part, reflects the younger women who are now working on women's issues. It also reflects the growing maturity and confidence of the feminist movement in Newfoundland and Labrador. Women are increasingly able to voice their concerns and write about their experiences openly.

As well as poetry, short stories and academic articles, we have also included some edited extracts from "reports" (Malone, Smith, Robinson, Johns et al). We have done this because so much excellent "policy related" work sees the light of day *only* as limited circulation reports or brochures, and then disappears forever. While much of this work is topical (and consequently becomes dated) it is such an important part of feminist work in the province that we wanted to include it as another form of "feminist knowledge." We have also captured recollections of women's lives and work in the 20th century. A series of letters and diary entries provide glimpses of local women's lives throughout the century – from nursing stations in France during World War 1 to teaching and travelling on the Labrador coast in the 1930s to upper-class family life in the capital city of St. John's in the 1950s. Shorter biographical pieces explore the life and work of specific women, Agnes Cowan for one, to round out this volume.

This volume is necessarily more selective than the previous one. There is so much more to choose from: young scholars producing theses, young writers finding an increasing readership for their work, women's organisations researching issues of vital importance to women. We have tried to present as broad a selection as we could, but obviously, there are gaps. Some gaps point to places where we failed to find relevant material; others point to areas, experiences or themes that have not yet been written about or studied. In some cases we found the creative writers more courageous in addressing sensitive issues than academic writers; in others we found patient research by academics that was not matched by interest from creative writers. There are some geographical areas where we know there should be writing — we have little from the west coast of the island, nothing from Labrador West, nor from Franco-Newfoundland and nothing that documents the experience of immigrant women.

We see the exciting mix of forms and approaches as a key strength of this book. In particular, we like the way in which poems and short stories pick up the subject matter and themes made in academic articles and take them in wholly new directions, and the way in which different kinds of writing focus our gaze in a variety of ways. For this reason, among others, we decided not to organise the book by theme or section. Instead, we have developed sequences or chains of writing, each of which connects to its neighbours in different ways — some obvious and some surprising. For example, Carmelita McGrath's description of her first communion and her subsequent or consequent loss of faith "fits" in obvious ways with Willeen Keough's academic account of the diversity of women's religious beliefs and activities, and some of their forms of resistance to the dominant (patriarchal) ideology in other Catholic parts of Newfoundland. Similarly, we like the way in which Louise Belbin's recollections of her life as a "beach woman" in Grand Bank connects with Brenda Grzetic's account of women's increased entry into the harvesting sector of the inshore fishery since the moratorium. Jane Robinson has collected together facts and thinking that point up the difficulties poor women in Newfoundland and Labrador face trying to find and keep appropriate housing. MaDonna Maidment approaches the issue somewhat differently by looking at the root causes of criminality in poverty. An important part of that poverty is unsuitable housing and the inability to escape from harassment of (male) family members. Susan Rendell's powerful short story "The Way to Get Home" shows us how the issue of poverty can come alive in a fictional account.

Sometimes it is hard to tell where one "sequence" begins or ends, and this is done on purpose. Clues about alcohol and violence appear in Helen Porter's extract from "Guns and Lovers." Sexuality and knowledge about sex is explored in Annette Johns, Karen Tweedie and Kathy Watkins' report about "Adolescent Sexual Decision Making." Alcohol appears in a different and savage form in Christine Poker's searing poem, "Firewater." We can gain further understanding of the violence of alcohol from Donna Malone's conversations with young women about their experiences of alcohol and violence in downtown St. John's bars ("Bars, Booze and Sexual Violence: Young St. John's Women Speak"). While alcohol is largely (although not completely) separated from male harassment and violence in Brenda Kitchen's account of the sexist treatment of women in the military, her piece provides us with further clues about the nature and origins of male harassment and violence towards women. From there, the sequence segues into a different account of life in the military and the experience of military violence in Frances Cluett's letter, written from France in 1916.

And so on...Readers are invited to make their own connections between the pieces, being aware that different approaches and styles enrich our understanding of any of the issues addressed in this volume. In putting together this collection we have, ourselves, learned much. In particular, we have learned to respect all the different ways that women have to express and analyse their experience; we have learned to admire the resilience and creativity Newfoundland and Labrador women show in adversity; we have wondered at the sheer volume and quality of writing that women in Newfoundland and Labrador have produced. We hope our readers share our enjoyment of the contributions to this book, remembering always that there is far, far more out there than we have been able to contain within its covers.

Linda Cullum, Carmelita McGrath and Marilyn Porter

The Pitcher

Sue Sinclair

Unafraid of the dangers
of perspective, of distance,
round as a fruit, sure
of its proportions,
it confides in us its secret:
an inch tall, an inch around,
dainty lip and handle
ready to pour.

You want to hold it in your hand
because it fits, and makes you believe
in a place as small and certain
as that, like the way we remember
childhood
            through a keyhole:
our tiny mother,
tiny father, the tiny bed
in which we slept. Did we dream?
We did not. The sun rose
again and again, digging up the day.
Endlessly we began. Our cheeks were rosy.
We cried tiny tears.

The pitcher shines, the persuasive
curve of its body leads you
into recollection. So small
there's no room for doubt.
But what doubt did you have? Some things
you never quite forgot, and some
you always believed were true.

1

Scarlet Girl – A Memoir

Carmelita McGrath

I. It's you in the yard, but who's in the window?

That's what the e-mail from my brother, Jerry, says. Apparently, there is an attachment which has disappeared, or I can't open. *Do you have an old computer? Confess.* This is what he says in his next e-mail, reminding me of how I hang on to obsolete technology. He has sent it a second time in a different format but once again it is–nowhere. I'm curious. *I'll send you a copy in the mail*, he writes. And now it's here, the photograph, on the table. It's me in the yard but who's in the window? I peer past myself, in, can't make out the shadowy face divided by a sash.

Is it Jerry?

Donnie?

Uncle Mike?

Dad?

It's male for sure. For a moment I even puzzle that it might be the devil, because he did show up on the day the photograph was taken, and maybe he was hiding in the house all the time. Outside, in the brilliant light reflecting from the new patio stones, I try to remember what the devil looked like, what his distinguishing characteristics were, the ways in which he was utterly unlike those familiar male relatives.

II. May • 69

That's the date in the left-hand border of the photo. I am eight but soon, after Our Lady drops the stone in the water that will make the bay warm enough for swimming, I will be nine. I have awoken early and been permitted to eat, there still being plenty of time before 11:00 Mass to get in the required hour's fasting.

It is a special day; its special clothes are hung carefully and waiting. There is a white nylon dress with a scalloped lace overlay. It slides on. Around my neck goes a fine chain with a small blue and white enameled medal of the Blessed Virgin, for May is her month, and even on schooldays we wear blue ribbons in her honour. On my hands go thin white gloves. In them is a prayerbook ordered especially for the occasion–hard, shiny, creamy, full-colour picture on the cover, the pages edged with gilt, special. There are red and green ribbon markers to find my place, to return to a prayer if needed. Why two? I pray to not encounter a two-prayer situation. Perhaps two ribbons were so that you could compare, have a choice. Even then I am aware of contradictions; two ribbons are not a bad thing. On my legs are openwork white tights; the girl in the catalogue had worn them with go-go boots. The shoes have disappeared in the border and in time, but I know they are white patent leather with composition soles. In the photograph I am crowned–a veil of nylon, tulle and lace is pinned to my peter-pan haircut; a circlet of white organza flowers sits just back of my bangs. I am ready. My mother has borrowed a camera from someone. She says, "Come out in the yard and I'll take a snap." I stand on the salty beachrocks in front of the house. Snap. She catches also her own handmade curtains–café style, cotton, polka dots of hot pink, avocado, turquoise and gold leaping off a white ground. She captures also someone watching through the window. I cannot puzzle who. We often do not know who is watching us.

III. Her Face

In her face now I can see my own daughter and she is beautiful; therefore I must have been beautiful too. But what I remember is that I thought I was ugly. A couple of older girls at school had assured me this was true. When I drew girls, I did not draw girls like me. I drew them with uptilted button noses, wide blue eyes and mouths like rosebuds. I drew them with golden tresses down to their waists. I drew them all in vaguely medieval costumes, dresses with low necks and trumpet sleeves, dresses that flared from hip to ankle and that were adorned with waist chains of gold and piping of velvet. Sometimes I placed conical hats on their heads and suspended from them long nylon veils, though even I knew no nylon existed in the Middle Ages. I sent these girls to tournaments where they watched jousts and were too brave to swoon at the sight of blood. I did not draw girls with peter-pan haircuts; I had cried when mine had to be cut because of the lice at school. Two nights of my head soaked in kerosene and confined inside an old step-in. If anyone saw me like that I would die. After, my mother said I'd have to cut it, she said, "you wouldn't want to go through that again, now would you? And who's the one sitting in front of you, spreading the dirt?"

I wouldn't say, but she had long hair with lights in it like my princesses had, and she liked to flick her beautiful, lousy mane back over the desk where I hunched over my exercise books. But despite the damage princesses could do, I drew no girls with dark hair, dark eyes and straight noses. I did not want any of my creations to hear what I had heard, "Where did your mother get you, you little Portugee?" Years later, when I saw the one who'd said it, I was ashamed that I was so pleased at how spectacularly she'd fallen to ruin.

IV. The State of Grace

On the morning the picture was taken, I was in the state of grace. There was not one black speck on my soul. I had made First Confession and I had tried not to sin in the interim. The state of grace was essential to making First Communion, which I would do shortly after my mother's snap in front of the house.

The state of grace was to be guarded, like virginity, a thing I had barely an inkling about but found fearful. It was a thing some martyr women had died horribly for in the olden days, even before the Middle Ages. Some of them had their heads and even–their female parts–cut off, their innards hauled out. Virginity would be an awful thing to have to defend, even if you were made a saint after because you died to keep the state of grace. In the state of grace, one looked in and saw one's own spotless soul shining like a white enamel sink. The soul I imagined was somewhere in my chest cavity, protected by the rib cage and keeping company with the heart. On that May

morning in 1969, I had done, I thought, everything in the world to safeguard my soul's purity; I turned my eyes backwards and looked and saw it in there, shining, beautiful.

V. Occasion

As we walked to church, we joined a crowd going up the steep, rocky lane. Other new communicants bloomed among the crowd, the girls' veils fluttering. I'm not near as pretty as that one there, I thought, but I certainly have one of the nicest communion dresses; you wouldn't know but we were shopkeepers. I pressed the prayerbook in my hand to push such sinful thoughts aside.

The church was decorated in white and blue–white for purity, blue for Mary, the mother of all of us who I wanted to love more than my own. There was something else in the church, something that made the air shimmer, the statues in their niches blur. So many candles burning in the huge votive stand; could they be consuming all the air? I must remember to light one later for Aunt Katie Turner in case she was still in purgatory for being prone to fits of temper and for working in a supper club in America.

I sat between my parents and tried to breathe. The Mass went on and on, Father Murphy's hands trembling and fluttering like fat white birds, flitting and alighting on gilded things. So many things to pick up and put down, he was like a queen in her kitchen. The consecration bell rang and we fell to our knees. Light flashed off a brass sun. Red and blue pinpoints of light dropped from stained glass windows. Some landed on my knees, hot like sparks. My mother said, "Go on up now." I looked up and saw the priest's fat little birds beckon us to the altar rail. I walked on someone else's feet, stiff and unfamiliar as if I had drawn them on one of my medieval beauties.

This was it–the moment. Christ's body, now flat and small and white, would dissolve in my mouth and travel through my tight gullet to some mysterious place where it would unite with my white soul. The priest's immaculate hands held the moon that was Christ under my nose; it smelled like cardboard boxes. Delicately, I extended my tongue to receive, then slowly slid it back into my mouth. The host stuck, which I had heard was a sign of unconfessed sin, to the top of my mouth. Near the back. I felt the gag reflex rising.

The priest gave me a queer look, then moved on. It was taking Christ an impossibly long time to melt. Christ have mercy. Lord have mercy. Christ have mercy and melt. There, done. The line of communicants all served now, all possessed of Christ in the breastbone. There, there. A blessing was cast over us; a prayer swelled; a hymn ran like a river. And the one at the end of the line was prodded, moved, creating a chain reaction that brought us back to our seats. I managed to get to mine before the faint took over. I did not fall; I simply dissolved into the pew.

VI. Instruction Preceding First Communion–Official and Unofficial

1. If you remember a sin you did not confess, please do not take the host. To accept the Lord knowing you have a sin on your soul is a mortal sin. A fellow did it once and his tongue turned all black and rotten.

2. Under no circumstances chew the host. The Lord Our Saviour is not a stick of gum.

3. The host will be dry, but under no circumstances spit it out. This would be a rejection of Our Lord Jesus Christ. The priest will kill you.

4. Do not say, "Thank you father." The priest says, "the body of Christ." You say "amen." That's all.

5. Did I mention avoid all occasions of sin between First Confession and First Communion? Thoughts are as bad as deeds.

5

6. Don't be thinking about how nice you look in your new outfit. This is pride, and it is one of the seven deadly sins.

VII. Go in the Peace of Christ. Thanks Be to God.

This was the view from the point of escape: the long gravel descent of lane, the eye-hurting lime of new leaves on fire in Mrs. Margaret's rose hedge. A ditch with mudpies baking along its rim. Fences of bleached longers, houses too brightly stepping down to the shore where the sea undulated in an amazing blue dress covered in diamonds. Our house seemed very far away. Someone ran into me, one of the boys careening from relative to relative collecting coins. Quarters and five- and ten-cent pieces flashed in the air and descended into pockets. A crooked uncle said, "Go away, I'm beggared, I got nuttin' only coppers." My mother was saying something to me but I kept stumbling forward. Then she bent down and looked right into my face. Her rhinestones blinded me. Her red lipstick hurt. She said very gently, "You don't look right."

The relatives were lined off on the daybed in the kitchen. My aunt and uncle from St. John's; that uncle, my godfather, giving me a whole dollar for my special day. Chicken sputtered in the oven, sent out a smell that nearly knocked me off my feet. A pot of potatoes boiled on the stove, loud as a skiff going out the gut.

"What's wrong with her?"

"She's white as a sheet."

"Must be all the excitement."

"Come here, honey dear, let me feel your head."

"Oh my God, i'nt she hot."

"Let me feel."

"Sacred Heart of Jesus sure, she's on fire."

My pale yellow room was cool. I took off my special clothes and folded them on the dresser. I watched with fascination the red spots breaking out all over me. I was trying to understand something, but thoughts kept running away like friends who suddenly didn't want to play with me. I felt confused and sad. I lay on the bed in my vest and step-in and pulled the sheet up to my chin. Chill clanged against fever. I could hear voices far away as I fell in slow-motion, descended to someplace deep and dark.

"She's some sick."

"I don't know what come over her."

"Keep an eye on her is all you can do."

"Give her some aspirin."

"Should someone go for the nurse."

"No, wait, it's liable to be excitement, that's all."

"No, she's right sick. She's after catching something."

"Well, at least there's one consolation. If God took her right now, this very day, she'd go straight to heaven."

NO! GO GET THE NURSE! I was yelling but no one heard me. No one came. Please, please, I tried to call. I had to get through to them. Because something was there to take me and it wasn't God. I tried to keep my eyes closed, but he was powerful and made me look.

VIII. In the Name of the Father, the Son and the Holy Spirit, I Command Thee to Leave

My arms, the sign of the cross on my chest.

Nights when vampires leered through a crack in the curtains, the cross and the invocation, something I heard in a movie, I think, were enough to send them away. I'd close my eyes until I heard the far-off flap of their retreating wings. But this was different. Here was the King of All Vampires, the Great Deceiver, the Commander of the Legions of Hell. The King of the Damned. He looked just like he looked in my Catechism. He crossed his legs, and his sooty muscles rippled. I noticed he'd brought his own chair, a chrome one. He sat on it too near the bed. He raised a taloned hand and scratched a horn. If he leaned any closer, I'd die. I closed my eyes, but he was there too, silhouetted sootily against the red silk backs of my lids.

"Did you forget something?" he said.

"No."

"Did you forget to tell the priest something? In your Confession?"

"No."

"What about down in the weeds?" he said. "Did you tell the priest that?"

"It wasn't my fault he hauled down his pants."

"You looked though."

"I didn't, no. Anyone'd look. And anyway I ran."

"The occasions of sin are so many," he said. "How do you think you're going to avoid them all?"

He clucked his tongue as if in sadness. "Poor little thing," he said, "you'd have a better chance with me."

My mother came into the room then, clutching a bottle of aspirin and a tumbler of water. "You gotta try to get some of these in you," she said. She bent over me; her bum was stuck up right in the devil's face.

"Mom," I screamed, "what's wrong with you? Don't you see him?"

"Here," she said, "drink the water."

"Watch out!" I yelled. I was choking on the water she pressed to my lips.

The devil was looking up under her dress where the tops of her stockings met her garters.

"Behind you, look," I croaked. A sourness rose in my throat. I hurled the aspirins in a sticky foam right past my mother and onto the bedspread. She took a cold damp facecloth from her pocket and rubbed my face with it. Then she cleaned the bedspread. She laid a cool hand on my forehead.

"If you can't keep the aspirin down," she said, "you'll have to fight this off yourself."

"Good luck," the devil said.

"What's wrong with you? Aren't you listening to him?"

"Ah you poor thing," my mother went on, "you're raving, I can't pick out a single, solitary word."

"But Mom—"

"Shush-hush, sure the best thing for you now is a good sleep."

I tried to grab her, but she folded the covers over my hands. And as she turned and left, I moved my beached-fish mouth and tried to call her back.

The devil said, "She's a fine figure of a woman, your mother."

"I'm going to sleep now," I said.

"Do you ever think you're going to die in your sleep?" the devil said. "Do you ever jump up at the last moment? That's what people do. They can't help it. It's their bodies doing it. People's bodies love the world and don't want to leave it, not even for God. But every time they fall to sleep, they don't know if they'll ever wake up again. So they jump, like this." The devil did a startled jump, a pretty real-looking one. "Poor, poor humans," he said, "I can't say I envy them."

But already I felt myself letting go, and no startle called me back.

Through red visions I moved, through worlds like the backs of my eyelids. Pulsating with light, worlds with no gravity. Green oceans crashed on violet shores, shattering the rocks. Horses whinnied. Sheet lightning split a black sky and showed Calvary on the rocks over the bay. Flowers of many colours throbbed and pushed out human limbs.

I'd wake to find him still watching with an expression of great patience.

"You're not pure of heart," he said.

"You're one to talk."

"Being saucy won't help," he said. "See, that's part of the problem. You'd like to be good, but your thoughts are full of things you shouldn't be thinking, and things you shouldn't say are always on the tip of your tongue."

A tidal wave full of writhing sea monsters crashed through the bedroom door and pulled me under. I fought, rose, felt it drop me in a dry place.

"Are you ready to come with me?" the devil asked.

"I am not," I shouted at him. I was in the worst temper of my life. "I am not. I won't. You're not even real."

"Oh, I'm real."

"No you're not, you're a fake. I don't believe in you."

"Yes, you do."

"No, I don't. You don't even look real. You're a thing someone drew. You're only out of a book. I don't believe in you."

"Oh," he said, "maybe you don't. But then that presents a problem. If you don't believe in me, you can't believe in God either. Do you see that?"

"No," I said.

"See, God and me, well, we're only two faces on the same coin." He fetched a coin from somewhere and spun it in the air. "Heads *and* tails," he said. "That's the way it is. If you don't believe in me, you can't believe in God. Now, do you believe in me?"

"No," I said.

He crashed his chair to the floor so hard it was like the time I kicked the nurse over when she tried to give me a needle.

IX. Scarlet Girl

The tail end of sunset. From where I lay, I could see the last red and purple streaks in the sky. I felt weak and tired, but cooler. When I was younger, I had been terrified of those colours. I'd been unwisely taken to a sermon where a visiting Mission Father had told us what the end of the world would be like. Just like sunset. I was no longer afraid; I had been in school long enough to understand that science can explain sunsets and all kinds of other things. I loved science and the way it named everything; that spring I was learning the names of minerals and stars.

Scarlet fever. That was the name my mother gave me for the horrible illness I caught on Communion Day. I was the first of several cases and the quickest to recover. My mother said she didn't worry too much because I always caught things hard and then got better in a day. She said when I was deep in the fever and raving and shaking, I was *delirious*. I rolled the word around on my tongue, *delirious*, a nice round sound for such a mixed-up thing.

I never saw the devil again. How could I, since I'd told him I didn't believe in him and sent him packing. But whatever he was, what figment of my worst fears and deepest dreads, he was right about one thing. I was an unbeliever, still am. A born unbeliever. All through those early years, as I struggled to take in the dark mysteries of Catholicism, its insistence on blind belief and the acceptance of contradictions, a logical part of my mind was steadily rejecting it. I could not believe in original sin, no matter how hard I tried. I couldn't believe that the Jews, after all they'd suffered, wouldn't go to heaven or that poor little babies, dead before they could be baptized, would go to a lonely place called Limbo. I didn't believe that thoughts were sins, for how could we control our thoughts? I didn't believe that Confession could wipe you clean if you were bound and determined to do the same wrongs before next Saturday. But I was also afraid that it was all true, and that even by thinking those things, I was damned forever.

The girl in the photo. Fallen woman, scarlet woman, scarlet girl. How she must have felt on that morning of her First Communion. She wants to believe but she cannot. She is afraid because she cannot. Somehow, she knows it is wrong for her to kneel at those gleaming altar rails holding her secret, unspeakable sin, the sin of doubt. For years, she will feel troubled and guilty.

I look at her now and try to imagine how she could have believed herself damned. There she is in her pretty dress. The sun is shining through her veil; she can feel its warmth on her hair. It'll be a nice enough day for popsicles and hopscotch. Her eyes are squinting a little in the May morning glare. She is smiling at her mother who loves her and who is holding a camera. She is the picture of innocence.

The "Old Hag" Revisits St. Brigid: Irish-Newfoundland Women and Spirituality on the Southern Avalon[1]

Willeen Keough

THE SPIRITUAL LIFE OF ANY GROUP IS A SITE of continuous negotiation between the natural and supernatural worlds.[2] The process is enigmatic; the issues, profound; the stakes, unfathomable. Those who are chosen as mediators must, therefore, enjoy considerable authority and respect within their communities. Such was the case for Irish-Catholic women on the southern Avalon Peninsula, who served as guides to the spiritual landscape throughout the eighteenth and nineteenth centuries.

The southern Avalon prides itself on being the most Irish corner of the island of Newfoundland, yet the "planter" population (resident fishing proprietors) there in the late seventeenth century was almost exclusively English — the demographic outgrowth of a West of England — Newfoundland fishery that was almost two centuries old. An Irish element was creeping into the migration stream, however, as West Country fishing ships began stopping at southeast Irish ports for cheap salted provisions and labour en route to Newfoundland. Irish numbers swelled through the eighteenth century with the development of an Ireland-Newfoundland trade in provisions and passengers, and as a sizable Irish population established itself on the southern Avalon, it began to assimilate the English-Protestant ethnic group. By 1845, the population had become 97 percent Catholic through the processes of intermarriage, conversion, and integration (Ewer, 1796; Fleming, 1836, 91, and 1837, 39; SPG, 1773, 1801, and 1845; Newfoundland Census, 1845; and Keough, 2005).

Irish-Newfoundland women played an essential role in these processes of early community formation. Given the highly transient nature of the male fishing population, it was the increasing presence of women that made permanent settlement possible. Furthermore, numerous English-Protestant family lines, especially within the plebeian community, were absorbed into the Irish ethnic group through marriage with Irish-Catholic women. Women were also an integral part of the economic life of early communities — in subsistence production, in hospitality and nursing services, as laundresses and seamstresses, as domestic and fishing servants, and as mistresses of fishing premises. Increasingly, they became shore crews for the family production unit in the fishery, replacing hired, transient male servants as they performed the vital work of salting and drying fish. Because of their role as co-producers in family economies, these women exercised considerable autonomy in the running of their households and were often the primary managers of household resources. They also had significant influence over matters outside the home, frequently directing male decision-making from behind the scenes and often engaging in verbal and physical confrontations that were commonplace mechanisms for informal conflict resolution in the days of early settlement. Add to this the image of women smoking and drinking in public and we can see that Irish womanhood on the southern Avalon was not engulfed by the constructions of passivity, fragility, and dependence that were increasingly constricting the lives of middle-class women during the period (Keough, 2005).

In this, they were similar to their counterparts in eighteenth-century rural Ireland, where women derived considerable status from their role as co-producers in a mixed farming and domestic textile economy. Rural Irish women performed heavy agricultural work, gathered seaweed for fertilizer and food, dug peat for fuel, kept livestock, sold eggs, and distilled and sold spirits. They also worked as domestic spinners in the woollen and linen trades, often providing the family's only cash income. Women were also conspicuous in the social sphere, where they participated in sports, drank in public, and took part in faction fights, often wielding stockings filled with rocks as weapons (Clarkson, 1993; Daly, 1981; Diner, 1983; Fitzpatrick, 1987; and Nolan, 1989).

Thus, there were many similarities in women's status and authority in rural Ireland and the southern Avalon, emanating from their essential contributions to family economies. While a facade of patriarchal authority was usually maintained in both cultures, women had considerable input in family and community decision-making. L. A. Clarkson describes this family power structure in Ireland as "matriarchal management behind a patriarchal exterior" (Clarkson, 1993, 30). The oral tradition on the southern Avalon has a more homespun equivalent: "She made the cannonballs, and he fired them."[3]

Given the paucity of evidence on early Irish-Newfoundland women in written sources, oral history can reveal contours and shadings that bring their lives into sharper focus. Take, for example, the following anecdote from Cape Broyle:

In the early 1900s, the Newfoundland railway was building a branch line along the southern Avalon. Mrs. Ellen T———, a Cape Broyle woman of Irish descent, held some land along the proposed route that she hoped to sell to the company for a tidy profit. Her ownership of the property, however, was disputed by a prominent local merchant, Michael C———. Lawyers were consulted, but the quarrel would ultimately be resolved on a less formal basis. Michael had her fence posts on the property torn down under cover of darkness; Mrs. Ellen set them back up again, and every night thereafter, she personally patrolled the property to discourage any further nocturnal tampering with the boundary lines. One night, she was knocked unconscious with the butt of a gun, and rumour had it that her assailant had been hired by Michael to strong-arm Mrs. Ellen. Advantage in the dispute see-sawed back and forth until Mrs. Ellen's mother, the widow Mrs. Anne A———-, entered the fray with an ancient form of conflict resolution: she placed a curse on Michael and his entire family. Shortly thereafter, one of Michael's sons was returning home from nearby Shore's Cove when his carriage overturned; several days later, he died of his injuries. Everyone in the community knew that he had fallen victim to the widow's curse. Michael promptly withdrew his claim and Mrs. Ellen's ownership of the land was secured (ESF, 1999 [paraphrase]).

This narrative illustrates several aspects of the lives of Irish-Newfoundland women that have also been encountered in documentary evidence: women's ownership of property and willingness to defend it, even against adverse claims from more powerful community members; women's physical assertiveness in protecting personal and family interests; and women's access to both formal and informal mechanisms of settling disputes. But perhaps the most striking element of the story is the motif of the widow's curse. This is not merely a storyteller's device, but evidence of a non-Christian system of beliefs and practices in which Irish-Newfoundland women acted as guides and mediators, even into the twentieth century.

Indeed, religion — in both orthodox and informal observance — was an important source of informal female power within the Irish community of the southern Avalon, particularly before the encroachment of ultramontanism[4] and the devotional revolution of the latter nineteenth century. Women played an essential role in keeping the Irish-Catholic faith alive in the eighteenth century, when the religion suffered under a penal regime similar to that of the British Isles. Catholics in Newfoundland were not permitted to hold office, bear firearms, hold property, or run public houses. The Catholic faith operated underground until Governor John Campbell issued a Declaration of Liberty of Conscience in 1784. Shortly thereafter, several Catholic missions were established on the island, including one on the southern Avalon, but there were still very few priests to serve the growing Catholic population.

There is evidence that with the scarcity of priests, Irish-Newfoundland women performed Catholic rites and assumed other religious authority. For example, Bishop Michael Fleming complained to his superiors that before the establishment of Catholic missions, "The holy Sacrament of Matrimony, *debased* into a sort of 'civil contract,' was administered by captains of boats, by police, by magistrates, and *frequently by women.*

The Sacrament of Baptism was equally *profaned*." He also expressed his dismay that midwives had taken the authority upon themselves to dispense with Church fasts for pregnant women (Fleming, 1836). And even after the priests had arrived, midwives and other women continued to baptize babies at birth to "tide them over" — a stopgap that reduced the urgency for performing the formal church rite. Dean Cleary of Witless Bay tantalizingly wrote about an incident (circa 1830s-40s) in which the women at St. Mary's took "the sacred fire from the altar to burn a house" — perhaps a rite of exorcism of some sort (Cleary, [1850?], 28). Furthermore, the oral tradition identifies women as the spiritual overseers of Irish-Catholic households. Women, more than men, had observed the rituals and kept the faith alive before the priests came. Indeed, as one informant stated and most others implied: "If it was left to the men, sure there'd be no religion at all" (EO, 1999). All agreed that women played a greater role in transmitting the faith to following generations, for "it was women who taught children their prayers." These references suggest that women played an important custodial role in relation to Catholicism and, by extension, the identity of the ethno-religious group in the period of early settlement.

In addition, female figures were prominent in the Irish-Catholic hagiocracy of the area — harking back to the powerful position of Celtic goddesses and female druids, a status that had carried over into early Celtic Christianity. To this very day, the Virgin Mary, St. Brigid, and "good St. Anne" are a triumvirate to be reckoned with on the southern Avalon. Mary, the mother of Christ, and her own mother, Anne, patron saint of housewives, have been represented by the Catholic Church as models for self-sacrificing Catholic womanhood. Brigid (circa 455-525) was possibly a female druid before she converted to Christianity. She founded a mixed sex religious community (not unusual for the Celtic world) at Kildare and may have been ordained a priest. She is said to have had intimate relationships with both a male bishop and a female member of her religious community. When she was brought into the formal Catholic calendar of saints, however, her life story was sanitized: she was made into a model of female virtue and piety; her mixed community was transformed into an exclusively female order of nuns. Aside from this whitewashing, her adoption by the Catholic Church provides an intriguing example of formal religion's co-opting aspects of pre-Christian belief systems. The feast day of the "holy woman of Kildare" is observed on 1 February, which corresponds with *Imbolc*, the ancient Celtic feast of fertility celebrating the coming of spring, the return of light after winter's darkness, and the beginning of the lactation of the ewes. The name of the Celtic goddess of fertility was Brigid (Ellis, 1995, 27-9 and 146-50; Toulson, 1996, 73-81).

These holy women were revered by both sexes on the southern Avalon.

Men and women plaited small straw crosses and erected them over doorways on the feast of St. Brigid for protection, and Mary's capacity as a powerful intervener between Christ and man was acknowledged by the entire Irish community. But Mary, Brigid, and Anne were (and are) particularly cherished by women — not as sanitized feminine ideals, but as women who once lived worldly lives and who could therefore empathize with the experiences of other women. When asked if local women prayed especially to these three entities, one female informant declared, "Oh God, yes, sure I'm still at it" (ESX, 1999).

Women and female figures were also central in an alternative pre-Christian religious system, transferred from the home country, that operated in tandem with, and sometimes overlapped, formal Catholic practice. Today, there is a tendency to look at these ancient beliefs and practices as quaint folk traditions — grist for the mill of the modern-day tourism industry. But they formed a "very real part of the mental world of large numbers of Irish Catholics" in the eighteenth and nineteenth centuries (Connolly, 1982, 100). On the southern Avalon, women were important navigators of this mental landscape.

A belief in the occult powers of certain women was part of the ancient belief system. Some women had special healing powers — the ability to stop blood with a prayer, for example. A widow's curse, by contrast, had the power to do great harm — to wither crops or drive fish from nets, to cause bodily harm or even death. And places like Mrs. Denine's Hill, Peggy's Hollow, and the Old Woman's Pond (named for the women who had died there) had supernatural qualities that could cause horses to pull up in their tracks and grown men to lose their way.

The local Irish community also believed in supernatural beings, and women were again central, either as symbolic figures or as intermediaries in deflecting evil from loved ones. Sheelagh — in popular belief, the wife or companion of St. Patrick — was attributed with the fierce ice storms and heavy snowfalls that battered the island on or soon after her feast day of 18 March, a phenomenon known as "Sheelagh's Brush." The "bibe," the local variant of the banshee, was a female figure — an ancient crone whose wailing cry in the night was the harbinger of death. So too was the "old hag," a supernatural creature who came in the night and sat on her victim's chest, producing a choking sensation or semi-conscious state from which her "hag-rode" prey could only be wakened by calling his or her name backwards.

Women also featured prominently in fairy lore. On the southern Avalon, the natural environment was filled with traces of the "little people," and "fairy paths," "fairy caps," and "fairy pipes" proliferated in the woods and meadows just beyond the garden gate. Fairies had the power to replace babies with changelings and render all humans, young and old, senseless or "fairy-struck." Women played a vital role in protecting their families from these troublesome creatures. They made blessed bread and tucked it in infants' blankets to prevent fairies from stealing their children. They placed "fairy buns" in the pockets of loved ones moving beyond the safety of the hearth to protect them from being "fairy-led" in the woods or back-meadows. Blessed bread made on Good Friday had special protective powers — a combination of practices from formal Catholicism and the pre-Christian belief system.

This overlapping of systems was quite common in Ireland. Some customary observances maintained their original content, but acquired Catholic labels, for example, the dedication of ancient holy wells to Christian saints. Conversely, some Catholic rituals were incorporated into magical practices such as the use of relics to verify oaths, or prayers to stop blood. The Irish-Catholic laity did not see the two systems as conflicting but, rather, mutually reinforcing (Connolly, 1982, 119-20).

This convergence can also be seen in many customary practices on the southern Avalon. Women used a Christian symbol (the sign of the cross) to give protective power to "fairy buns," and they made special batches on one of the most sacred days in the Catholic calendar. When telling fortunes, the efficacy of women's predictions, particularly the identification of future spouses, was greatest on St. John's Eve and All Souls' Night, or Allhallows Eve, in the Catholic calendar — or Midsummer's Eve and the Celtic feast of *Samhain*, ancient feasts for celebrating fertility and harvest. Women also combined formal and informal systems when they anointed their homes with holy water and blessed candle wax to protect their families from danger. Holy water could be obtained from the church, but ideally, it came from a holy well — reminiscent of the ancient belief in the power of sacred and magical sites. Father Duffy's well near Salmonier provides a local example. Blessed candle wax was obtained from a priest on Candlemas Day, 2 February.

Anglican missionary Lewis Anspach wondered at the devout observance of Candlemas by Irish Catholics, who crowded their chapels "to receive a few drops from the lighted blessed candles on their hats and clothes, and a piece likewise blessed by their priest, which they carry home and preserve with the most religious care and confidence, as a protection against . . . evil spirits" (Anspach, 1819, 474). The Catholic Church promoted these blessed candles as a symbol of Christ, with the flame representing "the union of the nature of God with the nature of man" (Boase, 1961, 262). However, the Irish community on the southern Avalon associated Candlemas with Mary and a fervent belief in her power to ward off evil. Thus, when women dripped blessed candle wax at the windowsills of their homes, they sought Mary's blessing and protection, and when they dabbed the wax into their children's shoes, they said a prayer to Mary to guide their children's footsteps. According to local belief, Candlemas was the day when Mary was churched. This was an unlikely event for a Jewish woman, but the fact that a holy day for venerating Christ was revised to honour his mother instead demonstrates the awe in which Mary was held by the Irish community. Intriguing also was the linkage of Brigid to the event, even though the two women were not contemporaries. According to local informants, Brigid walked before Mary as she was on her way to be churched, with rays of light pouring from her head to distract attention away from Mary's shame.[5] This, they say, is why St. Brigid's feast day is celebrated the day before Candlemas, on 1 February, which was also the Celtic feast of *Imbolc*. Here, then, was not only an intertwining of Celtic and Catholic systems, but a conflation of time itself. This custom of contemporizing Brigid and Mary also existed in Ireland in other variations. One compelling version held that Brigid was a midwife to Mary and wet nurse to Jesus — making her a favourite of pregnant women. Note again the connotations of fertility that hark back to the goddess Brigid (Toulson, 1996). The tradition plays havoc with the historian's love of time lines, but it was a tradition, with women at its core, that helped Irish communities on both sides of the Atlantic make sense of their spiritual and natural worlds.

Another striking example of the combination of ancient practices with Catholic belief on the southern Avalon was the wake. Here, women played an essential role in the rituals associated with death. The corpse was usually laid out by a woman, or group of women, who bathed the body, then poured the water on the ashes in the fireplace — a practice that suggests spiritual as well as physical purification — before dressing the body in a habit sewn by a female relative. Throughout the process, men clustered outside, waiting for the laying out to be completed before entering the wake-house — a spatial separation that suggests that they were remote from this ritual cleansing and preparation.

As in Ireland, the wake itself was a mixed gathering at which stories and practical jokes abounded, "God be merciful" pipes[6] were at the ready, and liquor was usually in good supply. Both sexes engaged in these wake-house practices; and while modern-day observers might view them as callous or distasteful, they helped mourners cope with the loss of loved ones and to re-affirm life in the face of death. Women as well as men sat up with the corpse overnight to guard its spirit until burial. And both sexes keened at the wake-house and graveside — a ritual lamenting to mourn the departed and mark his or her transition to the afterlife. Anspach observed the practice among the Newfoundland Irish, describing it as "crying most bitterly, and very often with *dry* eyes, howling, making a variety of strange gestures and contortions expressive of the violence of their grief" (Anspach, 1819, 472-3). But while keening often struck the outside observer as primitive and strange, it was an accepted mechanism for expressing grief within the Irish community. Indeed, this characteristic wailing usually punctuated a ritual eulogizing, sometimes in rhyming form that required a fair degree of literary finesse — an aspect not recorded by Anspach, but observed in contemporary Ireland (Connolly, 1982, 157-8; Diner, 1983, 28). There, it was common for women to lead this public demonstration of grief, and the various emotions expressed in their rhythmic lament — denial, anger, bargaining, sadness, and acceptance (not necessarily in sequence) — are recognized by modern-day psycho-analysts as necessary stages of the mourning process (Bourke, 1988). It was a practice, however, that was seen as pagan and heathenish by the Catholic church in Newfoundland and Ireland, and was aggressively discouraged. By the mid-nineteenth century, keening was increasingly being represented as self-indulgent caterwauling. One male informant on the southern Avalon, when asked about the predominance of women keeners, told me, "Yes, some of them were real bawlers alright" (XT, 1999). Thus, while most of the other customary practices related to death persisted well into the twentieth century, this one did not. Its disappearance marks a more general crusade by Catholic clergy to impose middle-class standards of respectability on their Irish congregation, particularly Irish women.

Indeed, there was an increasing effort by the Catholic church to undermine the alternative belief system in both Ireland and Newfoundland. As early as the eighteenth century, higher church authorities in Ireland were trying to discourage popular supernaturalism because it provided competing mechanisms for meeting the emotional and psycho-social needs of their flock. But many in their congregation were reluctant to part with their customary practices, and church disciplinary measures, such as public denunciation and exclusion from the sacraments, were effective only in as much as the congregation was willing to reinforce them through the shunning of non-compliers. Until the people, themselves, wished to abandon the ancient system, it would persist; the clergy could only lead the people where they, the people, wanted to go (Connolly, 1982, 119-34).

The tide turned for the Catholic church in Ireland in the second half of the nineteenth century, in part because of a devotional revolution that intensified church discipline and devotional practices (Larkin, 1976). But perhaps more significant was the dramatic shift in the profile of the Irish population that occurred during the great famine, when labourers, cottiers, and smallholders — groups that had clung tenaciously to the older belief system — were decimated by death and emigration, and the small farmer class emerged as the backbone of the population, with aspirations to greater respectability that meshed with the wishes of church authorities. Once again, the priests were leading the people where they wanted to go; the composition of their flock had simply changed (Connolly, 1982).

The Irish-Catholic population in Newfoundland also experienced the impact of the devotional revolution; but it did not experience a similar

18

demographic shift. As the nineteenth century progressed into the twentieth, many Catholics within rural, plebeian culture continued their customary practices in tandem with formal religion, and women's roles in this alternative system — as symbolic figures and as interpreters of the supernatural world — continued. But this alternative female power was perceived by church authorities as competing with, not complementary to, the church's own authority in the spiritual realm. It would be discouraged as part of the church's "civilizing" mission in the area — a crusade that focused on imposing feminine ideals of domesticity and dependence on Catholic women in particular as it attempted to locate women at the spiritual core of the home.

This campaign began on the southern Avalon with the establishment of the Catholic mission at Ferryland. In 1789, the newly arrived parish priest, Father Ewer, expressed pastoral concern to his archbishop about the irregularity of women's marital arrangements in the area:

The magistrates had for custom here, to marry, divorce & remarry again different times, & this was sometimes done without their knowledge, so that there are women living here with their 4th husband each man alive & form different familys in repute. I would wish to know if these mariages are but simple contracts confirmed & disolved by law, or the sacrament of matrimony received validly by the contracting partys. If the latter it will be attended with much confusion in this place, with the ruin of many familys & I fear the total suppression of us all as acting against the government . . . (Ewer, 1789).

What Ewer was observing were frequent incidents of common-law relationships and informal marriages, separations, and divorces — part of a local marital regime that kept fairly loose reins on female sexuality and, in effect, freed many women from the repercussions of coverture[7] (Keough, 2005). Intriguingly, Ewer framed the problem primarily in terms of women's multiple partners; apparently, the men's role in these irregular arrangements was not of equal concern. With the priests, then, came a concerted effort to bring women into formalized church marriages; and as their efforts met with increasing success, the options of cohabitation and informal separation and divorce disappeared. A dichotomized construction of woman as respectable wife and mother or temptress Eve was also part of church discourse. Thus, with the priests came the practice of churching women after childbirth: a perfunctory, shady ritual — usually a few prayers mumbled at the back door of the priest's residence over a woman who had to be "purified," regardless of marital status, for the "sin" of conceiving a child. With the priests also came a more systematic shaming of unwed mothers and adulterous wives — reflecting a double sexual standard that laid the "sin" of pre- and extra-marital sexual relationships overwhelmingly at the feet of "unchaste" women. Particularly in terms of illegitimacy, single mothers were punished more harshly than fathers, suffering public humiliation, even ostracism, as they were denounced from the altar and denied (at least for a period of public penance) churching and the sacraments.

Church efforts to control "unruly" womanhood gained momentum under the stewardship of Bishop Fleming. The monitoring of female respectability was his main objective in bringing the Presentation nuns to Newfoundland from Galway in 1833. Fleming was outraged at how "the children of both sexes . . . moved together pell-mell" in the island's schools, declaring coeducation to be "dangerous" and "impeding any improvement of morals" (Fleming, 1837, 3-4). He later explained his urgency in removing female children "from under the tutelage of men" and "from the dangerous associations which ordinary school intercourse with the other sex naturally exhibited." He hoped to protect "that delicacy of feeling and refinement of sentiment which form the ornament and grace of their sex." In separate schools, the nuns could "fix ... [their] character in innocence and virtue," prepare them for motherhood and domesticity, and lead them to their destiny as moral guardians of their families. A curriculum that included knitting, netting, and needlework (the three N's of women's education) would ease the transition from work on flakes and in gardens to pursuits more properly reflecting womanly respectability. And "solidly instructed in the Divine precepts of the Gospel," they would abandon the ancient customary practices that were an alternate source of female power (Fleming, 1844, 18).

The Presentation sisters did not actually come to the southern Avalon until the 1850s. But the effort to circumscribe women's lives within the parameters of gender ideology had begun with the arrival of sanctioned Catholicism, and was articulated as early as Father Ewer's expression of concern about women's living arrangements. The endeavor intensified as the nineteenth century unfolded, and some inroads were being made by the 1830s, when then parish priest Father Timothy Browne mounted a shaming campaign against a local woman, Peggy Mountain of Ferryland, for suspected marital infidelity. Over the course of several months, he repeatedly denounced her and convinced the local community to shun her (albeit reluctantly on their part) for an alleged transgression that would have been readily tolerated in the area not many years before. Ultimately, he succeeded in hounding her out of the district (*Mountain v. Mountain*, 1834-5; Carter, 1834-5; and Keough, 2002).

Within the framework of Catholic orthodoxy, the denial of female sexuality, the celebration of selfless motherhood, and the increasing pressure on women to transform their homes into spiritual havens, removed from the outside world, were impelling women to retire into genteel domesticity and respectability. Still, church constructions of femininity met with resistance from the local Irish community because they clashed with the realities of plebeian women's lives. The continuing need for women's work in household fishing production and their continuing status and authority in family and community acted as counterweights. Because the southern Avalon remained a pre-industrial society into the twentieth century, plebeian women's status did not undergo the erosion experienced by women in rural Ireland. There, the masculinization of agricultural work and dairying, and the industrialization of cottage industries led to the devaluation of women's labour, while the collapse of the potato culture led to a depreciation of women's worth as reproducers (Daly, 1981; Diner, 1983; Fitzpatrick, 1987; and Mageean, 1997). Along the southern Avalon, women's status as essential co-producers and reproducers of family work units within the fishing economy remained intact, and they continued to wield significant influence in family and community well into the twentieth century. And within the realm of belief systems, formal and informal, the old hag and St. Brigid continued to fend off the incursions of an increasingly patriarchal church.

Archival Sources
Carter, Robert. Diary. 30 and 31 December 1834 and 1, 5, and 12 January, 14, 15, 16, 19, 20, 21, 23, and 28 March, and 6 and 9 May 1835. MG 920, Provincial Archives of Newfoundland and Labrador [PANL].

Cleary, Dean Patrick. [1850?]. "A note on church history [1784-1850]." Series 103, Archives of the Roman Catholic Archdiocese of St. John's [ARCASJ].

CO 194 Series, Governors' Annual Returns of the Fisheries and Inhabitants of Newfoundland for the 1790s and early 1800s, PANL.

Fleming, Michael A. (1836). "The State of the Catholic Religion in Newfoundland Reviewed in Two Letters by Monsignor Fleming to P. John Spratt." 103, File 26, ARCASJ.

Fleming, Michael A. (1837). Report of the Catholic Mission in Newfoundland in North America. Rome: Printing Press of the Sacred Congregation.

Fleming, Michael A. (1844). Letter on the State of Religion in Newfoundland, addressed to the Very Rev. Dr. A. O'Connell, 11 January. Dublin: James Duffy.

Mountain, Peggy, v. Michael Mountain. GN 5/4/C/1, Ferryland, Box 1, 57-60 and 64, 23, 29, and 30 December 1834 and 2, 12, and 19 January and 23 February 1835, PANL.

Society for the Preservation of the Gospel Collection [SPG]: C Series, Box 1, 56, Petition of the Inhabitants of Bay Bulls, 19 October 1773, and Box 1A/18, 180, Rev. John Dingle to Rev. Doctor Morris, 22 November 1801; E Series, Report on the Diocese of Newfoundland, Mission of Ferryland, 1845; and G Series, vol. 1, 159, Bishop Edward Feild to Rev. Ernest Hawkins, November 1845. MG 598, PANL.

Notes

[1] The author gratefully acknowledges the financial assistance of the Social Sciences and Humanities Research Council of Canada and the Institute of Social and Economic Research, Memorial University.

[2] An earlier version of this paper appeared as "The "old hag" meets St. Brigid: Irish women and the intersection of belief systems on the southern Avalon" in *An Nasc* 15 (spring, 2001): 12-25. This material also appears in *The Slender Thread: Irish Women on the Southern Avalon Peninsula of Newfoundland, 1750-1860* (New York: Columbia University Press, 2005, http://www.gutenberg-e.org).

[3] Information from the oral tradition derives primarily from interviews conducted by the author between 1999 and 2001 with twenty-one male and female informants from seven communities in the study area, supplemented by material from Johnson, 1967-8 and O'Brien, 1967-8.

[4] Ultramontansim means advocating supreme papal authority. It was a conservative, spiritual, intellectual, liturgical, and political response of the church to the threats posed by the French Revolution and the ideas of the Enlightenment.

[5] On the southern Avalon, the churching of Catholic women was not perceived as a rite of thanksgiving, as in some Protestant faiths, but a rite of purification for the "sinfulness" associated with conception.

[6] These were communal pipes, shared by men and women at the wakehouse. After a smoker drew in the smoke, he or she exhaled it with the invocation "God be merciful."

[7] The English common-law doctrine of coverture dictated that the legal personality of a married woman was subsumed in that of her husband.

Sisters, Students, Teachers: A History of the Contributions of the Presentation Congregation in Newfoundland

Melanie Martin

W E WERE ONLY A FEW HOURS ON BOARD WHEN we got sick and were obliged to our berths. We were almost insensible. Nothing was left undone which could contribute in any way to our comfort. We had the vessel all to ourselves and when we recovered a little we went on deck. On the third day we had a storm which lasted three days, and we were very sick. Then another storm, on the tenth day...the sails were torn, waves were monstrous high. You would suppose every moment was your last... (O'Shaughnessy, 1833).

The above passage was written by Sister Magdalen O'Shaughnessy, one of the original Sisters from the Presentation Congregation in Galway on the vessel *Ariel* sailing to St. John's in 1833. This organization, founded in 1775 by Nano Nagle, was the first of its kind to establish an educational institute for young women in Newfoundland. When Michael Anthony Fleming was appointed Bishop of Newfoundland in 1830, education for poor Irish Catholics, especially young women in St. John's, became an important priority. In 1833 he secured thirty-six year old Sister O'Shaughnessy, twenty-one year old Sister Xaverius Lynch, thirty-six year old Sister Mary Bernard Kirwan, and fifty-one year old Sister Mary Xavier Maloney, while visiting the convent in Galway. The Sisters came to Newfoundland, the first foreign foundation of the order outside of Ireland, with only one condition set out by their Superioress, Reverend Mother Mary John: they could be recalled after six years of service (Howley, 1888, 279). Not one of them returned to Ireland. Instead, they stayed in Newfoundland and established 34 Presentation Houses, a dozen educational institutions, and delivered education to thousands of young girls throughout Newfoundland, marking 1833 as a milestone in the education of young women.

Newfoundland, a mere fishing station for hundreds of years, was a colony dominated by males — from the fishery to the patriarchal political structure, as well as an all-male church (McCann, 1989, 180). The role of women in Newfoundland history has often been omitted. Historian Philip McCann once wrote that, "[O]nly in the education system were numbers of women able to find a means of intellectual and social advancement, though even here female teachers were to find themselves subject to the adverse affects of patriarchalism" (McCann, 1989, 185). It is under the umbrella of patriarchy that the Presentation Sisters came to Newfoundland, due to the efforts of Bishop Fleming, an ultra-montanist[1] bishop, who was highly motivated to better educate the Irish and raise their status throughout the island. The core of Fleming's educational plan included securing religious organizations already well established in Ireland to deliver their unique, but high quality religious education.

The Most Reverend M. F. Howley described Bishop Fleming's undertaking to bring the Presentation Sisters to Newfoundland as the crowning work of his episcopate (Howley, 1888, 275). The church required the Sisters' presence in Newfoundland and they complied without question. Gender ideology proposes that women are nurturing, moral, and even pious; therefore, the most logical educators for children. This was one of the most important roles the Sisters held within the Roman Catholic Church. Bishop Fleming was pleased with his accomplishment as well, because the education of young women was an issue he had laboured over for some time. He often wrote to his colleagues back in Ireland that he:

> ... felt the necessity of withdrawing female children from under the tutelage of men, from the dangerous associations which ordinary school intercourse with the other sex naturally exhibited; for whatever care could be applied to the culture of female children in mixed schools, they must lose much of that delicacy of feeling and refinement of sentiment which form the ornament and grace of their sex ... (Howley, 1888, 276).

Fleming also felt that women exercised great influence over the moral character of society by helping mould the character of their own children. He intended to offer women great opportunities to gain a useful education and proper religious instruction. They would, in turn, pass these intellectual and spiritual tools onto the next generation ensuring the growth of moral and virtuous citizens. Fleming was convinced that acceptance and equality for his Irish Catholics could only be achieved through education and by securing the Presentation Sisters he started working slowly toward that goal.

Meanwhile, long before the Presentation Sisters, Bishop Fleming corresponded on several occasions with Edmund Rice, founder of the Irish Christian Brothers, about establishing an order of Brothers in St. John's. Rice repeatedly turned Bishop Fleming's request down and cited lack of resources as the main explanation. However, in 1876, some forty years later, when the Brothers finally consented, a series of negotiations between then Bishop, Thomas Power, and the Superior General of the Irish Christian Brothers took place. The Brothers were not keen on coming to Newfoundland without a number of guarantees in place: land and building ownership, teacher salaries, as well as an understanding that they would remain autonomous from all other institutions were the three most important issues (Slattery Papers, March 2, 1872; July 28, 1875). The Presentation Sisters and the Irish Christian Brothers were two religious organizations committed to similar educational mandates, however, the Presentation Sisters chose to come to Newfoundland with no guarantees. This move provided a new opportunity for these women to not only strengthen the Catholic church's position in Newfoundland, but to establish a quality of education and foster the growth of their own order outside the confines of their homeland.

The years before the Presentation Sisters who came to Newfoundland were interesting politically and socially. The Irish Catholic population of St. John's grew rapidly during the early 1800s when the Napoleonic Wars were at their height. In 1804, six hundred and seventy Irish emigrants landed in St. John's (Prowse, 1895, 378). Rapid growth brought with it social and economic issues such as lack of adequate housing, disease, and poverty. Tensions between Irish Catholics and English Protestants were still very much present and were tied to Newfoundland's cultural, political, and socio-economic situation. Education for the poor was an important issue, which was addressed in 1806 by the Benevolent Irish Society, a philanthropic organization dedicated to establishing relief to its own countrymen and others, but Bishop Fleming had his own plans to provide a "proper" Catholic education to his congregation.

When Fleming first came to Newfoundland in 1823, as a priest, he was struck by the similarities between Newfoundland and Ireland. Executive power was largely in the hands of Protestants, as was the case in Ireland. Catholics were excluded from most government jobs, as well as from the Governor's Council, unless they took oaths that were offensive (FitzGerald, 1997, 31). Patrick O' Flaherty (1999) argued that the Irish who flooded into Newfoundland in the early 1800s retained fresh memories of the rebellion of 1798 and, after arriving, realized they had fled one colonial system only to find themselves in another (122). To complicate matters further, Newfoundland was a three-tier society in the 1800s. There was a small merchant class, largely Protestant, who controlled the economy and the credit system.[2] There was a larger group of planters who owned small boats and property, some farmers and tradesmen, and a huge class of fishers, largely Irish-Catholic, who caught and cured fish as part of a family fishery (McCann, 1994, 22). The education issue was deeply rooted in the hearts and minds of Protestants and Catholics in a society struggling not only for social stability, but also political identity. The situation became more fluid as various denominations began to stake claims in each community. Fleming pressed for social, cultural, and political gains for the Irish in Newfoundland and was convinced that education was the most important foundation to achieve these goals, but more specifically, he desired separate education for girls and boys.

The four Presentation Sisters arrived in St. John's on September 21, 1833 and just one month after their arrival, on October 21, the first Presentation School opened its doors in the New World. The school opened in an old tavern named "The Rising Sun" that Bishop Fleming had rented for the Sisters. Howley suggested the tavern name was fitting because it symbolized the light of faith and education the new institution and the Presentation Sisters diffused throughout the country (Howley, 1888, 290). On their first day, the Sisters enrolled over four hundred girls. The Protestant newspaper, *The Patriot*, observed that, "… Seldom has it been our lot to witness a scene of such deep interest, … whether we regard the community of ladies of family and fortune, surrendering all the joys of life for the advancement of the Glory of Him to whom they have consecrated their lives, or the little applicant for admission …" (Penney, 1980, 44). The tavern proved to be insufficient as a result of the large enrolment and in December 1833 the Sisters moved to a new dwelling, formerly owned by Anglican Archdeacon Wix of St. John's. The new school accommodated 1,200 girls and the area took on the name of Nunnery Hill, which it retains to the present. After one more move, the Sisters remained there until they finally settled into their new convent at the head of Long's Hill on December 14, 1843. There they taught classes in a few rooms in the basement hall while a new school was erected nearby that would accommodate at least 1600 girls (Howley, 1888, 292).

In 1842, Sister Ignatius Aloysius and Sister Antonia joined the other six and arrangements were made for the now eight Presentation Sisters in St. John's to move into Mercy Convent (Howley, 1888, 293). Unfortunately, these plans went up in flames, as did half of St. John's, during the fire of 1846 and the new convent and school were both destroyed. Bishop Fleming was about to return home from England with two more Presentation Sisters, Mother M. Josephine French of the Convent in Galway and Sister F. de Sales Lovelock, Novice Mistresses. After hearing the news of the fire, he offered to release them from their obligation, but they chose to continue (Howley, 1888, 293). In 1848, plans were devised for a new convent and school, which were completed in 1853. After Bishop Fleming's death in July 1850, the Congregation flourished under his successor, Bishop Mullock, and a second convent and school were established in 1853. In 1855, Bishop Mullock stated in his Lenten Pastoral:

As regards the education of females, you have in St. John's and the principal outports, the Convents of the Presentation Order, the best institution ever founded for the useful education of female children. Persons of every creed, who have taken the trouble to inspect these establishments, and especially the Government Inspection of the National Schools of England and Ireland, have recorded their opinion that the Presentation Schools are the most perfect in existence. The advantage of communities trained to teaching by a long course of discipline, invariably insures an excellence which individual teachers cannot attain (Mullock, 1855).

Between 1851 and 1865 ten Presentation Convents were established outside of St. John's. The first Foundation[3] was established at Harbour Grace on July 1, 1851 by four Sisters and although school age girls showed up for the first day of classes, so too did girls twenty years and older. Sunday school instruction was provided for children and adults, and girls who could not attend school during the week were taught on Sundays (Penney, 1980, 68). Three professed Sisters and three postulants[4] established the next foundation at Carbonear in June of 1852 and in 1853 foundations at both Harbour Main and Admiral's Cove, Fermeuse were established. Mother Bernard Kirwan, one of the original foundresses of the Presentation Congregation in St. John's, was appointed Mother Superior in Fermeuse and in 1876, the foundation was moved to Renews (Catholic Women's League (CWL) Pamphlet). Further foundations were established in Ferryland in 1858, St. Mary's in 1859, Witless Bay in 1860, Placentia and Torbay in 1865, and Trepassey in 1882.

The Presentation Sisters provided a rare opportunity for young women to secure a secondary education at a time when this was extremely rare, but their efforts were not solely confined to education. Newfoundland was an incredible opportunity for the Roman Catholic church to ensure the propagation of the Catholic faith. The Sisters delivered quality education, but they also stressed the importance of religion and the preservation of moral values for women regarding gender relations. By extension, women ensured the Catholic faith within the family unit that resulted in higher attendance at church services, increased financial aid for the church, and a base of volunteers to help administer church affairs within the colony. A combination of factors attributed to the Sisters' popularity including their Irish homeland roots, which appealed to the Newfoundland-born women of Irish origin struggling to define their position within a burgeoning Newfoundland society, like those scattered around the Avalon Peninsula. Many Newfoundland families hoped their own children would follow in the Sisters' footsteps and approximately five hundred women followed the vocation to serve others in religious life establishing foundations throughout the island.[5]

The Presentation Sisters were the first religious organization to establish roots in Newfoundland and changed the face of education for females of the poorer classes. The Irish Sisters, many of whom came from wealthy families, were well educated even before they entered the convent (Penney, 1980, 161). Sister Kirwan, the first Mother Superior of the Convent in St. John's, was born into an influential family. She was highly trained in business, music, needlework, and French. Sister Lynch, the younger sister of Reverend Dr. Lynch, Bishop of Kildare, was also very accomplished. She taught needlepoint, oil and watercolor painting, singing, and French (Penney, 1980, 168). This type of education established a foundation and opened up a world of opportunity in the minds of the average girl from a Newfoundland outport, who normally would not have had many different lifestyle choices. Girls in St. John's, and eventually those in the outports of Conception Bay and the Southern Shore, gained a primary, and later, a secondary education equal to that of their merchant-class counterparts who were sent abroad for schooling.

Necrology[6] statistics at the Presentation Convent reveal that approximately five hundred Presentation Sisters were active in Newfoundland after the arrival of the first four Sisters in 1833. The Presentation Archives records show that ninety of these Sisters were of Irish origin including Sister Mary Philomena O'Connell from Lixnaw, County Kerry, the last Irish postulant, who arrived in Newfoundland in 1911. Over eighty percent of the Presentation Sisters were of Newfoundland birth. In 2005, one hundred and thirty-eight of the Sisters still spread throughout the island are Newfoundland-born, while a few are from outside of the province (Necrology Statistics).

A geographical breakdown is necessary to explain the origin of the largest number of Newfoundland women who joined the Presentation Congregation and why they chose convent life. Of those still living in Presentation Houses a brief survey reveals that thirty-seven women came from communities along the Southern Shore, twenty-eight from St. John's-Torbay, and eighteen from Conception Bay. Sixteen are from St. Mary's Bay-Placentia, as well as sixteen from Grand Falls-Gander, ten from Corner Brook, seven from Stephenville, five from the community of Conche on the Northern Peninsula, one from Brent's Cove, White Bay, and one from Harbour Breton on the south coast of the island. Sister Perpetua Kennedy, archivist at the Presentation Convent in St. John's, revealed that a great majority of women who entered the congregation since its beginnings on the island were from the Southern Shore.

By the turn of the 20th century three religious congregations, originally from Ireland, were well established in the colony: the Presentation Sisters, the Irish Christian Brothers, and the Mercy Sisters. The Presentation Sisters were firmly entrenched in the communities where the Irish were concentrated on the Avalon Peninsula, particularly in the St. John's area, the southern shore, Conception Bay, as well as the Placentia-St. Mary's Bay area, where the majority of the Sisters originated. For example, Sister Kirwan established a House in Fermeuse on the Southern Shore in 1853. Thus, by the time Newfoundland women made a commitment to enter the Convent they already had long-standing ties to the Presentation Congregation. Like their mothers, and possibly grandmothers before them, they had been pupils of the Presentation Sisters from primary school onward. Vocations to Religious Life were strongly encouraged in the Catholic outports of Newfoundland. As in Ireland, it was important socially and economically to have children in the family who committed their lives to the priesthood or to the convent. This transplanted Irish Catholic view was strongly encouraged by parents and other family members who were already part of a religious foundation. Sister Perpetua recalls that as a child she became extremely excited when a Sister came to visit, "[W]e would all crowd around and hang onto her every word. She would sit so prim and proper and all you could see was the tips of her toes sticking out from underneath her habit ..." (Kennedy, June 2004). So curious and fascinating were these women that Sister Perpetua and her real sister, Sister Josephine, both joined the Congregation.

Young women who entered the Congregation were expected to complete a one-year postulancy, which included training in religious life preparation for the profession she had chosen. The white-veiled novice, the second phase, lasted two years and included training in spirituality. At the end of this phase the novice took First Vows to enter into the next phase as a Junior Professed where she went out into the mission field and took yearly vows until she was ready to take her final vows and become a Sister. This time period for the Junior Professed used to be three years, but in later years it was extended to six to nine years or until the girl was ready to take her final vows and became a Finally Professed Religious (Kennedy, March 2005).

The Presentation Sisters were encouraged to achieve a high level of education and continued education was equally important. All of the current Sisters in Newfoundland have post secondary education of some kind, many have Master's degrees and six have doctoral degrees in education, music, or guidance. Sister Perpetua explained that the Sisters engaged in teacher training left immediately after classes finished in June to attend summer school in other parts of Canada and the United States in order to upgrade their educational standing. Others were encouraged to take educational sabbaticals, and when Sisters retired from one profession they often re-trained and began another (Kennedy, June 2004). This retraining was the pattern for many Presentation Sisters in Newfoundland in 1999 when the provincial government eliminated the publicly funded denominational school system.

Historian Philip McCann once wrote that, "[B]oth ethnicity and religion must be recognized as forces powerfully influencing the direction of social policy. Nowhere is this more true than in Newfoundland in the 1830s and 1840s" (1989, 181). This was long the crux of Bishop Fleming's argument and the reasoning behind his "cradle-to-grave" educational approach that he believed would raise the status of the Irish in

29

Newfoundland. Through the first four Sisters, who remained in the colony, and the women who followed, the Catholic church was able to strengthen its position in Newfoundland while it administered to the educational needs of young Irish Catholic females from the lower classes.

Forty-three years before the Irish Christian Brothers came to our shores women dominated Catholic education and fostered its growth within the Roman Catholic church. Five hundred Newfoundland women joined the Presentation Congregation between the 1830s and the 1980s and there were several reasons. Young Newfoundland women easily identified with the Irish Sisters, who were from the same roots, beliefs, and faith as the transplanted Irish in Newfoundland. Their eagerness to join the Congregation may well have been an assertion of their Irish Catholic identity, but like the Irish Sisters who came before them, it also indicated their search for wider educational opportunities for themselves and a vocation, which satisfied their family's social and economic needs as well.

We have only just embarked into the 21st century, but Newfoundland's societal needs and wants have changed drastically since the Sisters' arrival in 1833. Opportunities are more abundant today, for all classes and genders, and the Presentation Sisters Congregation, not unlike other Religious Congregations around the world, has experienced a lack of postulants in recent years. What role the Presentation Sisters will play in the future of the Catholic church is not known, but their significant contributions in shaping education, offering lifestyle alternatives and career advancement to female Irish descendants, are milestones in the history of women in Newfoundland.

Archival Sources

The Slattery Papers, Vol. 1. Letters dated: March 2, 1872, July 28, 1875. Mount St. Francis Monastery, St. John's, Newfoundland and Labrador.

Mullock, Bishop. Lenten Pastoral, 1855. Mount St. Francis Monastery, St. John's, Newfoundland and Labrador.

O'Shaughnessy, Sister Magdalen. Letters to the Convent in Galway. Presentation Convent, St. John's, Newfoundland and Labrador.

The Presentation Sisters Archival Collection. Necrology Statistics. Presentation Convent, St. John's, Newfoundland and Labrador.

Catholic Women's League (CWL) Pamphlet. Presentation Sisters Vertical File. Centre for Newfoundland Studies, Memorial University of Newfoundland.

Notes

[1] Ultramontansim means advocating supreme papal authority and was a conservative, spiritual, intellectual, liturgical, and political response of the church to the threats posed by the French Revolution and by the ideas of the Enlightenment.

[2] The "credit system", also known as the "truck system" in Newfoundland was an autocratic system whereby fishermen purchased their fishing supplies, as well as their groceries and other items from the local merchant. The merchant, who was paid in fish at the end of the fishing season, was also the person who graded the fish and established the price the fishermen would get, which often resulted in the merchant purchasing the fish for a lot less than he sold it for in other markets. Typically, a fishermen was lucky if he was able to write off his debt from the previous year before the cycle started again, and many a poor fisherman never cleared his debt at all, and it was carried over from year to year by the merchant.

[3] Foundation refers to the Presentation Congregation's establishment of a house for its Sisters, as well as an educational institution in a community.

[4] A postulant is a candidate being considered for admission to a religious order.

[5] The Presentation Sisters established a foundation in Harbour Breton in 1872, which later moved to the community of St. Jacques. This foundation was re-established in Harbour Breton in 1970. In 1925, a foundation was established in Stephenville and in Corner Brook by 1927. Over 25 years the Corner Brook mission turned into three separate foundations with 33 Sisters and approximately 1, 500 students. Central Newfoundland established foundations in Grand Falls in 1933, Windsor in 1943, Bishop's Falls in 1945, Badger and Buchans in 1953, Gander in 1957, St. Catherine's, Grand Falls in 1965 and Brent's Cove, White Bay in 1966. Other foundations were established in Port au Port in 1950, Deer Lake in 1953, Benoit's Cove and Cape St. George in 1962, and St. Alban's and Piccadilly in 1967. In St. John's, three more Presentation Houses were established between the late 1850s and early 1960s. In 1958 the Assumption Convent opened on Bonaventure Avenue, in 1963 Mary Queen of the World Convent opened in the west end of the city and in 1964 a Presentation Convent was established on Carpasian Road. Three more foundations were established on the Avalon Peninsula: St. Vincent's and Mount Carmel, both in St. Mary's Bay in 1962 and 1967 respective, and St. Bride's on the Cape Shore in 1968. By 1975 there were 34 houses of Presentation Sisters in Newfoundland. (Kennedy, June 2004)

⁶ Necrology Statistics is a compilation of the names and dates of all the Presentation Sisters, who have passed on during their years with the foundation, compiled by the Presentation Archives and housed there.

Oderin

Agnes Walsh

I

Pushing through water
dense air constant in my face
the smell of diesel churning my stomach.
Very pleasant all this near nausea.
Soft brine to bite into
hand over hand of raw rope
the roar of voice over engine.

My cousin likes this, showing me his pasture,
taking us around the island by boat
naming every point, rock and meadow.
I curve into his rhythms of speech,
hear how when he fits two words together
it sounds so different than the words alone:
SallyFootRocks BreadBox RunaboutBeach

II

The white tablecloth billowed and spread,
exhausted and collapsed onto our table.
My hands evened the edges,
patted my fears, my fortune,
my connection to this island of dreams.

Tears and salt, guts and blood.
Nerves taut, pain ripping the night sky.
"How could she cross over from one side
of the harbour as easy as all that?
Like walking from day into night,
white into black, catholic into protestant.
Cross over and forget she left me there.
Five years old. How could she forget that?
Shipped out to old people who were childish;
they didn't know a five cents from a ten."

Her words cut the moving grass before my feet,
drive the lap of water to the door.
Can I walk anywhere without voices?
Although it is the voices I came here for.
Now they cut too near the bone,

too much inside the soundbone
thump thumping into the blood.

And that other balance upset by coming here,
kicking at sleeping dogs, turning over tired bones.
These goddamn ghosts rattling under broad daylight.
Knowing summer is short they
shake their fists both day and night.

The hot potato tossed
from one generation to the next,
burned holes in my palms, left smoulders aching.
I watched tranced by the cult of blood.

I ask strangers: Was she cruel?
They turn away. Stare across the meadow.
Fidget with pipes and bandannas.
Then, finally:
Well, girl, she had a hard life.

So, she was cruel.

III

I walk backwards through the tall grass,
the voices crowd in on me.
I trip and fall into holes
dug by those waiting for me.

Remember how we played kick the block?
How we shoved our skirts into their Yankee faces,
rubbed our eyes into their naive hearts, remember?
And all I do remember is that
she worked for officers' wives
and slept with galley slaves.

IV

I sit on the fish stage at the splitting table
intent on writing, on making a history.
Young Phonse bounced up and said: Well, that's a first.
Writing on 200 years of fish guts, blood and guts,
guts and tears. No fish no more, my girl, my own.

Into the wind the anchor flies and sounds the deep.
A lonely fish eye gleams up,
meeting dreamy me still going backwards
into sunken oaken bottoms, into islands without end.

I tell you there is not enough time
to understand all I need to know.

Before the "Fogo Project" There Was Florence O'Neill: a Glimpse of Early Adult Education and a Dedicated Advocate

Katherine McManus

T HE "FOGO PROCESS" IN NEWFOUNDLAND BECAME well-known among adult educators across Canada. When adult education practice needs an example of an exemplary project, it is common to find reference to Newfoundland's Fogo Process — or "Challenge for Change" as it was formally called (Selman and Dampier, 1991, 50). The project was a mid-1960s experiment using videotape and community development processes. Field workers put video cameras into the hands of people on Fogo Island and the people recorded their lives and community needs. The tape was used as a tool not only to record the process but also to convey the community's wishes to government bureaucrats and others. People were able to speak for themselves and be heard by government leaders and others without having to travel outside the community. This technique was soon in great demand in developing countries and it became the "gold standard" for good practice in community development and non-formal adult education.

Justifiably, Newfoundland and Canadian adult educators are proud of the process developed and recognition received from the success of the Fogo Process. These and others are generally unaware, however, of the importance of the preceding decades and how the roots of the Fogo Process were nourished by a long history of good adult education practice in Newfoundland. In fact, the beginnings of adult education and community development began in the early part of the century through the efforts of three prominent educators: Vincent Burke, Levi Curtis, and W.W. Blackall, all superintendents of schools for the religious denomination they represented. It was continued through the efforts of a few organizations, the most important of them was the Newfoundland Adult Education Association (NAEA).

The NAEA discovered a level of community interest it had not anticipated and a compelling argument was made to the government for a larger program. In 1936, through a Commission Government department of adult education, itinerant teachers were hired to travel to communities, and spend two or three months to teach and promote community values. In 1944, with her newly earned doctorate in hand, Florence O'Neill became the Director of Adult Education in Newfoundland. Over the next decade, she attempted to establish an integrated, sustaining program to reach all communities and all adults who were interested. Through her vision, dedication, and hard work she nearly succeeded. The Fogo Project is the phoenix that rose from the ashes of O'Neill's "Plan for the

Development of an Adult Education Program for Rural Newfoundland" (O'Neill, 1944).

Florence O'Neill's story begins before she became an adult educator and began without her. In the second decade of the Twentieth Century, the Carnegie Foundation of New York provided a grant of $5,000 for a traveling library put on the coastal boat service that visited a thousand-plus isolated communities along the coast (Burke, 1930; Bellows, 1975, 5). The first funding was secured through the efforts of Vincent Burke. As the years pass, Vincent Burke, the Carnegie Foundation and Florence O'Neill converge several times. Here is her story.

Florence was born in the comparatively affluent community of Witless Bay in 1905. She was one of only two children in her family. Her father, a tradesman in the construction industry, was able to provide well for his family. She received an excellent education from the nuns who taught at the convent school in the community. Her early life was one spent indoors because she suffered from rickets and, as a result, was not a robust child. She described her childhood as living in her "own private dream world: my world of fantasy enhanced by the varying enchantment of a picturesque rural seacoast community, in which Shelley, Byron, Tennyson, Wordsworth, Dickens, Jane Austen, yes and Shakespeare played a major role" (O'Neill, 1971) In many ways she was fortunate, however. She enjoyed a childhood free from hunger and cold. She lived in a large, warm house and participated in adult conversation. From these beginnings, her mind was able to think about the world outside her own community and she was encouraged to act on her dreams.

By the time O'Neill was finishing school she recalled a "compelling restlessness" and a desire to "share in some small measure in Newfoundland's development" (O'Neill, 1956). Turning her desire into action required of O'Neill a plan that could ensure a safe and acceptable means for leaving home. The common avenues women chose when they preferred a career to marriage were either teaching or nursing. O'Neill chose teaching. In an interview on CBC radio in 1956, O'Neill described her choices thus:

> I had read the thrilling story of Florence Nightingale. Could I not be a Florence Nightingale? Teaching? An opportunity to make my favourite poets come to life for other boys and girls, an opportunity to help in the molding of character, in developing the future citizens. How well was I equipped for this sacred and challenging charge? By formal training for the job? By native ability? If sincerity, love of my fellow man, determination, definite ideas as to the 'know how' of teaching gained from my experience as a pupil, belief in the democratic process mean anything, I was generously endowed. (O'Neill, 1956)

O'Neill's sense of passionate connection with the world "out there" and her desire to be in it propelled her toward teaching. Compelled as she was by her desire to mold the lives of boys and girls, she accepted her first teaching position on Oderin Island.

Oderin Island, located in Placentia Bay, no longer exists as a community, but in 1923, Oderin Island was a somewhat prosperous fishing community. O'Neill was hired to teach in an all-grade school and received twenty-three dollars a month for her work. Twenty dollars of her salary was paid by the school board; the other three dollars each month was paid by the parents who sent their children to school (Quinton, 1962, 9). She traveled by boat to the small community on the very small island in the Bay. There she was confronted by children of all ages, many whom towered over the tiny framed O'Neill. The children had not had a teacher every year because it was hard to find anyone to come to the isolated a community. On Oderin, O'Neill learned her first lessons about the world outside Witless Bay. She recalls of this teaching experience that she was "terrified" of the children — some of whom "carried guns to school in the morning" because they had been hunting (O'Neill, 1971). She was also completely alone. Her contact with family and friends was completely severed during the two years on Oderin.

O'Neill decided that she needed more education herself during her first two years of teaching. She left Oderin to attend Memorial University College. The College had opened only one year earlier and it was the only post-secondary institution available to her. With her entry into the College, she began what was to be a long relationship with higher education, alternated with periods of work. Her enjoyment of her first college courses and her respect for the person who taught most of those courses shaped her life. O'Neill recalled that upon entering the College she "came under the influence of Dr. Paton" who she said was the "first great man — the only great man I've ever met" and one who had a "tremendous influence" on her life (O'Neill, 1971).

O'Neill attended Memorial College for one year, then taught again for two years, and, in 1929, returned again to the College for another year. Her next two years of teaching were spent on Bell Island at the Lance Cove school. Bell Island was a fairly prosperous island in Conception Bay. When O'Neill was there the Dominion Oil and Steel Company (DOSCO) employed thousands of men to work in underground mines that stretched far under the ocean floor. A committee organized by the mine management approached both the Church of England day-school teacher, Elizabeth Northover, and O'Neill, who was Roman Catholic, asking them to teach the miners so that they would "at least be able to read and write." Both women agreed to teach. O'Neill recalled that she felt very brave, but that she also wondered why the men came to school. She had forty students who came to her classes to learn the basics after they had spent an entire day in the mines. The experience had a lasting effect on O'Neill. She was moved by the life these men led and by their desire to learn. She was shocked to find that "they often came to class a little inebriated; they liked beer," but after one experience of seeing the men in their environment: "[W]hen I went down in the mine and saw them slaving with water pouring off their bodies . . . covered with ore, I understood." She said they "hadn't seen the day, the light of day for hours and hours, from early dawn to dark, but they came to night school." She recalled from her experience at night school that she "learned a lot about people," and she found the need for adult education was "pretty terrific" (O'Neill, 1971). While O'Neill's experience with the miners gave her a first taste of adult education, Newfoundland had already taken several giant steps toward introducing adult education opportunities for the individual and creating a structure to sustain programs at the community level.

I digress

In St. John's several organizations developed, just as they had in nearly every "colonial" outpost, to support "working men." Organizations such as the Mechanics' Institutes and the Llewelyn Club had existed from around the turn of the twentieth century and they offered to members a place to converse and read. It was not organized adult education but these organizations offered to individuals an opportunity to improve knowledge.

In 1909, a group of women, usually described as part of the St. John's "elite," formed an organization they called the Ladies Reading Room. They rented "a large and airy room" on Water Street in order to offer to women a place where between "intervals of shopping or business," they could find refuge to chat or read. The room held English and American newspapers and magazines and contained other books and materials to inform members regarding women's voting rights in other countries. The ladies in the Reading Room were suffragists and many were also members of the Temperance Union. It functioned as a "self-taught liberal arts college" in the sense that members were encouraged to speak, give presentations and papers, discuss issues, and develop analytical skills. Membership in the organization quickly grew to one hundred and twenty-five (Duley, 1993, 41).

Women continued to develop more organizations over the next years; the Women's Patriotic Association (1912), the Newfoundland Outport Nursing Industrial Association (NONIA) (1924), and the Jubilee Guilds (1934) were all formed in order to "improve" the lives of the members, or the community, or both. Often the "improvement" organizers sought was purely economic, but an emphasis on nutrition and health and education was also found in the goals of many of these groups.

Another education project of the Carnegie Foundation and Vincent Burke (along with L. Curtis and W.W. Blackall) was in 1931 (Burke, 1937, 287). This project sent five women to Clemson College in North Carolina to learn methods and strategies for teaching adults (Blackall, 1932, 11). Elizabeth Northover, O'Neill's protestant partner while teaching the miners, was one of the women who went to Clemson College.

The years from 1929 to 1932 were challenging ones in Newfoundland. By 1932, England had taken control of Newfoundland's finances and with that change also came a loss of the democratic process. During this upheaval, O'Neill continued her path and simply went back to school. From 1929 to 1930 she studied English, Latin, German, history and biology from her favourite teacher, Paton, and others at Memorial University College.

O'Neill Continues Her Path

At the end of the 1930 academic year, O'Neill spent the summer at her family home in Witless Bay. She then travelled to St. Mary's Bay to teach at the Mt. Carmel school near Salmonier. O'Neill's experiences as a teacher of children were usually not wholly positive. Children felt driven by O'Neill's intensity and her demands on them. She may have remembered being afraid of children, but it was likely that they were equally afraid of her. Former students recalled that she could be both a "slave driver" and the best teacher they had. She was familiar with corporal punishment as a tool to control children as it had been used freely when she was a student. She had no other model to follow and so used "strapping" as a method to get students' attention.[1] O'Neill taught from 1930 to 1932, and again returned to her own education, attending Dalhousie University in Halifax.

For Newfoundlanders who were determined to complete a degree, Dalhousie was usually the next step. Memorial University College was a two-year junior college and its founders created agreements with several other universities: Dalhousie University, the University of Toronto, and McGill University (Bellows, 1975, 5). For most Newfoundland students, travelling to Halifax was as much of an adventure as they could imagine. Few students contemplated travelling even further — to Montreal or Toronto. Paton, Memorial's Principal, wanted to facilitate the success of his students who chose to continue to a degree. In order to assist them as much as he could, he ensured that Memorial's standards of academic excellence matched those of Dalhousie. One shock the students would not have would be one induced by academic differences (Macleod, 1990, 58).

For O'Neill, entrance into a "mainland" university was a tremendous step. While O'Neill's courses at Memorial prepared her to continue as an "Arts" student, O'Neill's island life isolated her from the larger world.

She may have dreamed about seeing the world, but the reality of leaving the island was something else entirely. Crossing the Gulf of St. Lawrence was not only a journey from one location to another, it was a cultural leap as well. Life in Halifax would have introduced to her an entirely different social, cultural, and political environment and must have had profound effects on her ideas about the possibilities for her own future.

O'Neill returned to Newfoundland in 1933 and, for the last time she taught children. She accepted a position as an elementary school teacher in a school that was newly opened on the Blackhead Road just outside of St. John's. The new school was isolated from St. John's by poor roads and steep terrain. The community that grew up around the Road was largely comprised of "squatters" — poor people without permanent employment. They were victims of the terribly hard economic times. Most of the people lived on the "dole". Many of the families depended upon the woman's wages because the job of "charlady" to the wealthy families was one of the few sources of paid employment (Forestell, 1995, 76).

O'Neill's experience as a teacher in the Blackhead school was one of her worst as a teacher. Travelling to the school each day was in itself a challenge. She remembered having to take the streetcar to the end of the line, where today Water Street meets Waterford Bridge Road, and from the bottom of "this terrible hill" she walked up to the top following a "little cow path" to a community where "all the houses were made of tarpaper." The families, O'Neill remembered, had more than a few problems as well: "the fathers and mothers didn't always get along so well, so we had problems; the children were hungry and poor" (O'Neill, 1971). On the first day of school, after Mass had been celebrated, O'Neill recalled that the priest turned to her and said: "I'd sooner that you stay here than that I should" and then he left. O'Neill faced her class of "forty, fifty youngsters" whom mothers had pushed inside the door. Her reaction was again one of terror: "I was scared of them all" (O'Neill, 1971).

The Blackhead School was O'Neill's first encounter with the kind of extreme poverty that was abundant in the many isolated communities around the island of Newfoundland. Before this experience O'Neill found teaching positions in places that were wealthy enough to have a teacher. Oderin had been quite isolated, but fishing was good in Placentia Bay where it was located. In St. Mary's Bay communities, the residents may not have had luxuries, but they had food to eat and a substantial house that was warm and dry in the winter. Bell Island enjoyed equal prosperity because of the mine. In short, O'Neill's experience at Blackhead Road was different from any previous experience. It caused her to reconsider her future:

I wanted to know what made people tick. I knew about the outports,

41

and rural communities, I knew what made people tick there, but I didn't know what made people tick on Gower Street, let's say in the slums, and . . . this thinking was prompted, probably, from my experience on the hill, where I knew there was so much to be done. And that was at first a very, I don't know, very different experience (O'Neill, 1971).

After three months teaching on Blackhead Road, O'Neill collapsed from exhaustion. She made a habit while teaching there of sharing her lunches with the children and that, together with the long trek up the "terrible hill" each day from January to March, finally stopped her in her tracks. At this point she decided that it was "about time that I knew what I wanted to do with myself, permanently, careerwise" (O'Neill, 1971).

O'Neill returned to Dalhousie to finish her undergraduate degree, and in 1936, she returned to Newfoundland. There was new opportunity on the island. The NAEA, supported by funding from the Carnegie Foundation, and the Commission Government, Department of Adult Education, under the directorship of Vincent Burke, joined forces to offer an island-wide adult education program to any community that requested it. The Department of Adult Education was looking for teachers for this effort, and O'Neill was hired. She recalled that "the demand for the services of itinerant teachers became so great that they, in any one year, couldn't fill one quarter, so they increased the staff up to maybe ten, twelve, fifteen" (O'Neill, 1971). As an itinerant teacher, she was sent to communities all over the island. Each teacher spent approximately three months in a community and then moved on. Their role was to contact all of the adults, discover their needs in education or education related activities. For instance, teachers would help community members with literacy and numeracy skills by helping them to be better farmers, seamstresses, or better able to calculate amounts of credit they should receive in exchange for fish caught. O'Neill found this work deeply satisfying. She didn't seem to have the problems she experienced teaching children and she found adults eager to learn. As well, she believed that in order to raise educated children, she needed to develop educated parents so they could pass their interest in learning to their children.

O'Neill knew that she had not been trained to do this kind of work, but felt that she and the other teachers were "fine people, dedicated people, with experience in homemaking in their own lives as well as common sense" (O'Neill, 1971). From 1936 to 1939, O'Neill worked as an itinerant teacher, visiting communities on the Great Northern Peninsula, Port-au-Port Peninsula, Twillingate area, Conception Bay and others.

A Woman With a "Plan"

By 1939, O'Neill was ready to return to school. This time she entered

Columbia University in New York City. She entered first for a summer school term where she met several people with whom she continued to correspond so that when she returned to Columbia as a full-time student in 1942, she had a fully developed goal. For O'Neill to decide to go to Columbia was a step of immense magnitude. She may be the first woman from an outport community to earn a doctoral degree. O'Neill seemed unaware of the unusual step she was taking; instead, she seemed to be eyeing her goal. She intended to finish with a doctorate degree.

She arrived at Columbia at a good time. The adult education program was in development and she was fortunate to be able to take courses from those who shaped the field in the United States. Included among her teachers was E. L. Thorndike who pioneered work in understanding the psychology of adult learning. She also took courses from Lyman Bryson and Edmund de Salles Brunner, both of whom contributed to research that led the world to understand community function and dysfunction in farm and rural communities. During her last year, she settled on her own thesis topic: "A Plan for the Development of an Adult Education Program for Rural Newfoundland" (O'Neill, 1944). The "Plan" proposes an integrated program for distributing adult education throughout Newfoundland. She includes methods for training teachers, developing materials, and integrating services. Her focus is the coordination of the overlapping services already available and the integration of those services with new services that would be needed in order to replace the ad hoc system that had developed over time. Among O'Neill's objectives were:

1) development of citizenship and democracy, 2) improvement of educational and health standards, and 3) general improvement of life, i.e., "by awakening active interest in making homes more attractive, comfortable, convenient, knowing that better homes have a tremendous effect on the physical and mental health of the family" (O'Neill, 1944, 57).

Her expressed purpose in developing her plan was to develop an organization and administration system that could be distributed throughout Newfoundland. She wanted to develop a "functional relationship" between the government departments of adult education, public health, rural reconstruction, and fisheries. In addition, she planned to include the women's associations that had a strong network of education and self-help operating island-wide. She envisioned that all would work together to bring communities together and provide a basic level of education to those adults interested in learning (O'Neill, 1944, 58).

Her "Plan" was organized around the idea that both a man and a woman would be sent to each community as field workers, to assess and then respond to the needs of that community.[2] The responsibilities of each worker were assigned according to gender. Female field workers assumed responsibilities for domestic development such as cooking lessons, nutrition classes, child-care education. Male field workers were responsible for "boys junior and youth clubs," as well as the development of agriculture committees and the establishment of a cooperative for fishers.

O'Neill described the way in which a female field worker might approach her community once she got to know them:

> As an adult educator she is more concerned with what actually happens to people — she realizes the importance of individual and community-wide participation, she knows that programs must be built around the needs of the community (O'Neill, 1944, 77).

The roles of male and female workers followed the assumed gendered division of labour that was predominant at the time. O'Neill never protested that such division might be unfair or unnecessary, she seemed willing to follow tradition when it came to the predominant notions about men and women's differences.

One of the more troublesome elements of the itinerant teacher system was the constant and routine rotation of teachers. O'Neill in one of her more memorable postings requested to be allowed to stay in a community one month longer than the customary two months. She was granted this extension, but she also knew that one extra month was not enough. While she worked for the department as an itinerant teacher she was frustrated by her inability to be in a community long enough to ensure that steps the members in the community had taken toward their own betterment would last. She knew that when a teacher was placed for a mere two or three months in one place, much depended on the strength of the community members to propel themselves forward in order to finish the work that had only just begun.

In O'Neill's "Plan" she addressed the problem by developing within her system a continuing connection to help when it was needed. Rather than sending one worker to a community, she suggested that a man and woman would be sent to a region as coordinators and they would have an area within which they would work. Their work would be continual and coordinated, delivering courses, workshops, and other help as communities identified their needs.

O'Neill conceived her "Plan" in order to reverse the terrible effects of educational and economic poverty in her country. She believed Newfoundland's history could be viewed as government and education in perpetual crisis: she wrote "[g]overnment policies were not always constructive" and that there had "never been equality of educational opportunity" (O'Neill, 1944, 20, 24). But, she also felt great hope, in 1943, that these problems were the past and a bright new future was possible. She wrote that the Commission Government, which had been in place from 1932, had made some progress toward the development of departments and agencies that promoted the reconstruction of agricultural, forestry, and fishery sectors. It had also been the vision of the Commission Government (and Vincent Burke) to create a department for Adult Education (O'Neill, 1944, 50). As she reported on the state of schooling in her "Plan," the voice of one who experienced the severe conditions came through her writing:

Nor must we forget the role of the day school. We have 809 one-room schools and 218 two-room schools in Newfoundland. The sole charge school presents a most difficult problem. There is a need for creative supervision. Here teachers with least experience, least educational preparation, poorly paid, and with the least help, isolated and alone, struggle with the innumerable problems to be faced in conducting one-room schools. The aims of both adult and day-school teachers are interdependent and interrelated. It is to their mutual advantage to cooperate. (O'Neill, 1944, 50)

She knew first-hand the difficulties of teaching both children and adults. From her experience and her exposure to the theories and principles of adult education philosophy she conceived a plan that brought those working toward the same goals together to work cooperatively. She added a dimension to the plan for direct training and supervision so teachers would be equipped with more than dedication and good will. She also provided an organizational structure.

In 1944, with her doctoral degree from Columbia University, O'Neill returned to St. John's and was hired as Assistant Director of Adult Education, working under Vincent Burke. Later, when Burke was promoted to a new role under the new Smallwood government in 1949, O'Neill became the Director of Adult Education. She dedicated her days to implementing her "Plan". Her success was documented in a *Survey* of Memorial University of Newfoundland completed in 1951 by Robert Newton at the request of the Board of Regents. Newton wrote that "a good programme" of evening classes, rural youth and adult clubs, and community art and drama groups had been developed by the Director of Adult and Visual Education — Florence O'Neill. Newton explained that there was variety in the approaches used, depending on the needs of the community: "The field worker does not arrive with a ready-made programme, but very wisely works with the people on the spot" (Newton, 1951, 60). His observation suggests that O'Neill was well on the way to successfully developing significant parts of her plan.

Newton's role was to assess how well the university was meeting its objectives and goals. One topic included in the *Survey* was Extension

Services, an area that O'Neill had been openly and loudly supporting from her position in Adult Education (Newton, 1951, 59). The purpose of an Extension Division was to bring people not closely or usually connected with the university into its sphere by extending some of the benefits and services of the university beyond the boundary of the campus. Newton observed that within the area of adult education "such field men and women as are already numbered among government staffs should count on university help in appropriate enterprises" (Newton, 1951, 62). It is evident that Newton saw the structure of the adult education program developed by O'Neill as sufficient to serve the needs of a community, and that left the university to bring disparate groups together for the mutual benefit of all concerned. For instance, an Extension Division could assume the responsibility for training field workers for Adult Education by using appropriate university faculty, and leaders from health and welfare organization. Such training would contain more depth and breadth because it would be both academic and practical.

Memorial University of Newfoundland created an Extension Services Division in 1958. The same year, O'Neill received a lateral transfer to a position as Director of 4H programs. In the next few years, the government eliminated adult education as a department or division, and, ultimately O'Neill took a new position in Ottawa. Memorial University continued to build upon this legacy of community development work and trained Field Workers to achieve great success with the widely promoted "Challenge for Change" project, more commonly known as the "Fogo Process."

Archival Sources

O'Neill, Florence. My First Job. CBC Radio Broadcast, 13 June 1956. Transcript. Centre for Newfoundland Studies, Queen Elizabeth II Library, Memorial University of Newfoundland: Collection 212, file 6.01.

O'Neill, Florence. Interview with John Hewson. 22 December 1971. Transcribed. In the Centre for Newfoundland Studies, Queen Elizabeth II Library, Memorial University of Newfoundland: Collection 212.

Notes

[1] Malcolm, David. A friend and colleague of Florence O'Neill, David Malcolm began to document her career and her work with adults in 1991, shortly after her death. He interviewed several people who remembered her as a teacher or co-worker and he shared some of these interviews with the author. They are not available to the public at this time.

[2] The model that O'Neill followed was that of the "county agent" and "home demonstration worker" used by agricultural extension. See

46

Malcolm Knowles, "The Field of Operations in Adult Education," in Gale Jensen, A.A. Liveright, and Wilbur Hallenbeck, eds. *Adult Education: Outlines of an Emerging Field of University Study*, (New York: Adult Education Association of the U.S., 1964) 41-67.

Letters and Diaries

FRANCES CONROW PYE (1904-19?), a young woman from Kansas, USA, arrived in Muddy Bay, Labrador on October 26, 1926, as a replacement teacher for the International Grenfell Association Boarding School. Frances signed on to teach for only one year, but stayed for two, teaching first in Northwest River and then in St. Mary's River. In the summer of 1927 she met her future husband, fisherman Hayward Pye, and married him in 1932. They settled in Mount Moriah, near Corner Brook and had four children. Frances wrote many poems and stories on all aspects of her life, including her work in Labrador. This is an excerpt from diaries kept during her time in Labrador.[1]

Arriving At Muddy Bay

Thru the growing dusk the monotonous "putt-putt" of the motorboat came strangely to me. It seemed we were passing into a new world. If ever I longed to turn back, it was now. However, I had come some three thousand miles and was only a mile from my goal, so I braced up.

"There's Winter's Point," someone spoke.

I strained my eyes thru the dark. What was I coming to?

"Here we are," another voice spoke.

Lights in the window greeted us as we rounded the point. The engine stopped and we came slowly to the wharf. Then such talking and laughing and taking of bags and baggage. There seemed to be nothing but children, they were in front of us, behind us, surrounding us. We walked up the wharf. A huge building loomed ahead, a flight of stairs, open doors, down a long hall and into a dimly-lit room. Packages and mail and confusion were everywhere! After formal introductions were over we struggled through supper, then everyone disappeared into his or her mail, coming out occasionally to announce or question.

"See what Miss Goodyear sent the children for Christmas."

"Did the cow's feed come?"

"How do you like my new dress?"

"Did you have a good trip?"

With neither chance nor expectation of answer. I had received my mail on the steamer and it had been devoured long since. I might just as well not have existed, for what was the arrival of a new teacher compared to the last mail boat before Christmas?

From Day to Day

The busy hum of every-day life prevails over the huge house. Here is the clatter of dishes, there the murmur of children's voices, with happy shouts at times. Perhaps the sewing machine is going at a mad pace to finish a belated party dress. There might even be a dolls' tea party in full

swing, or an excited game of marbles at its height. Below, in the basement, the steady chopping shows that the fires are not to be neglect-
ed. Suddenly, a bell rings. Such a scampering up-stairs, bidding of good
nights, and wild excited tumbling into bed. Then again, we noticed the
affairs downstairs quieter now that the younger ones are safely
tucked into bed and supposedly sound asleep. The more serious things
begin for the older ones. Perhaps it is study night, or Girl Guides and Boy
Scouts are holding meetings. Whatever it is, the time soon passes and
soon another bell rings. There follows a sound of singing, then quiet
prayers before retiring. After a cheery good night to each and all there is
a general rush for drinks before going to bed. Quiet begins to settle slowly over the house. Only a murmur in the older children's rooms and talking in the staff room. The staff relaxes cautiously, and begins with interest to rehash the day's events. It may be Mary's sudden angelic disposition, or John's noticeable improvement, or Rush's latest tantrum. Perhaps
it is plans for changing certain rules or a new schema for dining room
management. One by one the remaining staff depart. The last one takes
a look around, puts out the hall light, and settles down for the night. The
great household is asleep. It is as great beast slowly relaxing, finally giving a last sigh, and becoming still in a dreamless slumber.

The night moves on slowly, surely, silently. The first hint of dawn
tinges the eastern sky and an alarm clock rudely awakens the one who
first must struggle with the day. She soon rouses the kitchen girls, who
light the fires, and start kettle boiling. The beast has stirred in his
sleep. Pattering footsteps in the hall: a knock.

"Time to get up, Miss."

The beast is rousing and slowly opens an eye. He blinks, stirs and rises
slowly. In six dormitories some forty children wake and begin dressing,
while the chatter increases. After they are washed, dressed, and inspected, they pass quickly downstairs, their voices again sound as they gather
in groups about the fires. Another bell rings. A song and prayers come as
a pleasant routine of the morning. The line of children passes to their
breakfast and another long, busy day has began.

The First Visit

Nearly a month had passed since my arrival and I was just beginning to
get my bearings. I had found out that the bungalow had a piano, a bath-
tub and a bed with box springs. That a "bight" was a small cove or bay.
That the "Stent" was a low-water crossing between the bight and the
pond. That the red berries, blue berries, and black berries on the hills
were all very good to eat. I had admired the many varieties of more we
had discovered before the first heavy snow, the lonely colors of sunset,
and most of all the blue hills in the distance. When I say blue, I mean the
bluest blue of any dress I ever owned, not the grey blue I had always

49

thought "blue hills" meant. I had found that we at Muddy Bay were composed of thirty-eight children, aged seven to fifteen, five kitchen staff, a principal, two teachers, a dentist, a nurse, an industrial worker, and Mr. Bird, our handy-man, and his wife and his family. One Sunday, my co-worker asked if I would like to visit our nearest neighbor, a mile away. Of course I would, so we set off on the newly frozen bight. Half-way across she stopped, turned and said, "Now you can really see Muddy Bay." It was spread out in a semi-circle before us. The laundry and warehouse to the left, then the big two-storey schoolhouse, the henhouse and barn, Mr. Bird's house and, last but not least, the bungalow. The buildings, all red and white, with the snow in front and the dark hills behind made a lovely picture. We faced again the low hill in front, made our way through a narrow ravine, and came out on a small marsh. There at the river's edge nestled a tiny house, already partly covered with snow. A woman appeared at the door holding a baby, while two small children peeped out beside her.

We went though a low, back porch into the main room. Benches were our chairs. A stove, on which a kettle boiled merrily, occupied one side and a table and cupboard the other. One window served for light and ventilation. A baby's cradle stood in the middle of the room. Through the open door of the other room we could see a cabin bed built from wall to wall. Another window was there. Newspaper formed the wall-paper of the rough lumber. Mrs. Burden greeted us most cordially, asking questions about the work and events at the school, especially of the coming Christmas concert.

Her hospitality was sincere and when we rose to go she wished us luck and insisted that we must come again. It was my first glimpse of the true land to which I had come, for the school was imported and quite American.

Notes

[1] CNSA, MF-396, Memorial University of Newfoundland, and *The Humber Log*, 6 March 1985, 5. Sources do not consistently identify her birthplace as Kansas, as in *The Humber Log*. The International Grenfell Association Boarding School, formerly the Labrador Public School, burned to the ground in 1928. A version of this excerpt first appeared as "Muddy Bay Sketches," in *Among the Deep Sea Fishers 26* (4) 1929, 147-150, then, an expanded version appeared as "Fifty Years Ago at Muddy Bay" in *Among the Deep Sea Fishers 74* (2) 1977, and finally as "Sketches of Labrador Life" in *Them Days Magazine 5* (1) 1979. Thank you to Martha A. Dzioba of Schulte Roth & Zabel LLP, New York, for permission to reprint from *Among the Deep Sea Fishers 74* (2) 1977.

Letters and Diaries

FANNY RYAN FIANDER (1889-1962) was born in Harbour Grace and educated there, in St. John's and in St. Pierre. She trained as an accountant and stenographer, working with Thomas Bond at Bay L'Argent before marrying George Thomas Fiander, and settling in Trinity, Trinity Bay. The family, including four children, moved to Harbour Grace in 1940. An ardent supporter of Responsible Government, she made radio broadcasts and public speeches around Conception Bay during the confederation debates in the late 1940s. Fanny was a prolific writer, contributing to the *Evening Telegram* in the 1930s and 1940s, writing poems, stories, and letters, sometimes under the pseudonym "Shannie". In the early 1940s, Fanny sent the following account of a 1924 voyage on her husband's schooner to Joey Smallwood, The Barrelman, in response to one of Joey's "Big Fish" stories.[1]

Dear Mr. Barrelman,

A few nights ago I listened in to a big fish story of yours, and I was wondering if you would find this one interesting. In 1924 I made a trip to Halifax in a sailing vessel, the Captain was a relative of mine, that is if you can call your supposed better half a relative. For the first 3 days and nights I almost died with sea sickness. I think I would have died only I overheard a conversation between two members of the crew in which they avowed solemnly that the Captain was going to sail the missus back to St. John's the very first chance. I aroused myself enough to obtain an interview with the Captain, the result of which was, I was given the option of either eating or leaving. Suffice it to record that I ate, and continued my sailings. Incidentally, my first order, to the cooks joy, was a small piece of roast salt cod fish, one thin piece of hard bread and a cup of tea containing neither milk or sugar.

After vainly trying to partake of the menu, the captain presented me with a half gallon jar of lime juice, which much to his sorrow led to my final recovery. To his sorrow, did I say Mr. Barrelman, yes to his sorrow, as I deprived him of two hours fishing on St. Pierre Bank, and jigged — ah that's the story ...

We were, what one of the crew said, soaking[2] out over St. Pierre Bank. There was very little wind, but a heavy swell. I had been trying to crochet, but every time the vessel would roll down, I'd drop a stitch off the hook, and so I gave it up and enjoyed the motion of the ship as she rolled in the swell.

Suddenly, I remembered St. Pierre Bank spelled fish and so I commenced my search for a jigger. I could not find one, and I was afraid to ask the Captain for one fearing I would loose the chance to do a little fishing, as he

Fanny Fiander with grandchildren Claudia (standing) and Elizabeth (in arms). c. late 1940s. Courtesy of Elizabeth Fiander Woodrow

was an enthusiastic fishermen. At last, I found a jigger and line, and I went up on deck. On my husband's face, when he caught sight of me, was written dismay, and no doubt inside he was using some fancy French, but he gallantly prevented me from taking a flying leap overboard, as the ship rolled over, and advised me in future to watch where I was going. As a reward for saving my life he asked for the jigger. I was grateful, but gently refused.

Well, the crew gathered around, and I commenced fishing. An hour passed, my hands burned from the line and salt water. My back ached, my arms pained, my dress and feet were wet, still I fished.

I almost went over the side of the vessel twice, still I held on to the line, another half hour passed and then Mr. Barrelman, I hooked something which almost took me overboard ....
Recovering my balance I declared I had struck a fish, but at this the skipper smiled, and seating himself nearby lit a cigar. I began to pull in my line; it was coming in so easy, not a move to indicate that I had hooked a fish.

Hand over hand I brought the line in, and then Mr. Barrelman, some oh's and ah's to the rhythm of strong, yes, very strong language, began to float around.

It was for the benefit of a huge cod fish which was lying just beneath the water. The jigger had caught in its gills and it had swam up. Now it lay motionless, a grand sight.

It was claimed by the crew that it was too heavy for me to land. I knew it was; I did not want to land the beautiful creature. I was content to watch it palpitating there a few feet beneath the water.

My husband was more practical, he demanded that I give the line to him, so that he could secure the prize, but I began gently to take in more line. Suddenly there was a splash, a flash, and almost over my head came hurtling a monster fish. My husband had landed it, but I jigged a cod fish measuring 5 feet 4 inches and of tremendous girth!

Shannie

Notes

[1] CNSA Collection 028, 2.01.002 and *Encyclopedia of Newfoundland and Labrador, V2*, St. John's: Newfoundland Book Publishers (1967).

[2] According to the *Dictionary of Newfoundland English*, to "soak along" is to go at a steady, continuous pace. When applied to a vessel, as Fanny does here, it means to sail steadily and smoothly.

Recollections
Louise Belbin: Beach Woman
Introduction by Helen Woodrow and Frances Ennis

IN 1995, THE NEWFOUNDLAND AND LABRADOR Women's Fishnet set out to produce a book about women's work in the fishing industry. We, Frances and Helen, were the project's architects and editors. We dreamt of a book that resonated with the sounds of shoreworkers and shore skippers, brokers and buyers, supervisors and owners, filleters, floor ladies and fishers. We saw folios draped in a rich pattern of historical and contemporary photographs. We hoped it would reveal many telling moments for women in the industry. Above all else, we wanted a publication that celebrated the work and contributions of rural women.

In the end, ten women worked with us to develop oral histories about their work in the industry. Each woman reflected on her own work environment, and how her labour was valued. They analyzed the relationships between managers and workers, and husbands and wives. They considered society's view of women's work, and of fisheries workers. Many critical themes emerged from their chronicles.

Strong as the Ocean (Harrish Press, 1996), does not tell the whole story of women and their work in the Newfoundland and Labrador fisheries, but the stories that were told — of cold November days on the beach, rough days at early morning and tired feet at shift end — teach us about women's endless days of work in the industry, at home and in the community.

In this short article, we honour the life and memory of the book's oldest contributor and feature an excerpt from her story.

Louise Belbin (1897-1999) was ninety-eight when she spoke to us about her working years as a "beach woman" at Grand Bank. Her daughter, Violet Green, later joined in the conversation to discuss the art of fish making.

Louise
Jacques Fontaine was me home. Years after, I was here in Grand Bank I went working at fish down on the beach. I was married and had children then. The whole 14 years I was on the beach, I was a piler. Everybody couldn't make the piles, but I was used to the fish before I come to Grand Bank — not on the beaches, but on the flakes. You had to go on the beach to earn a few dollars — do the best you could to make ends meet. I wouldn't like to ever see it come back again. That was in the depression years and we knowed it was depression too. Some hard going days them times, but I conquered the big battle to be alive like I am

54

today and got me right senses. I got a lot to be thankful for. The dear Lord was good to us, we hold our health.

My husband was skipper. We was married a month and a half when he went away and I never see him no more for 11 months. When the schooner was going, he had to be gone. The first five years we was married, I hardly see him much at all. One time the doctor come over because one of the children was sick. He asked where me husband was to, and I told him. He said, "You're the mother and father of a family, your man away like that."

I was 25 when I got married, and I had three children when I was working on the beach. I could work with anyone, but in the morning sometimes I sat on the bed and me legs be that stiff and tired I could hardly get me stockings on. 'Twas hard managing it. I used to have short nights. I had to be up every night to do for me children and the house 'cause when it was daylight I was not in the house. Then every night, stars in the sky, you'd take your two buckets and bring in a barrel of water for the next day. I used to set me gardens too in among that.

Now there was no odds how much food you had in your house, you wouldn't be able to get many days long enough to cook. You had to go early in the morning, and you'd come home, get a lunch, and go again. 'Twas hurry up and boil the kettle and go again so quick as you could get there when you had the two lots of fish come the same time. I'd be trying to stir up the fire to get the kettle to boil, put tea in steep, going about the house with me overall jacket, sun shade and all on.

When we had two lots of fish, you'd come 11:00 and get something to eat to go back again noon, and be there the rest of the day. There was no supper hour. I used to have food put out for the children to eat till I get back. That's what you had to do 'cause you had no set time to get back. It might be dark. We often come home 9:00 when we had the two lots of fish going. I mind one evening I come and the three of them was sat down. When I come in, 'twas getting dark in the house. They said, "Mom, we didn't think you was going to come home tonight."

When I was going to have Emma, I was on the beach all that summer. She was born the 10th of October and I was off the beach no time when she was born, perhaps two or three weeks. I tell you, I used to be some miserable some times. The man loading the cart sometimes he'd say, "Don't give that woman a big yaffle of fish like you carries in. You got better sense than that." 'Cause he see I was carrying a baby; hard to work on the beach like that, so much bending over. I always thinks that's the reason Emma was the shortest one in the family.

Sometimes we went on the beach in March. There was patches of snow we'd have to swim between. I know what 'twas like on the beach Good Friday. Poor old Mrs. Matthews up the brook used to say, "The bells is ringing and only the good ones is going to church," and we was all on the beach at fish.

One year we got clear the last of our fish just before Christmas Eve. It was late in the fall — in October — when we got the last fish from Labrador. The schooners brought it in and they wanted to get it dried out. 'Twas some cold in November and December out on the open beach. And we only had a overall jacket to wear on over our clothes, 'cause they was stronger than our rubber clothes, and a pair of rubber boots. I had the sleeve wore right out taking the fish they used to bring in to me.

One time when the schooner come in from Labrador with the fall fish, I said we should've had more for to suffer the cold. And I said to the boss, "Come on, Jenny Grant, I'm going over to Mr. Carr."

"No", she said, "I'm not going."

"Nobody going to come with me, what's wrong with you?" I said, "I'm going."

So when I went in the shop, I said to the girls, "Is there anyone in the office with Mr. Carr?"

And they said, "No." I had on me beach clothes, see, and me sun shade and they thought there was a stir up over on the beach.

I said, "Can I go in and see Mr. Carr?"

"Yes," they said, "you can go in."

I went in, and I said, "Mr. Carr, we got a lot to face now for the time of year coming on, fall of the year and that wet fish. Can't we have a little raise in our pay, 'cause we needs more now for to wear in the cold weather than we did all summer, and we needs better boots. It all takes money and we haven't made much the summer."

"I must say, you're right," he said. "Yes, I will give you a raise."

When I went back, I was going to clap me hands at them. "Guts enough for nothing," I said, "I went over to Mr. Carr — he's only a man like our own men. You got to have a bit of gum into you to get through this world."

Well, I thought 'twas right when I made the move and we got the raise 'cause we did deserve it. I don't think I done wrong there.

When you get off the beach, you didn't know the first thing to do — house cleaning and doing things for Christmas, and then doing work all through the winter until the time you went on the beach again in March. You were steady going. Sometimes the boss woman would come down to the house. She used to say, "What's news Louie?"

I'd say, "I been nowhere since I come off the beach, only at me work."

You never had time. Your time was occupied by your family and your home.

Louise and Violet

The first thing, the fish was brought out from the schooners and washed clean. Now that was what we called "water our fish." Men and boys used to wash the fish. That was what they called the green fish, cause 'twas wet. Then all the women would work at that putting it on the beach to dry. It was a long time drying a load of fish in them days 'cause people had a lot of fish.

You had so many women working at dry fish in piles and so many working at the green fish. There was eight and nine and sometimes ten women — that was the crowd for the beach. One of them was a boss. She would tell you what to spread and how much.

We spread it out if 'twas fine enough and then put it in faggots — that's like small piles. There'd be five or six or seven fish in a small faggot. They was spread up and down, heads and tails, not around. We spread fish every day till you get it dry enough to start making big round piles. You couldn't pile green fish. I suppose it'd be in faggots a week sometimes and when it'd get a bit nice and dry, then you'd start piling it.

Those piles were round and we took pride in the shape of the pile. When it got up so high we used to make it up almost like a sharp roof, like a peak on a house. This was a real art and had to be done just right or it didn't suit.

The boss would get $10 more for being boss than her women what were working with her. The last summer I worked on the beach, I made over $100. Not very often I made $100 in the 14 years I was at it and they'd only give you $10 cash. You had to take up the rest of it in their store. Only $10 and a paper, what they used to call a credit note. Every time you want something to their store, you had to carry that paper. That was the wrong part of it. 'Twas not even a fair play 'cause they had two prices. If you went in with $1 you got a different price than you would if it was on your credit note. That's the way it was — two prices. It was hard for your work, 'cause you wanted to get what you could for every dollar and stuff used to be expensive. They wouldn't get that to work today on people, no my dear.

Between Life and Death: Fisherwomen in Newfoundland and Labrador

Brenda Grzetic

Introduction

Since the mid 1980's, inshore fishing families in Newfoundland and Labrador have been hit hard by the decline of groundfish stocks, and the subsequent restructuring of the fisheries. This restructuring has been driven by a view of economics and progress that benefit a select few. Committed primarily to market practices and technologies of efficiency, these new fisheries policies and practices loosen their ties to rural communities and diminish their commitment to inshore fishing families, which have constituted the backbone of the traditional Newfoundland fishery.

In this chapter, I will focus on a particular aspect of the fisheries, that of women's increasing presence on fishing boats throughout this period of restructuring. Drawing on interviews and discussions that took place between 2000 and 2002, I will explore the complex reasons for their increasing numbers and their experiences of working aboard small boats. The interviews were conducted with sixteen fisherwomen from the south and west coasts of the Island who work in the small-boat inshore fishery. These were first presented in my Master's thesis (Grzetic, 2002), and later in a book entitled *Women Fishes These Days*[1] (Grzetic, 2004). All these women fish mainly with their husbands, but some also fish with other crew members on larger boats.

Here I will take a feminist political economy view that considers the backdrop of issues noted above, but focuses on gender as a social relation within fisheries restructuring policies and practices. The institutional scope includes fishing families as well as state and fisheries institutions. These are all locations where the construction of differences create unequal wealth and power between women and men. This view also allows for consideration of the potential health effects of fisheries restructuring on fisherwomen in Newfoundland and Labrador.

Women in the Fisheries

Much of women's work in the fishery can be characterized by the division of labour on the basis of sex: traditionally, women have worked on shore while men have worked at sea (Wright, 2001). A persistent characteristic of their work is that it has been undervalued, unpaid and made invisible by a male-focused and capitalist bias related to how "productive work" is defined (Nadel-Klein and Davis, 1988, 7). Feminists have long challenged this male-bias in valuing the types of work considered "productive" and institutionally recognized. Yet, women in fishing households have been living in this strange space where their fishery work onshore and aboard boats has been essential to the success of the inshore fisheries but invisible and uncompensated by governments and institutions. Such undermining of women's work has characterized fisheries policies in Newfoundland and Labrador since their origin.

During the 1980s and 1990s, economic, social and environmental restructuring created a particular context that shaped the choices available to women in fishing households. When the collapse of the groundfish threatened family incomes and increased outmigration, increasing numbers of women once again stepped up their efforts to secure family incomes and began fishing with their husbands. They were drawn into the industry as a cheap source of labour and by 2000, there were over 3,100 women fishing. Regardless of whose idea it was that they go fishing, most women said they were left with little choice in the matter. Prior to the collapse of the groundfish fishery, the husband might have paid a man from outside the household to work with him aboard the boat. Now, the financial pressures resulting from downloading of costs onto fishing families with restructuring and the increasing cost of living have made it increasingly difficult to support multiple families from one inshore fishing enterprise. Most women said they went fishing in order to have that second income to offset the increasing fisheries-related fees, the cost of living, and the costs associated with their children's post-secondary education. Working aboard a boat fits their needs as well, given that they have little post-secondary education with which to compete for the fewer and fewer jobs available now in these fishery-dependent communities. Their presence in fishing has also been made possible by the decreasing manual labour associated with the shift in the main species harvested from the labour-intensive ground fisheries to crab. The installation of hydraulic equipment aboard boats, for example, has helped reduce heavy manual labour and made the work more accessible to women.

If we think about women's presence on fishing boats in terms of agency, we must consider their actions in terms of both compliance and resistance (Moore, 1994). Indeed, these patriarchal households in crisis and under considerable financial pressure[2] require their compliance in order to survive. There are ways, however, that working on a fishing boat can be seen as resistance. Fisherwomen have been influenced, like women elsewhere, by the women's movement so that they can realistically envision themselves working in male dominated environments like fishing boats. Some have been influenced by a small number of persistent fisherwomen who have been working on fishing boats for years and who are said to be: "almost as good as their husbands." Equality issues are important to fisherwomen and they occasionally used equality arguments to convince their husbands to let them go to work on the boats: "Well, he needed somebody to help him so I said, "Why can't I go out"? Women fishes today, so why can't I go out?"

Given the economic imperatives of their lives, it is understandable that their main reason for fishing is to secure the household income. However, women also want to work and they feel better and are healthier when they do (Pavalko and Smith, 1999). It also seems that these fisherwomen are using their limited power within fishing families to interrupt common ideas and discourses about not only women's work but also about aspects of fisheries restructuring schemes that target their livelihoods and the future of their communities. Together, they pose a collective challenge that will at least slow down the effects of fisheries policies that attempt to decrease the number of inshore fishing families.

"We Were Forced in There Big Time, Sink or Swim"

The invisibility of women's work in the fishery has been institutional-ized most prominently at two locations: within patriarchal fishing house-holds where males hold 97.7% of fishing licences (Grzetic, 2002), and in discriminatory Unemployment Insurance (UI) regulations that credited a woman's fishery-related work to her husband, and denied UI eligibility to women who fished with their husbands (Connelly and MacDonald, 1995, 391). Since the 1980s, fisherwomen have successfully posed legal chal-lenges to the federal government for fairer assessments, recognition, and compensation of their work, particularly with regard to UI.

Today, Employment Insurance (EI)[3] probably affects the work dynam-ic within fishing communities and fishing households more than any other policy. The Fishing EI regulations define a fisher as someone doing a variety of tasks related to the fishing enterprise both on land as ground crew, and on the water (Human Resources Development Canada, 2001, Part 1). The regulations restrict recognition and compensation for ground crew work unless those workers are also actively involved in catching fish. This regulation has made it difficult to compensate women who are more likely than men to do only ground crew work because EI benefits will only compensate work done on the water, realized through fish sold. The result is that women, who have done fishery-related work for years, have been ineligible for EI.

When the collapse of the ground fishery threatened their livelihoods, fishermen began to find ways to compensate their wives. Here Bernice[4], a fisherwoman, describes what fishermen did to secure household incomes and the consequences of this for women in fishing families:

The way the EI system is set up, …you're an independent business as a fisherman so there's always been room to manoeuver that with com-panies, where you can go out and get your catch and put it in whoev-er's name you saw fit. So, with the decline in the quotas …, the per-fect opportunity was there to sell fish in your wife's name even if she didn't fish. Now I would look up to you and say that she might not

60

fish but it's likely that she did the bulk of the work for that business on land. So if that fish was going in her name, she was only helping with it anyway to start with but a stigma got attached to us.

While fishing provided the second income to a household that desperately needed it, some women described pressures, including the Fishing EI regulations, as forcing them onto the boat, leading one fisherwoman, Gloria, to be concerned that women who have been entering the fishery in recent years during this period of crisis to be: "there in body but not in mind." It seems that women's increasing presence on fishing boats is being driven by tighter pressures on them to conform to certain expectations, mainly through EI surveillance, stigmatizing, and reporting measures. Their reputations and incomes are on the line, so they need to be seen to be fishing, and have the documentation to prove it to people inside and outside their communities who monitor their whereabouts[5]. While fishermen are often skeptical of women when they first go fishing, one woman said, "if women do what [fishermen] think you should be doing, … they look at you a little differently than they did in the beginning."

A Typical Day for Fisherwomen
Most women who fish are up and about by 4:00 a.m. and on the water by 5:00 a.m. Women who combine their work in the fishery with raising children adjusted the times they went on the water in order to get the children ready and off to school. In such cases, the husband would go out at 4:30 a.m. and come in for breakfast at 8:00. When the children were sent off to school, the two of them would go fishing together until the afternoon. Once the children were a little older and more mature, women would lay out the children's breakfast and lunch, and go fishing with their husbands at 4:30 a.m.

The distance they go out on the water varies somewhat depending on the size of the boat and the species fished. Four women worked on 34'11" boats and went out from eight to twenty-three miles, depending on the species they were fishing. Twelve women fished from smaller, open boats and went out from a few miles to fifteen miles, but one woman regularly went out twenty-three miles.

The season opens with lobster; then they usually move on to lumpfish, cod (for those allowed to catch it) and then crab. For those still fishing cod, later in the summer and fall they will try to fish it again, depending on the weather. Due to the distances to the fishing grounds, four women spend most of their time during the fishing season away from their communities, living in small cabins with their husbands. Being away from home for extended periods of time causes additional worry and stress, especially for the women who have young children at home. In these cases, the women hire people close to them, usually relatives, on whom they can depend, such as family members or neighbours who live nearby, to help take care of the children.

Fisherwomen talked about their work load both inside and outside the fishery. Assuming a six day fishing week (weather permitting), the women spend an average of sixty-three hours a week on the water. Each day, when their work on the water is done, all but two women have a second job tending to onshore duties that have to be done every day they are on the water. This involves ground crew work at the wharf and around their communities, such as offloading fish, purchasing and gathering supplies and equipment, cleaning the boat, preparing bait, baiting nets at the wharf, and interacting with buyers and occasionally representatives of fishery organizations, as well as keeping financial records, paying fees, ensuring they are up to date on safety requirements, filing income taxes, and taking care of other incidental paperwork. The workday does not end when they are done their fishing work. All the women leave the fishery work and go home to a third job taking care of the home, children and elderly relatives, and some also volunteer with non-profit and fisheries organizations.

Fisherwomen's Work And Identity

The gender division of labour aboard fishing boats reflects the traditional gender division of labour in the home so women's duties aboard the boats are often different to those of men. They measure and band lobster and crate crab. They take care of bait, set traps and nets and keep the boat clean. Some women said that both they and their husbands occasionally repair lobster pots aboard the boat. Women are rarely in charge of the boat — navigating or maintaining the engine — although they do operate the hydraulic equipment that brings the nets and pots aboard the boat. They act mainly in a "helper" capacity, doing most of the fast-paced, fish-processing work such as sorting, cutting, and icing. In fact, women do a lot of the labour intensive work aboard the boat. As Bridget explains, this work is most intense when they're catching cod:

> My husband hauls the trawl and I got to cut the fish's throat right away. I got to bleed the fish, wash it, put it in pails, ice it down and start all over. Cod is a very long job. That's the worst about fishing is the cod. You got to make sure everything is clean because we're on a grading system so it's really hard because you got to have so much ice on it, you can't leave it out in the sun. ... If you leave them there too long they're going to go soft. It's certainly a lot of work especially if they are big, right? I does all that. He just hauls the trawl and drives the boat. Now the hydraulics does most of it — it's a beautiful system my dear, but I does all the cutting and icing. But last year was wicked — 1,000 pounds of fish cleaned and I did all that.

Women's invisibility in the fishery stands in stark contrast to the labour-intensive work that Bridget describes above. In contrast (and at least publicly), the men are in control of the boat, as they are in control of the fishing enterprise and it is important that they be seen to be in control. When women's presence aboard boats is acknowledged publicly, local fishing talk sometimes targets women in derogatory ways. "A lot of people say that's a woman's job, just women's work — the crab. You just go out and you pull the string on the bottom of the pot, dump the crab and pack them away in the locker."

As helpers, women assist their husbands in various tasks aboard the boat. While they acknowledge this "helper" role, they nonetheless struggle to find their place in the fishery and learn more skills to help them in their work in order to become more competent workers. These struggles are both external and internal as women insist on being respected as workers and "helpers" while at the same time, challenging themselves and others to look beyond the limiting "helper" identity. One fisherwoman, Bernice, talked about her own struggle with the devaluing of women's fishing work and the significance of women adopting limited conceptions of themselves in their work:

> I think about that sometimes because, in the beginning, I thought my work wasn't that important. I remember talking to another woman in the fishery and I asked her about her work. She said, "I don't do very much. I just measures the crab." And she went on and on about the things she did. I said, "Without that being done … that was important." But she figured that what she was doing wasn't as important as what the men are doing because they were men. Even me, even though I knows better … deep down there's times I even think that. It's true and I don't know how we're going to get away from it. More and more I'm coming to realize it.

Job Satisfaction

Most fisherwomen said that there were aspects of the work that they really liked and that they felt healthier as a result of their work aboard the boats. They spoke positively about learning new things, the improvements in their physical and emotional health, being able to spend extra time with their families during the winter months, and having more income in the household. Others talked about their relationships with their husbands and how they have grown closer since they started fishing together. They get along well with their husbands and this is very important to them: "Having a good job in the fishing boat comes right down to whether you got a good relationship at home, basically. If you're blessed to have that, it's a little different than if you're not." Another woman commented that cooperation aboard the boat, between women, their husbands, and other coworkers is: "between life and death." While most women said they enjoyed their work, their expression of this enjoyment was often qualified by the increasing stress on small inshore fishing families. In particular, they noted the uncertainty in the industry, poor catches, feeling forced to be on the water in bad weather, going further offshore to fish, and their concern about their role as mothers and their obligations to the children at home.

Women's feelings about their work must also be seen in the context of their previous gender and class experiences with education and work. While they feel good about being able to earn an income and provide for their families, some women clearly do not feel that fishing is something to aspire to as a career. Careers, especially ones that physically take them away from their home communities come second to household responsibilities. It is therefore possible that while women have to be seen to be aboard fishing boats (for EI reasons), their primary roles as mothers means they also cannot be seen to be enjoying this work too much. The role of mother is very powerful both ideologically and emotionally. Angela's oldest son understood the importance of the role of "mother" in her fishing work: "He was very responsible ... I know he used to say, "Mom is not out there doing this for herself. She's out there doing this for us." Angela went on to explain her mixed feelings about fishing in terms of her primary role as mother, because she is not there in the mornings to take care of her children. Yet, there are obviously things that she has come to enjoy and, over time, her feelings have changed:

Well, [fishing] is not something that I want to be at, but I love it. Well, it's not that I love it. I got to do it. It's not as much of a burden right now as it used to be. It was bothersome to me back when I started, but I guess I was younger then. Now it seems like it made my kids more responsible. My oldest [at home] is fourteen and when he leaves the house he makes sure the other kids have their shoes tied, their jackets on, and clean clothes on that they laid out the night before. In that sense it has made me feel better about them because I know that I can trust them a lot more than I normally would.

Women's stories speak to their habitual or everyday knowledge about fishing but their tangible experiences of fishing are probably best illustrated not by the money that immediately evaporates with the endless household bills, but by their ability to prepare food for the winter — the act of touching, eating, and sharing a meal of fish solidifies their own acts of labour that are: "doing something good in many ways."

Safety on the Water

One of the most difficult aspects of working in the small-boat inshore fishery involves learning how to respond to the constantly changing conditions on the water and make the right decisions about when to come ashore. Most of these women go fishing whenever they can, unless the weather is so bad that they cannot go out. Often they are on the water when the weather turns bad. All these women depend on and trust their husbands' judgement about the weather. Some of them leave the decision about what to do solely up to them, but a majority of them insist on having a voice in the decision. Over time, many of them have begun taking a more active role in deciding what to do in bad weather.

First, they have learned to use dependable information about the weather by listening to the forecast, keeping an eye out for changes in weather patterns, ensuring that all safety precautions are addressed aboard the boat, and by gaining enough confidence in their knowledge of fishing to really know when it is time to go ashore. Knowing how to dress warmly is also important. A common theme in women's stories was their faith and need to pray while on the water. While most women pray that they will make it home safely, Gloria says that after fishing for twenty years, she no longer prays out of fear. The ocean has become a place where she feels closer to God and, for her, prayer is interconnected with location, good fishing practices and experience.

Beneath the practical knowledge, prayer, and other things, lie women's attitudes towards the environment and the species they fish. They tend to be consciously conservative in their fishing habits: they describe themselves as less aggressive when fishing, and less willing than their husbands to take unnecessary risks on the water. Based on these values, they negotiate their safety and are quite content to err on the side of caution in both sustaining the fish stocks and keeping themselves safe during bad weather.

While these women have been learning to cope with rougher weather as they spend more time on the water, they appear to be more likely than their husbands to initiate the decision to come ashore, regardless of the length of time they have been fishing. Sometimes this causes arguments between women and their husbands. When asked how she felt about fishing work, one core fisherwoman said, "I like it on the water as long as it's not too rough. When we go out for crab, we go out fourteen miles in a twenty-foot, open boat. I usually watch out for when the sea is high and I want to come in. [My husband] disagrees but usually he gives in."

Tensions are also the result of different working styles, especially situations where women want a more egalitarian (non-hierarchical) working relationship. When I asked women if they considered their husbands to be their bosses, they all said no, but when I asked them if their husbands tried to be their bosses, most said yes.

Skill Levels

Women's level of comfort on the water is strongly related to their skill levels and general knowledge about the environment in which they work. When describing the kinds of skills they need in order to do their work, women's first inclination was to say that there were no "skills" needed to do their work on the water: "You have to watch what you're doing all the time, but other than that, there's no skill needed, I don't think." Some women talked about the more technical aspects of the work they have learned, mostly from their husbands, such as navigating the boat, dressing the fish, and cutting bait and adhering to conservation measures and grading requirements.

It is well known that crew members in small-scale fisheries are responsible for and dependent on one another. Given that there are usually only a small number of workers on one boat, this means that they all need to have certain critical skills. Some fisherwomen reported no problems with learning a wide range of skills from their husbands and co-workers. However, eleven women work in situations where they usually are the only other crew member aboard the boat with their husbands. When describing their skills, eight of these women felt they did not have adequate navigational and engine maintenance skills, even though they worked alone with their husbands. If an emergency occurred, they said they might not be able to bring the boat ashore safely on their own or do basic repair on the engine should it stall.

Many of these women depend on informal training, on their husband's and co-worker's willingness to teach them navigation and basic maintenance. They are clearly not content with just their husbands having these skills, precisely because, at times, there are just the two of them on the water. The other option, formal training in navigation and engine maintenance, require funding. The restructuring of the post-secondary training system and increased course tuition seems to have put this out of reach for many of these women.

Given that some husbands are reluctant to teach the women particular skills, women have had to strategize ways to improve their skills. Some try to convince their husbands to teach them the skills. Others though, have been fishing for years before their husbands began teaching them navigational and mechanical skills. It was evident that some of these women are learning slowly and under very dangerous conditions.

Perceptions of Risk

Many women felt they were taking risks on the water and this was especially true of the women who worked in open boats. Their perception of risk, however, is subjective, shifting, and related to their position as "helper" on the boat. Their often subordinate position means they have less control over decisions affecting their health and safety and are therefore more at risk of increased worry, stress, illness and injury. Perceptions of risk are related to control and it is usually the husbands who are in control even when women have some input into decisions related to safety. Women rarely have opportunities to operate the boat independently and their perceptions of risk interact with the degree of control they have and their skill levels. Over time, as they learn more about fishing and the mechanical equipment aboard the boat, their comfort levels and competency have increased and their perceptions of risk change. The two women who have been fishing for almost twenty years said they rarely take risks but one of these women said, "There's times probably when we do [take risks] but we don't consider them risks. Probably we would do things one time that we wouldn't think about doing now because back then you didn't know the difference."

For some women, their perceptions of risk may also be influenced by the degree of risk in the occupation in general or the amount of risk that their husbands take while on the water, rather than anything specific to the work women do aboard the boats. These understandings of risk have historical and social meanings that are different for men and women. It is obvious among many of these women that they are not comfortable with the degree of risk in the occupation, or the macho attitude among fishermen and fisheries management that promotes increased risk-taking.

Some of these women have been trying to reduce the level of risk aboard the boats. They realize that they cannot do much about broader fisheries policies that compromise safety but within their scope of influence aboard the boat, they do challenge their husbands and co-workers on safety issues and their risk-taking behaviours, especially in relation to going out or staying out in bad weather. They also make sure that safety equipment aboard the boat is up-to-date. Although at one time, it was common for children from fishing families to grow up without a father, many of these women will not take the risk that their children will have to go through life without a father or a mother. They will do whatever they can to make sure that does not happen. Some women felt that having more fisherwomen was a good thing precisely because they tend to be more conscious of safety issues. The "watching" that is taking place is not solely of others watching women's activities in the fishery: most of these women carefully watch what the men are doing too, and some women say they alone enforce safety protocols.

All the women but one said they wear life jackets and most have been wearing them since they started fishing. They also described ongoing attempts to try and convince their husbands to wear life jackets. One woman who has been fishing with a crew for ten years described how she had been trying over the years to encourage her husband, father and brother-in-law to wear life jackets. Only in recent years have they agreed to her requests. The men around her consider wearing life jackets to be an admission of fear that will just erode their nerve to go on the water in their small boats because, if you fall overboard in the water off Newfoundland, you "either get out or die." Wearing a life jacket is metaphorical — an admission of vulnerability, and resisted by fishermen because it means letting go of some aspects of a male work culture that visibly promotes high risk-taking. Of course, women have not been part of the construction of this work culture on the water and, therefore, do not have the same type of investment in it.

Conclusions

Women's presence aboard fishing boats helps offset some of the insecurity felt by fishing families with the loss of the groundfishery, the subsequent restructuring of the industry, and increased outmigration from rural Newfoundland and Labrador. Their presence poses a challenge to the collective imagery about fishers, disrupting male-defined ideas about skill, work culture and place that are closely tied to gender. However, it is likely that this challenge is most intensely felt among fisherwomen themselves as they struggle to find a place in this dangerous male-dominated industry. Many of them never expected to be fishing, say they are "still in shock" that they are doing this work and occasionally dream about having their time back again. They downplay their injuries even as they happen but over time, most have adjusted to the work. They are caught in a strange gendered space where fishing is: "not something I want to be at but I love it." And it is likely that as fish stocks become more scarce, costs associated with fishing increase, access to fishing more restricted through professionalization and other measures, and women are seen as a cheap and only source of labour, their presence aboard fishing boats will continue to increase.

Most considerations and discussions of fisheries policies do not consider their effects on women's lives or women's experiences, perspectives, or needs. Here, I have attempted to close this gap somewhat by exploring how fisheries policies and practices change women's lives in rural Newfoundland and Labrador, how their health has been affected by such changes, and how they have met the challenges that so often undermine their work and needs both within their communities and in larger institutions.

Notes

Special thanks to Barbara Neis and Rosonna Tite, my thesis supervisors, and Marilyn Porter and Linda Cullum for helpful feedback on this chapter. Thanks to the faculty, staff and students in the Women's Studies program at Memorial University. For funding and support in carrying out the initial research with fisherwomen, I would like to thank the School of Graduate Studies and the "Coasts Under Stress" research project at

Memorial University. The fisherwomen who participated in this research were tremendously supportive and giving of their time. Without their commitment and guidance, this work would not exist.

[1] Sections of this chapter have been taken from my book *Women Fishes These Days* (2004) with permission from Fernwood Press.

[2] In 1990, the average total income in one-earner fishing families was $16,946 before taxes, well below the low income cut-off of $21,000 after taxes for a family of four living in a rural area. A second income, which often comes from women's work, literally raises the family out of poverty. Two-earner fishing families earned an average of $28,666 in 1990, putting them just above the low income cut-off (Task Force on Incomes and Adjustment in the Atlantic Fishery [the Cashin Report], 1993, 174).

[3] In 1996, the federal government renamed the Unemployment Insurance (UI) program the Employment Insurance (EI) program.

[4] All names given to fisherwomen are pseudonyms.

[5] Compare the way ground crew workers are recognized in Canada with practices in Norway where they are hired as ordinary crew members on a boat. They follow a formalised system where their pay is based on an agreement between the boatowners section and the crew section in the Norwegian Fishermen's Association. The "landmen," like other crew onboard on the vessel are paid through a share of the catch, and they also share the costs, even though they work on land.

Rosella and Bride

Mary Dalton

When they marched up from the cove to the Cross
They'd dazzle a blind horse with blinkers on–
Rosella and Bride rigged out in full sail–
In bright blue and yellow, red jumpers
Or green, rouged cheeks and the
Ear-rings as long as a jigger
Sure when they laughed they lit up the very
Gravel on the road.
The women tsked. The men grinned.
A mile and a half of eyes behind curtains
As those two set off for the shore.

Professional Bodies: The Control and Discipline of the Female Body at Work

Onar Usar

I'm supposed to be dressed well, present myself well. I would think that … I would probably be expected to wear nice clothes, shoes and stuff a lot of times … [Because] well, I think, Hall Inc. is really big on appearance, and I guess if somebody is coming in to the office and I'm sitting wearing a t-shirt and jeans or whatever, that's not gonna … that's not gonna look well … But I just can't afford to have that wardrobe for work. So I try my best … I try to wear, you know, a skirt and a blouse and basics expected of me …

(Interview with Nancy, receptionist, September 17, 2003)

DRESSING OUR BODIES IS A SIMPLE FACT OF LIFE. It is also a significant part of social and moral order. Through dressing we perform our gender and sexual identities and negotiate power relations. It is a symbolic activity through which we challenge or reinforce gender, class and all other markers of being (Rubinstein, 2001; Entwistle, 2000, 2002; Brewis, Hampton, Linstead, 1997; Dellinger, 2002). As a part of the complex systems of signs and symbols, our clothing and bodily adornments may tie us to certain groups while distancing us from others. In this regard, all work organizations adapt more or less formal dress codes and establish gender appropriate appearance norms. However, as Rubinstein emphasizes, clothing images or dress codes are meaningful and significant only when they are located and interpreted in a specific social and geographical context (2001, 8). In this article, I explore how the discourse of professionalism produces, and is a product of, gender appropriate dressing and appearance norms in a particular organization, Hall Inc., located in Newfoundland and Labrador. I examine how these norms are used to maintain hierarchical levels, negotiate power relations and discipline the female body in particular. I investigate how heterosexuality is maintained and normalized in the on-going process of creating professional, gendered and (hetero)sexed bodies. Finally, I discuss the notions of agency and resistance during this creation process. While this article is divided into subsections, I am aware that the practices and dynamics discussed are interdependent and occurring simultaneously.

Hall Inc.: "A Modern Type of Company"[1]

In the early 1950s, Mr. Hall started a small, residential electrical contracting business in the basement of his St. John's home. Little did he know then that by the turn of the 21st century his small business would become one of the largest privately owned contracting companies in Atlantic Canada. Now as "a major player in the contracting and servic-

71

ing of electrical and instrumentation systems in the offshore energy industry" (Ocean Resources, 2002), Hall Inc. employs approximately 250 skilled trades people, and undertakes both national and international projects. With various offices located in Newfoundland, I conducted my fieldwork in the head office, where 14 women and 21 men carry out administrative, financial, and technical tasks.

Hall Inc. expanded its operations to the offshore energy field in the early 1990s, and established its reputation quickly in a highly competitive industry. This is not a small accomplishment for a local business in Newfoundland, where "the economy has always been a problem" and "the manufacturing sector is underdeveloped" (House, 1985, 18, 118). As J. D. House noted, the discovery of the Hibernia oil field, located off the southeast shore of St. John's, led to an influx of national and international companies to the region (1985, 141). These companies, equipped with the required capital, experience and reputation for expensive offshore oil projects, became the major operators in the province's offshore energy industry. Consequently, local businesses with limited resources faced the problem of breaking into this highly competitive environment, which is inherently hostile to smaller companies (House, 1985, 141-49). It is against this background of monopolizing corporate power that the discourse of professionalism becomes an extremely important strategy to the success of Hall Inc. With their well-groomed and disciplined, heterosexual appearance, the women of Hall Inc. play a crucial role in the achievement of the modern and professional image of the company, and in the maintenance of the professionalism discourse.

Professionalism Discourse in Hall Inc.: Professionalism as the Management of Appearance and Self-Presentation

...We have earned [our clients'] confidence in the professional management of projects and delivery of high quality results... The professionalism of our work speaks for itself...
(From the Company Catalogue, 2003)

Victor [the owner of the company] is extremely, extremely big on professionalism. He portrays that through all its ... you know, all the companies and the people he works with know that he expects a high level of professionalism from everybody...
(2nd Interview with Dianne, the executive assistant, February 9, 2004)

Undoubtedly, "professionalism" is the most influential and dominant discourse at Hall Inc. On the surface, this is most evident in both the exterior and the interior design of the main building, as well as in the clothing and appearance style of its female employees. While this strong emphasis on professionalism is a deliberate effort on the part of the upper management, it is widely accepted and embraced by almost everyone I interviewed in the building. Interestingly, while the professionalism discourse can be produced and maintained through various metaphors, organizational structures, and daily interactions such as formal company policies, social activities and rituals, the most obvious and frequently invoked metaphors are "appearance" and "self-presentation". For instance, when I asked Dianne, the executive assistant, what she meant by "a very professional place," she replied, "I mean, appearance, it's a very professional appearance ..." (Dianne) and then continued to talk about how this appearance was cultivated through particular self-presentation and interaction styles. Other employees as well emphasize the importance of the professional look with phrases such as, "Hall Inc. is very big on appearance" (Nancy), or "We have a very professional image here" (Doug).

Sociologist Eliot Freidson argues that the notions of "profession", "professional" and "professionalism" have ambiguous meanings and contradictory uses (1994, 101). In general, when a "profession" is defined as a concrete historical occupation, it refers to an occupation with specialized knowledge, skill, and training, with a right to control its own work and outcomes. Professions gain power and establish their legality and credibility through "strategies of social closure" that usually require membership in a specific association or regulating body (Deverell, 2001, 16). These associations examine and license individual organizations, and establish rules and guidelines for the operation and maintenance of the specific profession in question. In this regard, Hall Inc. is a professional organization, "providing wide range of services to support the full life cycle of a [construction] project" (Company Catalogue, 2003). This is a very simplistic way of defining a professional organization however. How one "accomplishes profession" or becomes "professional" is a more complex process that requires a closer look at the mundane aspects of professional practice. According to Katie Deverell for instance, professionalism is both a "social construct" and an "identity marker" as it "not only says something about what people do, but also who they are" (2001, 16-17, 136). Consequently, professionalism can also function as a discourse through which organizational members make sense of their everyday experiences. Discourses "structure the person's subjectivity, providing him/her with a particular social identity and way of being in the world" (Alvesson and Deetz, 1996, 205).

The Professional (Female) Body: Organizational Power and Self-Discipline

...[While waiting for Mr. Payne] I noticed a few women constantly going up and down the stairs. They rather have a conservative, traditional female look: short to medium hair, blond or sometimes with varying shades of blond highlights, long or knee-high skirts and dresses with matching half or long sleeve blouses, with a limited variety in styles and colors. Perhaps because it is only my second time, they all look the same to me. Their height, weight and body shape are all within a certain range. No one is visibly overweight, too short or too tall. They're all white (possibly local people, I don't know for sure yet), with a similar complexion and facial features. But then again, I reminded myself that I didn't see all the women in the building yet ...

(Second Visit to the Company, Field Notes, May 22, 2003)

The adoption of detailed dress and appearance rules is one of the most common and direct ways of maintaining employee control and discipline in the service industry jobs dominated by women[2]. Explicit regulations and strict guidelines put forth by management on how a female employee should dress, carry her body, do her hair, and apply her make-up are commonly found in these types of jobs, and breaking rules might eventually lead to lay-offs (Adkins, 1995, 122). However, in so-called professional and managerial jobs it is less common to find such formal, written regulations and dress codes (McDowell, 1995; Rubinstein, 2001; Kaiser, 1997). Similarly, among various company policies and procedures, from maternity leave to internet usage, no single policy specifies a dress code in Hall Inc. This does not mean however that employee appearance and dress is not regulated or that there is no negotiation of power through appearance norms. Rather, the organizational power operates in more subtle and complex forms, making it more difficult to recognize initially. In this case, the Foucauldian notion of "modern power" and its re-interpretation by some feminist theorists, provide better analysis of how power relations operate, especially, as Susan Bordo says, "when it comes to the politics of appearance" (1993(a), 27).

Foucault conceptualizes modern power as non-authoritarian and non-coercive, but still able to produce relations of dominance and subordination. Power is not something concrete that belongs to only one group but rather a dynamic "network of non-centralized forces" (Bordo 1993(a), 26). These forces are shaped by the dominant ideologies of the time and are challenged and recreated through history (Foucault, 1977,155 cited in Bordo, 1993(a), 27). Furthermore, modern power is deployed not through repression or coercion but through numerous "techniques of power" such as "surveillance" and "self-discipline". As a result, self-induced discipline and surveillance, or what Bordo calls "power from below" comes to replace the coercive assertion of authority, or "power from above" (Bordo, 1993(a), 27). Joanne Entwistle suggests that the Foucauldian notion of power can be extended to the analysis of modern forms of self and dress "to show how institutional and discursive practices of dress act upon the body, marking it and rendering it meaningful and productive" (2002, 147).

Bordo's and Entwistle's re-interpretations of the Foucauldian concept of power are particularly useful in exploring the power dynamics at Hall Inc. Due to anti-discrimination legislation, there is no formal or written rules specifying height, weight, complexion, or gender of the employees deemed appropriate for certain positions in the company. Nor is there any formal company policy indicating what can or cannot be worn, or what kind of hairstyle or body shape is appropriate for professional appearance. Nevertheless, my daily observations suggest that every woman knows what to wear and how to look or present herself in a strikingly similar, "professional" fashion. In Bordo's terms, the organizational control of the female employees' bodies and their heterosexual appearance are achieved and maintained through the dominant discourse of professionalism in Hall Inc. The discourse is embraced by most of the women as it provides meaning and pride in what otherwise might be called low status "female" jobs. The women already monitor themselves and each other's dressing and grooming practices by embracing the professionalism ideal, regardless of whether their actual position is defined as professional or not. As a result, management at Hall Inc. does not have to exert its power through strict, explicit dress codes[3]. The techniques of surveillance and self-discipline effectively reproduce the discourse of professionalism and the existing power relations, without too much resistance. Dianne, the executive assistant, puts it very clearly:

You are never told [how to dress] ... but you don't need to be! You really don't need to be. You can tell by the atmosphere, you can tell by the building itself. How it's built, how it's organized, the decor ... you know when you are walking ... We just take our cue from the type of business people we deal with and the professional look of the office itself ...

(2nd Interview with Dianne, February 9, 2004)

Men, on the other hand, do not experience the same level of scrutiny on their dress and appearance. The professional male body comes in all different sizes and shapes. I could observe several men, especially estimators, coming to work with casual pants or jeans and t-shirts on any given day. Their informal look is neither a threat to the overall professional air of the company, nor is their competency as professional workers questioned because they do not dress formally. Their casual attire is usually explained in terms of the spatial organization of the building — that men are usually located upstairs, so no one sees them anyway — or the nature of the job they do — that they go to the construction site, so it is more convenient to wear jeans. Similarly, it would be more convenient for the

IT (Information Technology) staff, both of whom are women, to wear more casual/practical clothes as well, "... because they may be crawling under desks working on computers at any time" (Dianne). While Dianne explains that "[the IT staff] very rarely wear dresses or skirts," nevertheless they maintain the full image of professional women with pantsuits (instead of skirted suits), high-heeled shoes and makeup.

However, it would be wrong to assume that the regulation of the female body is mediated by the organizational ideology exclusively. As Carla Freeman illustrates, broader cultural values as well as specific corporate ideals simultaneously shape the dressing and appearance rules for women (1993, 177). Situating the women at Hall Inc. in a larger socio-cultural context helps to explain why diet and exercise are the most popular conversation topics among women in the company. While the western cultural ideals of beauty, health and productivity dictate vigorous exercise, dieting and body management for women[4], the company encourages and maintains this self-endorsed bodily discipline through the professionalism discourse, and through recruitment practices. The absence of different sizes or shapes of women at Hall Inc. sends a message to women, both inside and outside of the company, that only the physically fit, slender, young and well-groomed female body can be appropriately professional (Trethewey, 1999).

During my three months of fieldwork at Hall Inc., I participated in numerous conversations about low-fat meal recipes and the essentials of healthy weight loss, and took part in lunchtime jogs in the neighboring park. These were all exclusively female activities in the company. While it can be argued that these activities are forms of surveillance and endorsement of bodily discipline for women, they can also be interpreted as a pleasant way of socializing with, and relating to, the women in the company. However, the following excerpt from my research diary shows the extent of the pressure self-control can take.

While I was chatting with Dianne and Shelly by Dianne's desk, to my surprise and amazement, Heather put a little, gray, handbag-like thing on the floor and stepped on it. Only then I realized that it was a scale and Heather was weighing herself in the company lobby! She then turned to Shelly, who was next to me, showing her four fingers and her mouth moving quietly 'I lost four pounds' she said. Shelly shook her head and said it wasn't that good. She then went on saying how much weight she lost, except the previous week because it was her birthday so she ate a lot. Dianne made a joke (perhaps to ease the tension) and said 'I think I put on all the weight you lost!'

(Field Notes, July 14, 2003)

This seemingly ordinary exchange between Heather and Shelly clearly illustrates the operations of modern social and organizational power on women's bodies.

Professional Dress(es): Maintenance of Organizational Status Quo and Hierarchy

Despite the considerable resemblance in terms of the physical appearance and dressing practices, the women at Hall Inc. are not an homogenous category, nor are their jobs and positions within the company. How they dress and present themselves varies within a certain range depending on personal taste and organizational status. Among the 14 women in the building at the time of my fieldwork, only one was in a managerial position. The others were employed in administration (2), accounting and finance (5), information technology (2), purchasing (1), reception (2), and executive assistant (1) positions. As Dianne said, "… because women [are] in varying office roles they wear clothing equal to their roles" (Dianne). While she makes the distinction between relatively different styles according to the amount of public exposure — more public exposure was equated with more formal dressing — the appearance and dressing styles also reflect and reproduce the occupational subcultures to which women belong, as well as their place in the organizational hierarchy.

Several researchers argue that the women in managerial or senior positions pay particular attention to their overall look in order to distinguish themselves from other women on the lower end of the hierarchy (McDowell, 1995; Sheppard, 1989; Dellinger, 2002; Pringle, 1988). In addition, they claim, female managers make a special effort to minimize their feminine look and sexual attractiveness by adopting a sombre, serious, business attire in order to relate to and blend with the dominant male managerial culture. At Hall Inc., it is very unusual for Laura, the only female manager in the building, to wear jeans on designated "jeans days", while almost all the other women do. Laura's constant care and attention to her full professional image, even on more casual days, indicate her actual or desired membership in the higher level, male, managerial culture. This may also be one of her non-verbal strategies to establish her boundaries with, and assert her authority over, the women in the company. In my brief interview with her, Laura talked about the difficulty of balancing her friendly, easygoing approach to everyone in the building and her need to assert her authority when necessary, especially in relation to other women. Once, she noted, she was "on the edge of [her] boundaries" (Laura) and even the owner of the company noticed a few of the women held a "disrespectful" attitude towards her. Distinguishing herself from other women through her more serious appearance, especially in the absence of more concrete authority symbols, might serve to remind other women of her distinct status and authority in the company. This is a well-documented method used by several female managers demonstrated in the literature (Sheppard, 1989; McDowell, 1995; Dellinger, 2002).

Sarah, the purchasing assistant, usually comes to work with minimal make-up, sporty, casual pants and large clothes that cover and minimize the contours of her body. She is located on the fourth floor and her location away from the "public eye" plays a role in her clothing choices. However, it is her relatively equal working relationship and status with her male colleagues that permits her more casual appearance. Her education and training are comparable with that of the male estimators, and like them she is working on company projects rather than taking care of routine office business. Similar to the male estimators, who dress very casually, Sarah's dressing style and appearance mimic the general look of the floor on which she works.

Like Laura, Sarah's clothing choice and appearance style de-emphasizes her femininity and sexuality. Sarah realizes this through her casual appearance, approximating the general look of the men she is working with, while Laura dresses in more elegant, serious, and tailored suits to achieve and maintain her authority in the company. On the other hand, women's clothing, particularly in junior administrative assistant positions, prominently marks their femaleness and sexuality. The female assistants work for the male managers, organizing and taking care of the everyday routines of the office in general and the divisions they work for in particular. Unlike Sarah, they are working for the men, who have more power, authority and status. As a result, the assistants' immediate working and reporting relationships with the men are based on an apparent structural power imbalance[5]. The subtle organizational norms that prescribe an appropriately gendered and heterosexualized look for women are maintained through this imbalance. Whether they do so knowingly or not, the assistants conform to these norms through their more feminine appearance, which in turn reproduces the assistants' subordinate status in the company.

The Professional Dress: Normalization of Heterosexuality and Gender Binaries

As I have demonstrated, there is a complex relationship among the operations of organizational power, appearance norms, gender identity, and the status quo. All these dynamics are woven together by the assumption of universal heterosexuality. Entwistle claims that the notion of a professional woman and the strict monitoring of her visual appearance "articulates a very particular kind of body: one that is feminine *and* professional at the same time … a relatively recent historical invention" (2002, 141, original emphasis). "Compulsory heterosexuality" that manufactures and normalizes the traditional gender binaries lies at the center of this articulation (Butler, 1990, 23). In heterosexual ideology, the disembodied, rational male worker comes to represent the logical order and values of the bureaucratic organization. His body and appearance do not endanger the rational command, as his mind is claimed to suppress his body and any bodily desires. Of course, this is true only as long as he maintains a certain form of heterosexual masculinity (McDowell, 1995, 85). Women on the other hand, are defined by their bodies and constructed in opposition to the rational (male) mind. If women want to have higher authority and power within the modern organizational hierarchy, or to assert their "professionalism," they have to refrain from overt display of their bodies. (Green, 2001; Entwistle, 2000, 2002; Trethewey, 1999).

The proper display of the heterosexual professional female body usually poses contradictory and complex tasks for women. On the one hand, the professionalism discourse claims a disciplined, not too feminized or sexualized appearance. As women they have to downplay their "distracting" sexuality, and demonstrate self-control, and logical thinking to validate their place in the company and confirm their professionalism. On the other hand, as a main organizing principle of workplace relations and interactions, heterosexuality requires women to be pleasant and attractive to the male gaze, regardless of their position in the hierarchy. For instance, even though Laura dresses in suits akin to those of male managers, with her high-heeled shoes, makeup, medium-length hair, and accessories she is still unmistakably "female" and "heterosexual", at least in her appearance. Thus, says Bordo, "with a 'softening' fashion touch to establish traditional feminine decorativeness, and continually cautioned against the dire consequences of allotting success higher priority than her looks, she represents no serious competition (symbolically, that is) to the real men of the work place" (1993(a), 209). Unlike Laura, most of the women at Hall Inc. are support staff positioned at the bottom of the organizational hierarchy. This provides them a wider range of possibilities to present themselves, as it is evident in "jeans days," since they do not have to fit in to the male managerial culture. However, the display of their femaleness and (hetero)sexuality is circumscribed by yet another appearance rule endorsed by the professionalism discourse. The widespread notion of "professional workplace" enables the organizational power to control the overt display of female sexuality that would otherwise present a threat to the so-called non-sexual, impersonal nature of the bureaucratic organization.

Jeans Days: Subversion or Compliance?

[During this Friday's lunch] Shelly said that, Victor [the owner of the company] had noticed a few of them with jeans and asked 'Is this that Friday again?' not amused at all. 'He doesn't like us wearing jeans,' she said. I asked the reason. She replied: 'Victor doesn't think it looks professional.' Speaking directly towards me she continued, 'We've been fighting for a year [over the issue of wearing jeans to work]'. She seemed upset [by him]. I was glad that I was wearing my jeans as the other women at lunch were also all wearing jeans ...

(Field Notes, July 25, 2003)

As a lesbian, I was well aware of the "heterosexual norms of feminine appearance" in modern capitalist work organizations even before I started my research (Dellinger and Williams, 1997,162). I carefully planned the details of the image I wanted to present through my external appearance in my first visit to the company. After the research project was approved, one of my initial concerns was about arranging and buying clothing suitable to wear at Hall Inc. This, I thought, would help me both to establish my credibility as a competent organizational researcher and to blend well with the other women at work. Consequently, like most other women in the company, I played a part in the reproduction of the dominant organizational ideology and status quo. However, as several scholars argue, resistance is always possible and there is a dialectical relationship "between processes of organizational control and acts of resistance" (Ashcraft and Mumby, 2004, 103).

Bordo notes that resistance exists simultaneously with power and "prevailing norms themselves have transformative potential" (1993(b), 191). Similarly, John Fiske adds, "no bodies are completely docile" (1993, 64) while Dellinger and Williams discuss women's capacity to resist and to "transform institutionalized norms"(1997, 168). Dellinger and Williams claim that "makeup can be a topic of conversation that bonds women together" and that "some women ... use makeup to promote their goals of personal enjoyment and bodily pleasure" (1997, 169, 171). Brewis et al. argue that professional women's dress at work is gender inappropriate and it provides an example of "a deliberate modification of gender identity" (1997, 1288). The adaptation of the male suit for the professional women, they believe, takes the attention away from their femininity and puts the focus on "their (masculine) abilities" (Brewis et al., 1997,1287). Accordingly, the "jeans day" at Hall Inc. can be interpreted as a subversive practice on the part of the women. "Jeans day" was initiated by the Social Committee, an almost all-female group. On the last Friday of each month, anyone can come to work wearing jeans if they donate two dollars to charity. Since men usually come to work in casual dress and jeans on any given day, the "jeans days" are significant for the women. Therefore, they take active responsibility to implement and carry on the practice. It would be misleading however, to construe the "jeans day" as an utterly subversive practice.

Bordo warns us that while the Foucauldian notion of power makes resistance possible through the creation of alternate discourses and practices, the new discourses may paradoxically help to maintain established norms. In other words, the experience of power through subversion of dominant discourses can be illusory (Bordo, 1993(a), 28, 179) and thus, the negotiation of power relations and the practice of resistance may become double-sided (Pringle, 1989,168). Brewis et al. recognize power dressing is not "particularly subversive" as it still perpetuates traditional gender binaries and heterosexual ideology (1997, 1288). Similarly, Dellinger and Williams accept the limits of their argument by stating that comments about appearance and makeup are not always comforting or bonding (1997, 169). In the same way, the meaning of "jeans days" becomes fluid. Nancy explains on "jeans days" "[they] usually put a little sign up on the [reception] desk that tells everybody coming in that 'we're wearing jeans today in support of a local charity' " (Nancy). Dianne adds an important piece of information to this. She states that "giving back [to community and charities] is something Victor is extremely big on ..." and gives numerous examples of donations (Dianne). Clearly then, contributing to the charities is a significant social component of becoming a "professional organization" at Hall Inc. As a result, the "jeans days" quickly become a medium through which the professionalism discourse at Hall Inc. is maintained and expressed, albeit in a different form. By notifying every visitor to the company about the "jeans days" and their charity activity, women still function within the same discourse, yet with a different appearance rule. The female employees are also capable of manipulating the discourse for their own interest. Four months after I finished my fieldwork, Dianne informed me that "jeans days" were extended to every Friday instead of once in a month, a direct result of the efforts of the social committee.

Conclusion

The female body and by extension its external, dressed and adorned appearance is highly charged with sexuality and constructed as a main site where the dominant discourses, power relations, and gender binaries are negotiated and maintained (McDowell, 1995; M.E. Bailey, 1993; Bordo, 1993(a), 1993(b); Entwistle, 2000; Sheppard, 1989). At Hall Inc. the existing power relations, organizational status quo and the discipline of the female employees' bodies are maintained through gender appropriate heterosexual appearance norms. These norms shape and are shaped by the dominant organizational discourse of professionalism as well as the Western ideals of health and productivity.

Given Newfoundland's peripheral economic and social status, the successful construction of the professional and modern image of the company is vital for its survival and growth in a highly competitive industry. The creation and display of well-disciplined and groomed, slender and heterosexual female bodies is a main vehicle through which this image is achieved. This does not mean that women's bodies are passive constructions, nor that women lack agency to resist or manipulate the dominant discourses for their own benefit. Rather the construction of body and interpretation of its experiences are dynamic processes where conflicting discourses are negotiated and new ones are formed. In this regard, the women at Hall Inc. embrace and reproduce the professionalism discourse, while simultaneously challenge it by creating alternative discourses of professional appearance.

Notes

[1] All the names and identifying details of the company and the employees have been changed to protect their anonymity.

[2] According to the latest (2001) Canadian and provincial labor market statistics, in Canada 65.7% of sales and services workers are female. In Newfoundland, sales and services industry employs the greatest percentage (36%) of women who are active in the labor market (Adapted from: http://www.statcan.ca/english/Pgdb/labor45a.htm).

[3] This is true with the exception of two cases. The two women who were both performing the receptionist duties mentioned that they were told how to dress in one way or another by the upper management.

[4] While one can argue that the same standards apply to men as well, it is certainly not to the same extent. Slim and slender appearance is not a necessary condition for men to show their professionalism either.

[5] However, as Pringle notes, organizational structures are only one of the dynamics among many, and power relations "cannot simply be read off from these structures or be said to reflect them" (1988, 28). In general, the assistants are quite resourceful in their negotiations of power with their superiors.

Did I Choose to be Marginal? Structural Constraints on Individual Agency in "Career Choice"

Linda Parsons

A S A CONTRACTUAL WORKER AND MOTHER for many years, I continually encounter an assumption among employers and others that women in my position *prefer* part-time or temporary work. Because of this assumption, we are often considered "less capable" than full-time workers and are subsequently marginalized in the workplace. This is problematic for many reasons. While the flexibility of contractual work is undeniably attractive to young mothers, it is difficult to see how this justifies their continuing marginal status as workers. Moreover, this assumption overlooks the structural constraints of work and family that inform the "choice" to work part-time or on a temporary basis, and it ignores the fact that such contingent work is designed to meet the immediate needs of employers and not those of workers.

My question in this essay is whether women *choose* to work in contingent jobs solely out of a sense of "individual agency", defined here as the personal power to choose one's career path, or because of structural constraints and necessity. I argue that it is the *situational context* of workers that circumscribes such choice and that this context is established through both structure and agency.

I am using my own experiences as autoethnographic data. Although my work as a contractual teacher in a post secondary institution differs in its relatively high level of pay, I share a sense of precariousness (Vosko, 2003) with many other contingent workers in that we anticipate being "laid off" when demand falls or when we can be replaced by cheaper workers. In this essay, I combine authoethnography with a brief review of the sociological literature to trace the effects of this precariousness on career choice.

Autoethnography draws on the principles of feminist research by linking personal experience and social patterns and then using this intersection to develop "reflexive understanding" in research (Goodall Jr., 2003; Sparkes, 2002; McRobbie, 1994; Smith, 1987). Furthermore, autoethnography "... unsettle(s) the moral dualisms which are thrown up by the narcissism of "common sense" and its normative closures" (Hills, 2002, 81). Here, one moral dualism lies in the tension between the idea that women are individually free to choose the conditions of their work, but must do so in deference to a structural "motherhood imperative". Another moral dualism occurs when women are expected to prioritize mothering even when the contingencies of their work provide little support for caregiving and motherwork. I hope to clarify how such moral dualisms and the same structural constraints faced by working mothers throughout Canada influenced my personal choice — or rather, decision — to work contingently.

The Argument: "Breakdown" or "Boundaryless" Career Biographies?

Despite the myth that knowledge workers are unaffected (or even positively affected) by globalization, the "restructuring"[1] of human resources has extended even to post secondary institutions over the past few decades and has, without doubt, led to greater contingency and precariousness in all jobs. Temporary, short-term, and part-time work is now a common business strategy to stimulate efficiency and profitability, often at the expense of work security (Lowe, 2000; Rinehart, 2001; Livingstone, 2001).

There are a number of ways of looking at how this trend affects the career decisions of women: I consider two of these here. The first argument is that contingency in the work of well educated knowledge workers has undermined traditional career paths of upward status mobility and better-than-average incomes. Instead, knowledge work is becoming progressively more "proletarianized", with status inconsistency, increasing workloads, decreasing relative wages, underemployment, and the degradation of many jobs to part-time "contractual", "casuals", or "temps" (Rinehart, 2001; Sennett, 1998; Livingstone, 2001). No longer depending on a predictable career path where their specialty skill sets would be scarce and in demand, many knowledge workers are currently facing "flexible" workplaces and short term contracts rather than long term security. Choices are redefined as individual "risks" and for Beck (1999, 12),

> one thing is clear. *Endemic uncertainty is what will mark the life world and basic existence of most people - including the apparently affluent middle classes - in the years that lie ahead* (italics mine).

The element of risk in career biographies means that "All too swiftly, the 'elective', 'reflexive', or 'do-it-yourself' biography can become the breakdown biography" (Beck, 1999, 12) and uncertainty over income and advancement may lead to feelings of disassociation among knowledge workers. Younger workers are encouraged to take risks rather than stick with an inflexible plan of career progression that appears stagnant and archaic. Such risks might include choosing self-employment or contractual work but as Jurik (1998) points out, these types of work are more often structurally *forced* through unemployment, underemployment and the overall casualization of work rather than *chosen* by individuals. From this point of view, contingent and self-employed work are attempts to deal with job insecurity and exploitation, with varying degrees of success.

84

A counter argument to the breakdown biography is the "boundaryless career". Here, the "growing disarticulation between worker and workplace" as a result of restructuring can be re-interpreted as *facilitating* the power, control, and personal agency of knowledge workers over their own work. The "casualization of the employment relationship" means less mutual commitment between management, and workers and worker solidarity is undermined by the "shift from collective bargaining to individual bargaining" (Cornfield, Campbell, and McCammon 2001, xi - xiii). This also gives knowledge workers more autonomy in shaping their own experience of work. No longer committed to one employer, they are free to play the field; no longer committed to bargaining along with co-workers, they can seek their own maximum advantage.

In the "boundaryless career" argument, the life chances and workplace relationships of knowledge workers are continually in flux, but they are better able to take advantage of whatever "structural gaps of opportunity" exist in the new form of work organization (Cornfield et al, 2001; Sennett, 1998). Instead of viewing career decisions as individual *risks*, a positive connotation emphasizes individual agency and responsibility in career choices. Here, the alternatives of contingent work and self-employment are preferred choices in a rational labor market. The worker is assumed to be unfettered by other life concerns and chooses employment to suit her own maximum self-interest. This is part of what Carr (1996) and Waring (1995) refer to as the "male model" of employment. Within this boundaryless career, the worker is a "liberated innovator" (Jurik, 1998, 152), and is better off in terms of autonomy, control, and managing work and family. By extension, she is also more productive and profitable.

Which of these views of career choice among contingent workers best explains my own motivations for entering contingent work? Am I the author of a boundaryless career or the subject of a breakdown work biography? I argue that my career choices, like those of countless other contingently working women in Canada, reflect (and are reflected in) social structures. I consider these social structures in the following sections.

The Situational Context: Work Restructuring in the Postsecondary System

Within the university setting, limited term teaching contracts have become a mainstay and an important part of "neo-Fordist" business policies of university administrations throughout North America. The academic labor market has been divided into at least two tiers — tenured full time faculty and contingent, part-time or temporary lecturers and sessionals.[2] Many argue that this has also led to the overall proletarianization of academic labor where *both* full-time and contingent faculty have been assigned increasing workloads and have experienced a decreasing "quality of work life" (Parsons, 2002; Tirelli, 1997; Rhoades, 1996;

Goyder, 1992; Rosenblum and Rosenblum, 1990).

Sessional and contractual teachers in my university assume several distinct categories that vary by status, level of education, and degree of commitment. The lowest paid are "per course" contractuals who teach one or two courses on campus with no health or pension benefits or seniority status. Contractuals who teach solely by distance education are paid "per student", again with no benefits or seniority status. "Per course" and "per student" instructors usually combine contingent teaching with other jobs or with study in academic programs: few can actually live on the income made while teaching on contract.

In contrast, term and sessional appointments involve a full time commitment to teach at least three courses per semester with no research or administrative duties required. These jobs are paid relatively well as a proportion of an annual salary. In my institution, benefits are also included if the term contract extends beyond six months. The actual pay varies by length of contract and by the education and experience of the sessional, with a ceiling that usually ends at about the beginning of the salary scale for assistant professors (Canadian Association of University Teachers [CAUT], 2004). With experience one becomes a relatively expensive worker, and administrations have recently preferred to risk a high worker turnover rate and to hire more but less costly "per course" contractuals on a semester-by-semester basis. Thus, even at the level of relatively cheap term appointments, knowledge work is becoming more insecure.

Along with insecurity there is a question of status: While our teaching experience is acknowledged within departments and to some extent on the pay scale, it counts for very little in status within the larger academic community where sessionals are routinely deemed "marginal workers". As Church (1999) notes, this stigma is often attributed to personal failure. Sessionals have been

> made invisible in the university caste system by disappearing as "professional failures" according to the ideals of meritocracy ... Performances of professionalism subtly demand that tenure track faculty forget the structural conditions in which these temporary laborers work and naturalize success and failure as a matter of personal merit (251).

This is further exaggerated by gender. Despite the strong overall position of academic women since 2000 (Statistics Canada, 2005), the proportional representation of women goes down as professorial status goes up: Only 28.4% of those in the top category of "full professors" in my field were women in 2000-2001 (CAUT, 2004). The Canadian Association of University Teachers found that almost 80% of faculty in the "other" category in my field were women. "Other" is distinguished from full, associate, and assistant professorships and includes term, sessional, and contractual appointments, all of which are contingent on administrative demand.

Why are women predominant in contingent academic work? One reason is that the post secondary system has always been based on a "male model" of work. Women often find its stipulations difficult to meet in addition to family role expectations (Harman and Remy, 2002). For example, the imperative that academics "publish or perish" demands ample time for reflection and writing and offers little remuneration in the early stages of one's career. To accomplish this, one can remain single and childless until established or find a very supportive and understanding spouse who will assume most of the family role responsibilities, as many male academics do. Family women, and to a lesser extent men, often find themselves postponing the doctoral degree and taking up contractual and sessional work to keep a foot in the door (Litner, 2002; Harman and Remy, 2002), as I did. Despite these structural constraints, however, this decision is still viewed as a "choice" to work contingently. Do all contingent workers in Canada make this "choice"? Are these voluntary personal choices or involuntary structurally influenced decisions?

Statistics Canada on "Reasons for Voluntary and Involuntary Part-time Work"

The question of whether contingent work is "chosen" or involuntary and necessitated by structural factors has been the subject of wide scale quantitative research at Statistics Canada since at least 1993. Statistics show that 68-80% of the "total *involuntary* part-time population from 1993 to 1996" were women in their child bearing years, with the highest proportion in the 35-44 year old group (Noreau, 2000, 10: emphasis mine).

In a 2002 survey of part-time workers, Statistics Canada (2003) researchers found that only 26.2% of women and 22.3% of men stated "personal preference" as the reason for working part-time. The remaining part-time workers cited other reasons such as "caring for children", "other family responsibilities", and "attending school". Common assumptions often attributed these reasons to individual choice rather than to social structural constraint but a closer look indicates that gender roles are likely influential. For example, only 2.3% of the men but 20.6% of the women stated that "caring for children" and "other family responsibilities" were the combined reasons for working part-time in 2002. "Going to school" was the reason for 41.9% of men and 24.9% of women who worked part-time (Statistics Canada, 2003). The fact that there is an increasing number of women citing school as a reason might indicate that the "educational imperative", once attributed to the family breadwinner, is now keenly felt by women. Support for this can be found in Lowe's (2000) study where more women than men engaged in learning activities that were supplementary to their paid work. Few would now argue that education is simply an individual choice in light of the growing credentialism in the labour market (Livingstone, 2001).

In the 2002 Statistics Canada survey, the numbers identifying involuntary (structural) reasons for working part-time — "business conditions and inability to find full-time work" — were more approximate, accounting for 30.2% of the men, and 25.6% of the women who worked part-time (Statistics Canada, 2003). Nevertheless, gender remains significant as both the absolute and proportionate numbers of women in part-time work overall are much higher than those of men. In 2002, only 10.9% of all employed men worked part-time, while 27.7% of all employed women fell into this category (Statistics Canada, 2003). This means that the 25.6% of women working part-time because of "inability to find work" will far outnumber the 30.2% of men working part-time for the same reason[3] and is an indication that more women than men are disadvantaged in the workplace.

The idea that contingent work is a rational career choice for women is further compromised by the fact that long-term part-time and contingent work results in lower levels of cumulative lifetime income, work security and promotion, and pension remuneration among women (Drolet, 2003; Statistics Canada, 2002b). Statisticians have also found that contingent working women have greater difficulty "repositioning themselves in the full time job market after an extended absence (... coupled with) the general difficulty for women to find full time employment" (Noreau, 2000, 10-11).

Most working women are aware of these disadvantages from the outset and of the fact that these are *structural* outcomes of the intersection between work and family. Few see contingent work as a rational career advantage, despite our cultural discourse[4] that we are making voluntary, non-gendered choices. We decide between alternatives on the basis of what we feel is best, for ourselves and our families, and this situational context changes constantly.

In my own experience, these statistics do little to clarify the shifts that so often occur in career biography. Had I been interviewed for these Statistics Canada surveys at the beginning of my working career, I would have answered that I *decided* to work contingently to care for children and admitted my susceptibility to that larger "motherhood imperative". If asked many years later when I was still working contingently, my answer would be an "inability to find full time work". At neither point was contingent work totally voluntary, and the gendered aspects of my family and work roles were always considered when making the "choice". In the next section, I consider some of these aspects.

Gender Differences in the Experience of Work

The decision to work contingently is at least partly affected by the fact that women still experience labour force constraints that are different from those of men. The most persistent of these differences is the wage gap where women earned an average of 80% of men's aggregate wages in 1999 (Statistics Canada, 2002a), despite wage equity legislation in Canada. According to Statistics Canada, only 24% of this wage gap was due to "worker characteristics" like experience and occupation. The vast majority of women have equivalent levels of experience and occupational training as men. About 20% of the wage gap in 1999 was due to the segregation of women in low wage occupations and 18% was associated with workplace characteristics such as the predominance of contingent work. The remaining 38% of the age gap could not be accounted for in the statistical models that did not include "gender discrimination" as a category (Statistics Canada, 2002a). Even when similar jobs and hours of work are compared, women make less money than do men. This has a significant effect on the decision about who is to care for the newly arriving babies or drive the children to their never-ending activities. The family allotment of this work, usually to the mother, is determined both by traditional gendered expectations and by who would lose the least in opportunity costs (Fox, 2001; Lowe, 2000; Drolet, 2001, 2002).

"Role overload" is another gendered experience that informs the decision to work contingently. Defined as having too much to do in a given amount of time, role overload is associated with work restructuring and with both physical and mental health problems such as job stress, absenteeism, illness, and decreasing work satisfaction. In Duxbury and Higgins' (2003) quantitative survey, higher proportions of all workers in lower level white and pink collar occupations, and of women workers at all levels, reported poor mental health including stress, depression and burnout. This was correlated with intensified role overload, high "work to family interference" and "negative spillovers" from work such as caregiver strain. Family and gender expectations have an interesting impact here: Male workers in managerial positions, where role overload is quite high, usually experienced *fewer* mental health problems than did their female managerial counterparts or all workers in lower level positions. In addition, motherhood was strongly correlated to higher levels of depression and lower levels of life satisfaction among workers in this study and others (Duxbury and Higgins, 2003; Hochschild, 1997; Simon, 1995).

Again, women's choice of working contingently must be framed in the situational contexts of workplace and family demands. In my own experience , the role overload associated with being a full time academic was daunting. An academic career involves an enormous investment of research and writing time in the first ten years *after* a doctoral program has been completed, and the two enterprises together can easily account for close to 20 years of an adult's working life. After my children were born, I found even the prospect of this overwhelming.

Individual Responses to Structural Constraints: Is This "Agency"?

For many theorists, the focus on structural constraints such as I have described above obscures a reality where the individual *does* derive power from individual agency and actively creating meaning (Hills, 2002; Muggleton, 2000; McRobbie, 1994; Flyvbjerg, 2001). According to this argument, individuals are fully aware of the cultural contradictions they must live with and *negotiate* meaning that allows them to survive within the "hegemonic discourse" and structural constraints.

The strategy of *subjective* containment is one means of reappropriating some measure of agency and power by contingent workers who feel excluded from an apparently "more legitimate" full-time labour force. In academic work, sessionals sometimes feel stigmatized by their part-time status and, as McRobbie (1994) notes,

> black, female, or working class intellectuals ... are experiencing the enforced fragmentation of impermanent work and low career opportunities. Far from being overwhelmed ... there is evidence to suggest that these social groups and minorities are putting it to work for them (by) invent(ing) the self (23, 72).

In dealing with gendered role overload, the subjective containment of work helps. Indeed, part of the attraction of sessional and other types of contingent work is that it can be subjectively contained to allow at least a few moments for reflection and leisure. Sessional work is easier to balance with other aspects of life, such as raising children or devoting time to a spouse than is full time work (Enke,1999), mainly because it excludes research and administrative responsibilities. During the semester, teaching work time can be arranged to suit family and other demands as long as one is willing to work nights and weekends![5]

In recruiting workers, employers in all industries often cite the flexibility of contingent work as a woman's resolution to the contradiction in combining work with family responsibilities. Oddly, however, it is rarely proffered as a resolution for men and it can have unintended consequences for anyone. For example, self-employment is a similar type of resolution that women often attempt, but with varying results according to their *social location*.[6] This occurred in Jurik's (1998) and Carr's (1996) studies where women respondents chose self-employment to escape workplace discrimination and enjoy autonomy, self fulfillment, a balance between work and child care, and flexible hours. Many considered themselves to be secondary earners in the family whose primary responsibility was child care[7] and they were more likely to choose self employment if they had the adequate resources to support their choice — specifically, if they were educated, had a "fall back" income, enjoyed child care support, and maintained a separate office.

Like contingent workers, those in Carr's (1996) and Jurik's (1998) studies who were without these resources soon realized the insecurity of self-employment in having to accept lower earnings, routine "bread and butter" work, and self-exploitation to meet their own goals of profitability or expansion. Contrary to its allure, self-employment, like contingent work, involved *reduced* work satisfaction and flexibility, especially in areas where unemployment was rising. For these women and others (see Lowe, 2000; Mirchandani, 2000), balancing work and family was actually exacerbated by working at home unless they could draw on family or friends for help. Few could find any time for themselves.

My experience as a contingent worker aligns with this. Although sessional teaching is attractive in its flexibility, the allure is often compromised by circumstance. Hired for a specific and relatively short period, sessionals frequently work long days and weekends to get the job done. This easily translates into role overload that affects health in terms of stress and "burn-out", and in physical ways. For example, Gadbois (2002) described placing herself at risk by ignoring health complications that accompanied a broken ankle on one occasion and a uterine cyst on another, in the interests of ensuring that her term appointment work was fulfilled. Working contingently often involves such individual "choices".

I anticipate that, as with self-employed workers, the social location of the contingent worker affects how these experiences become part of one's self-identity. Autonomy, self-fulfillment, and defining oneself as "successful" were higher among the professional women of Jurik's (1998) study, and professional and middle class women had a larger pool of resources to use in maintaining a degree of control over their work process. So, if health problems from role overload and stress can occur among academic sessionals, I speculate that they would be exacerbated in those social locations delineated by lower income and education levels.

The Intensification of Gender Roles

For women, the pressure of role overload and the displacement of family and leisure time by work is problematic but so, too, are the solutions. Some analysts believe that role overload is partly a result of the "penchant" of women to intensify their gender role performance when faced with competing demands. According to this argument, we spend more time in child and elder care than do men because we continue to subscribe to the gendered social imperative for women that places caregiving before work. Viewing work and family roles as independent of each other, and therefore as conflicting, we working women feel we are cheating our families with every moment spent at paid work. We compensate by continuing to take responsibility for the bulk of unpaid work in the home[8] (Duxbury and Higgins, 2003; Simon, 1995; Noreau, 2000).

These analysts recommend that women must change their attitudes, share the burden of housework and caregiving with men, and seek better working conditions. While these are all excellent points which would undoubtedly contribute to greater equity in paid and unpaid work, I am left wondering who will pick up the slack? Statistical and qualitative research has long documented the struggles (and difficulties) women have had convincing others, principally men, to take more domestic responsibility and obtaining better working conditions for all women (Fox, 2001; Luxton, 1997; Ross and Wright 1998).

Another argument is that contingent work better suits the self-identity of women than of men, but this ignores the fact that the majority of women still *prefer* full time employment (Lowe, 2000) so that working conditions like contingency are not fully "chosen". It also ignores the complex, situational, and intersubjective contexts (Flyvbjerg, 2001; Cullum, 2003) of the decision to work contingently. For example, not only did the situational context of my decision to work contingently change over the years, but so did the intersubjective meaning of part-time and temporary work. This meaning varied over time and sometimes within the moment, according to whom I was meeting. With my full time mothering friends, my work decision was framed by the difficulties of maintaining a family life and finding good child care while working. We agreed that if family income permitted, contingent work was preferable to full time work in hopes of avoiding the very real problems that have been associated with "latch key" children. The decision was cast in terms of our mothering responsibilities and the lack of adequate childcare alternatives, both structural elements.

With friends who also worked, the decision to work contingently was still framed by the lack of and expense of viable daycare and the difficulties of juggling work and home, but we acknowledged the attraction of flexible work in dealing with these structural constraints.

When alone, my sense of personal agency disintegrated and contingent work really seemed like my best option: It provided a reasonably well paying job in employment-poor Atlantic Canada that afforded me some measure of a life, albeit at the expense of work security, status, pension, and other work benefits.

I still believe in all of these meanings, seeing them not as contradictory but as responses to specific life events and situational contexts. These "complex, shifting ... discursive practices" create a "shifting identity formation" where identities are admittedly complex, sometimes contradictory, and always adapting to the expectations of surrounding people and circumstances (Cullum, 2003, 49, 55). In our culture, the identity associated with motherhood is juxtaposed with the identity of "worker" and the choice between the two is left up to the individual. This assumption of individual agency obscures the fact that gendered identities affect and are created from both work and family structures which are, themselves, fluid and are continually "... taken up, regularized, institutionalized, resisted, contested, transformed" (Marshall, 2000, 162) through individual identity construction. As Flyvbjerg (2001) points out, elucidating such situational contexts leads one to question the validity of the "structure versus agency" debate — can we really attribute our actions to only one side or the other?

Conclusion

The positive effect of regarding contingent work as an individual choice and part of one's "boundaryless career" is that this encourages a sense of agency and empowerment in dealing with the contradictions of that work. Nevertheless, it also glosses over a "strategic disavowal of the vicissitudes of (our) ... own reality" (Church, 1999, 257). Those who value "opportunism" and "risk" tend to ignore the *dis*utilities of contingent work. The ideals of individual choice and meritocracy become "point(s) of dislocation", according to Willis (1977/81, 163), obfuscating "... a centered world of oppression from a specific and determinant social organization of thought, production, and interest (e.g. the corporate profit logic) ... (Instead) we have the naturalistic world of a thousand timeless causes."

From my own experiences, I conclude that the structural needs and contingencies of work and family are concealed by the ideals of choice and individual agency. I agree with Giddens (1994) that the better term for "choice" is "decision". We are not so much availing of a free choice as making decisions between the limited options available in work and family structures which "... refract back upon the pre-existing power relations" (76). Work and family constraints are undoubtedly changing, becoming much more fluid and difficult to pinpoint (Bauman, 2000) but they are also still definitive and cannot be hidden under the rhetoric of free choice. For women working contingently, individual agency is a double- edged sword. We gain a sense of control when choosing our life path (the boundaryless career), but this individual choice then becomes a rationale for our marginalization in the workplace (part of the breakdown biography), and often for an unequal and gendered division of labour at home (Marshall, 2000). Terminology is important when "individual agency" and "choice" hide structural inequalities (Luxton, 1997), such as those enumerated here, and the increasing casualization of work on all levels of the occupational hierarchy. The importance of the distinction between "choice" and "decision" is twofold. Individual choice has too long been used as a justification for restricting social support to women and men who are balancing work and family, and for the disparaging notion that contingent workers, having opted out of full time work, are only marginally capable and are less deserving of "quality" in their working conditions (Lowe, 2000).

Although I cannot describe the experiences of other contingent workers in the knowledge industry or otherwise, I do feel that my experience is fairly common among working women in Canada. I believe that both the "structure versus agency" discourse and the stress on personal choice do little to truly address the concomitant problems of precarious and contingent work. Rather, a focus on the *situational context* of this increasingly prevalent form of work will better elucidate these problems and their possible solutions.

Notes

[1] Work restructuring refers to such modifications in the workplace as the globalization of production, outsourcing, "just-in-time" production, and labour force downsizing and delayering (of middle management). These are accompanied by (or elicit) the "influx" of women and temporary/contingent workers (Sennett 1998; Rinehart 2001; and Cornfield, Campbell, and McCammon, eds., 2001).

[2] The information for this paper focuses on teachers within the post-secondary system. This does not include the myriad of researchers and other student and faculty support workers who are also part of the academic labour market.

[3] That is to say, 25.6% of the 27.7% of all working women is a higher real number than 30.2% of 10.9% of all working men.

[4] For the purposes of this essay, 'discourse= refers to the myriad ways that cultural ideas and values, like the work ethic or the motherhood imperative, are transmitted and received.

[5] "Flexible" work is project-oriented and schedules are often non-linear, even though "flextime" rarely translates into less — or less difficult — work (Rinehart, 2001; Lowe, 2000). This flexibility in scheduling is one of the attractive features of academic work in general, so this in itself does not distinguish sessionals or contractuals from full time faculty.

[6] "... The term *social location* ... specif(ies) the way in which political and economic conditions interact with class, ethnicity, culture, (age), and sexual orientation to shape the meanings and strategies of working men and women" (Jurik, 1998, 152).

[7] Interestingly, those men in Jurik's study who chose self-employment to be more involved with family did not, subsequently, adopt greater domestic or child care responsibilities than they had before.

8 In 2002, women working full time averaged 4.4 hours of unpaid (domestic, child care and volunteer) work per day while men working full time averaged 2.7 hours per day (Statistics Canada, 2004). And although women have higher rates of absenteeism due to caregiving and other demands outside of work, it is revealing that only 10% of all workers, both men and women, actually reported "family to work" interference from their jobs in Duxbury and Higgins' (2003) survey.

Light Fingers

Beth Ryan

PHILOMENA'S MOTHER IS UP TO HER ELBOWS IN BREAD dough when the phone rings. It's an old-fashioned phone, squat and black, with a stiff rotary dial. Philomena wishes they could get a modern phone, a coloured one with push buttons. The Flynns have a harvest gold wall phone in the kitchen of their split-level house in St. John's. It was one of the first things Philomena noticed when she went to work for Mrs. Flynn right after she finished Grade 11 back in June. Everything there is colour-coordinated. The kitchen is all done in harvest gold, right down to the canisters and the electric can opener. The bathroom has a mauve bath-tub and toilet, and there are purple towels on all the racks. Even the soaps match.

"Are you going to look at that phone or are you going to answer it?" her mother says after the third ring. Philomena picks up the heavy receiver and says hello.

"Could I speak with your mother?" says the woman on the other end.

It's Mrs. Flynn. Her voice is crisp, precise, cold. Philomena does not say anything. She simply passes the phone to her mother and walks out the door.

It's a quarter to two and the lunch crowd at Woolworth's has dribbled away. A few old men streel in for a bowl of soup, and the secretaries from up the street are here for a quick sandwich. Philomena pushes a grungy cloth in a lazy circle over the counter top.

She hauls off her hairnet and tries to fix her straggly pony tail. It's hard to feel beautiful when she's wearing a brown polyester uniform and a hairnet. It's one of the worst things about her new job. On her break, she sneaks to the bathroom to sponge the grease from her face with a damp wad of paper towels. She applies fresh makeup — a dab of creamy blush-er, blended high on the round part of her cheeks, a slick of shiny lip gloss. She sniffs her underarms and sprays on some Love's Baby Soft, a cotton candy-smelling cologne that she got from the woman who runs the cos-metics counter. The bottle was a tester, the one the customers use to try out a new perfume. Winnie looks out for Philomena and gives her stuff that would only end up in the dumpster out back. Philomena treats it like it's Chanel Number 5.

She is talking to one of the old men, pouring him another cup of watery coffee, when she sees Miguel sail past the front window and into the store. She stops pouring for a second just to watch him move. He is not like the boys she grew up with around the bay. They came in two varieties – big, thick and stunned or small, sly and weasel-faced. But Miguel is like nothing else she's ever seen at home. He is soft-eyed, beautiful, exotic.

By the time he gets to the counter, Philomena has already poured a coffee for him and is cutting a slice of lemon meringue pie. He has tried all the pies that Woolworth's sells, and he says the lemon meringue is his "very most special favourite."

"Hello, Philly," Miguel says, as he slides onto one of the low stools at the counter and leans over the formica surface to look right into her face. Nobody calls her "Philly" but him. At home, the kids would shorten her name to Mena, which usually turned into Meanie. But Miguel says "Fee-lee" and it sounds beautiful, like a soap opera name. Philomena sighs his name as a form of greeting, and he gives her a smile that makes her catch her breath.

"Are you a very busy lady today?" Miguel asks. That's the thing with him. He's always asking about her. How is she feeling? Did she have a good morning? Do her feet hurt from standing up so much?

"Oh, I'm not doing too bad. I was nearly drove off my head at dinner-time. But now, it's slow," she says.

Miguel has been coming to visit her for over two weeks now. The first time, he was in the store with a crowd of Portuguese sailors, his fellow crewmembers. They were buying jeans, toys for their kids, presents for their wives. Miguel is only 21. He has no wife or children to shop for. So, while his friends searched the aisles for treasures, he sat at the counter and chatted with Philomena. Now he comes in every afternoon, telling her stories of Portugal, his family, his dreams to be captain of his own boat one day. But he doesn't hog the conversation. Miguel asks about Philomena and what she wants from life. It's the first time anyone has ever asked, and Philomena is embarrassed to realize that she does not have an answer.

Miguel is eating his pie, taking one small, neat bite after another.

"Mmm," he says, letting the meringue melt on his tongue. "You bake such a good pie, Philly."

She blushes at the compliment, even though it's not really hers. If only her mother could hear this! She says Philomena is so useless in the kitchen that she'll be lucky to ever get a husband.

"Thanks, Miguel," she says, any excuse to say his name, to let that melt on her tongue.

A gaggle of girls come into the store then and flounce past on their way to the home entertainment department. Philomena knows their routine. First, they look at the new 45's and giggle over their choices. Then, they go to the cosmetics department to smear on blue eye shadow and dip their baby fingers into pots of lip gloss. They wrap it up by sashaying out to the porch to get their photos taken in the coin-operated booth, screeching with laughter as they jockey for the best spot in front of the invisible camera before the flash goes off.

All of these girls look the same. They wear short, plaid bomber jackets with fake fur collars, which expose their skinny bums and reedy thighs. Their hair is long and shiny, thanks to endless bottles of shampoo and creme rinse, parted in the middle and flipped back with the help of a curling iron. Philomena is thinking about buying a curling iron for herself. It would force her to give up something this week. But, if it would make her look better, she'd make the sacrifice. She feels a flutter of resentment towards these girls, who have everything they want and don't even know it. They live in newly constructed bungalows and split-level houses in the east end. Philomena knows because they are just like the kids she used to baby-sit. The Flynns have two girls — ten and twelve. They each have their own room, with Shaun Cassidy and Leif Garrett posters on the walls. They gather with their friends in the family room to watch TV and play records. They take turns doing each other's hair and makeup, trying to make themselves look like teenagers instead of girls.

Philomena longs for nice things. It's not that she's greedy. She just wants something of her own, straight from the store. A tiny gold heart on a chain, a long coat that flares out on the bottom, a pair of jeans – girl's jeans, with a flower embroidered on the pocket, not ones passed down from her brothers. That hunger got worse when she worked for the Flynns. Every day she was surrounded by things she wanted, and seeing them made her desperate, even reckless. It started small. She pocketed a perfumed guest soap from the tiny bathroom off the front hallway. Then she would slide her hand over the pile of loose change on Mr. Flynn's bureau. Eventually, Philomena found herself sitting in front of the dresser in Debbie's room and admiring her jewellery box, filled with cheap, beautiful necklaces and earrings.

Miguel has finished his pie, running the edge of his fork along the plate to catch the last of the lemon filling.

"Thank you very much, Philly," he says, pushing the plate to one side.

Philomena smiles at him and fills his coffee cup for the third time. Her boss would give her a hard look if he saw that.

"I have a question I am wanting to ask you," Miguel says, dipping his head slightly and looking up at her through a fringe of dark hair.

She gives him a warm smile, what she hopes is an encouraging smile.

"I would like to take you to the movie show at the Paramount Theatre," he says, earnestly extending his invitation.

"That would be very nice, Miguel," Philomena replies quickly, before he can change his mind.

They make plans for the next evening, both of them eager to make it official. He will meet her at her boarding house on Bond Street, and they will walk to the movie theatre. Miguel touches her hand, a sweet, cautious gesture.

"You are making me very happy, Philly," he tells her before he slides the money for his pie and coffee across the counter and gets up to leave.

When her shift is over, Philomena makes a stop in the cosmetics department and sizes up the curling irons. There is one on sale for $5.99, one that features a tiny dot on the handle that changes colour when it has reached the right temperature. She knows how it works. Debbie and Tina Flynn each had one just like this sitting on the ornate, white dressers in their bedrooms. When they were at school, she would experiment with new hairstyles and try to copy the ones she saw in the girls' teen magazines. She wonders sometimes which one of them tattled on her. How did they even notice the few things missing from their bedrooms? They had so much. She had taken things carefully, one item every few weeks, storing them in a shopping bag in her bedroom closet in the Flynns' basement. A necklace, a hair clip, a red transistor radio. It was as if each thing had found its way into her hand, and once she was holding it, she couldn't let go, clutching it to her chest as she raced to her room to hide her treasure. It hurt to give everything back. She felt a real physical pain as her mother grabbed the bag from her hands and wrenched it away.

Philomena shakes her head to dislodge that memory and thinks instead about sitting in the darkness with Miguel at the Paramount, his hand laid gently over hers on the armrest, his shoulder touching hers. She closes her eyes and imagines him stroking her hair, hair that's been transformed into silky coils by the curling iron. Maybe he will whisper into her ear and tell her how pretty she looks tonight, how nice she smells, how soft her hair feels.

"Are you going to buy that or are you just going to drool over it?"

She whips her head around to see Derek King, one of the young guys from the sports department. He normally towers over her head, but he has stooped to speak directly into her ear. She turns so quickly that her cheekbone smacks into his chin, causing them both to clutch their faces in pain.

"Oooh, you're a dangerous one," he says.

But he is laughing, and that makes Philomena smile, too, forgetting for a moment that she is usually dumbstruck around Derek. This is the kind of guy that the Flynn girls will have as their boyfriends when they get to high school. He lives in the suburbs with his parents and two brothers, drives a brand-new yellow Pinto and spends his days at the Trades College, where he takes the Electronics Tech course. Woolworth's is just a pit stop on the way to his real life, a place he works part-time to help pay for his car. He has never spoken to Philomena before, other than a curt greeting when they happen to be punching their time cards at the same moment.

"So whatcha doing? Getting ready for a big date?" he teases her.

Derek is never at a loss for a date. Girls are always trailing into the store to say hi while he's on his break. They stand and look up at him with worshipping gazes, taking in his hockey player build and long hair, cut short at the front and sides. Philomena finds herself turning into one of those girls on the spot, giving Derek a coy smile, delighted that he's even interested in her after-work activities. He leans in close to her face again and lowers his voice.

"But please tell me you're not going out with one of the Portuguese," he whispers, and his breath on her ear makes her face grow hot.

"What?" she mumbles. "What do you mean?"

Derek stands back then and assumes his normal stance, pulling his long torso up and his wide shoulders back. His expression is not friendly anymore.

"I mean, the only girls who go with the Portuguese are the whores. Don't you know that? Haven't you ever heard of the girls who go down to the boats?"

Philomena looks at her feet, wishing he would walk away now, wishing she could get away from him without ever having to lift her eyes. She feels red-hot shame creeping up her neck on its way to her face, leaving bright, mottled patches on her pale skin. She knows the feeling of being caught. This is just how she felt the day Mrs. Flynn called her mother.

"No, I don't know about those girls," she says.

"Well, then, let me tell you all about it," Derek says, speaking to her as if she is simple. "They go to bars with the Portuguese and get drunk, and then they go back to the boats. They take money from the Portuguese, and then they lie down and open their legs for them."

Philomena steps back from him then, one hand to her mouth as if he had reached out and smacked her across the face. She can't imagine why he's saying this to her. She wonders for a moment if this is a joke, if he will throw back his head and laugh, poking her in the sides and making her laugh, too. The laughter would be such a relief.

"So come on, Philomena," he says, stepping into the silence and filling it with another hoarse whisper. "Please tell me you're not going out with one of the Portuguese."

"No," she says. "Don't be so foolish."

Derek grins at her and chucks her under the chin as if she was a child.

"I knew you were a smart girl," he says.

"I have to go now," she tells him.

Philomena calls goodbye to Derek over her shoulder as she walks towards the door. Her voice makes a thin sound that disappears into the air. She pushes the glass door open and walks out onto the sidewalk. She walks two blocks on Water Street before she looks down and sees that the curling iron is still in her hand. Philomena does not hesitate before she opens the crumpled Woolworth's bag that holds her dirty uniform and puts the long, narrow box inside. Then she heads for Bowring's.

As soon as she walks in the door, she knows she's in a different world, one where the scent of real perfume hangs in the air instead of the grease from the cafeteria. Instrumental music murmurs to her from unseen stereo speakers. No one is screeching on the intercom, paging the stock boys to come with a trolley. On the main floor, she examines the glass shelves that display dozens of hats and gloves, and matching scarves. She has been eyeing a tam made of pale pink angora wool, a hat that costs more than the winter jacket she bought on sale at Woolworth's before Christmas. Her hand darts out to touch it, to smooth its silky hair. It curls around her hand like a kitten, and with one swift move she scrunches it into a ball and presses it into the bag under her arm.

The next afternoon, Miguel comes in a bit later than usual. Philomena has been watching the clock since one, wondering what she will say when she sees him. He slips onto one of the stools while her back is turned, and she jumps when she sees his face, beaming at her.

"Hello, Philly. I could not wait for tonight," he says, reaching for her hand.

But she pulls it back, jamming both of her hands into the pockets of her uniform. Miguel looks bewildered.

"I don't think I can go out with you," she tells him.

"What is wrong? Are you unhappy with me?" he asks.

Philomena folds her arms firmly across her chest, trying to look stern. She turns away from Miguel's crumpled face for a second, ashamed that she's the one who is making him look so sad. She sees Derek King watching her from his post in the sporting goods department. He's leaning on a pile of boxes, staring a straight line across the store that burrows right into her forehead. She looks down and closes her eyes, blotting out both of their faces. When she looks up again, Miguel is leaning towards her over the counter.

"What is wrong?" he repeats.

Philomena opens her mouth, and the words spill out before she's even planned what to say.

"I can't go. I just can't. I should never have said yes in the first place," she says.

Miguel stares at her, and he looks so surprised that she instantly regrets saying anything. She has made a mistake. Maybe Derek was wrong after all.

"Why? Why do you say this?" Miguel asks.

"Because, we are different. We have no business being with each other," she says, but she sounds stupid, as if the teacher had called on her and she didn't know the answer, so she started making one up.

"No business? What do you mean 'business'?" he asks.

Philomena looks at her feet, studying the scuffed toes of her sensible work shoes. She wishes Miguel would stop asking her questions that she can't answer. Finally, he obliges. He stands up and takes a package out of his pocket, a tiny, black box with a pink ribbon tied around it.

"For you, Philly. It is a gift for you. Just for you," he says.

Philomena holds the box in her hand and watches him leave. It is from Silver's Jewellery across the street. She has spent many an afternoon in there, peering into the display cases that line the walls, pressing her nose to the glass to get a closer look at the earrings, the necklaces, the beautiful glittery pieces made from silver and gold, with stones set in them. Derek is still watching her, so she slips the box into her pocket and starts wiping down the counters.

Her shift goes on forever. At five o'clock, Philomena changes her clothes, punches her time card in the heavy metal clock and shrugs on her coat. The box from Silver's Jewellery is carefully nestled at the bottom of her Woolworth's bag. She clutches the bag close as she leaves the store. Down the street at Shelley's Restaurant, Philomena orders a Pepsi and a plate of chips, which will allow her to sit in the front window for at least half an hour. She uses her paper napkin to polish a spot on the table in front of her until it gleams. She takes the box out of her bag and lays it on the newly shined spot. It sits there almost vibrating, with an energy that begs her to open it. But she waits, eating her chips one by one, dipping the tip of each one in a puddle of ketchup. She drinks the Pepsi slowly, savouring each mouthful. Twenty minutes pass before she wipes her fingertips clean with her napkin and unties the ribbon. She lifts the top off and opens the folded tissue paper, pulling out a fine gold chain with a wafer-thin heart dangling from it. She holds it up to the light that filters in from the street lamp and sees minuscule ornate script engraved on one side. *Philly.* She rubs the smooth piece of gold between her finger and thumb, stares at her new name etched in gold.

The morning that Mrs. Flynn called her mother, Philomena ran from the house without even putting on her coat. She walked down to the wharf and sat there in the cool, damp breeze, trying to come up with answers for her mother, for the questions she would inevitably shriek at her. No, she didn't know what she thought she was doing. No, she didn't think about what Mrs. Flynn was going to do when she found out. Yes, she knew she would have to find herself another job and a place to live when she went back to town on Monday. Yes, she knew very well that she was an ungrateful girl who didn't deserve the opportunity the Flynns had given her.

Philomena leaves the restaurant and steps outside into the cold evening again, walking towards the waterfront. She isn't sure which boat is Miguel's, but she scans the name on the bow of each one, looking for something that sounds familiar. About a dozen men are playing soccer on the harbour apron, running and panting, their breath puffing out in front of them in wispy clouds. They are laughing and calling to one another in Portuguese as they kick the ball and dart around each other. But the action slows to a crawl when Philomena stops walking and peers at their faces in the dim light.

"Hello there, beautiful lady," one of the sailors calls and does an exaggerated swagger as he walks toward her. "I am the man you want!"

The others laugh and poke each other in the sides with their elbows. A voice calls out something in Portuguese that makes them all stop. A man is standing on the deck of one of the boats, looking down at the soccer game and at Philomena.

"Are you looking for someone?" he calls to her, and his voice is kind.

Philomena tilts her head back and peers up at the man's face.

"Miguel. I'm looking for Miguel," she calls up to him.

"Sorry," he says, shaking his head sadly. "He's not here."

Women and Water Street: Constructing Gender in the Department Stores of St. John's, 1892-1949[1]

Carla Wheaton

OVER THE COURSE OF THE LATE NINETEENTH and early twentieth centuries, a revolution in retailing occurred in St. John's with the growth of department stores on Water Street. On a street once crowded with the premises of fish merchants and small shops, grew large retail establishments, organized along departmental lines and utilizing modern retail techniques such as fixed prices, sales, newspaper advertising and credit plans. Simultaneously it seems, women came to be identified as the primary household consumers and, by extension, the main targets of store attempts to attract customers.

The feminization of consumption was a western trend, a central component of a spreading consumer culture. With increasing regularity and growing insistence starting in the latter years of the nineteenth century, the women of St. John's, like their counterparts in much of Europe and the rest of North America, were subjected to a campaign by city retailers, one which sought to delineate their consuming role in society. They did so through the merchandise displayed in store windows and on shop floors, as well as through sales, services and special promotions, but most effectively through their advertisements, which reveal that retailers' expectations of women, reflecting those of the larger society, were manifold and exacting. They were to be attentive mothers, attractive wives, efficient housekeepers and inveterate shoppers, their commitment to the latter being inextricably linked to their success at the former — if women were not efficient, economical, and eager shoppers, they were unlikely to be good mothers, wives and housekeepers. And despite the growing number of working women in St. John's, the roles of consumer and worker were considered mutually exclusive — a woman could not be both shopper and wage-earner. In this way, the stores were central to the construction of gender identities in Newfoundland.[2]

The Department Store in St. John's

The development of the department store in St. John's must be seen within the context of the socio-economic changes taking place on the island in the latter half of the 19th century. The nature of the Newfoundland economy was changing as the fishery declined and the results of Industrial Revolution began reaching the island. The mass production of new and cheaper goods in Britain and North America made "luxury" items more accessible to the average Newfoundlander. The Newfoundland government began turning its attention to diversifying the country's economy through the introduction of new industries offering alternative forms of investment and employment to that of the fishery; and, as part of its plan for development, the government, following leads in Britain, the U.S. and Canada, hired the Reid Company to build a railway (Alexander, 1980, 25-7). The impact of these changes was felt mostly in St. John's and, later, in the few industrial towns — such as Wabana, Grand Falls, and Corner Brook — created as a result of the government's efforts to encourage development of the island's resources.

In these centres, opportunities for waged labour outside the fishery contributed to the growth of a working class, employed in mines, factories, and mills, and in a service sector expanding to meet the needs of a rising urban population. The middle class also increased, employed in managing shops, offices and factories, and within the growing bureaucracy overseeing the government's development schemes. The rising numbers of people earning cash wages and the availability of cheaper goods expanded opportunities for retailers, a fact reflected in the changing nature of the island's imports which included a growing variety and a rising volume of non-staple, luxury goods in this period.

As the Newfoundland economy expanded and diversified, new businessmen employing new methods and catering to city consumers entered the St. John's retail trade, introducing new modes of retailing already gaining prominence in the department stores of Europe and North America. The growing popularity of low, fixed prices, fast turnover of stock, cash-only policies, sales, promotions, extensive advertising, and an emphasis on customer service and store appearance, meant that the old-time merchants had to adapt in order to survive by altering their operations and embracing a new mode of retailing to consumers — the department store.

From Home Production to Mass Consumption

Based on scant descriptions of consumption in nineteenth-century Newfoundland and the practices of their contemporaries in Canada, it seems likely that Newfoundland women actually did little of the household purchasing until the late 1800s. In communities where long-term credit enabled family survival, men typically purchased supplies that could not be made in the home from merchant stores. This was as true of farming families on the Canadian Prairies as of fishing families in Atlantic Canada. Yet, with urbanization, industrialization, mass production, and the growth of a cash economy, patterns of consumption were altered so that women assumed a greater responsibility for household purchasing (Strong-Boag, 1988, 128).

By the early 1900s, it was becoming increasingly clear to many in St. John's that a shift in consumption patterns had occurred. A 1909 Trade Review article, for example, noted that there was no longer a need for stores to stay open past six since,

In the old days men bought most of the domestic dry goods, and they were not very particular as to shades and styles, and hence, gaslight was just as good as daylight for them. But things have altered a bit the last few years, and purchasers are more exacting as to fashion, patterns, and colors, and very little purchasing is done in the night as compared to twenty years ago.

This would seem to suggest that women were now doing much of the purchasing, necessitating new retail methods to serve them. That store owners believed that women, generally married women in charge of households, constituted the majority of their customers by the early decades of the twentieth century is easily discerned from the services they offered and the nature of store advertisements. The addition of rest rooms and tea rooms for the comfort of lady shoppers and the hiring of salesladies to serve them are an indication of their growing importance to city retailers. By 1936, "The Roving Shopper," a *Daily News* columnist offering information and advice to St. John's female consumers, estimated that women did ninety per cent of household buying.

While there were other factors contributing to women's growing responsibility for consumption, retailers throughout Europe and North America were instrumental in defining that role. Although they clearly viewed women as the "home directors," they also believed that women had to be educated in how to consume. Not only did they, therefore, help guide the shift from home production to mass consumption, but it has been argued that advertising campaigns encouraging the purchase of mass-produced goods also led to the deskilling of women, who were encouraged to buy ready-made items which were "better" and "more economical." In consequence, the importance of women's domestic skills declined while that of their appearance rose, illustrated by the rising numbers of advertisements telling women that their goals ought to be "daintiness, beauty, romance, grace, security and husbands," all of which could be "fulfilled in the marketplace" (Ewen, 1976, 47, 79-80). Many of the store advertisements appearing in early twentieth-century St. John's newspapers seem to support these assertions. Not only were women told that they could not possibly make clothes, preserves or baked goods as cheaply or efficiently as they could buy them in the stores, but also that, in most cases, the factory-made item was superior to that which was home-made. Some of the time thus saved could then be spent on maintaining a fashionable, attractive appearance that advertisements argued was an essential attribute of the modern woman.

This growing emphasis on appearance in store advertisements was no doubt a consequence of retailers' efforts to create a market for the new ready-made apparel and accessories and the steady increase in the fre-

Exterior of Ayre and Sons, 231-235 Water Street, ca. 1900. CNSA Coll-137, 2.01.009

Interior of Ayre and Sons, Water Street, ca. 1920s. PANL, B16-152

quency of advertisements for such merchandise from the late 1800s onwards is an indication of their importance to store profits. Through such advertisements, the stores helped define the standards by which a woman's appearance was to be judged. Suggestive of the tone of early advertisements, a 1901 Royal Stores advertisement warned the women of St. John's that, "Beauty in the boudoir must have the proper toilet accessories to fit her for her place in society, otherwise she must do an injustice to her friends and herself." There was more for a woman to worry about, however, than the approval of a nebulous "society." In order to fulfill her proper role as a wife, mother, and shopper, she had to capture male interest, a goal best achieved with a stylish new hat according to several other Royal Stores advertisements for, "To storm the citadel of the male heart no weapon is so effective." Clearly reflecting middle-class notions regarding female propriety, advertisements suggested a lady's character was revealed by what she wore, her "head dress", for example, reflecting either "loudness and vulgarity" or "quiet taste and gentle upbringing." Attempting to appeal to middle-class consumers, and those with middle-class aspirations, stores emphasized the refinement and taste of their clientele but also offered themselves as guides for those unsure of what to buy. If their advertisements were to be believed, practically everyone a woman encountered throughout her day would be evaluating her appearance.

As the years passed, store advertisements became larger as well as more frequent, sophisticated, insistent, and explicit in their shopping "advice" to women. This was particularly true of those selling feminine items as advertisements became increasingly specific in their descriptions of how a woman should look and what she should wear. Everything down to her underwear had an impact on a woman's appearance, determining how she was viewed by others. As an Ayre & Sons advertisement for Kabo Corsets declared, "The impression you make is governed a great deal by the corset you wear. No maker of fine gowns would ever attempt to give you a stylish appearance unless you wore the right corset." That the changing fashions seemed to constantly require new corsetry made matters all the more confusing, not to mention costly, but the right corset promised everything from "better health and priceless comfort" to an "untroubled mind" brought about by the knowledge that one was "looking her best." In 1924, George Knowling, Ltd., went so far as to bring in an expert from a Canadian company to have corsets individually fitted for the "woman who really cares about her personal attractiveness."

By the 1920s, then, advertisements were targeting, and likely contributing to, women's insecurities about aging and weight gain, earlier advertisements having rarely mentioned either. A 1923 Ayre & Sons advertisement for "The Miracle Re-duc-er" promised a "safe and scientific method" to remove weight and mould "the figure into youthful lines." A 1930 London, New York and Paris advertisement for corsets, phrased the issue more bluntly:

How lovely are the new soft, fluttery frocks when worn over 'proper foundations.' However, a slovenly figure line simply ruins them. The bearing of these new dress creations depends on their being worn correctly — and this means that the figure must be properly controlled and moulded.

By 1940, corsets were giving way to the more flexible girdles to suit women's rising participation in the workforce and various leisure activities, but the emphasis remained on controlling one's figure:

Today's smart figure is a natural one ... casual, young, alive. Achieve it the Playtex way with this amazingly different girdle! Not a corset, not an out-dated rubber garment, but a modern method of figure control, as natural as your own lines slimmed down. It slims you for everything from an evening gown to a bathing suit!

Advertisements were, therefore, central to establishing the standards by which all women were measured, promising dress styles that were "youthifying" and "individual," hats that were "feminine" and "pretty," underwear that was "exclusive" and "refined." According to store advertisements, being fashionable was the goal of every woman with taste and style and, while the need for most women to economize was often recognized, it was argued that thriftiness should not be an impediment to being well-dressed.

Still, the question of how consumers were to keep abreast of fashion trends remained. The stores, through their advertisements and displays, promised to show them, holding themselves up as the city's arbiters of fashion. Advertisements were meant to inform, to tell consumers where, how and what to buy, retailers believing it was their responsibility to educate consumers. The fact that fashions originated in far off cities, determined by the amorphous "Dame Fashion," being brought to St. John's by the stores and their buyers, made their dictates difficult to contradict. Therefore, Ayre & Sons, the self-named "recognized authority," could claim to stock the "... styles most in vogue in London, Paris and New York" and suggest that "Ladies who like to keep abreast of the times, should make an early visit to our show." The Royal Stores also advised women to visit their Fashion Exhibits to see "the accepted and authoritative fashions" that would give women "a correct idea of the styles worn this season." By inviting women to "Come in and look around to [their] heart[s'] content," assuring them that the clerks and salesladies would "be only too pleased to show and explain everything," the stores presented themselves as sources of knowledge and advice, thus protecting women from the shame of being deemed unfashionable or the disgrace of bad taste. This does not mean that women wholeheartedly accepted their fashion dictates. Still, women could only choose from the products made available to them and, in the absence of alternative sources of information for consumers, retailers could successfully guide their consuming habits through their advertisements, store displays and fashion shows (Miller, 1991, 264).

"Controllers of the Home Purse"

Although most of the stores' advertisements in the late 1800s and early 1900s were for clothing, by the 1910s and 1920s, store advertisements pitched a growing variety of consumer goods, the majority of which were directed at women for family, home or personal use. Advertisements explicitly linked marriage and motherhood with consumption so that, despite providing an opportunity to escape the home and participate in public life, shopping, seen as part of women's domestic responsibilities, did little to challenge traditional gender roles. Consequently, in addition to advertisements appealing to a woman's personal needs and wants, many others addressed those of the family and household, often using the appeal of middle-class respectability and family values to sell goods. Advertisements suggested that "Every good housekeeper ... [should] make her house comfortable, attractive and in keeping with her ideas of 'HOME' " for her family's happiness depended upon it, another advertisement declaring that "... love of home is engendered in the young by tasteful surroundings in the household." And just as her appearance was constantly being judged, so was that of her home, one Ayre & Sons advertisement warning, "When You Consider that YOUR WINDOWS are more in the 'public eye' than any other portion of your home, you naturally want to have them above criticism." A later James Baird, Ltd. advertisement also advised women, "Just as your wardrobes and complexions need a thorough going over from time to time .... so do your homes."

Furthermore, advertisements told women they should take pride in their domestic work, presenting a pleasant demeanour and an attractive appearance as they went about their household chores. As a 1917 Martin-Royal Stores Hardware Co. advertisement for mops declared: "Make Your Work a Pleasure. You like compliments, to be told you have a cheerful disposition; how scientifically you do your work; that your home is clean, bright and beautiful." The assumption was that housewives had a special attachment to the home, that they "yearned" for new furnishings, and that a "good" housewife enjoyed shopping for things to "make cosy ... that place she cherishes and loves to call 'Home Sweet Home.'"

The demands on women to be good mothers were just as exacting, everything from her family's health to her son's success at school depended upon her buying the right products. One early advertisement dramatically declared, "Stolen from home has many a bright young life been, by the non-appreciation of the necessity for warm head covering in cold weather. First the cough, then the coffin and the vacant chair." Only slightly less melodramatic was a later advertisement for rubber boots:

Every Man, Woman, Boy, Girl and Child should always have a pair of our good Rubbers at this season of the year. Wet feet always travel the road that ends in Hospital and its [sic] usually a short trip.

Other advertisements advised "careful" mothers to ward off illness and ensure the safety and comfort of their children by buying warm blankets, Dr. Denton's sleepwear, Vanta baby garments and Pedigree prams, at times invoking scientific and expert authority to lend credence to their claims. In this way, male advertisers and their "experts" helped sell products by creating "standards of domestic cleanliness, all in the name of protecting family health." This was particularly true of household appliances, which were initially seen as luxuries and conveniences but came to be viewed as necessities by raising the standards according to which domestic abilities were judged (Miller, 1991, 264-287). As one 1934 Royal Stores advertisement told the housewives of St. John's, "You'll bless the day you bought one of these Refrigerators. It isn't enough to provide good food for your family. You must be sure it's safe for them to eat. The only way to be sure of that during warm summer weather is by refrigeration."

In no area were advertisements more specific or demanding in their domestic advice to women than when it came to child care, and Cook's (1995) study of the children's wear industry in the U.S. provides an interesting insight into the American influence on St. John's retailers. Through an examination of *Infants' Department*, a trade journal published by George Earnshaw, owner of the American company Vanta Baby Garments, Cook illustrates how the publication advised department stores on the most advantageous ways of merchandising infants' clothes and accessories, in turn influencing society's view of their target consumers, mothers. Along with the creation of a department devoted specifically to infants, the journal urged retailers to give mothers information and advice on caring for their children. The resulting image created by staff writers of the "consuming mother" was as "a self-sacrificing being motivated by love and instinct to carry out her duty as purchasing agent for the family." According to the journal, mothers would make any sacrifice to buy things for their children and so advertisers urged them to express their love through goods. Distributed free to those who bought, retailed, and manufactured children's wear, *Infants' Department* likely had some impact on how baby products were promoted in St. John's since at least one Water Street store carried Vanta baby clothes. Although the connection cannot be made definitively, several of the journal's suggestions such as selling layettes, celebrating baby week with special displays of merchandise beneficial to infant health, and invoking expert opinion in advertisements were used by St. John's retailers (Cook, 1995, 505-522).

Nor did the stores restrict themselves to advice on infant care. If babies survived the many threats to their health to become toddlers and young children, mothers then had to worry about choosing clothes beneficial to their educational and future prospects for, according to store advertisements, how they dressed could determine both. Yet, the concern was always for boys as one Royal Stores advertisement illustrates:

> We Have A Suit For Your Young Hopeful. Start your boy back to school in one of these good suits. Watch him hold his chin up and sail into his studies like a regular fellow. His appearance makes a lot of difference in his attitude ...

Advertisements also called upon every "proud" mother to give her son self-respect by dressing him in "stylish looking clothes" so that she could rest assured not one of his playmates would be better equipped for the coming season. Although there were advertisements for girls' school clothes, they never urged mothers to ensure daughters' success with a new outfit but rather appealed to the feminine love of fashion supposedly shared by mothers and daughters by virtue of their sex. Such advertisements hint at the early socialization of children into traditional gender roles since, like their fathers, boys required clothes that would give them the confidence to succeed whereas girls needed them to fill the female "craving" for fashion. Because children had little or no purchasing power, mothers were the target of advertisements for children's merchandise but advertisements and in-store contests still encouraged children to accompany their mothers on shopping trips. In this way, children, especially girls, were educated into their proper societal roles at an early age.

Working Women and Consumption

While early advertisements addressed women almost solely in terms of their domestic roles, as female participation in the workforce rose during and after World War I, more advertisements appeared in the newspapers directed at young, single, working women. Such advertisements did not promise professional success with the right dress but sold smocks and uniforms for a variety of acceptable female occupations, suggesting that the range of jobs open to women during the period was largely limited to maid, office or shop clerk, beautician, waitress, nurse and teacher. Since single, working women were among the few with the time and money to spend in the pursuit of fun, other advertisements sold clothes for leisure activities such as dances, movies, card-playing, skating and hiking. Because there were actually higher numbers of young women living in St. John's than young men throughout much of the period, this meant fewer marriage opportunities and a longer stay in the workforce, thereby adding to their importance as consumers and making them worthy of retailers' attention.

Despite this, most store advertisements continued to target housewives and mothers for several reasons. The vast majority of working women continued to live with parents or other relatives, the remainder living in boarding houses, negating the need to buy household items. Furthermore, most were expected to hand over a portion of their wages to help support the family while the rest paid board and, given the low wages paid to women amidst the depressed conditions of the 1920s and 1930s, their spending money would have been limited. Finally, going out to work was considered a relatively brief stage in a young woman's life, bridging childhood and marriage (Forestell, 1987, 68-71, 99, 103). Most would eventually leave their jobs to become wives and mothers, exchanging wages for more substantial spending allowances and advertisements reflected this social reality by continuing to target women primarily in terms of their domestic duties.

During World War II, with male enlistment and rising employment opportunities on the bases, more women entered the workforce but few advertisements addressed them in their capacity as wage-earners. When advertisements targeted single women, it was still largely in terms of their leisure activities. One change, however, was the increased number of advertisements encouraging women to buy dresses for dates, a response, no doubt, to the presence of foreign troops and their romances with local women. As one 1942 advertisement advised, "More than ever before you'll want pretty dresses for party-going, movie dates and dinner."

Advertisements frequently promoted items sure to attract male attention, the Model Shop promising dresses that "he likes to see you wear ... the kind that makes him proud to show you off before his friends." The London, New York and Paris also advertised "beau-catching dresses" while Bowring's told women to "Dress Up to His Expectations."

For those women successful in their quest to find husbands, stores also advertised bridal gowns and gifts for the "most important occasion in any girl's life," one advertisement stating:

Newfoundland needs women like you who have the courage and determination to go ahead — make a home for your soldier husband — raise a family — the new generation we are fighting for. We are proud we can be of service to the future Mrs. Newfoundlands.

Four decades earlier, a Royal Stores advertisement used similar rhetoric to sell women's undergarments suggesting, "Healthy womanhood is the prospective hope of a young country. To have healthy women, we must have healthy clothing, clothing made on scientific and hygienic principles." It appears that, in spite of women's greater public role as consumers and to a lesser extent as wage earners, little had changed over the intervening years in attitudes regarding the role of women in society: a woman's destiny was still marriage and motherhood.

Yet, despite the development of their consuming role within a framework of traditional gender roles, it is clear that women wielded a significant degree of economic influence through their buying. Even when it came to typically masculine products such as fishing tackle or car care items, or major purchases such as furniture and appliances, advertisements often appealed to husbands and wives, and sometimes just wives, suggesting store owners believed women would have a say in what was bought. And during World Wars I and II, women were made to feel that, through their role as household purchasers, they, too, could have an impact by buying British-made goods or war stamps, thereby supporting the mother country and demonstrating their patriotic spirit. Advertisements for a "buy local" campaign in the early 1920s also targeted women in their role as the primary consumers:

To-day, the Newfoundland house-wife, if she is thoughtful, loyal to her home interests, anxious to keep her fellow-countrymen independent and self-supporting, INSISTS on seeing local-made goods first, every time, and whenever possible, purchases them....

Another advertisement suggested that by buying local products, a portion of the money a woman spent would return to her own purse via her "husband's pay envelope." That such advertisements were directed at housewives and not their wage-earning husbands indicates an awareness that women were indeed responsible for the bulk of household purchases and were, therefore, important economic agents. At the same time, however, women faced great pressure to manage household accounts responsibly, to balance advertising rhetoric, family needs, and society's expectations with often limited budgets. Increasingly over the period, store advertisements emphasized thrift and economy, suggesting it was every woman's duty and responsibility as the family shopper to maintain a strict budget — "you owe it to yourself, to your family, to the wage earner" — while urging them to buy all the same.

Conclusion

The demands placed on women as the primary consumers continued to increase over the period of study as discretionary incomes rose, the variety of available merchandise expanded, and competition among retailers grew. The consequences of this feminization of consumption were mixed. Store advertisements clearly established that women were the "Controllers of the Home Purse" and were therefore in a position to influence the local economy by determining how the bulk of household funds were spent. At the same time, however, advertisements also reinforced traditional gender roles that confined women to domestic pursuits. This is the irony of women's identification with consumption: although performing an important function in the public sphere as consumers, it was within the context of their domestic duties thereby reinforcing middle-class gender roles with the female as housewife and male as breadwinner. During the latter part of the period under study, as the numbers of women in the workforce rose, stores began directing some of their appeals to the young, single, working woman but the emphasis remained on women's domestic role, the assumption being that a woman's participation in the workforce would be short-lived, ending upon marriage. So, while the world of industry and production continued to be male, the world of consumption, seen through store advertisements, was very much female domain. In this way, the St. John's department stores were central to the construction of gender in Newfoundland. Whereas men, according to stores' advertisements, were producers, breadwinners and only reluctant consumers, women were naturally avid and impulsive shoppers who, through wise consuming habits cultivated through careful scrutiny of advertisements, could be attractive wives, good mothers, and efficient housekeepers.

Notes

[1] For a more detailed discussion see "'As modern as some of the fine new departmental stores ... can make it': a social history of the large Water Street Stores, St. John's, Newfoundland, 1892-1949," unpublished Ph.D. thesis, Memorial University of Newfoundland, 2002.

2 This article is based on analysis of advertisements run by the large Water Street stores in the *Daily News* (1894-1949) and the *Evening Telegram* (1892/1949).

Unfinished Houses

Bernice Morgan

FOR YEARS THE THOUGHT OF GOING BACK — "coming home" her mother would say — ran like a subtext through their marriage. Lenora and Dave talked about it every time they visited, agreeing that St. John's was more interesting than it had been when they were growing up. Nowadays the town had art galleries, theatres, even a symphony orchestra. Still, returning was just a thought–a nice way to end a visit. "We'll be back to live some day," they would say as they waved goodbye. Then Dave got the job offer.

By now Dave had been with DeChem Canada for twenty years. They were financially secure, owned a small sailboat and a condo overlooking the lake. In summer they sailed and played golf, in winter Lenora taught flower arranging three afternoons a week just for the fun of it. They had a congenial circle of friends in Mississauga. Dave had been President of the Chamber of Commerce twice and that year he was also on the board of the Society of Ontario Chemical Engineers. There was no reason, really, to move, nothing except a vague restlessness, an awareness of being in their fifties, of Dave's having gone as far as he was going to go with DeChem. And the children were gone, their son transferred to California, their daughter married and living in Vancouver.

"Besides, it's a hell of a compliment to be asked to head up a new government laboratory," Dave said. Lenora knew then that he wanted the job, knew he was thinking how it would be to return to St. John's, move into a big house in the old part of town, buy a larger boat, join the yacht club, entertain, show old school pals how successful he was. Success, she imagined, must be sweeter in a place where people know how far you've come.

Aware of her husband's unspoken wish, Lenora flew down to join him in St. John's as soon as he accepted the job. On her second day in town she went scouting around with her sister Pam, looking for a house she and Dave might buy. They were due to move permanently in two months, and Lenora hoped she would have an appropriate house ready and waiting. "Appropriate" was a word she held onto during four hours of house hunting with her sister. It seemed like a good word to use, inoffensive but understandable. It had not been understood, and the afternoon had not been a success.

Still, an hour back in the hotel room, a bath and a fresh application of makeup had restored Lenora's confidence. Expertly recurling wisps of blonde hair, she reflected that the unsuccessful afternoon was her own fault, she should never have asked Pam along. Looking at houses together only confirmed how different she and her sister had become. Pam just assumed Lenora would want to live within walking distance of her and their mother — although there wasn't one house in the Pennywell Road area she'd consider buying. And she could imagine what Dave would say about the one bathroom, two storeys Pam had dragged her through — handyman's specials, these square boxlike houses outport carpenters built in the 1940s. Lenora could have found her way around in any of them blindfolded.

If Dave had not insisted on taking a shower before they went down to join the Deputy Minister and his wife for dinner, Lenora would never have seen Marion Fifield on television. To pass the time, she'd poured herself a weak drink and flicked ont he television set. From the bathroom, Dave, his voice fogged by steam and water, was telling her about the new lab. Located just behind the university, he said, and more up to date than anything he'd seen in Ontario.

Lenora kicked off her shoes and, taking care not to wrinkle her dress, slid back on the hotel bed. Half-listening to Dave, she sipped her drink and watched the announcer's lips as he delivered the day's dose of gossip, news and propaganda to the citizens of Newfoundland and Labrador. Her optimism started to seep back. She decided that tomorrow she would call one or two real estate agents, go around by herself. There must be something available on Rennie's Mill Road or out Waterford Bridge way — houses she would really enjoy looking at.

She might not have recognized the blur on the TV screen if the grey haired woman coming out of the court house had not paused and blinked into the sun, surprised, apparently, that it was still day. "Good God, it's Marion Fifield!" Lenora shouted.

Marion, as if she'd heard her name called, turned and looked right into the camera. There was no mistaking those eyes, blue and stupid, like the eyes of women who gaze out from old paintings. Eyes that accept the world without understanding a thing about it.

In the bathroom Dave stopped singing. "See any decent houses?" he called over the sound of running water.

Lenora didn't answer. On the screen a police woman took Marion's arm and led her gently, almost protectively, to the van — a modern version of the vehicle she and Marion used to call the Black Maria.

From Grade Five, when the Fifield family moved to Pennywell Road, until the second-last year of school, Lenora and Marion had been best friends. For those six years they had told each other everything — which boys they liked, when their periods began, what they thought about God, about sex, about other girls in the class, what they wanted to be when they grew up, when they washed their hair, even which shampoo they used. They had owned one tube of lipstick between them, Pond's Harem Orange. They baby-sat together and shared the money fifty-fifty. One year, in the final exams, Marion had slipped Lenora the solution to three algebra problems. Another year, Lenora made Jim Tobin choose Marion

117

as partner in the square dancing sessions that, for some reason, had replaced school skating that winter.

The girls sat beside each other in class, walked home together. Two afternoons a week they went to Lenora's house, to the bedroom she shared with Pam, to work on what they called "projects." The bedroom had no lock, but Pam, who was five years younger, could be excluded by simply pushing the bureau against the door.

Lenora and Marion spent hours in that icy cold bedroom cutting pictures of movie stars out of old magazines and pasting them into scrap books. They had books for each of their favourite stars — June Allison, Paulette Goddard, Elizabeth Taylor — women smiling from the arms of handsome men, women pressing their footprints into wet cement, sitting before gold framed mirrors, sweeping down marble stairways. Other projects included the construction of toy houses out of apple crates and the making of fragile furniture from match boxes and scraps of cloth. Sometimes they simply looked at old pattern books that Lenora's mother — who took in sewing — kept under the stairs.

Once, with some idea of setting up a display in the bedroom window, the girls made a Victorian street. It took weeks and weeks to contrive shops and houses from old Christmas cards, to arrange the tiny buildings along a fence paling covered with cotton wool to look like snow. The plan was to have horses and sleighs on the street, lampposts and children and Plasticine shoppers looking into store windows. But one day, after Marion had gone home, Lenora stood in the cold room staring at the rickety arrangement, and suddenly saw how ugly it really was. She put her foot down on one of the tiny red houses and crushed it. Then she jumped up and down on the other buildings until they were all smashed, reduced to bits of coloured cardboard ground into cotton wool and glue. Afterwards she splintered the paling, gathered it up and took it to the basement where she tossed it into the coal bin.

"We'll be finished the Christmas Street pretty soon — what'll we do then?" Marion asked after school the next day.

Although Marion was the one who understood Algebra, the one who got 100 percent in spelling every week, the one who could twist crepe paper into flowers and paint intricate patterns on toy furniture, she always asked what they would do next — as if she didn't have an idea in her head. The way she asked — so meekly — sometimes made Lenora want to punch her friend, hit her. Make her fight.

"How do I know what we'll do next? Anyway, I threw the Christmas Street out," she said.

"Threw the Christmas Street out?" Marion hadn't seem particularly surprised, or even angry. She just stood there on the school steps in her old rust jacket with the too-short sleeves, waiting for an explanation.

"It was under the window and the rain came in. It got all wet–the colours ran together — it was a mess!" Lenora said, and Marion nodded, seeming to accept the lie she was surely too smart to believe.

During the school year the girls allotted certain activities to each day. It gave a pattern to their lives. Every Friday they went downtown after school and walked the full length of Water Street. They started on the water side, going into the big stores, gaching at the dresses and shoes, feeling the yard goods, knowing to the minute how long they could linger before some brisk clerk would approach asking if she could help. When they reached the Sally Shop they would cross and walk back east on the other side past little stores they dared not go into, but stood outside of, studying the windows.

Sometimes they would ride home on a bus because Lenora's father worked for the Golden Arrow Coach Company and drivers let each other's children on for free. Usually though, the girls walked home, dodging slowly up Long's Hill in the half-dark, trying to decide which — of all the things they had seen — they would buy if they had the money.

On Saturday afternoons Lenora and Marion always went to the Paramount. They arrived early, picked the best seats: not too near the front where little kids dashed around changing comic books, not at the back where grade elevens sat necking in the shadows, but just far enough back so they could wave to classmates, see what girls from the big schools were wearing, note which girls arrived with boys and which couples had changed partners during the week, watch and whisper about the boys who came in groups, choose the boy they thought most handsome, the one they would go out with if they were asked.

Once the lights went out and the big double curtains, gold and red, swung majestically apart, not a word passed between the girls until the last credit rolled up on the screen. Then the lights came on, blindingly, and with great crashings and bangings the fire exits were pushed open, and hundreds of children stumbled blinking into the street. Lenora and Marion walked home, their heads so filled with visions — of girls (not much older than themselves but infinitely more beautiful) dancing along neonlit New York sidewalks, flirting with boyfriends on leaf-shaded verandas, or running, often through snowflakes, beside trains, calling farewell to handsome men — that they were hardly aware of each other or of the narrow streets they walked through.

Saturday night was usually hair washing, skirt pressing, shoe cleaning night. But once or twice a month the girls babysat for Lenora's Aunt Marge and Uncle Jim, who paid twenty-five cents an hour, their main source of income.

On Sunday night Marion and her twin sisters, Ruth and Roma, were obliged to go to Bible Chapel under the supervision of their father. Marion's mother did not go. Lenora's family, who were not church people, could never understand why Lenora was always waiting, dressed and

119

ready, when the Fifields came out Pennywell Road. As Lenora ran out of her door Marion would drop back; they would wink at each other and fall into step, walking sedately behind Mr. Fifield and the twins.

These were the only times Lenora ever saw Marion's father. Mr. Fifield worked at a place called the Ropewalk. But each spring he bought a piece of land on which he would immediately begin building a house. In the long summer daylight after supper and on Wednesday afternoons (in those days a half holiday) the sounds of Mr. Fifield pounding and sawing could be heard all over the neighbourhood.

"The man works like a nigger," Lenora's father, who played darts in his time off, said; "Mark my words, he'll be rich as Dan Ryan one of those days."

Because of Mr. Fifield's house-building, Lenora and Marion didn't often see each other during the summer. When school ended, Marion, her sisters and their mother had to help with the new house. Each morning, before he went to work, Mr. Fifield allocated jobs for the day: sort nails, throw rocks into the foundation, stack wood, or scrape concrete off boards that had been used for cribbing — horrible, dirty work, worse, even, than the floor scrubbing and baby tending expected of other girls during school holidays.

As soon as he had the walls up and roof on, usually just before school started again, Mr. Fifield would sell the house his family was living in and move them into the house he was working on. Through the winter he worked inside the house at night and on half holidays, installing partitions, flooring and stairways around his family. Despite her father's predictions, Lenora could never see any change in the way the Fifields lived or what they owned. The house they moved into was always identical to the one they had just moved out of — except it was an unfinished shell.

Mr. Fifield was a short, stocky man. Lenora thought he looked as if he'd been stuffed into his dark serge suit and starched Sunday shirt. His face, shiny and red, was cheerful enough, although he never spoke on the way to church, only nodded at Lenora and tipped his hat to her mother if she happened to be watching from the window.

After church Mr. Fifield stayed on for something called private testimony, so Marion, Lenora and the little girls were free to walk home on their own. They would almost run up the steep hill from the Bible Chapel, then slow down at the top, detouring along LeMarchant Road with Ruth and Roma trailing behind. Every church in town got out about the same time so the lower side of the road — the side with street lights — would be crowded with boys and girls, pushing and jostling along past each other. It was like a play, or a movie, Lenora thought: little groups meeting, merging, gathering in coveys, exchanging jokes, then moving on, overflowing onto the street and into the front yards of irritated homeowners who would yell from windows that the police had been sent for.

On a Sunday night in summer, with every young person in St. John's strolling along under the trees, Marion and Lenora wouldn't have exchanged LeMarchant Road for any street in the world, not even the sidewalks of New York. They would walk slowly through the warm evening, arm in arm, pretending not to notice boys leaning against fences or sitting on gateposts, snatching tams and whistling at every girl who passed.

If they had babysat the night before, the girls would have money and could buy chips, chips drenched in salt and vinegar and piled in twists of brown paper, from a van at the bus terminal. They bought chips for Ruth and Roma too, part of an understanding that nothing would be said about this buying and selling on the holy day, or about beating the streets on the way home from church.

When she thinks about Marion, it is hard for Lenora to remember the order of things they did together. Impossible to know, for example, if they'd been twelve or thirteen when they made the Victorian street, or to pinpoint which had been the square dancing grade, even to be sure what year they had begun breaking into Fifields' house to act out dramas after school.

In memory, Lenora thinks of the dramas as going on for a long time, months of unhooking a makeshift shutter, of squeezing through the glass-less basement window and dropping onto the dirt floor. The foundation of the house would be still damp, would smell of raw wood and concrete and something else, something dank and unpleasant that had been dug up before the footings were poured. Feeling their way along rough concrete walls that left white dust on their fingertips, the girls would move slowly, silently, towards a faint light glimmering down from the floor above. It seemed to take hours. Could they have done such a thing for months? Or had it been one of those adolescent fads that lasted only a few weeks, or even just days?

When they came to the ladder they would climb up through the hole into the stillness of the first floor hallway, pulling their legs up quickly, suddenly sure something was watching from the shadowy pit of basement down below.

The bright emptiness of the main floor always shocked Lenora. Only the kitchen had canvas, clean shiny squares of cream and red. Only the kitchen had furniture — stove, a green wooden table and five cream-coloured chairs. There was no kitchen couch, no rocker, no mats on the floor, no calendars on the unpapered walls, no toys, no dirt, no litter any-where.

Lenora and Marion would pull their boots off and pad in stocking feet to the pantry next to the kitchen. In the pantry doorless cupboards and topless counters had been studded in around a sink. Below the open counter sacks of potatoes and turnip, bags of beans and peas sagged against the wall. Marion would take a handful of split peas, dribble a few into Lenora's hand and toss the rest into her own mouth as if they were peanuts. They would then walk back into the hall and climb another ladder to the second floor. This ladder was homemade and nailed at the top; it went straight up, a separate ladder but directly above the first, occupying the space where the stairs would be. They would climb very carefully, knowing one misstep would plunge them into the black basement.

Since no windows had yet been cut into the walls of the top floor, the bedrooms were quite dim. There were no ceilings either, so the girls could see the wide planks holding the slope of the roof. Small beams of light. shone in at the corners of the rough, red brick chimney that came right up from the ground. Rooms would not be properly partitioned off, only separated up to eye level by green sheathing paper tacked around the studs. Even here, everything would be tidy. Woodhorses, lumber, tins of nails and Mr. Fifield's tools would be stacked in corners. In the doorless rooms beds would be neatly made, clothing hung on four inch nails driven into the outside walls. Although the floors were always gritty, no shavings or wood chips could be seen.

Having decided they must have bit players and an audience, Marion and Lenora had reluctantly admitted their little sisters to these dramatic presentations. The three younger girls got out of school earlier but were told never to go into the house alone. They were usually waiting impatiently by the basement window when Lenora and Marion arrived. Although Ruth and Roma were twins, Ruth was thin and plain and Roma plump and pretty. Roma knew the power of beauty; she lorded it over her twin sister and over Pam; she even tried to boss Marion and Lenora around.

One day, for some reason Lenora could not remember, she and Marion had been alone in the house. It was November, already dim at four o'clock. Marion, finger to lips, had led Lenora into her parents' bedroom. This room had a vanity with a heart shaped mirror and a little curved stool where you could sit and look at. yourself. Marion eased open the drawer on the left of the knee hole. It was a deep, square drawer and, as Lenora leaned forward, Marion reached in and quickly pulled out a dead animal. Lenora screamed before she realized the thing was just a fur. Marion draped the animal around her neck and snapped one small paw into the hinged mouth. They stood then, side by side looking into the mirror, admiring the gleaming fur, the same blue-black colour as Marion's hair. Above the fur her friend's face seemed unreal, pale and misty as the faces of movie stars, her eyes startling blue in the dimness of the room.

"Marion! You're pretty as Elizabeth Taylor!" The compliment came unbidden. Lenora had always thought of Marion as unredeemably plain.

"Not me — Mom's the pretty one." Marion seemed embarrassed. She pulled off the fur and stuffed it back into the drawer. "My mother is beautiful," she said softly, formally. She smoothed down the fur and closed the drawer.

For all their shared confidences, that comment was the only one Lenora remembers either of them ever making about their parents. No one talked about parents. Parents were just there, the unknowable, mysterious foundation that supported their lives.

"Want ta see something else?" Marion whispered. "Swear not to tell?" She waited until Lenora wet her index finger in her mouth and crossed her heart, then she pulled at the drawer on the other side of the vanity table.

Only it was not a drawer but a door that swung open revealing six separate drawers. Marion opened them one by one. The drawers were narrow and lined with red satin — like little coffins — each holding one item: a pin with a red stone, a pair of white kid gloves, a jet and turquoise necklace, a gold locket, an atomizer painted with tiny violets. Marion squeezed the gold-laced bulb of the empty container and a breath like the memory of violets wafted across Lenora's face.

When Lenora pointed to the remaining unopened drawer, Marion shook her head. It was locked, she said. Unlike the others, it did have a tiny keyhole but Marion didn't even try to open it.

"What's in it?"

"Promise not to tell!"

When she nodded, Marion leaned forward, her mouth touching Lenora's ear: "There's a gun in that drawer!" She made her voice deep and dramatic like they did when they were acting.

Lenora pulled back; she could smell split peas on Marion's breath. "That's foolishness — nobody in St. John's got guns! Where would you get a gun to?"

"Uncle Derm had it in the army — twas in his stuff that got sent home."

"They don't send dead people's guns home — the army keeps em!" Lenora said with assurance. She was recovering from the surprise of seeing such things as a fur and jewellery in the Fifields' house. Sensing that she'd lost some advantage over Marion by being so impressed, she reached out and yanked at the drawer. But it truly was locked.

Suddenly they had heard giggles from below. Marion pushed shut the door hiding the six little drawers. They moved quickly out of the bedroom into the hall and slid down with their backs against the wall, facing the hole where the stairs should be. They waited. Within a minute Roma, followed by Pam and Ruth, climbed up the ladder and rolled over onto the floor in front of them.

Roma jumped up and, with one hand pressed to her eyes, screeched, "Sweet Mercy! What will Lord Roland say? I've promised to marry Keith!"

"Stop that this minute, Roma Fifield!" Lenora was indignant. "We didn't leave off there — you're s'posed to be thirteen in this play — you can't promise to marry anyone for weeks and weeks yet!" She pointed dramatically at Roma: "Begone from my sight, wretched child!"

"Oh mother dear, don't send Camille away — that rich Mrs. Jamieson has promised to leave her a diamond ring, and we'll be able to rescue father from jail!" Marion declaimed. And they were off.

Following no script, the five girls flung themselves around the hallway, sobbing, laughing, screaming — suddenly unconcerned that their voices bounced off bare walls and echoed up from the cavernous hole at the centre of the house.

Thinking back, Lenora wonders if there was any sense to it all. If someone had written the words down or taped them, would they have found some gem of dramatic creativity in their histrionics? Or had it all been an outlet for something else? Some kind of sexual hysteria? She remembers having dull headaches each day when the dramas were over.

When it was almost dark, when only a faint light fluttered up from the lower hall, the little girls would falter, go suddenly silent. They would move back, sit on the floor close together and watch their sisters. Lenora and Marion would flail around for a few more minutes, determined to wrestle some order into the plot, to force it back to their will so that tomorrow they would still be the powerful mothers, the controlling wives, the Scarlett O'Haras of the story.

But soon the chill silence gliding up from the lower hallway would swallow even their voices, and the girls would all creep down the ladders, back down into the dark basement. Fumbling their way towards the window they would climb one by one out into the cold blue twilight.

Once outside, Marion and her sisters would go without a word and sit on the back steps to wait for their mother. Lenora and Pam would start across the field, hurrying toward their own house.

Often, then, they would see Mrs. Fifield walking in the road. She walked slowly, not hurrying or carrying packages. A woman by herself, walking as if she didn't have a husband coming home to supper or children waiting on cold back steps. Lenora and Pam always stopped to watch. So self-contained, so alone she looked walking in Pennywell Road. Lenora would reach out and take her sister's hand, glad to hold onto something alive and warm. They would stand in the darkening field and watch until Mrs. Fifield reached the house. There were no steps leading up to the front door and, without pausing, without seeming to look at the house, the woman would turn, walk around to the back, step between her daughters and unlock the back door. They would all go in. Lenora and Pam always waited until the kitchen light came on. When they could see the light, a small sun dangling on its black cord, they would turn and run across the field to their own untidy, cluttered house.

Lenora can remember the precise date of one event — the last day of November the year they were in Grade Ten. They had been walking home from school when Marion said: "I won't be in school no more."

Lenora stopped, but Marion had just walked on, explaining matter of factly that she'd gotten a job serving in Thorne's grocery store on Golf Avenue. "Edith Pye's leaving to get married — I got her job. Old Mr. Thorne told my father that he'd pay me ten dollars a week — fifteen after the first year."

Lenora was angry. She could not credit such a thing was happening — and without Marion having said one word. Without them talking it over! The two girls had walked all the way in Pennywell Road without speaking. Outside Fifields' house they stopped, stood facing each other. Marion kept her eyes down, watching her boot make a pattern of hearts in the slushy snow.

"But we promised to take Commercial together when we finished Grade Eleven!" Lenora said. "We was gonna work in a big office — travel around the world!" She was on the edge of tears.

Marion looked up, her face blank. "Yes, and we was gonna be movie actresses too, and write books, and design dresses! All just foolishness — pretend stuff — like that old fashioned street you broke up, like them plays we used to do!"

This house didn't yet have steps, front or back. Marion had to climb awkwardly up onto the slab of concrete, school books falling from her arms into the wet snow.

Lenora began to pick the books up. "Don't be botherin with em — I don't want em — I'm sick of school anyway," Marion said before she turned and went into the house. Lenora piled the books against the door and went home.

Lenora's family dealt at Thorne's Grocery, so for a little while she and Marion talked each time she bought bread or milk. But there wasn't much for them to talk about, and after awhile Lenora refused to go. "Make Pam go," she'd say whenever her mother tried to send her on a message to Thorne's. Although the Fifields stayed in the same part of town, they moved each year. Soon Lenora wasn't sure where Marion lived, had almost forgotten her.

One night, in Lenora's final year of high school, Marion had phoned. She didn't say hello, just: "I thought I better tell ya I'm getting married tomorrow."

"No! Who to?"

"Who Too — the Chinese laundryman," Marion said.

For a second Lenora thought she was serious. Then they both began to giggle.

"Well!" Lenora had tried to sound the way she supposed you should sound when a friend tells you she's getting married. "Well! Aren't you going to tell me Prince Charming's name? Roland or Keith, I suppose!"

"No, his name is Vic — Vic Tulk," Marion said, keeping her voice flat, letting Lenora know she'd heard the false gaiety.

"Can I come and see you married?"

"No," she said, then again, "No!"

Lenora almost asked why she'd called but didn't because she knew. Marion could not have gotten married without telling her.

"Have a nice wedding!" she said. Then after a pause, "And Marion — have a wonderful life!" she made a kind of kissing sound and hung up.

She bought four china cups. Transparent things with pale green leaves circling the rims. She wrapped them carefully and took them over to Fifields' house one day after school.

Roma came to the door, took the package, smiled pertly and said: "Thank you, your ladyship." She didn't ask Lenora in. The house behind her seemed as empty and unfinished as any house the Fifields had lived in.

When she asked where Marion and Vic were living, Roma rolled her eyes. "They got this flat down off Long's Hill, alongside the taxi where he works. All Marion ever does is scrub and wax and paint and paper — she's at it all the time."

That June Lenora finished high school. She refused to answer to the name Nora anymore, saved enough money to buy a grey Gor-Ray skirt and pink twin-set. She registered for Commercial. By then she had a new best friend, and a boyfriend she'd met while working after school at a bike rental place. But he was only temporary. Lenora knew this because she had her eye on a handsome university student boarding in the house next door. She was enjoying herself so much that sometimes she wondered if she'd fallen asleep at a movie, if any minute the ghostly curtains might pull together, the lights come up and she and Marion would be shuffling out into Harvey Road.

About five months after the wedding, Pam told Lenora she'd heard that Marion had had a baby. The very next Saturday afternoon, without phoning ahead, Lenora went to visit. Marion lived one flight up, in the middle house in a row of three that had once been painted deep yellow but were now grimy with coal dust. There was no doorbell. Lenora stepped into a hallway so dark and damp it reminded her of the Fifields' basement. She called out but no one answered. Feeling uneasy, almost afraid, telling herself not to be silly, she climbed up the narrow stairway. At the top of the stairs there was a pink door. Pinned to the door was a page from a child's colouring book, a picture of two birds perched on a heart — birds and heart were encircled by ribbons. The picture had been carefully crayoned, and inside the heart Marion had written"The Tulks" in round swirly letters.

Before Lenora could knock, the door opened and there was Marion staring solemnly out at her. She'd put on a lot of weight yet her face seemed thin, almost sunken. Her hair was pulled back behind her ears and there were dark circles below her eyes. She looked so strange, so womanly, that Lenora had to force herself to stand there, not turn away, hurry downstairs and out of the house.

"Come in." Marion hadn't smiled, not even when Lenora passed her the beribboned package and congratulated her on the baby.

The flat surprised Lenora. It was nice, a pretty kitchen and, Marion told her, a bathroom and bedroom. She did not show Lenora these other rooms or the baby — a boy, she said, asleep in on the bed.

Everything in the kitchen was pink and pale green; even the stove was green. A border of green leaves had been stencilled all around the pink walls up near the ceiling: "I copied them leaves from the cups you gave us," Marion said. She was proud of the kitchen and Lenora didn't wonder. They sat at a half circle table whose flat end was pushed up against a window. Marion pulled back the pale green lace to show Lenora how she could see right out to the harbour.

"Lucky you," Lenora said, "a husband, a flat and now a lovely baby!"

"I guess so," Marion said. She seemed mystified, a reaction Lenora didn't understand until months later when Pam told her that the baby had been born with something wrong with its brain. Pam had been angry, said Lenora should have known.

The visit didn't last long. After admiring the kitchen and the view there was nothing to say. Marion didn't offer to get tea. They sat there looking down over the odd shaped roof tops out to the harbour where the white Portuguese hospital ship and several small fishing boats were tied up.

Lenora had never seen Marion again. Over the years, news of the Fifields came to her from Pam, and sometimes from her mother. Mrs. Fifield had died suddenly in her late forties. Ruth and Roma had both married and Roma had moved away. Marion and Vic had four more children, but the first son was badly retarded and had never learned to walk.

Later, Lenora's mother told her that Mr. Fifield had moved to Florida to live year round. "So maybe he did make money on those houses he was all the time slavin over," she said.

Pam, who was still good friends with Ruth, reported that Marion had gone queer. Even when Vic Tulk could have afforded any house in town, Marion refused to move from their first squatty little apartment off Long's Hill. Eventually Vic gave up, bought the old row house and added rooms on back.

Then, a few years ago, just after their youngest got married, Vic and Marion broke up. Pam, having always maintained that Vic Tulk was "plain as an old boot and stunned besides," conceded he must have been smarter than she figured — after all he'd acquired a chain of taxi stands — and membership in Bally Haly Golf Club.

"Now," Pam wrote, "he's left, and according to Ruth, Marion never sets foot outside the door — won't even answer her phone half the time."

Pam had seen Vic downtown with some girl half his age. Ruth said they were living together in one of those big new houses out by Virginia Waters.

None of this had made much impression on Lenora. Her mother and Pam talk continually about people she can barely remember. She tries to look interested, says yes and nods, sips tea. But Lenora has lived in five provinces and met a lot of people. She's learned to play golf, to sail, has raised two children, managed a large flower shop and travelled twice around the world since she and Marion were friends. She can hardly be expected to remember someone she knew in Grade Ten, someone she hasn't seen for over thirty years.

It all comes back to her though, every bit of it. As Lenora crawls across the hotel bed to the television, spilling her drink, swearing, as she fumbles for the sound button, she remembers all about herself and Marion. If she doesn't get sound she may never find out why Marion, who is, after all, still young, has turned into this grey-haired old woman being led towards a police van.

The announcer's voice blasts into the room. Lenora twists a button and the voice moderates: "Mrs. Tulk had just come from the funeral of her eldest son. Apparently, she and other family members went straight to the airport to say goodbye to Mrs. Tulk's father who was returning to his home in Orlando. The following remarkable footage, taken just moments after the shooting, was filmed at the airport by our cameraman who was awaiting the arrival of the Premier. We apologize for the uneven quality of this clip."

The inside of Torbay airport appears on the screen — people pulling back, a baby crying, a tanned woman in a fur coat (could it be Roma?) screaming. The camera jerks downward, grey floor tiles, a man's hand curled inward. The camera travels up the sleeve of a dark blue suit, across the white shirt front, lingers on blood clotting along the edge of the tight collar. There is a split second view of Mr. Fifield's dead face, of his wide surprised eyes, his blood-spattered cheeks. The camera pulls away, searches wildly and focuses on a woman sitting on the edge of the baggage carousel. She has dropped the gun; it lies on the floor near her feet. She reaches into her pocket, takes out a package of cigarettes, sticks one between her lips and lights it.

"She smokes!" — for a moment Marion's smoking seems more shocking than the murder of her father. Then the woman sitting on the carousel looks up, straight into the faces of the people standing in a semicircle around her. She takes a deep draw on the cigarette.

Back in Mississauga, trying to reconstruct the events of that evening, Lenora is still not sure what part Marion's murder of Mr. Fifield had in her change of heart about coming back to Newfoundland. Other things had to be counted in — all those square houses, all that dull cosiness between her mother and Pam.

Dave was annoyed at first. He told her she was being hysterical, over-reacting. He is over it now, says they probably did the right thing after all. A new job would have been very stressful at his age.

But it had lain like a rock between them for a long time. "Look — a bit of shared past doesn't connect you with what someone does years later! Your being friends with that madwoman in year dot has bugger all to do with us!" Dave told her more than once.

He is wrong. Lenora knows he is wrong. The past can pull at you like bog water, haul you down from any ladder you've climbed. She's never been able to say this to Dave, of course, doesn't have words to explain, doesn't want to explain either. But she knows. The past is a dark hole, it can draw you under until you don't know who you are, don't know what you might do.

Letters and Diaries

MOIRA GORDON BAIRD BOWRING (1916-1990), daughter of David and Emma Baird, was born into a merchant class family in St. John's. Her marriage in 1940 to Derrick Bowring, son of a successful merchant family of England and Newfoundland, thus linked two prominent St. John's families. They had four children, David, Paula, Vivian and Norman. In this letter, Moira, who frequently signs letters as Gordon, writes to her mother-in-law, Clara Maria Pferdmenges, widow of Cyril Bowring who died in 1949. Although this letter contains family news — presents received, children's schooling, health concerns — the central theme is Moira's need to hire a good and reliable German maid for their upper-middle-class family. At this time in Newfoundland, more paid work opportunities were available for young women, and domestic service was less desirable as a "clean" occupation than it was prior to WWII. Derrick's sister, Sonia (Bowring) and her husband, Ronald (Prentice), are the expectant parents mentioned and "Uncle Eric" is Eric Bowring, brother of Cyril. Broad Halfpenny Farm, Moira's home, was located on Portugal Cove Road, near St. John's.[1]

Broad Halfpenny Farm
St. John's, Newfoundland
January 19th, 1950

My darling Mother

Your letter of the 15th arrived this morning and was received with great delight. It also had the proper effect on my very nagging conscience, so here I am, at last, to thank you so very, very much for all your lovely presents to me and all the children. My blouse is simply lovely and fits me perfectly. It is a heavenly colour and such a beautiful material, such as we never see on this side. All the children's clothes fitted perfectly, except David's pullover, which is a little large, so I am keeping it until the spring, when it will be more suitable. He wears breeches in the winter, and those he has now are brown, but when the weather gets warmer, he will go into grey flannel shorts and your pullover will be very nice. I got some Clydella shirts from John Norman, which are also grey, so he will be very smart when spring comes!

Regarding your suggestion of a German maid, I really think that is the only solution, as it is absolutely hopeless to get a local one. They are so independent and quite a few of our friends living in town are without maids now, so I know I would have no hope.

As for transportation, we could arrange that out here. She could either fly direct from Frankfurt (or some other German airport) to Gander and then into Torbay, or come by sea, which would mean coming from

Moira Gordon Baird Bowring with children Vivian, Paula and David.
CNSA, Coll-170, 5.01

Germany to England and taking the Furness boat from Liverpool. Naturally, Derrick would pay her passage out.

We would want good personal references, and if possible, a photograph, and a guarantee that she would stay with us for two years. As far as the girl herself is concerned, I would like one about 30, or at least young enough not to be put out by the children, but old enough to have a bit of sense and be able to take responsibility.

As far as the work is concerned, I think you have a fair idea of what is done here. One maid alone cannot do the children and the housework and cooking as well, but I am usually here and if she can cook, I am quite willing to do more for the children. If she can't, then I should have to go do the cooking and would expect her to do more for them, if you see what I mean. There is not much dirt here, as you know, and no fire to lay. I have the electric stove, a washing machine, vacuum cleaner and electric floor scrubber and polisher, all of which is extraordinarily labour saving, but there's still a fair amount left for what hands are available! Of course, as the children get older, there is less to do, in the way of washing, dressing them and various other aspects.

The average wage here is $30 or £10 per month, but we would be willing to go up to $50 or £17 although I would rather start a bit lower, in order to work up to that amount (ie $50) as time went on. However, if you think that £10 would not be attractive enough, you could move up the scale as you thought fit. I would not like to have the chance of a good maid for the sake of a $5 bill!

When we have had local maids, I have given them every second evening off, with one afternoon a week from lunchtime to 11p.m. and every second Sunday from lunchtime on. As you know, we have had to drive them into town, but don't want to do that if it's not absolutely necessary. There are a few houses on the road to which she could go, once she had learned the language, and would probably be satisfied to go to town only on her afternoon or Sunday off. However, once again, we wouldn't quibble about that if it meant the difference between getting and not getting.

I imagine this just about covers all you would want to know for now, but if there is anything else, you can let me know and I will answer at once.

It would be marvelous to get someone to help. Mrs. Bennett comes most days, but she isn't here when I need her most — e.g. she never comes on Sunday, so that Derrick and I can't even go for a walk together. I have to get breakfast and get the children up and dressed every morning, and she goes at 6 p.m, which means that we can't go out together. Really, the worst aspect of it all is that Derrick's time at home is pure drudgery instead of the pleasures he should have from his home and family. At present, it just stretches endlessly through the years, which is not a very happy outlook.

Things are much better now that all hands are well, but while Derrick and the children were ill, everything was black and sometimes I wondered how long I could keep going at that pace. What a priceless jewel health is. The children are all fine now and Derrick is much better, so all is well. I really feel that most of Derrick's asthma is a result of our domestic situation and that he would be much better if I could only get a maid of some sort.

Uncle Eric was very worried about Derrick and went to all kinds of trouble arranging for us all to go to the West Indies (Barbados) for a couple of months, but Derrick wouldn't consider it, although he did appreciate U.E.'s concern and the trouble he went to.

I am glad you had a nice Christmas with Sonia and Ronald and so thankful that you were all in new surroundings. 1950 begins a new decade, and for you, a new mode of life, but I do hope that you will find in it a new, if vastly different, happiness, to which we can contribute, in some small measure, here at Broad Halfpenny. You know how very welcome you will be at any time, but please make it soon. When Sonia has laid down her burden, perhaps you will make some plans to come here to us for a nice long while. I guarantee you that you won't be bored! Exhausted maybe, but not bored!

We had a letter from Grandma telling us of Ernest George's return. What celebrations they must have had. If not in the way of good food, etc., in their hearts. Ruth has had such a rotten time. I hope she will get happiness in full measure now to make up for it.

The children are all well and growing like hops. They all seem to be at a sweet age, and are a source of constant mirth. Paula is now picking up the nursery rhymes and the songs she hears on the radio. Her musical talents are well under the bushel, but she enjoys herself and gives us much entertainment. She is her usual sweet self and being affectionate.

David is back at school after a two month break. He seems to be catching up what he missed and is fast approaching the stage when his homework is beyond Mama! Father, with his superior brain, is still able to keep up! Tell Sonia she's in for quite a bit, and I would advise her to start learning now how to explain multiplication and division! Phew!

Vivian fell last Friday and gave her mouth a nasty cut, but it is better now. As you know, it was Friday, the 13th, and being of Irish ancestry, I spent most of the day keeping them out of trouble. Just before taking them up to get them ready for bed, I left her alone in the library. She climbed into the armchair and reached for something on the desk, overbalanced and fell to the floor. On the way, she hit her chin on the edge of the desk and clamped her top teeth into her lower lip. I took her into Tom Anderson on Saturday morning and he told me to see his father in the afternoon to get it stitched, so in I hobbled again, but Dr. A. would [not] stitch it, as he said he would pucker her lip if he drew it together when it was swollen. As usual, he was right, and it is now nearly healed.

Vivian is very advanced for her age, and says everything. She can do messages for me and loves to go to the kitchen to tell "Benna" (as they call Mrs. Bennett) something for me. She is very mischievous and very cute, but not a bit like Paula. She reminds me very much of David at that age, although she is more advanced than he was. Neither of them have Paula's placidity.

I think Norman will be more like her. He has grown tremendously. I haven't weighed him, but I think he is about 20 lbs. He is terribly fat, with bright red cheeks, although he never goes out, and curls so blonde they're almost white, which stand up in a cockade on the top of his head. He has 6 teeth and is a very happy wee fellow. He is a real Bowring, with a head like Uncle Eric's, rather than Derrick's or Father's. He is awfully strong and wiggles and roots out of the bedclothes no matter what I do. He digs in with his heals and head, arches his back, and travels all over the floor in this weird fashion. He can sit up by himself, but it's a highly uncertain and wobbly affair. I think his tail is too round!

I must have my supper — prepared and served by my domesticated spouse — as I have to water my lilies and then to bed. Love to Sonia and Ronald. I will try to write to them soon. Much love from us all.

Ever your loving
Gordon

133

Notes

[1] CNSA, Collection 157, 1.01.016 and Collection 170, 2.02.001.

Escaped Domestics

Robin McGrath

Foxglove, lupin and monkshood:
These are the escaped domestics,
Flowers that have seeded and soared
Out of colonial gardens
Into ditches, meadows and hillsides.
I see these flowers from the corner of my eye
As I speed down the highway
Making sharp turns onto country roads,
And each time I think I see
Mary, Madeline, and Phoebe
Dropping paring knives and hay rakes,
Buckets, baskets and bread pans,
Abandoning their duties,
Knocking over soap suds,
Leaving dinners to burn,
And racing out over the barrens,
Aprons as white as seagulls' breasts,
Hair as red or gold or black
As embroidery threads,
Skirts whipping out behind,
Arms flung high, feet dancing.

Something's Got To Change: A Case Study of Community Efforts to Change Gendered Housing Policies

Jane Robinson

IN DECEMBER 1996, MARGUERITE DYSON was murdered in her unsupervised boarding house in St. John's. The weapon was a screwdriver. The man later convicted of her murder was a resident of the same boarding house. Marguerite was an Inuit woman from coastal Labrador and had lived in St. John's for many years. At the time of her death, she was working as a volunteer at the St. John's Women's Centre. The murder of Marguerite Dyson made women in our community more aware of the vulnerability of women living in many of the city's boarding houses and bed sitters.

Less than a year after Marguerite's death, the St. John's Status of Women Council (SJSWC) adopted a focus on housing and related income issues. *The Hammer and Nail Project on Women and Housing* received funding for a 3-year period from the Urban Issues Programme of the Samuel and Saidye Bronfman Family Foundation. The goal of the *Hammer and Nail Project* was to improve housing supports and services for low-income women by making housing more safe, secure and equitable, and to promote women's sense of control over their housing.

The *Hammer and Nail Project* offered skill development to help single mothers, single women and widows carry out common household repairs. We held seven public "Repair Fairs for Women" where women instructors demonstrated basic household skills involving carpentry, plastering, painting, electrical, plumbing, and automotive. Participants got hands-on experience installing a peephole in a door, changing a door lock, fixing holes in walls, repairing a tap or toilet, fixing a flat tire, and a chance to develop many other survival skills.

There was also an action research component to investigate women's housing issues in St. John's which was completed in the winter of 2001. Women's Centre staff Michelle Boutcher and Madeline Lewis interviewed 26 women on low incomes who lived in boarding houses, bed sitters, shared apartments, and in public housing. Some were clients of the Women's Centre; others called when they saw the Project advertisements in the media.

The *Hammer and Nail Project Action Research Report* was released in the fall of 2002. It was the first extensive study of women's issues in rental housing for women on low incomes in the city. The Women's Housing Factsheet summarizes the findings of the study.

WOMEN'S HOUSING FACTSHEET

The *Hammer and Nail Project* interviewed 26 women about their housing in St. John's in the winter of 2000-01. The study focused on women living in boarding houses, bed sitters, shared apartments and in public housing.

- 7 women lived in bed sitters, 7 in boarding houses, 8 in private apartments (3 of these were shared), 3 in public housing, and 1 with relatives.
- 40% of the women were under 40 years old. Of these, 50% lived in rooms or bed sitters.

Affordability
"It is really hard for a single person to find housing. Social assistance doesn't give me enough money to afford anything nice. It's very difficult."

- 90% of women in the study were receiving income support (social assistance) from the provincial government. Their incomes (for single women) ranged from $417 to $617 per month. To get the $617 rate it is necessary to demonstrate a disability or severe illness.
- 88% of the women in the study spent over 30% of their incomes on rent, and 40% spent 50% or more of their incomes on rent. This is shocking, though not surprising, as it costs approximately $300 a month to rent a boarding/bed sitting room.
- Most of the women could not afford apartments of their own. Because of low income support, the only options open to them were boarding and bed sitting. The only women spending less than 30% of their incomes on rent were living in public housing.

Safety
"The knob on my room door didn't work properly and I was sexually assaulted as a result."

- 31% did not have access to a telephone in their dwelling.
- 61.5% of the women in bed sitters and boarding houses did not have locks on their room doors.
- 24/26 had smoke detectors.
- 50% had fire extinguishers.
- 7/14 women living in bed sitters and boarding houses said they had no means of escape if there was a fire in the building. Five of these lived in boarding or bed sitting situations where there were more than four residents. They said they would have to jump out of the window. One said she wouldn't be able to get out.

Living Conditions
"It's very cold and uncomfortable and it keeps me up all night."

"Mildew is still a big problem after ten years [in public housing unit]. Both my son and I have to use inhalers."

- 15/26 women (58%) reported dampness or mildew. Of these, 11 reported extreme damp or mildew, and this occurred over a range of housing types — bed sitters (3), boarding (2), apartments (2), public housing (3). Notably, the problem of extreme dampness/mildew existed in all of the public housing units in our sample.[1]

The *Hammer and Nail Project Action Research Report* made ten recommendations to the City of St. John's, the Province, and the federal government. The Project's advisory committee, composed of women from a number of community groups, met with government officials to inform them about the findings, and to ask for their support in resolving the problems. We focused our efforts at the municipal level and met with St. John's City Councillors and the representatives of Building and Property Management to discuss key issues.

One such issue was the recommendation for deadbolt locks on the doors of individual rooms in boarding houses and bed sitters. This example clearly illustrates the difficulty of resolving housing problems for low-income women. At first, City Hall told us that this provision of locks would contravene fire regulations. For example, they asked how a firefighter might remove a person from their room if the door was locked. We argued that the absence of secure locks on the doors meant that women's privacy and safety were often being violated. The city officials responded that it would not be a problem to address the deadbolt issue on a voluntary compliance basis. In other words, individual landlords could be asked to comply, but the City did not have the resources to enforce this.

The Gender-Inclusive Analysis and Housing Policy Development in Newfoundland and Labrador (GIA) Project

Recognizing that the housing crisis affects different populations of women differently, the St. John's Status of Women Council developed a second piece of work on housing in 2002: the *Gender-Inclusive Analysis and Housing Policy Development in Newfoundland and Labrador*, or *"GIA Project"* for short.

The *GIA Project* was provincial in scope and committed to a gender-inclusive analysis, which looks at the diversity within each gender due to income, cultural identity, ability/disability, age, sexual orientation, family status and other factors.[2] The *GIA Project* researcher Susan Williams consulted with 83 people through focus groups, conference calls, and telephone interviews around the province to find out about housing issues.

The Project was directed by an Advisory Committee composed of women from the SJSWC, the province-wide Coalition of Persons with Disabilities, the Association for New Canadians, the Consumers' Health Awareness Network, the Multicultural Women's Organization, the St. John's Native Friendship Centre, the Provincial Advisory Council on the Status of Women, the Provincial Association Against Family Violence, the Women's Health Network, the Lantern, and the Newfoundland and Labrador Housing Corporation.

In November, 2003, the SJSWC released the study *"Something's Got to Change": Research Report: Gender-Inclusive Analysis and Housing Policy Development in Newfoundland and Labrador.* It was the most comprehensive study on housing issues of people on low incomes in the province to date. In addition to the primary research, the report integrated previous research studies by the Coalition of Persons with Disabilities, the St. John's Community Advisory Committee on Homelessness, the Consumers' Health Awareness Network, the Interdepartmental Committee on Social Supportive Housing and the St. John's Status of Women Council into its analysis. The "Something's Got to Change": Housing Factsheet (2003) presents some of the key findings of the *GIA Report.*

The *GIA* study made 13 policy recommendations that the SJSWC decided to workshop with a group of community and government representatives. We held a Workshop on Gender-Inclusive Analysis and Housing Policy Development, in November, 2003 in St. John's. The workshop planning committee, Mary Ennis, Susan Williams, Kaberi Debnath, Madeline Lewis, Dr. Phyllis Artiss and myself, developed an agenda that included a lot of participation and group work.

The workshop was co-chaired by Phyllis Artiss of the SJSWC and Mary Ennis of the Coalition of Persons with Disabilities. Marie White, of the St. John's Advisory Committee on Homelessness, acted as facilitator. About 60 people attended, coming from diverse groups involved in housing issues, such as Inuit Women of the Torngats, the Association for New Canadians, the National Anti-Poverty Organization, the Seniors' Resource Centre, the St. John's Advisory Committee on Homelessness, the Bay St. George Women's Centre, the Newfoundland and Labrador Housing Corporation, the Stella Burry Community Services, and provincial and municipal politicians and civil servants.

On the first day, the community participants met to discuss and prioritize the recommendations contained in the report *"Something's Got to Change": Research Report.* Government participants joined in on the second day for skill development sessions on The Inclusion Lens, Gender and Diversity Analysis, and The Policy Development Process. Panelists from women's centres in Bay St. George and Labrador West, mental health services in Grand Falls-Windsor, and Inuit Women of the Torngats presented the priority issues from the first day. Then in small groups, we looked at the five areas of concern: Availability; Affordability; Adequacy; Public Information and Services; and Provincial Housing Division and Strategy.

Government officials were asked to give their input on which policy recommendations were most practical or "do-able," who was responsible for them, and what was possible over the short, medium, and long term. These discussions were summarized in a final document called *Summary*

"SOMETHING'S GOT TO CHANGE": HOUSING FACTSHEET

Affordability

"The greatest problem was the lack of rent cap, or maximum rent that could be charged [in social housing]. We went from a social assistance level, and my husband got a job so he went to probably $14 an hour. The next month, we went from a humble amount of rent to over $900. He only worked for several weeks and was laid off again." (community worker)

"We have single mothers trying to get into less suitable housing so that they don't have to choose between heating and eating." (community worker)

- Women are more likely than men to have housing affordability problems.
- In 1997, 71% of Canadian single mothers were renters and 60% of them had housing affordability problems — spending 30% or more of income on shelter.
- 50% of Canadian single fathers rented, but only 40% of them had affordability problems.
- The number of senior households in Canada with affordability problems increased by 16.3% between 1997 and 2000.
- Small apartments range from $450 - $550 per month in Newfoundland and $550 - $650 in Labrador.
- Heat bills were as high as $400 - $500 per month in the winter months.

Availability

"I'm on the waiting list to get into Housing, but there's just nothing. They say yes, I'm on the top of the list, but nobody's moving." (single parent)

"There's no housing for homeless outside of St. John's." (community worker)

- Rental vacancy rates in Newfoundland and Labrador dropped from 5.7% in 2000 to 3.0 % in 2002.
- There is a serious shortage of housing for people with disabilities in all parts of the province.
- Mental health consumers have few supports for living in the community and they frequently don't qualify for disability income or home support in Newfoundland and Labrador.
- Mental health consumers are being housed in hospitals and seniors homes in central Newfoundland due to the shortage of suitable housing.
- In 2002, the Salvation Army reported a 10% increase in use of their emergency shelter in St. John's, especially by young people and single parents with children.

Adequacy

"Single women don't want to go into bed sitters because of the safety issues, for instance, drinking and violent behaviour of other residents." (senior)

"From the bathroom all the time comes water... I clean everything, sometimes all night ... the water in the floor. My carpet now is very black. It's not healthy for my baby." (new immigrant, private housing tenant).

- Women are less likely to be among the visibly homeless, due to personal safety issues and the fact that women with children cannot live on the streets for long without the intervention of child protection agencies.
- 61.5% of women living in bed sitters and boarding houses in the *Hammer and Nail* study did not have locks on their room doors.
- Women and their children escaping domestic violence make up part of the hidden homeless.
- In some regions, women have no practical access to shelters.
- In Labrador's north coast communities, where houses are small and in short supply, young families were crowded into parents' homes waiting for housing.
- Tenants are afraid to make a complaint because they are afraid of eviction.

Discrimination

"A single parent was experiencing some negative comments from landlords, talking about the kids going to be lighting fires and sniffing gas, and things along those lines, just your typical stereotyping of Aboriginals." (community worker)

" 'Oh,' the landlord said, 'I've got professional people in this building, we can't take you in here.'" (community worker)

- There were cases of landlord discrimination against single mothers, youth, Aboriginal people, new Canadians, people with disabilities, people on income support, mental health consumers, students, lesbian women, ex-offenders and others.
- There were also landlords who did not want the inconvenience of children or the cost of making a dwelling accessible.

Health

"What we're seeing with the single moms is that the places that they're living in, they're drafty, there's mould, that type of thing. No fridge, no stove. Landlords aren't doing a lot of repairs in a lot of the cases." (community worker)

"Years ago, there wasn't as much known about asthma and mould and dampness and how it translates into illness, but given our current understanding of what's happening, and knowing that we don't know enough about it, there should be a lot more inspections of buildings for health reasons, for everybody." (community worker)

- Many people noted that inspections occurred less often and that enforcement was weaker than five to ten years ago.
- Some towns appeared to be lax about slum landlords and unlicensed apartments while others routinely inspected apartments before new tenants moved in.
- Budget cuts in Newfoundland and Labrador Housing Corporation resulted in fewer staff covering larger areas, with fewer resources for inspection and maintenance.
- There was evidence that bad housing conditions affected physical and mental health.
Physical: cold, no control of temps; asthma and allergies related to cold, dampness, mildew; poor repair causing danger of tripping, falling, burning. Mental: unsupportive housing, violence, fear, financial stress, disruption of family life, leading to depression.
- The Department of Health and Community Services Act only permits an inspection of health conditions of a dwelling if it is vacant.[3]

of Proceedings and Guidelines for a Strategy for Change in Housing Policies. On the third day of the workshop a Housing Policy Working Group was formed, with government and community representatives from around the province.

The *GIA Project* is now in Phase IV. This phase involves the Housing Policy Working Group (HPWG), which provides a forum for discussion and resolution of housing issues of women on low incomes and other disadvantaged people in the province. The HPWG mandate is to recommend and implement changes to housing policies and practices, and to develop a provincial housing strategy document in response to the recommendations and directions from the *"Something's Got to Change": Research Report* and the Workshop.

The Working Group is a province-wide network that has met by videoconference almost every month from January 2004 to September 2005. About 20 people participate in each video-conference from sites in Labrador West, Happy Valley-Goose Bay, Port aux Basques, Stephenville, St. Anthony, Grand Falls, Gander, Marystown and St. John's region. Provincial government officials from Human Resources, Labour and Employment, Government Services including Residential Tenancies, Women's Policy Office and the Newfoundland and Labrador Housing Corporation take part from the site at the Confederation Building. Participants represent women's centres and shelters, organizations of persons with disabilities, mental health agencies, international students at Memorial University of Newfoundland, individual Members of the House of Assembly, seniors, anti-poverty groups, housing service providers, immigrants and refugees, seniors and women in training programs. The HPWG uses an electronic list-serve to communicate between meetings about housing issues in the province. Members of the Working Group provide links and share information with national groups of housing activists, such as The National Working Group on Women and Housing, The National Housing and Homelessness Network and The Canadian Housing Renewal Association.

The major achievement of the housing policy working group has been the development of the document *A Housing Strategy for Newfoundland and Labrador.* This document draws from the *"Something's Got To Change": Research Report,* and two research studies commissioned by the Working Group which were carried out in coastal, central and western Labrador, and with new immigrants and refugees in St. John's. The strategy proposes five goals, with a detailed implementation plan identifying the agencies responsible for each step. The goals are as follows:

Goal 1: Availability
Increase and enhance the supply of adequate and appropriate housing for low-income residents.

There is a need for more decent, affordable housing in the province, and a growing need to repair existing housing stock. Governments should invest directly in social housing and provide more incentives for private and non-profit groups to build low-cost housing that will remain affordable. Initiatives are needed for low-income people to purchase homes. Housing is needed that is suitable for seniors, people with disabilities, single adults, and newcomers to Canada. More housing is needed on the Labrador coast where overcrowding is a severe problem. More shelters and transitional housing are needed for homeless people and for women and children escaping violence. The barrier of discrimination must be eliminated.

Goal 2: Affordability
Remove housing affordability barriers.
Changes in the economy and in government policies have put decent housing out of the reach of many low-income people. Housing needs have changed due to an aging population and the growth in new kinds of households such as single-parent families. Rising home energy costs are placing people at risk of homelessness, indicating a need for long-term energy efficiency solutions. Rental costs have increased exponentially and rent controls are needed.

Goal 3: Adequacy
Enforce existing laws related to building conditions, fire safety, public health and the responsibility of landlords to provide adequate private rental housing. Increase funding for repairs and re-fits to ensure that public social housing is preserved and can accommodate a wider range of households as well as provide shelter for homeless people and victims of violence.
Many private rental units are in poor condition, presenting fire, health, safety and security hazards. They also increase energy costs to tenants due to energy inefficiency. Many tenants hesitate to complain for fear of eviction, and there is less inspection of rental housing due to government budget cuts. Much of the province's public social housing is deteriorating due to shrinking maintenance and repair budgets, increasing problems such as mould and leaky roofs and foundations. Funds are also needed to divide the larger units to accommodate smaller households and/or make them accessible for people with disabilities. There is a province-wide shortage of supportive housing services to enable people with disabilities, seniors, mental health consumers and others to live independently in the community.

Goal 4: Government Information and Services
Introduce policies and practices to increase the housing knowledge and choices of low-income people and others with housing barriers.
People lack information about who can help them get repairs done and

who can help in the case of unfair eviction. Information on housing rights and responsibilities as well as income support policies needs to be more accessible to people with housing problems. Most agencies see housing as outside their mandate, and they need to recognize the links between housing, economic security, health and human rights. Equality-seeking groups must be able to participate in government decisions that affect housing. Housing information and supports are needed for new immigrants, international students and out-of-town students at post-secondary institutions.

Goal 5: A Provincial Housing Strategy
Provide a mechanism, an analytical framework and resources to implement and monitor a government-community provincial housing strategy to address the needs of low-income and marginalized residents in collaboration with community partners.

Government must adopt a provincial housing strategy to address the problems of people who are inadequately housed. The strategy should involve agencies and community organizations working together. Gender- and diversity-inclusive analyses should guide implementation of the strategy. The strategy should include revision of existing policies and programs, development of new models to meet housing needs and the dedication of resources to eliminate inequities and barriers to healthy housing for all residents of the province.[4]

The Housing Strategy was presented to Joan Burke, Minister of Housing and Responsible for the Status Of Women, in July, 2005. Further meetings are planned with the Newfoundland and Labrador Housing Corporation in November, 2005, and with the Social Policy Committee of Cabinet.

Over the last seven years, the housing work of the St. John's Status of Women Council has developed from the local focus of *The Hammer and Nail Project* to a province-wide scope. Our research work has moved from a feminist analysis, through gender-inclusive analysis to a gender and diversity analysis. Our collaborative work has expanded to include community and government groups and agencies.

While keeping up its work on the Housing Strategy, the St. John's Status Of Women Council has also taken a new direction in its housing programme in 2005. We are developing plans for a multi-service facility for women who are at risk of homelessness in St. John's. This new dream is named after Marguerite Dyson. According to Lisa Zigler, Executive Director of SJSWC, "Marguerite's Place will offer a space where women can feel safe, have quality housing and avail themselves of a range of support that would meet their needs. We will strive to create a place that will promote respect, healing and hope." It could be said that this has been the vision for all the housing work of SJSWC. [5]

Notes

[1] St. John's Status of Women Council (SJSWC). 2002. *Hammer and Nail Project: Women and Housing Issues Action Research Report.* St. John's: SJSWC.

[2] Hebert, Cheryl. 1998. *Guidelines for Gender Inclusive Analysis.* St. John's: Women's Policy Office, Government of Newfoundland and Labrador.

[3] St. John's Status of Women Council (SJSWC). 2003. *"Something's Got To Change" Research Report: Gender-Inclusive Analysis and Housing Policy Development in Newfoundland and Labrador.* St. John's: SJSWC.

[4] Housing Policy Working Group. 2005. *A Housing Strategy for Newfoundland and Labrador.* St. John's: St. John's Status of Women Council and Women's Policy Office.

[5] For further information, visit www.sjswc.ca and www.margueritesplace.ca

Traversing the Fine Line of Conformity: Reflections on Researching the Lives of Criminalized Women

MaDonna R. Maidment

If you have come here to study me, you are wasting your time. If you have come here because your liberation is bound up with mine, then let us work together (Pate, 2003, 169).

FEMINIST EPISTEMOLOGIES HAVE CONTRIBUTED to the growing practice of researchers locating themselves in their research to demonstrate the often subjective and biased nature of social science. This both enables the reader to examine the interconnectedness between the topic and the researcher's social location and the researcher to grapple with preconceived notions about the study and its results. Positionality refers to researchers locating and sharing their particular standpoint with their readers. Hertz (1997, viii) gives the following rationale for positionality:

> Through personal accounting, researchers must become more aware of how their own positions and interests are imposed at all stages of the research process — from the questions they ask to those they ignore, from who they study to who they ignore, from problem formulation to analysis, representation, and writing — in order to produce less distorted accounts of the social world.

Reflexivity is another tool used to produce a fuller and more accurate understanding of the social world. As articulated by Mauthner and Doucet (1998, 121), reflexivity translates into:

> Reflecting upon and understanding our own personal, political, and intellectual autobiographies as researchers and making explicit where we are located in relation to our research respondents. Reflexivity also means acknowledging the critical role we play in creating, interpreting and theorizing research data.

Locating my own personal, political, and intellectual biography has been an ongoing process as I traced the pathways into and out of prison of 22 criminalized women in Newfoundland and Labrador.

As an urban, working-class, white woman who grew up in St. John's, I have long recognized the fine line I traversed between the official status of "offender" and "non-offender." The question driving my research reflects my attempts to understand: "How it is that some girls/women from lower working-class, disenfranchised backgrounds avoid the criminalizing process in the first place (or avoid getting caught and subsequently labeled) while others do not?" The question formed as I took inventory of fellow classmates and neighbours who have ended up on the "other side of the law" while I managed to escape the same fate.

My political journey to this research was somewhat uneven. I realized relatively early in life that in order to effect social change I needed to position myself to influence macro social policy development. The conversion of "private troubles" into "public issues," as formulated by C. Wright Mills (1959), was the driving force behind my thinking.

My intellectual journey began in earnest as, nearing the completion of a Bachelor of Arts, I conducted a study of women on house arrest and was alarmed at the incongruency of their dual status as prisoners and caregivers in their own homes. It became evident that the criminal justice system did not account for the gendered realities of women's lives (Maidment, 2002). Subsequent graduate research reinforced corrections as an enterprise in which the experiences of men are taken as the starting and finishing point by which women are judged and processed.

"Re-integration" became a major area of inquiry for me as I watched women return to the same socially and economically disadvantaged locations in their communities which had brought them into "conflict with the law" in the first place. As an active member of the Canadian Association of Elizabeth Fry Societies[1] (CAEFS) and co-founder of the local branch, I became increasingly aware of the neglect of criminalized women internationally, nationally, and locally. The realities facing women returning to their home communities and the growing number of social, cultural and economic forces competing to bring women down made re-integration seem unlikely.

I came into this research with quite a number of perplexing questions and concerns which have not been satisfactorily addressed in the literature on women's "corrections".[2] Personal standpoints sought to inform and drive the direction of the research agendas. This is very much the impetus for this study.

Poverty Trap

Often the common denominator among criminalized women is a chronic cycle of poverty and dependence on welfare. Moreover, education, sex, age, and geographic location are strongly correlated to poverty. In a recent study by Statistics Canada (2004) workers with high school education or less were approximately three times more likely to live below the poverty line than those with a university degree. Consistently, women are more likely to be employed in low-paying, part-time jobs relative to men. Age of workers is also strongly correlated to the incidence and prevalence of poverty, with women aged 16-24 experiencing low-paying jobs almost twice as often as those aged 25-34. Furthermore, workers in the Atlantic provinces had the highest incidence of low weekly earnings. Given that criminalized women are generally mirrored on all these demographic variables accounting for an increased prevalence of poverty, it is not surprising that economics plays a key role in women's criminal pathways.

Indeed, the criminalization of poverty has become an international trend for women. As articulated by Wacquant (2003), "prisons of poverty" are due to:

> the increased use of the penal system as an instrument for managing social insecurity and containing the social disorders created at the bottom of the class structure by neo-liberal policies of economic deregulation and social-welfare retrenchment.

While Canadians often hold the misguided perception that homelessness and poverty are nowhere near the levels of our southern neighbours, as DeKeseredy et al., (2003, 2) point out, the percentage of Canadians living in concentrated urban poverty parallels, and in many instances, exceeds that of our US counterparts. Canada now has one of the highest rates of family and child poverty in the developed world, with an increase of 33.8 percent between 1990 and 1995 (DeKeseredy et al., 2003, 5). Evidence of the criminalization of poverty is being felt in all advanced capitalist societies where those at the bottom of the class structure are penalized by draconian, neo-liberal state policies targeting the poor. Moreover, as Table 1.1 shows, the realities of poverty are most acutely felt by lone parent families (overwhelmingly headed by women) in their

TABLE 1.1

Population Size and Social Assistance Rates for Unattached Individuals and Lone-Parent Families in Newfoundland and Labrador, 1999-2003

	1999	2000	2001	2002	2003
Total Lone-parent and unattached	29300	28930	27480	27205	27900
Average benefits	$5,300	$5,400	$5,100	$5,100	$5,300
Average duration (months per year)	9.1	9.2	9.3	9.3	9.3
Lone-parent families	9255	9085	8485	8150	8175
Average benefits	$7,200	$7,300	$7,400	$7,300	$7,400
Average duration (months per year)	9.4	9.4	9.4	9.4	9.4
Unattached individuals	20075	19850	19000	19055	19725
Average benefits	$4,500	$4,500	$4,200	$4,200	$4,400
Average duration (months per year)	8.9	9.1	9.2	9.3	9.3

often failed attempts to eke out a living on inadequate welfare incomes. Furthermore, the numbers of single-parent families headed by women in Newfoundland and Labrador has grown 13 percent since 1991, now comprising roughly one-fifth of all families with children (23,000) (Statistics Canada, 2004).

Experiences of absolute poverty and the stressors associated with trying to manage the basic survival needs of a family contribute to many women's criminal pathways. As Sarah said:

You are way below the poverty line living on social services and a woman to go out and have to buy extra fruits and vegetables and things for a child to eat to keep a child healthy they cannot do that on the budget they are living on. You take it, like I was getting $179 every two weeks. Now I was struggling with that. To buy your groceries and ... [t]hen you got a child going to school and they get in there and [you] can't afford to buy things. And then if someone comes around and things are stolen and says 'Want to buy a pair of jeans for $20?' and they fit my daughter, yes, I'll take them.

Affordable housing is an ongoing challenge for many women. In a recent gender-based analysis of housing policy in Newfoundland and Labrador, the St. John's Status of Women Council (2003, 1) pointed out that almost half of the tenant households in this province spent 30 percent or more of their gross income on shelter and thus were classified as "core housing need" as defined by Canada Mortgage and Housing Corporation (CHMC). Low-cost housing is scarce. There are lengthy wait-lists for social housing; many rentals are in poor condition; there is a lack of short-term housing for abused women and their children and a lack of emergency shelters; and not enough accessible and supportive housing for people with disabilities and seniors.

Increasingly, single women and their young families are becoming part of the "hidden homeless," staying temporarily with friends and relatives ("couch-surfing"), or in shelters (St. John's Status of Women Council, 2003, 1). Nicole described the affordable housing crisis in St. John's:

Most one-bedrooms wants $400 or $500 a month. They want damage deposits on top of that. Then they wants you to pay your own utilities. It's going to be costly to set up. It's still $350 or $400 for a bedsitting room.

As Rebecca articulated, the choice often comes down to food or rent.

I have gone out on days and just stolen enough stuff to put food in the house for the kids. And I don't care. I will be 90 years old and if I don't

have food in my house I will go and get it one way or another. If my kids are hungry, I am going to go and get it. Plain and simple.
Charmaine provided an economic rationale for her criminal activity:

The only real way I can explain it is like I said when I started out shoplifting it was for survival. But now ... [l]ike to go out and pay $90 for a pair of jeans when I can get them for nothing. I'd go out for half an hour and I'd have myself three or four hundred dollars and people are out there working their ass off for two weeks for that. Which is pathetic?

The lowest minimum wage in Canada doesn't provide much of an option. And for women on welfare, the drug plan available through Social Services is a valuable benefit they would not have if they worked. Victoria provided an example of the trap of dependency on welfare benefits.

I am asthmatic. My inhalers is 100 and something dollars a month. I get a drug card through social assistance. I wouldn't be able to make it [without that]. That's why I am hanging on to this welfare. I want to work. It makes me feel better. I don't want to be on welfare for the rest of my life.

Women wage earners now earn 65.2 percent of the incomes of their male counterparts, are more likely to be concentrated in low-wage service jobs with little security and benefits and are over-represented in part-time, temporary work. Three-fourths of part-time workers in Canada are female (Statistics Canada, 2004). Rebecca saw little incentive to join the ranks of the working poor:
There is no incentive to work for minimum wage. Maybe it's alright for a single person, living at home but it ain't no good for a family. I'd be worse off if I went that route.
The psychological consequences of being poor are not lost on these women. Many, like Rachael, connect the emotional anguish of poverty to a decline in their overall physical and mental health.

I guess being poor and not having a lot leads to overall depression ... [a]nd of course the depression leads to not having any money. So that's why so many people drinks and gets involved with drugs because you can afford it. Most drugs you can afford. Like a gram of weed that lasts hours and hours is only $20.00. And you stay so high that you don't really know if you are in the world and you are so happy.

The cycle of poverty is reinforced by state-sanctioned impediments to climbing out of it. One of the strongest correlates to poverty is low levels of education. In 2003, for example, families headed by individuals who did not graduate high school were at least twice as likely to fall below the Low Income Cut-Offs (LICOs)[3] as those headed by people who had either a university degree or college diploma *(Canadian Council on Social Development,* 2004*)*. The oft expressed desire to return to school and "make something of themselves" is waged against the reality that in doing so women will be cut off from their only source of income. Jessica discussed the short-sightedness of government fiscal policies with regard to the welfare trap.

> I had to quit school because Student Aid didn't come through. You are trapped there [on welfare] and you got no way out of it. You are stuck there and you are staying there. You are not getting anywhere else. If they sat back and said, o.k. fine, go to school and then maybe in a year or two they would be rid of me altogether. They don't look at it like that. There is no choice.

Once women are criminalized, the criminal record stands as a major impediment to getting even a minimum wage job, as Rebecca pointed out:

> There is no second chances here. You got a record no one will look at you. I can't even work at Tim Horton's or nothing because I am not bondable.

Poverty for many women also creates unwanted dependencies on male partners as breadwinners. In a recent study connecting abused women and their experiences of the welfare system in Ontario, Mosher et al., (2004) denounce neo-conservative policies which drive women further under the control of their abusers and acknowledge that:

> Women who flee abusive relationships and turn to welfare seeking refuge and support frequently find neither. Women's experiences of welfare are often profoundly negative ... They encounter a system that is less than forthcoming about their entitlements, and about the multiple rules with which they must comply ... They are often subjected to demeaning and humiliating treatment from workers within a system in which suspicion and the devaluation of recipients are structured into its very core. For many the experience of welfare is like another abusive relationship ... Disturbingly, the decision to return to an abusive relationship is often the "best" decision for a woman, in a social context of horrendously constrained conditions (Mosher et al., 2004: v).

Remaining in unhealthy and abusive relationships based on economics was echoed by a number of women, including Corrina:

> You wonder why everybody is scamming welfare. I'll tell you why. They won't let you get ahead at all. They won't give anybody a break. They get you in the rut and they keep you there. I am stuck here now 15 years in an abusive relationship and I am sick of it. They try and keep you down ... [I] don't know what I would do if he [partner] ever left me. I wouldn't be able to make it here alone without him. Otherwise, I'd be gone out of here for long ago.

This financial dependency is sometimes the only viable (and non-criminal) means of economic security. Failing to take this route, many like Victoria find themselves living on the streets or turning to crime.

> I did stupid stuff because I did not want to go back [to my parent's] home. I wrote cheques to have a place to stay in B&B's and hotels. I didn't want to go home because my family background was so dysfunctional and I didn't want to ask people for things. You don't do that right. You are supposed to make it on your own. You're not supposed to screw up. So I wrote cheques. That was my first offence. After the first time going inside I learned about how to get prescriptions and stuff and then I started writing prescriptions, fraud, whatever I could. Then I moved in with him to get off the street and things went downhill from there ... I wouldn't be able to live in this apartment if me and him split up because I definitely would not have enough to live off.

Physical and Sexual Abuse

The high prevalence of criminalized women with histories of physical and/or sexual abuse has been well-documented. The Task Force on Federally Sentenced Women (1990), for example, found that over two-thirds of women interviewed (n=191) had been physically abused as children or adults; over half this number (53%) had been sexually abused. These figures are considerably higher among aboriginal women where 90% had been physically abused and 61% sexually abused (Heney and Kristiansen, 1998). Similarly patterns of abuse were evident in the experiences of women in my study. Kathleen drew the links between trying to cope with abuse and criminalization.

> I've got to start dealing with all the shit that is going on and deal with [childhood] sexual abuse issues. I'm 33 years old now and I can't take this anymore. I've got to get away from my common-law. I have left

him before but he was in jail when I left him. He got a load of assault charges but he never gets any big time for it. A few months here and there in weekends and then I writes a cheque for $52.80 and I gets eighteen months. Figure that one out. The highest sentence he ever, ever had was 13 months for assault. I don't know but it is just a homicide waiting to happen. I've got to get away from him [common-law partner]. When I get out things are alright for a little while. Then things start to get abusive again and I start using [drugs].

For some women, like Emily, troubles with the criminal justice system began later in life, often as they began their journey towards a realization that the sexual abuse they suffered did not constitute a "normal" way of life.

I never drank until I was 31. I had been doing stuff growing up but I hadn't realized until seven or eight years ago that that was a way of coping with things that happened when I was growing up. I never knew that. We were always taught that wrong was right and there was no arguing. To be raped and molested and all that was normal.

Past abuse is often the marker for early state intervention. Reporting abuse often begins a downward spiral of state-sponsored control. Jennifer chronicled the cycle of foster care and mental health interventions in her young life as a result of *her* sexual victimization.

My first suicide attempt was at 11 years old. We lived in this big old two-story house and the boys were in one room and the girls were in another but because there was no room in the girl's room for me I was put in the boy's room with the boys. He [live-in relative] used to come in and do a lot of things and it wasn't until I made the suicide attempt he [abuser] was kicked out of the house. Then, of course, unfortunately child protection got involved ... I ended up in the Janeway [Children's Hospital]. I don't remember how long I was there but I was going back and forth for counselling for years. And then when I was 14 I was admitted to the Waterford Hospital.[4] To this day I am the youngest person ever admitted to the Waterford Hospital.

The emotional trauma of childhood sexual abuse leaves many women struggling to maintain any semblance of healthy adult relationships, as Olivia recounted.

I married when I was 18 but it was kind of hard because it was kind of hard in a sexual way because he was trying to get my clothes off and going down around my crotch and stuff. Oh God. Thinking back then it was hard. I got in the bed with my clothes and all on and turned in. He was there like trying to turn me out and trying to get my clothes off. Oh, come on now. We just got married. But he didn't know [about my past sexual abuse] so I turned around and I told him so.

In the end, Olivia faced the additional trauma of discovering that her husband was sexually molesting family members. The discovery of this abuse eventually led her to violence towards this man.

When I was married I found out after seven years that my husband was a child sex offender. I was going to leave him was because it was two of my nieces that he was trying to get a hold to. Six months old and the other one was nine years old. He was caught feeling them up and everything ... So after I grabbed the gun and I went from there. I was going to shoot him and shoot myself ... Then a few years after all that I ends up with another guy I was going with for four years and lo and behold he was up on charges from Bell Island for sexually assaulting kids. I said every man I gets involved with is always a child molester.

Olivia spoke openly about the pain she continues to suffer as a result of her horrific experiences.

To tell you the truth I have been going in so many different directions, wrong directions. I am reaching for the bottle. I am reaching for someone to put their arms around me and say yes by I understands exactly what you are going through. What I wouldn't give. There is nobody on this god-earthly world who can ever take the pain away. It's just myself. I am the one that got to go to sleep and I am the one who got to face it the next morning. And to tell you the truth there is no bottle and there is no medication that can help that.

Incarcerated and 46, Olivia is so haunted by the sexual abuse and the losses it led to that she still cannot sleep without a light.

I am after turning a few times to the doctors in the hospital but they didn't understand exactly what I was going through. I lost my education. I lost my home because I ended up in hospital a few times. They turn around, back in them days, they say I was unfit to look after a child. [They said I] was in the Waterford quite a few times. So they used that against me and took my child away. So then I turned more to the bottle and more to the pills and everything.

Turning to drugs and alcohol is often a "damage control technique" (Comack, 1996, 42) to help women cope with the pains of past abuse.

Well over half of women in prison report substance abuse or addiction concerns (Morash and Schram, 2002). Leanne talked about her connection between drugs and crime.

Where I live [in public housing] there is a lot of people addicted to OxyContin.[5] My best friend is on them the past year. It is hard for me to stay off the drugs when I am living life like this. What have I got to look forward to?

Olivia described her attempts to medicate her pain and the lack of support she received:

I did the wrong things. Facing the bottle. Facing pills. Taking four or five of this kind, this kind and that kind. And before you know it I am all loaded down with different kinds of pills. You figure that them two things, the bottle and the pills are you biggest friends. In the long run you are hurting yourself. And in the long run it don't make any sense because you say, 'Is they worth it?' You know. These people who hurt you, are they worth hurting yourself for? But in the meantime you just don't care. You got to turn to something because some of these people on the outside don't understand exactly what you are going through.

For Olivia, no deterrence tactics or punishment inside or outside the prison could take away the pain.

Like I said, I would be lying if I turned around and said to you there is no way in bloody hell that I will end up back in here, in this hell hole. They could turn around and they could put you in one of those fancy [restraint] chairs they got in there and they could beat the soul right clean out of you. But that's not going to change anything.

For many women, their addictions are closely tied to the commission of criminal activities in the first instance. In Canada, 69 percent of federally sentenced women indicate that drugs and/or alcohol played a major role in their criminalization (*Canadian Association of Elizabeth Fry Societies*, 2004). However, long before patterns of criminalization are established, women have encountered other state control interventions stemming from their dysfunctional family backgrounds.

Histories of State Controls

Most women who end up in penal custody have been under state supervision at an earlier age and usually for non-penal reasons (Carlen, 2002, 126). These formal agents of control predominantly included child protection services, mental health agencies, foster care, and social services. Carlen (1988, 74) discusses the prominence of foster care in the lives of criminalized women. In a study of 39 women prisoners, Carlen found that nearly two-thirds had been through the "care/custody mangle." A disproportionate number of young women go directly from foster care into prisons. This pathway was prevalent among the women in my study, as Yvonne's account demonstrates.

Well where my criminal history comes in, it comes from my past abuse and I where I have been in foster care all of my life and where I have been, physically, sexually and mentally abused which led me into the criminal justice system. Getting involved with breaking the law. Because from my past abuse I had a lot of anger which causes violence which caused me to a lot of emotional issues which I had this negative attitude about life. I said to myself people don't care about me and I don't care about them. So anyway, from my past, all the abuse I have been through led me to a lot of anger. I was a very angry person. For a good 15 years of my life I have been in and out of prison.

For some women, the abuse began in foster care. As Maggie recounted:

I have been in foster homes since I was six months old. Every day I was beat and beat and beat. I was ignored. No communication. I would get beat around all the time. Then my foster father sexually abused me. I couldn't stand up for myself. I went through a hard time. There is a book out called *Suffer Little Children*.[6] I was in that home. I know first hand.

Following a lengthy history of being bumped around from one foster home to another, Yvonne attempted to escape the abuse.

At 16, I start running away. Then I got into a girl's home and that's where it all started. The violence actually started in there. For the next 15 years I was in and out, in and out, in and out [of prison]. I didn't care. The abuse numbs you. You can't think.

Christine detailed how social support systems failed her throughout her life.

At 11 years old I was taken out of my parent's home. I was put in foster care. The first time I was in a juvenile jail I was 12 years old. It started off when I was mentally ill one time when I was in a foster home and I went out to K-Mart. I stole some products. A 50- cent eye pencil I got caught with. I was supposed to write a letter of apology but I couldn't because I was dyslexic and they couldn't understand that so they shoved me juvenile.

Admissions to psychiatric institutions are all too often a precursor to criminal pathways. For Valarie, prison was the lesser of two evils.

I went into the youth centre in Pleasantville[7] for girls and boys when I was 13. I was in a psychiatric unit when I was 11. I've mostly been in hospitals, institutionalized. I would go to court and they would put me in hospital on a normal ward. Whatever you call normal in there. So I got in trouble in BC and they put me on a forensic unit. I was always in hospitals until 1996 or 1997. That was the last assault with a weapon. They wanted to do a report with the psychiatrist and I wouldn't do it because I knew what would happen. I would spend the rest of my life in a forensic unit.

Child protection agents also played a significant role. Either women were wards of the state during their own childhoods or had encounters with child welfare as mothers. Child welfare removed Maggie from her family home, placed her in foster care, and subsequently diagnosed with a psychiatric illness, which led to her losing custody of her own child.

When I was 18 I had my first child. They [child welfare] took my child away because I was in the Waterford a few times and they used it against me ... [T]he welfare turned around and took him away on me. I tried to get him back but no, no. They used the same thing on me as before. I was an unfit mother. I shouldn't have him and blah, blah, blah.

While under the control of the state, any act in perceived defiance of authority can have very serious consequences and result in disciplinary action. Maggie's resistance to authority in open custody landed her further criminal charges and a persistent record of violence for which she was subsequently classified as maximum security in the adult prison system.

When they put me in open custody, I done some violent acts at the juvenile jail. They were trying to put me in a suicide watch cell to calm me down. And they were trying to rustle me to the cell and so I hit them to get away from them. They charged me for when they were trying to rustle me to the cell and I touched them and they took my clothes off and put me under suicide watch. So they charged me with that and I got months added on. If I was in open custody I would say,

157

'I'm not fucking listening to you. You know, you're not my mother or you're not my father so go to hell.' They would tell me to go to my room. I would say, 'I'm not fucking listening to you. Go to hell or I'll fucking kill you.' They thought I was serious but it was only a figure of speech ... I am not using my mental illness as an excuse but that's just the way my mind worked, my adrenaline.

Not surprisingly, there is nothing linear about women's varied experiences with confinement in state and community-run agencies and their past abuses, addictions, and mental illnesses. Maggie described her history of cycling in and out of formal control systems.

I was in a mental hospital for three months first because I was hearing voices saying burn that unit down and you will die. They will evacuate everyone else and you stay in your room and they will think that you are gone and you will die in the fire while they're gone. That was my first crime as an adult ... After that, about a year and a half later I was feeling sick again ... I got married to a really wrong man and I was after having a child. I was having problems with post-natal depression and psychotic depression. So I thought in my own eyes anyways. Then I married a man after I lost my child to adoption. I married a man who was physically and mentally abusive. And the other way too [sexually abusive]. And so we separated after he beat me. He was after beating me that day. So I went to the Waterford and asked them for admission and they wouldn't admit me. [Halfway house] wouldn't talk to me because I had been away from the [criminal justice] system for years. And I had nowhere to go so you have to do what you have to do. So I went down to the phone by the Waterford hospital and I called them and told them I had a gun but really it was only a plastic toy thing I had in my hand. I was crying out for help.

Defiance of Gender Norms

Gender norms are a powerful societal tool for ensuring conformity (Andersen, 2003). The informal processes of routine social interaction through which women are personally discredited or "put in their place" often result in "labeling women deviant" (Schur, 1984). Women's deviance, then, is a social construct which results from a particular kind of definition and response. As Howard Becker (1963, 9) argued:

[s]ocial groups create deviance by making the rules whose infraction constitutes deviance, and by applying these rules to particular people and labeling them as outsiders. From this point of view, deviance is not a quality of the act the person commits, but rather a consequence

of the application by others of rules and sanctions to an "offender."

Becker (1963, 17) notes that labels are applied unequally and are largely a matter of some persons or groups (in this case men) imposing their rules on others (women). Deviant designations get assigned by those who hold the political and economic power. Women who "offend" specific gender system norms by behaving in ways deemed inappropriate for females receive the label of "deviant."

Beauty norms are one such example of the antisocial control (Carlen, 2002) exerted over young girls. Beauty norms govern the visual objectification of women and, as Schur (1984, 68) makes clear:

[p]hysical appearance is much more central to evaluations of women than it is to evaluations of men; this emphasis implicitly devalues women's other qualities and accomplishments; women's "looks" thereby become a commodity and a key determinant of "success" or "failure"; the beauty norms used in evaluating women are excessively narrow and quite unrealistic; cultural reinforcement of such norms conveys to the ordinary woman a sense of perpetual "deficiency."

Failing to satisfy the stringent requirements associated with physical appearances can lead to a dual designation of deviance. Violation of beauty norms results in a deviant label in and of itself, and attempts to renegotiate the boundaries leads to "secondary deviance." As Corrina recounted:

I never considered myself very pretty. Now I look at myself and if someone don't like me they don't have to look at me. But back then I was a teenager and I wanted to be like everybody else. Small and pretty. So what I could do to fit in I done. That was my humor. And doing whatever, bend over backwards, doing whatever anybody wanted me to do. That included being taken advantage of by all the guys [for sexual purposes].

Other women employed resistance strategies to gender norms by turning to "formally sanctioned deviance." Rachael, for example, took steps to compensate for her "deficiency" and sought alternative means of gaining acceptance by becoming a "runner" for her peers, providing them with an ongoing supply of stolen goods.

All my life I was told I was ugly. That I would never get anywhere. That I would never amount to anything. So I took it in my head that I would have to do things a bit different. Do what I had to do to get accepted. And that's just how it went.

Another powerful tool for ensuring gender norm conformity is the notion of women as "passive" and "nurturing". A "masculine character structure" requires self-confidence, independence, boldness, responsibility, risk-taking, and aggression/violence (Messerschmidt, 1986, 40). Such characteristics are shunned in women and transgressing these boundaries results in a deviant designation, as it did for Katharine and several other women in my study.

I was basically on the other end of any abuse. I was the aggressive person. Men, I didn't bother with them. Boyfriends came and went at that point. I was one of the guys. I was out beating around. We had our fun and I was out beating around and I had a really bad temper. And growing up in [Mundy Pond] there was a lot of people to meet. I was just out having fun, just like the guys but because I wasn't a guy I drew a lot of attention. The wrong kind of attention.

Non-conformity to heterosexual relationships becomes another form of antisocial control. Speaking to the objectification of women, MacKinnon (1982, 533) asserts that "sexuality is the linchpin of gender inequality." She further argues that:

[a] woman is a being who identifies and is identified as one whose sexuality exists for someone else, who is socially male. Women's sexuality is the capacity to arouse desire in that someone (MacKinnon, 1982, 533).

Homosexuality then becomes a major site of exclusion and isolation. Not surprisingly, lesbians told of having to "compensate" by seeking out other forms of social approval, often by turning to drugs or alcohol.

Another of the pivotal regulators of women's conformity are maternity norms (Welch, 1997; Schur, 1984). Maternity norms govern what is often viewed as women's primary traditional role, that of mothering. Despite changing family patterns and society's claim of loosening the traditional family construct, women are still expected not only to bear children but also to do so within the approved context of conventional marriage. As Schur (1984, 83) points out:

[t]he very terms used for childbearing outside of marriage — "unwed" or "unmarried" motherhood, and also "illegitimacy" itself — indicate both the character of the norm-violation and the strong social disapproval attaching to it.

Violation of this gender norm is uniquely a motherhood "offence". April talked about her rebellion against maternity norms and her 'breaking out' period.

> I wasn't a hard kid growing up ... I was only young when I got pregnant and I more or less said, fuck, like my life is gone now anyways. I was young. I was free ... But now I was supposed to go a certain way that I didn't want to go. I was expected to stay home and look after a youngster. Even though I had a child I didn't want to be tied down.

Conclusions

Women's trajectories into prison are remarkably similar and often characterized by longstanding patterns of poverty, physical and sexual abuse, drug addictions, histories of state interventions, and defiance of gender role norms. These factors converge in non-linear ways to produce a lifestyle of (mostly unwanted) dependencies on the state. In turn, these dependencies become further entrenched in a criminal justice system which fosters a culture of dependency and does nothing to contribute to women's economic and social empowerment.

To come back to the feminist epistemological framework which launched this essay, it is most troubling to reunite with women who once sat in an elementary school classroom alongside me, and have been swept up in a system of formalized regulation and control based on a capitalist patriarchy which marginalizes women's productive and reproductive labour, medicalizes and infantilizes their past histories of abuse, and perpetuates gender role stereotypes. There is a 'shadow line' between the pathways of criminalized women and the directions in which they might otherwise have gone had it not been for the layering of structural and social inequalities which precipitated their encounters with the criminal justice system. Women's equality is a struggle we are all in together and therefore our collective liberation is truly what's at stake when researching the lives of criminalized women.

Notes

[1] The Canadian Association of Elizabeth Fry Societies (CAEFS) is an "association of self-governing, community-based Elizabeth Fry Societies that work with and for women and girls in the justice system, particularly those who are, or may be, criminalized. Together, Elizabeth Fry Societies develop and advocate the beliefs, principles and positions that guide CAEFS. The association exists to ensure substantive equality in the delivery and development of services and programs through public education, research, legislative and administrative reform, regionally, nationally and internationally" (Mission Statement). In Canada, there are 25 local Elizabeth Fry societies. For more information on the workings of this organization see: http//:www.elizabethfry.ca/caefs_e.htm

2 The "corrective" nature of the competing goals of incarceration (e.g., punishment versus rehabilitation) is challenged throughout this research. As Horii (2000, 107) clearly argues, "[c]orrections is plainly a misnomer since reformatories, lockups, jails, prisons and penitentiaries correct nothing, rather they err."

3 Statistics Canada determines whether a family is low-income by "comparing the income of an economic family to a low-income cutoff (LICO), which varies according to family size and the size of the area of residence. The LICO values are chosen by estimating at what income families spend 20 percentage points more than average on food, shelter and clothing" (Canadian Council on Social Development, 2004).

4 The Waterford is the primary psychiatric hospital located in St. John's and offers acute, rehabilitative and continuing care to those 16 and older with mental health problems and mental illnesses. This historic hospital located on Waterford Bridge Road in St. John's was first opened in 1854 as the Hospital for Mental and Nervous Diseases. It was renamed the Waterford Hospital in 1972 (Health Care Corporation, n.d.).

5 A recent epidemic of OxyContin abuse in Newfoundland has resulted in the creation of a provincial task force to identify the nature and extent of the problem related to OxyContin abuse. OxyContin is a prescribed drug used in acute pain management. Because of its controlled-release property, OxyContin contains more oxycodone and needs to be taken less often than other oxycodone-containing drugs. This feature of the drug has led to a 400% increase in the quantity of OxyContin tablets prescribed in the province from 2000 to 2003 (Newfoundland and Labrador, *OxyContin Task Force Report*, 2004).

6 This chilling autobiography of a foster child uncovers the abuses by the Roman Catholic church in the delivery of foster "care" services, written by a former resident of Mount Cashel Orphanage in St. John's (O'Brien, 1991).

7 The 10-bed Pleasantville Youth Centre is the only other secure custody facility in the province, besides Whitbourne. It primarily serves the greater St. John's Census Metropolitan Area (CMA) and accommodates young persons temporarily detained by the police, short-term remands, or those awaiting psychiatric assessments.

The Way to Get Home

Susan Rendell

For he shall deliver the needy when he crieth: the poor also, and him that hath no helper.

–Psalms 72:12

TODAY JESSIE BROUGHT ME A TOOTHBRUSH SHE GOT at a church. I almost asked her why she didn't keep it for herself, but it skipped my mind. Later I remembered that she has no teeth. When you first meet someone who has no teeth it is the most prominent thing about them like baldness or a wheelchair. But after your friendship has gestated you fill in the missing bits, teeth, hair. Legs that work.

Jessie doesn't have teeth because Welfare will only give her a pair if she signs her name Marie Skanes and she won't. Because she not Marie Skanes, she is Jessica Horwood, wife of the Anglican Archbishop, Dennis Horwood. Marie Skanes is a mad woman from Bell Island. She follows Jessie around, sleeps in the room next to her at the boarding house, tells people that she is Jessie: Marie is trying to drive her crazy for some unfathomable reason. But Jessie is smarter than Marie. And stronger. *They all try to drive me crazy but they'll never do it. They'll never drive Jessie crazy because I have a good friend who looks after me.* She points upwards, her knobby arthritic forefinger parodying Adam's on the Sistine Chapel ceiling as she stretches it towards the Son.

Jessie's hair is sparse and thin, hanging from her head in inch-long yellow-white tendrils like alfalfa sprouts. She always covers her head with a baseball cap, her head that is like an old frayed baseball discarded by some boys who have worn it out reducing their testosterone levels under a macho August sun. Even when she is wearing her garden party outfit, a lavender dress with a white acrylic shawl and purple pumps, Jessie has a cap on her head: the shape stays the same, only the logos vary — Pepsi, Blackhorse, Errol's Groc and Conf. Jessie gets invited to the Lieutenant Governor's garden party every year because Prince Philip is her uncle. Jessie's mother was Prince Philip's sister, the Lady Marion, who once played the harp in an opera house in Montreal, her fine white fingers making the sharp strings shiver out Greensleeves.

Alas, my love, you do me wrong
To cast me off discourteously;
When I have loved you for so long
Delighting in your company.

A man who came here from Quebec told Jessie that, and she cried because the Lady Marion had died giving birth to her, her only child. When Jessie was ten she asked her father if he was sorry she wasn't a boy. He hit her and told her to go to her room. *Because he loved us more than anything, me and my mother; he never remarried, he wasn't that kind of man. And he put death into my mother along with my life, and he felt so bad; men, they have so much to feel bad about, I wouldn't want to be one.* After Jessie's father died, they locked her in a room in the palace, not to punish her but because she wouldn't behave; she kept crying and screaming that he wasn't dead. *And that is not the way a member of the Royal Family is supposed to act.* Jessie puts an *h* on *act*; it sounds French. Or the way someone from Bell Island might produce the word if they chopped it, 'hacked' it off through rock-hard gums.

Jessie says she has her father's eyes. When she was young she also had his coal black hair, good French hair. Jessie's father was a French diplomat who was assassinated during the Korean War. Jessie was twelve when he died; she had just gotten her first pair of penny loafers the day before they told her. *Shoes the colour of my hair, and two new pennies shining up at me. And then he was dead and they didn't shine no more.*

One night a man walked up to Jessie in a bar and said, "Jessie, that was the worst assassination I ever saw, your father." Jessie tells me this story once a week; it means that her existence is large and true, bigger than the lives of the teenagers who taunt her — "fifty cents, Trixie" — and the grown men who pelt her with raw potatoes. Greater than that of the woman who threw a quarter on the ground and told Jessie she could have it if she would pick it up. Jessie stepped over it. But afterwards, she turned around to look, knowing what she would see: the woman in her blond wool coat crouched on the icy sidewalk, plucking at the metal sliver with leather-tipped fingers. And Jessie laughed her silent laugh, audible only to dogs. *And to sad small children, and the moon when it is thin and grieving for the sun.*

Jessie's eyes can see farther than anyone else's. She can see beyond the hills that hunch around the harbour to the coves on the other side. The light in Jessie's eyes beams in from somewhere so far away and old that the suns of Bootes are juveniles in comparison, this light that shows her seagulls suspended over distant promontories, and even the Stairway to Heaven rising over the Narrows, a silver band floating in a sea of brilliant colours; so lovely, she says, like the little cross of stars that dangles outside her window sometimes. And the moon following her, and sometimes even the sun. *The sun follows me because it is the Son, you know, the Son of God, my Lamb.*

Jessie says a prayer for the moon when it shines in her window, a prayer of thanksgiving because it has brought her home safe. She told this to a nun once and the nun said that the moon is the Virgin's lamp, and that she, Jessie, was special, beloved of the Mother. A chalice is kept for Jessie at the Basilica. *Although it is the cup of the Lamb it is more like a basin than a cup. And it is pure gold, not brass like the regular one. I go up first, alone, before the rest of them, and drink from my special cup; I don't share the same cup like the others.*

I do not tell Jessie that she is singled out because they are afraid of her, afraid of her old bald gums and her madwoman's spittle. She wouldn't believe me. She would put me in the same category as the quarter woman or the Bishop's false wife. And I would never see her again in my house, shining the kitchen sink, polishing the little life I have left.

The only thing that ever casts Jessie down is her husband's treachery. The Bishop has spurned her: some hussy has taken Jessie's place in the Bishop's house, a harlot who calls herself his wife. This woman has given him drugs that make him forget his true wife; he won't even let Jessie into the Cathedral anymore. And she loves the Cathedral; it reminds her of the forests of her English childhood, cool and dark and mysterious, the light coming down slanted from the little sun of the rose window high up behind the altar, falling between the dark mahogany columns, lighting up the clearing in front of the case that holds a marble sculpture of the dead Christ. Jessie used to prostrate herself in front of this glass mausoleum, lying there for hours sometimes. But they won't let her in now; they tell her she is upsetting the parishioners, but she knows this is a lie: it is all the doing of the Bishop's woman, who is afraid of Jessie, afraid and jealous because of her husband's love for his true wife. Jessie's eyes well up when she tells me about her lost husband, but the tears never descend. I don't think they ever have, because there are no lines in her face for them to run along, although she must be somewhere on the thin dry road between fifty and sixty.

I used to be beautiful and my husband loved me; now I am ugly. But this is the way God wants me to be. He has not forsaken me, it is just a different part of the story He is making up, He needs me to look this way now. And I love my ugly face because He does.

The other thing that makes Jessie's eyes creep back into the hollows beneath her eyebrows is when children call her a witch and run away from her. Or when parents tuck their offspring behind them as she walks down the street, swinging her crucifix like a yo-yo. Last Easter Sunday when Jessie went to church she tried to talk to a man with a baby in his arms, but he turned away from her, growling a curse over the naked head of his child. Jessie loves children, even the ones who are mean to her. Because they are not always mean: the little boy who mocks her one day may give her a candy the next, or even the gum out of his mouth. Once Jessie picked up a pigeon that had been hit by a car and carried it until it was dead. *It looked up at me and then its eyes closed, like going to sleep.* She laid it in the grass and said a novena for its soul.

The first time Jessie came to me she was wearing a mini skirt and a blouse cut to there and way too big for her; her breasts kept sliding out of their silky sack like two withered turnips. She told me she was eleven; *I am visiting with my father from St. Pierre, bonjour.* I said *bonsoir* because it was a sweltering July evening. I was sitting on my front steps while the city danced and sang, drunk as ten lords on the humid heat. Sitting slouched like a discarded effigy, listening intently to the murmuring of the pigeons at my feet, their throats throbbing with the sound a mother makes when she is stroking her infant with quiet words to calm its fear.

I need the toothbrush Jessie brought me this morning; mine is two years old and worn to the bone. Two years ago I had a new toothbrush; a year ago I had a job, only a small one, but we looked after each other. As did my lover and I, who said that nothing in this world would ever part us. Who asked me to wait by Cassiopeia's Chair for him if I died before he did. Now I have only two things, essentially: a son and a small stretch of life to walk, or crawl or slither on my belly down until I come to...

Until I die.

One fat cyst of a year left, perhaps even two, if I'm lucky.

That's what they said to me — one year, two if you're lucky. "Where's the luck in that?" I asked the two in white coats who had just handed me my death as though it were a sterile instrument. "Where is the rabbit's foot dangling from this death sentence, where is the sound of bells signalling three gold bars in a row? All I hear is ring around the rosy, pocket full of posies, ashes, ashes all fall down," I said, doing a bitter parody of the old childhood dance while they backed away from me; politely, of course. "Would you rather die right now, or watch death parade in front of you every minute of every hour for seven hundred days? Which one — which would you choose?" They looked at each another, and at the floor, and then they said to the wall, "Well it all depends on your attitude doesn't it? Keep busy, think positive thoughts." It is useless for the dead to converse with the living, whose ears are stopped up like those of Ulysses' men against the siren song of death, that fatal lullaby.

My son calls me every week from Scotland, where he pulls the bright mackerel out of the sea for a living. I haven't let him know yet; I am reluctant to put the shadow of death into my son's head by telling him about the shadow that is in his mother's: a grey penumbra on my brain, no bigger than my thumbnail. But big enough to end the world. And to confine me to the valley of the shadow; this is the first death, the introductory chapter. I am afraid of the last chapter, even more afraid that there will not be an end at all, that I will go on like this forever, a dull ash of despair floating in some vast black vermicular eternity — god I hate that word — I hate all words now; how merciful God has been to dumb beasts, that die without knowing they ever lived.

The day I found out that life had no more use for me, my lover and I were in bed, inside a perfect arc of passion. And then the phone rang, squealing through the quiet house; my lovebird in its wicker cage lifted its head from its white breast and opened its beak, but no sound came out. "Let it ring," my lover said to me: he was crouched over my breasts, his penis homing towards my mouth; it had a drop like a tear hanging from its tip. I pushed him away; there was something in the sound of the phone that was more compelling than desire — what could it be? And then Death said hello over the wires.

When I got off the phone I went and lay back down by my lover's side. "What is it?" he said. "You look like a ghost." And then he shook me because I wouldn't answer. Shook me and shook me, but my body was not inhabited: it was unyielding and heavy in his hands, a dead weight. Eventually he stopped shaking me and got between my legs, driving himself into me with sharp quick jerks as if he was trying to start a stalled car. And then a sound came out of me like the one I made when my son's head was crowning twenty years ago. My lover slapped my face and I started to cry. And I told him what the doctor had said: nothing at all, really, except that he needed to talk to me about the results of some tests I had had the week before. But I knew — I had known for some time. The same way I had known I was pregnant with my son the moment his father removed himself from me and turned away into sleep. The body knows immediately when it has been invaded by life or death, and sometimes the quiescent mind can hear the snapping into place of the new element: a fertilized egg, a rogue cell. A door creaking open deep in the substrata of the self, a glimpse of nascent life awakening. Or death stirring, waiting its hour to be born.

My lover got up and pulled on his jeans. "I need to go for a walk," he said. "Stay in bed, keep warm, I won't be long." He came back the next day with a dozen roses from the supermarket. The kind that are perfect buds which never open, blackening on the stem after a few days.("O Rose thou art sick./The invisible worm/That flies in the night/In the howling storm/Has found out thy bed/Of crimson joy,/ And his dark secret love/Does thy life destroy.")

I hated God that morning, a God I didn't even believe in. Jessie hated God when He took her son, Raymond; she hated Him for years, soiling herself with prostitute sex and alcohol and drugs to get back at Him. But one night He sent an angel to wrestle with her. *All night I struggled, fighting the angel that had me pinned to the bed, but that angel was as strong as Hulk Hogan. And he loved me so much, just like my father.* Now Jessie loves God's Son the way she used to love her Raymond, who was only two pounds when he was born, ethereal as a cherub. *You never see old angels. They don't age because they have to go to work every morning.* Last week I gave Jessie a picture of the Annunciation a Catholic cousin had sent me when I was pregnant with my son. *That is the Angel Gabriel. Look how happy Mary is, but she's embarrassed too because she's not married. And she's sad because she has to marry that old man. But you never know with God, you just have to do what you're told.*

A month after I was sentenced, I saw my lover and a young red-haired

girl walking along the harbour apron. We had been apart for two days—
he told me he had to go to Halifax for a week on business. "Rest," he said,
"keep safe until I come back — how can I miss you if I don't go away?"
I saw him only once again, as a part of me, my life. Five days later he
came to my house for his sunglasses — and a Judas kiss. He lives with
the girl now, in a house by the polluted river that slides through the heart
of the city like a soiled snake, blindly seeking the ocean in which to
slough its foul skin.

When I told Jessie about my lover, she said that the girl must have
drugged him like Bishop Horwood's false wife did to him or else he
would never have betrayed me, never abandoned his true love. Yes, I told
her, I do believe he was drugged. She asked me if I thought it was Haldol,
which some doctor had put her on once; it had made her so crazy, she
said, that she used to sit in her boarding house room rocking back and
forth and praying to her Lamb that she wouldn't kill herself. No, I said, I
don't think it was Haldol, I think it was Spanish fly. Or Ecstasy. Jessie
laughed and laughed at that one, her big alien's eyes as wide as windows,
her toothless gums gleaming like pink roses wet with the dew.

Before Jessie came, when the snow was throwing itself down in fistfuls
for the wind to toss around, I used to think about driving out to Salmon
Cove with a picnic basket full of pills and wine. There is a place on the
top of the cliffs near where the eagles have their nest, a dark bed in the
bracken, broad enough for two. My lover and I used to go there on summer days the colour and intensity of Jessie's eyes and pick each other
clean. Afterwards, we would walk to the edge of the cliff and watch the
two eagles, male and female, fierce hieroglyphs of fidelity wheeling
against the mandala of the sun.

On those winter days, I would look out my crusted front window at no
one coming up the steps, and imagine the bed I would make in the wine-
stained snow, how I would lie down and fold my hands across my breast
like a marble effigy on a tomb. And let the clicking sleet knit itself up
around me, like a baby's bunting bag. Bye bye baby bunting, Daddy's
gone a-hunting.To find a living woman's skin to wrap his joy and hunger
in.

I had managed to forget about death for a little while on the evening
Jessie came, her hands and breasts crisscrossed with silvery white scars
from the fire that consumed Raymond when he was five months old. The
fire the Bad Man set. One of Jessie's hands is more afflicted than the
other; *sometimes I go wild with the pain in it, it is like it is still on fire.*
The only thing that helps is when the priest anoints it with holy water and
the divine atoms in the drops exorcise the memory of the flames that
burned her baby to death while she held him.

Jessie won't tell me who the Bad Man was or why he set the fire, or
what went before or after. When I bring up the subject she will say she is

a Syrian Jew, which according to the Bible means she is more precious than rubies. Or she will describe to me what the ten tribes wear on their heads, how the colour and shape of each person's headgear corresponds to his rank. Or she will tell me about being a Korean war orphan, and having the mark on her foot that all war babies have. All the orphaned babies of all the wars that have ever been have this stigmata on one foot; it is the shape of a crescent moon and red as blood. Jessie never shows me her cicatrix and I never ask to see it. I am careful when she is barefoot in my house, cleaning the floors or sitting at the kitchen table with her legs crossed, a child's sandal dangling off her crimson-tipped toes; I never look down.

The evening Jessie came to me I had taken a handful of pills of all colours, like Sweetarts: pills they gave me to control the seizures, sleeping pills, Aspirin and old odds and ends of discarded medication I had found at the bottom of my bathroom cupboard. I imagined that the pills were lover's candies, but instead of saying "You're Mine" in pink letters they were mute and black-bordered. I was sitting on my front steps, waiting for the pigeons who live in the eaves of the building across the street to descend. I had put bread on the sidewalk in front of my house, the ends of three loaves I had been living off for two days, rye and flax and raisin. And little winged packets of birds were dropping at my feet when Jessie appeared in the middle of them like some freaky St. Francis.

I thought the pills had conjured her up until she sat on the lowest step and leaned her head against my shin. *Bonjour*, she said; I said *bonsoir*. And then she began to tell me about her father and her dead son, about her Lamb and the newly lit moon chasing her all over the city until she came and sat down by me because God told her to. *I think I must go there, I don't know why, God says go here, go there, so I go.*

I sat up then, and listened to her like Sheherazade's husband; but after a time I began to feel faint and I excused myself and went inside the house. The front hall was strobing, pulsating with the colours of the pills I had taken; it took me a long time to find the phone. When I called the hospital they seemed happy to hear from me, excited even. "We're coming for you, don't move," they said. "You're going to be fine." I would be fine: it had all been a mistake then, a stupid practical joke, a puerile prank by some big dumb goof of a god who had had his fun and was letting me go. I lay down on the floor and wept while life bounced around, licking me all over. Several hours later I woke up in a hospital room with death lying next to me as if we'd never been apart.

When I came back to my house the next day, Jessie was there again. Or still. *What you did last night — that is not the way to get home.* In her hands was a purple sash, from the altar at the Basilica. When we went inside, she said *Put it around Jehovah*, mistaking the bust of Zeus on the top of my bookcase for her god. And I took it from her and tied it in a bow around his neck. And then she cleaned my kitchen and made me tea in a Christmas mug. *Look, there is a French Santa on it; see, he has a long robe and a tall hat. One time I got a talking doll for Christmas; "I love you," she said, you had to pull out a string on her neck to make her say it.* The tea Jessie made was stronger than I usually have it, but it was hot and sweet and my body took it like an embrace, even the residue at the bottom. And then she made me come and look at the kitchen sink, which she had scrubbed with Javex. *We say Javel in St. Pierre; look, look how it shines! Like silver, like the moon when there are no clouds over her face.* Jessie and I peered into the sink together; two shimmering women as beautiful as the souls of stars looked back at us. And we laughed. *Better than in the mirror.*

Jessie died herself once, but she didn't go home because it wasn't time. She was hit by a car in front of her boarding house, hit in the head; people gathered to see the great mystery of death, and someone called the police. The bumper of the car that hit her was dented; bits of her hair pasted on with blood decorated the chrome cavity. *It was all black, everything was black, but it was not cold black, it was warm like hiding under the covers when you are small. And then an angel pulled me up out of the blackness and I was alive again. The woman who hit me with her car was crying, 'Jessie, we were sure you were dead.' 'No, not me,' I told her, 'I have a friend, a very good friend who looks after me. I am in good hands, don't worry about me.'*

The police called an ambulance but Jessie waved it away and asked for fish and chips. The woman who had killed Jessie gave a little boy a twenty-dollar bill and he ran to Johnny's Diner and got Jessie two of the biggest orders they had. And she and the boy sat down on the side of the road and ate them, with everyone gathered around, amazed as anything. *There wasn't a mark on me the next day, not a scratch. When the police came to Mrs. Lynch's in the morning, they are looking at me* (she does an impression of a perplexed cop, taking off her baseball cap/police hat and scratching her head), *they can't believe it. Everyone says it is a miracle, a miracle.*

What is a miracle? That some live when they shouldn't, or that others must die when life is beside and behind and before them and they feel as safe as houses inside its radiant circumference? Are these both miracles, or only one of them? Or is it all a miracle, every sublime horrible idiotic unquantifiable leap life takes? On the mornings Jessie is with me, saying *look, look at the cat rolling in the grass!* and I look — really look — at the blissful conjunction of cat and grass and Jessie's toothless joy, it seems to me that everything in the universe is perfectly aligned and singing like a nightingale — it's all good, very very good a voice far away and yet inside me says, and I believe it. And then Jessie goes away, and I think that maybe everything is an illusion — perhaps even the hand with death and sorrow scribbled on it that Jessie gives me to hold on to when I cry — and that there is no rhyme or reason to any of it, no point; no great shining Point, waiting at the end to scatter the small shadows that are our deaths. But then she comes back — *look, look! see how many flowers are on that tree; so small, such a small tree, but so many flowers. Like little stars, baby ones.*

One night last week Jessie and I talked about heaven. *I can see the Golden Gates, and past them where it is quiet and there are colours you can't see here. And you never grow old there; you grow young.* And then she told me about the thing that is going to happen to all the countries, the bad thing. There was a meeting about it, she said, with the military and the men of god, priests and ministers and rabbis; even her husband the Archbishop was there. She says she may be leaving for East Germany next week. *But don't worry. You will have eternal life because you have been good to me, and I am a Syrian Jew, more precious than rubies, and also a war alien baby.*

When she left, Jessie told me to lock the door because you never know who might try to get in. I smiled; she doesn't know that she is the thing most doors and minds are dead-bolted against. And then she hugged me and said *I love you; don't forget me if I can't come back.* I watched her out of the window as she walked away, and then I looked up into the sky, at the moon bouncing along behind her like a child's ball.

More Than Just Going to the Doctor: The Health of Women and Girls in Newfoundland and Labrador

Diana L. Gustafson

The major barrier for women to the achievement of the highest attainable standard of health is inequality, both between women and men and among women.

(United Nations, 1995)

THIS CHAPTER INVITES YOU TO THINK about the health of girls and women in Newfoundland and Labrador. What does it mean to be healthy? How healthy are women and girls in this province? Are some of us healthier than others? If so, what accounts for differences in our health and wellbeing? What supports are needed to ensure that all girls and women in Newfoundland and Labrador lead long, healthy, and productive lives?

These questions are addressed in four sections of this chapter using health research carried out in Newfoundland and Labrador between 1995 and 2005. Some of these materials identify health disparities among women and track trends in rates of disease, disability, and injury between men and women. Other materials explore a range of biological, social, and environmental factors that influence girls' and women's wellbeing and quality of life. To breathe some life into this discussion and to convey a sense of women's health and illness narratives, these findings are organized around a fictionalized case of three generations of the Johnson family: Mary, a 57 year old recently divorced woman born and raised in St. John's and her child Jennifer who is 24 and the single mother of 6-year old Rose.[1]

What Does it Mean to be Healthy?

Definitions of health have evolved over time and vary among groups of people (Chamberlain, 1997). When you ask Mary Johnson what it means to be healthy, she tends to focus on her physical state and her ability to go to work at the local grocery store, carry out her daily living activities, and spend time with her granddaughter. Healthy is what she is when she is not suffering from one of the frequent chest colds that she attributes to years of smoking. Healthy is how she feels now that she is not treating the cuts, bruises, and in one instance, a broken facial bone she got at the hand of her now ex-husband. She admits that living with violence made her feel unhappy and depressed for most of her 30-year marriage. Mary's "dualistic" definition of health separates the physical aspects of health from the emotional and mental aspects of health (Chamberlain, 1997).

172

By contrast, Jennifer integrates all aspects of her wellbeing into what might be described as a "complementary" definition of individual health (Chamberlain, 1997). She attributes this way of thinking to the case worker who helped her deal with parenting and substance abuse issues. Four years ago when Jennifer's parents moved to Ontario to find work, she felt angry, isolated, and overwhelmed. She felt ill-equipped for the full-time job of parenting a child with spina bifida. Her occasional weekend use of street drugs escalated to more regular use and she became less able to care for herself and Rose. Today, Jennifer strives for a greater state of balance in her life. Yet she faces an every day struggle to be healthy in a social system with limited supports for poor single mothers.

Another way of thinking about health was adopted by the World Health Organization (WHO) in 1948. This United Nations agency that specializes in global health issues defined health as a complete state of physical, mental, and social wellbeing and not merely the absence of disease or infirmity. This definition of health is still cited over fifty years later by government policy makers and health researchers in Newfoundland and Labrador, Canada and around the world.

Some critics of this early definition argued that health was being equated with well-being, human development, and quality of life, and that interventions aimed at improving health were beyond the scope of medicine. And indeed, the World Health Organisation was calling on governments to take responsibility for the health of their people through adequate health and social measures. Others argued that health is more than a state of being and is "the capacity of people to adapt to, respond to, or control life's challenges and changes" (Frankish et al., 1996).

A *population health perspective* is currently used by the Public Health Agency of Canada (PHAC, 2003), formerly known as Health Canada. The PHAC assumes that health is an individual and collective experience, an important life goal, and a valuable resource that enables people to be contributing and productive members of society. If we can agree on this broader, more inclusive definition, how healthy are women and girls in this province? How is health measured?

Most of us have heard the results of medical research that list, for example, rates of breast cancer (*Strategic Social Plan* [SSP] 2003, 6) or the risk factors associated with heart disease among women (Power-Kean, 2001). Statistics tend to measure health by quantifying the pathological changes in a woman's physical body from Mary's allergy to aspirin to the zygomatic bone fracture caused by spousal abuse; from the symptoms of Jennifer's drug abuse to various treatment options; from the genetic changes occurring during Rose's fetal development to the germs that cause her recurrent bladder infections.

When considered critically, such tools measure disease, injury, and disability or the absence of health. With the exception of self-reported health and quality of life indicators, we have few tools for measuring the *pres-*

ence of health. Given these limitations, the next section describes the health of women and girls in this province.

How Healthy are Women and Girls in Newfoundland and Labrador?

On average, Canadian women are healthier than women in many countries, and much healthier than women in countries of the South. One way to measure this is life expectancy. *Life expectancy* is the average estimated life span predicted for those persons born in any given year. Women who make up more than half the Canadian population have one of the longest life expectancies in the world at 81.7 years (SSP, 2003, 4).

How do women in this province fare on this measure? Life expectancy has increased steadily over the last 20 years but remains lower than the national average at 80.2 years (SSP, 2003, 4). Although Newfoundland and Labrador females as a group are living longer lives than their male counterparts, many women and girls are at a disadvantage for attaining and maintaining optimal health.

Years of potential life lost (PYLL) measures premature death from any cause as the difference between actual life span and life expectancy. Thus, the younger a woman is when she dies, the more potential years of life lost. Far fewer Newfoundland and Labrador women are dying of heart attacks and strokes than 25 years ago meaning that the PYLL from heart disease is dropping. Although this is a positive trend, rates of heart disease are higher in this province than in any other province, claiming more lives than any other disease including cancer. Provincial rates for heart attack and strokes exceed national rates by 20% and 18% respectively (SSP, 2003, 7).

As the Johnson women know, living long and living well are two different things. Disability, chronic disease, and hospitalization are measures of *morbidity* or the incidence of disease in a given population. When looking at these health indicators, Health Canada (2003) data suggest that the average Canadian woman fares as well or better than the average Newfoundland and Labrador woman, and significantly better than the average aboriginal woman. Therefore, it is important to note regional differences that distinguish women in this province from women in other geographic settings, as well as cultural differences among women such as race, ethnicity, aboriginal identity, country of birth, shared language or religious beliefs, and so on.

Are there cultural differences among Newfoundland and Labrador women? The health literature typically describes Newfoundland and Labrador as a culturally distinct and homogeneous population. Mary shares this opinion as do many "from away" whom she met when working in Ontario. The settler populations who came from Ireland and France to establish small coastal communities on this large rocky island share traditions and practices that reflect their strong ties to the sea, the

Christian church, and each other.

There is another sense in which Newfoundland and Labrador might be considered culturally homogeneous. Both the settler and aboriginal communities of Newfoundland and Labrador have experienced markedly low levels of *in-migration* or movement of people into the province. Consequently, St. John's, for example, has retained a predominantly white, Christian population compared to other Canadian cities such as Toronto, Montreal, and Vancouver that have experienced relatively high in-migration of racially and religiously diverse populations (Shah, 2003). The aboriginal population accounts for about 8% of the Newfoundland and Labrador population. Low levels of in-migration account for the genetic homogeneity that is of considerable interest to biomedical researchers mapping the genome.

Notwithstanding these forms of homogeneity, there is considerable diversity among Newfoundland and Labrador women in terms of age, sexual orientation, functional ability, income, social affiliation, urban and rural location, and so on. These social, economic, and political factors are associated with health differences between aboriginal and settler women, between settler women and recent newcomers, and among settler women (Health Canada, 2003). The Johnson women are in this latter group.

The Johnsons like other women and girls living in poverty, those who are differently-abled, and those who hold certain jobs have shorter life expectancies and fare less well on quality of life indicators than women as an undifferentiated group. Some essentials for healthy living that white, middle-class women take for granted are in limited supply for the Johnson family. With inadequate income and limited access to safe affordable housing, opportunities for socializing, exercise, and recreation, and sufficient amounts of nutritious foods, these women are more likely to have poor health and suffer from preventable disease (Health Canada, 2003).

What accounts for differences in health among Newfoundland and Labrador women and girls?

There are differences in the health of women and girls because there are differences among women and their access to power, money, and material resources. The population health perspective recognizes twelve health determinants that contribute to good health and, conversely, influence the incidence of disease and other measures of ill-health. They are:

• gender
• biology and genetic endowment
• healthy child development
• income and social status
• personal health practices & coping skills
• employment and working conditions
• culture

- physical environments
- social environments
- social support networks
- health services
- education and literacy

While each factor has an independent impact on health, each interacts with the others to influence the health status of individual women and groups of women (PHAC, 2003). The dynamic interrelationship among factors is one key to understanding disparities in health status, quality of life, and the biological and social processes through which these differences are expressed in women and girls.

Income is arguably the single most significant factor influencing the health of women and girls here as elsewhere. Women with a household income of more than $75,000 report better health than those in the middle income bracket who, in turn, report better health than those women in a household with less than $20,000 income (SSP, 2003, 30). Most likely to live in poverty are aboriginal families, families headed by young parents, and lone-mother families. Almost half the children living in poverty in this province are from lone-mother families. Also among the province's poorest are senior women and women with disabilities (Health Canada, 2003).

How is poverty measured? The *low income cut-off* or LICO is the most commonly used indicator of poverty in Canada. Individuals and families who spend at least 20% more of their pre-tax income than the Canadian average on food, shelter, and clothing are classified as low-income. LICO takes into account the number of family members and the size of the urban or rural area where the family lives (Statistics Canada, 2000, 140). An adequate income determines access to the necessities of life such as good nutrition. Because women as a group earn less income than men (SSP, 2003, 17), some of us have less money to buy nutritious foods for ourselves and our children. Ten percent of Newfoundland and Labradorians say they worry about not having enough to eat. Fifteen percent say that lack of money prevents them from eating the quality or variety of foods they want. Newfoundland and Labrador has the highest per capita rate of food bank use in the country (Cost of Eating, 2003).

Women who are food insecure are less likely to be healthy or to be able to nourish healthy children. Women have greater need for some nutrients than men during pregnancy, lactation, and when performing certain types of work. Today, Jennifer like other food insecure mothers feeds her daughter before herself, lowering her own resistance to disease (Clarke, 2000). When she was pregnant and breastfeeding, Jennifer did not get sufficient amounts of dietary iron, iodine, and Vitamin A to support healthy fetal and infant development. Poorly nourished women are more likely to bear stillborn or low birth weight infants. Low birth weight babies have higher mortality and morbidity rates; moreover, birth weight is also an important predictor of future health (Clarke, 2000).

Poorly nourished women are also more likely to bear children with neurological impairments. Research on birth defects shows that poor maternal nutrition and low levels of dietary folate (one of the B vitamins) increase the likelihood of having an infant with a neural tube birth defect such as spina bifida. Many years ago, policy makers responded to these findings by mounting educational campaigns directed at females of childbearing age. Women were advised to take supplementary folic acid to reduce the risk of neural tube defects. Since then, the frequency of neural tube defects has fallen in many parts of the world. However, Newfoundland and Labrador has not enjoyed the same downward trend in the incidence of neural tube defects. What accounts for this finding? Are women like Jennifer uninformed or do they intentionally make unhealthy choices? A critical look at the conclusions reported by some Newfoundland and Labrador researchers suggests that we should focus less on women's obligations as individuals and more on food insecurity and the systemic factors that structure women's lives.

One study compared the dietary record of 25 mothers of children with neural tube defects with a comparable group of mothers of children without this diagnosis (Friel, Frecker, and Fraser, 1995). Like previous studies, this research demonstrated the link between poor maternal nutrition and poor pregnancy outcomes. Of particular interest, this study found that mothers of children with neural tube defects were younger, heavier, and had a lower socioeconomic status than the comparator group. Although not stated explicitly, this study suggests that women who are young and poor must be aware of healthy choices and financially able to make healthy choices.

National guidelines for healthy eating such as those adopted by Health Canada assume that women like Jennifer will act in her own best interests by adopting those ideas and practices that result in her good health and that of her unborn fetus (Rail and Beausoleil, 2003). Although health educational campaigns can increase awareness and contribute to changing individual behaviour (Shah 2003), they simultaneously reinforce the notion that women like Jennifer are responsible for their health and conversely, responsible for their *ill* health and that of their children.

Educational campaigns can contribute to mother blaming and a pathologizing of women's health experiences. *Mother blame* emphasizes individual responsibility for parenting and holds women responsible for negative child outcomes even though parenting is an interrelational activity. Mauthner (1999) calls for a "relational reframing" of women's health experiences in the context of their lives, family relationships, and social supports. To be more effective, educational campaigns must be supported by healthy social policies and programs that support mothers and families (Shah, 2003). One such example is the Canada Prenatal Nutrition

Program that funds nine *Healthy Baby Clubs* across the province. Jennifer was able to receive prenatal and postnatal support in the rural community where she lived with her boyfriend until the two-year relationship ended. Financially destitute and isolated from her friends and family, she returned to St. John's to be closer to the health services her daughter needed.

Children disadvantaged by their family circumstances are more vulnerable to developing emotional and behavioural problems, poor coping skills, and unhealthy behaviours. Growing up in a violent home, Jennifer experienced poor performance at school, mental health problems, and drug abuse. Rather than relying on her own knowledge and experience of being parented, Jennifer wanted to learn positive parenting practices that would have a protective effect on Rose's development (Crill, 2003). On the suggestion of her case worker, Jennifer attended the *Nobody's Perfect* parenting program funded by Health Canada. Like parenting initiatives in general, this program is attended mostly by female parents because women more often than men are deemed responsible for the care of children in and outside of civil unions (Donovan and Gustafson, 2005).

Next year, when Rose starts school full-time, she will be among the 16,000 children in kindergarten to grade 12 across the province who will receive breakfast and lunch through programs supported by the *Kids Eat Smart Foundation Newfoundland and Labrador*. Rose is not the only one who will be attending school in the fall. Jennifer is eager to complete her high school diploma before going on to complete a two-year business related diploma or a degree in the arts (SSP, 2003, 17). Although high school drop-out rates in Newfoundland and Labrador fell sharply during the 1900s (SSP, 2003, 9), Jennifer was not among those who completed. When she was 17 and could no longer cope with the stress of witnessing her mother's abuse, she moved to a rural community to live with her boyfriend. Within months, she learned she was pregnant. After her relationship ended, Jennifer became one of the single-parent families who receive more than 38% of their income from government transfers such as child tax benefit, social assistance, or employment insurance (SSP, 2003, 17).

Today, Jennifer knows that women with post secondary education have more employment opportunities and earn on average more than those without it. She was frustrated to learn that regardless of her educational attainment, she would earn about 74% of that earned by a male counterpart (SSP, 2003, 17). Having formal education, a good job, and a secure income will give Jennifer and her daughter greater access to the resources that support health. Two-thirds of those who were employed reported very good to excellent health with less than 10% reporting fair to poor health. In contrast, about half of those who were unemployed reported very good to excellent health with 21% reporting fair to poor health (SSP, 2003, 31).

Mary is among those who rate their health as fair. Like other women with little formal education, she is in a job where she earns less than $15,000 per year, not a living wage (SSP, 2003, 17). The grocery store pays minimum wage. At $6.00 per hour, Newfoundland and Labrador has one of the lowest minimum wage levels in the country. Mary has no health benefits, no pension plan, and no opportunities for promotion. With less after-tax income, she is unable to put money into RRSPs, pension plans, or other types of savings. This shortfall means that Mary will age in poverty (Keresztesi, Aucoin and Gustafson, 2004). In a province known for its high rates of seasonal work and unemployment, Mary feels lucky to have any job. She suffered the financial problems and feelings of uncertainty that came with massive employment during the cod moratorium (Murray, Gien, and Solberg, 2003). It was with her eye on their economic future that she and her then husband left for the mainland to find work four years ago.

Over the last few years, provincial and local governments in Atlantic Canada responded to the depressed economic climate by creating incentives to small businesses. Today, many women in the province work in workplaces with fewer than 20 employees. To have an income to support themselves and their families, women like Mary work in small workplaces with unhealthy environments that predispose them to higher rates of injury, and acute and chronic illnesses (Kosny, 2005). Mary suffers from varicose veins, and back and foot pain from standing for long hours at the cash register. Her doctor warns her that repeating the same monotonous tasks without adequate breaks puts her at risk of repetitive strain injuries in her hands, arms, and shoulders (Kosny, 2005). She says she has little autonomy over what she does and how she does it. Mary does not want to complain to the store manager or lobby for workplace change for fear of losing her job (Kosny, 2005).

Her only other work experience was at a downtown pub. There, she had to deal with unpredictable work schedules, sexual harassment from customers and other staff, and second hand smoke (Kosny, 2005). Smoking and exposure to second hand smoke are clearly linked with lung cancer. Lung cancer represents 21% of all female deaths in Canada from cancer (Health Canada, 2003). While Newfoundland and Labrador women's rates of lung cancer are about half the national average, provincial mortality rates for women from lung cancer are about the same (SSP, 2003, 3).

Rates of tobacco use are higher than the Canadian average (SSP, 2003, 3). Mary knows that she should quit smoking and points to the anti-smoking campaigns directed at changing individual health behaviours. She found it difficult to quit when she worked at the pub. She supports legislation that extends the smoking ban in public places to include bars and restaurants. This legislation addresses the issue of second-hand smoke affecting the predominantly female workforce (Kosny, 2005). It also addresses the cultural pressures that influence women's smoking habits and supports individual smoking cessation and prevention programs. Still, Mary understands that owners opposed to the legislation are afraid of losing their businesses in one of Canada's poorest provinces.

The employment future is grim for Mary's granddaughter. A recent study indicates that even well-educated and highly motivated women with disabilities are less likely than able-bodied women to get long-term, satisfying employment (Murdoch, Gustafson and ILRC, 2005). Many are unemployed for long periods. For others, work tends to be short-term with little more than a living wage and often without pension and health benefits.

Securing long-term paid employment requires modification of the physical and social organization of work including adaptive technology that enables a woman to effectively perform her work. While accommodation is essential for women with disabilities to meet their optimal productivity, these accommodations are an expensive investment for the small workplaces that make up over 90% businesses in Atlantic Canada (Kosny, 2005). Consequently, many well-educated women with disabilities who are eager to work and contribute to the community find themselves living in poverty, marginalized by their disability, and at greater risk of mental and physical ill-health (Health Canada, 2003).

The physical environments where women and girls live, play, and go to school also influence health. The WHO says that poor environmental quality is responsible for about 25% of all preventable diseases in the world (as cited in Morris, 2001). Clean water, pollution-free air, adequate sewage, safe housing, and opportunities for recreation are prerequisites for long-term health. Finding stable, affordable housing in a safe community with established social supports is more difficult for aboriginal women and their families, those with a disability, lone-mothers like Jennifer and older, unattached women like Mary. Mary currently rents a bed-sitting room in an old downtown house a few blocks from Jennifer. Jennifer is on a long waiting list for subsidized housing that will accommodate Rose's wheelchair.

Rose's mobility poses a greater challenge now that she is too big for Jennifer to carry onto the bus. Yet public transportation is the only reasonable option for getting to and from doctors' appointments or doing the shopping. Paying for a taxi puts additional strain on their already limited budget. With more box stores shutting down local independent businesses, Mary and Jennifer are finding it increasingly difficult to shop for the things they need in their local neighbourhood. Recreational outings are limited to walks in the park that is within walking distance of home. According to Health Canada, inactivity can be as harmful to health as smoking (as cited in Morris, 2001).

Social support by community, friends, and family is an important determinant of physical and mental health (Morris, 2001). Mary says this is why she returned to the province after her divorce and one of the reasons why Jennifer and Rose returned to St. John's. Women who have positive connections to family and community tend to lead happier, healthier lives. When ill or injured, having an established social network speeds recovery. Family and friends can offer emotional support as well as the physical necessities of life such as food, housing, and transportation. The strength of social support networks and a sense of belonging to the wider community are reflected in the high rates of volunteerism, the variety of non-government organizations, community agencies, and informal social practices in Newfoundland and Labrador (SSP, 2003, 21).

Another reason that Jennifer left rural Newfoundland was to have better access to health services. Health services cover a continuum of care. At one end of the continuum is *primary prevention* that includes services such as prenatal care that promote health and prevent health problems before they occur. *Secondary prevention* includes services such as breast cancer screening that are directed at early detection and treatment of health problems. At the other end of the continuum is *tertiary prevention* that involves the treatment and rehabilitation of persons with health problems. Discussion about health services tends to focus on this latter aspect of care and the organization, quality, and accessibility of the curative health services (Botting, 2002).

Rationalization and regionalization of health care services in Newfoundland and Labrador, as in other parts of the country, resulted in cuts in local services and longer waiting lines for women in need of emergency and specialty services. If, for instance, Jennifer had wanted to terminate her unplanned pregnancy, she would have had to travel a long distance for a therapeutic abortion (Botting, 2002).

Restructuring also increased the already disproportionate burden of unpaid care work done by women (Botting, 2002). When Rose needed surgery at two days old to repair her spinal defect, Jennifer travelled the long distance from a rural hospital to the children's hospital in St. John's. Without paid employment and a strong social network, she incurred considerable out-of-pocket expenses. *Out-of-pocket expenses*, those not covered by provincial health insurance, include prescription dispensing fees, travel, parking, and accommodation while receiving outpatient treatment (Mathews and Edwards, 2004). Providing unpaid care work has serious consequences for women who lose time from paid work, reduce the number of paid hours worked, and accept changes in job duties. These losses jeopardize their paid employment, reduce earnings, diminish pensions, and increase the likelihood that women will age into poverty (Botting, 2002).

Restructuring of the health services also resulted in severe shortages of health care professionals (Botting, 2002). As the numerical majority in Newfoundland and Labrador and in Canada, women frequently access health services for themselves and their family members. Almost all

Canadian women make at least one visit in a year to a health professional. However, women living in rural communities were less likely than their urban or semi-urban counterparts to have a family doctor (Mathews and Edwards, 2004). Especially hard hit are women like Mary and Jennifer who live in precarious financial and social circumstances and those living in rural, remote, and northern areas of the province that historically have been underserved.

The Johnson family story, though fictionalized, is based on documented disparities in the health of Newfoundland and Labrador women and girls. The story dramatically illustrates that good health is more than just going to the doctor. True, a single health care provider such as Jennifer's case worker or Rose's surgeon can make a difference in individual lives. More importantly, significant health gains for all Newfoundland and Labrador women and girls will only be achieved through interventions aimed at the determinants of population health. That means addressing the difference that difference makes in the health of women and girls.

What supports are needed to promote health for all girls and women in Newfoundland and Labrador?

The quote at the beginning of the chapter says that inequality is the major obstacle to good health. It stands to reason that addressing inequality is the key to promoting good health for all girls and women. This means developing, implementing and evaluating healthy social policies and programs that address the differential access to power, money, and resources that determine health status.

Healthy social policy is the responsibility of the public, private, and voluntary sectors. It emerges from alliances built by concerned citizens, corporate policy makers, health professionals, and government bureaucrats. It is produced by coordinating intersectoral activities in health, environment, education, law, and employment. Healthy social policy supports and sustains healthy social programs. Broadly speaking, healthy social policy and programs aim to provide all Newfoundland and Labrador women and girls with fair and equal opportunity to:
• Live in a safe, prosperous community with sustainable resources and opportunities for education, satisfying employment, and recreation;
• Have sufficient income to meet daily needs for comfortable housing, a varied and nutritious diet, clean air, soil, and drinking water, and efficient waste disposal and sewage treatment;
• Engage in positive relationships and meaningful activities with supportive friends and family and the larger community;
• Have ready access to high quality, affordable health care services offered by a variety of competent care providers;
• Enjoy a sense of power, autonomy, and control over one's life at home, work, school, and in the community;
• Participate actively in the development and implementation of the best options relating to any policy or program decision affecting their health;

and
- Have the political, religious, and cultural freedom to practice their beliefs without fear of reprisal (Shah, 2003).

Notes

[1] I thank Drs. Pauline Duke and Cheri Bethune at Memorial University, Faculty of Medicine for their permission to expand on a case study they developed and use with first-year medical students.

Beyond Sarah Gamp[1]: Agnes Cowan and Hospital Nursing in Nineteenth Century St. John's

Terry Bishop-Stirling

IN WESTERN CULTURES, NURSING HAS ALWAYS BEEN regarded as a proper and "natural" role for women who were expected to tend to family and neighbors. Additionally, in many communities certain women were recognized as particularly gifted healers and midwives. Whether termed midwives, practical nurses, wise women, or just "grannies," such women were valued as essential members of their communities. Before the twentieth century, the great majority of such work took place in private homes. Hospital nursing, on the other hand, has generally been portrayed as undesirable work for any woman and as unsuitable for a respectable middle class woman. Hospitals themselves were not yet seen as "healing institutions" but as places where those who were unable to afford home care went for treatment, and often, to die. Hospital nurses before the last quarter of the nineteenth century were hired and paid as "institutional domestics."

Their background as domestics led to frequent attacks on nineteenth century untrained nurses as careless, slovenly, drunken and incompetent. Often originating from complaints by attending physicians, these portrayals have been challenged by the "new" nursing history. The leading historian of Canadian nursing, Katherine McPherson, notes that even Dr. William Osler, a major critic of untrained staff in nineteenth century hospitals, acknowledged that their domestic experience often prepared them to take good care of patients. Writing about nurses at the Montreal General, he admitted that despite their "Dickensian" looks, they were, "in behavior, in devotion and in capability equal to the best I have ever met" (McPherson, 1996, 28). While drawing attention to working and living conditions in nineteenth century hospitals, historians acknowledge some truth in the negative portrayal of nurses in these institutions. A recent study concluded that generally, "few but widows, uneducated, excluded and otherwise disgraced women at the margins of society," chose to work there (Gagan and Gagan, 2002, 131). Nevertheless, little is really known about the background of these hospital workers. Frequently information comes from physicians and social reformers anxious to upgrade the image of hospitals to attract a better class of patients, or from records surrounding dismissals, scandals, and investigations of suspicious deaths — sources with an obvious inherent bias.[2] Osler's reluctant praise cited above raises the possibility that many early nineteenth century nurses did serve their patients well. McPherson further points out that the presence of nuns in some hospitals also complicates the picture of the nineteenth century "outcast nurse." The nun/nurses were educated, skilled, and widely respected (McPherson, 1996, 29). The background and work of nineteenth century nurses, therefore, must be separated from extreme depictions and placed in the broader picture of women workers in the past. Between the drunken outcast and the nun, it is likely there were many working class women who did their best in a very difficult job, under frequently appalling conditions.

The supposedly ignorant and slovenly hospital nurses of the pre-Nightingale era were supervised by a matron, usually an experienced nurse drawn from their own ranks. These women lived at the hospital, cared for patients, supervised staff and generally saw to the efficient administration of the hospital. While they may have been viewed as exceptional among their peers, these women further bring into question the negative portrayal of early nurses. The life and career of Agnes Cowan, the first matron of the St. John's General Hospital, offers a more positive perspective. Cowan was a nurse and an administrator who earned the respect of doctors visiting the hospital and of her community as a whole. Her career spanned the years when Florence Nightingale and other nursing pioneers in Europe and North America were working to establish nursing as an acceptable career for educated young women of the middle class. The effect of this change was not really felt in Newfoundland until the 1890s but Agnes Cowan, an untrained "practical" nurse, was certainly recognized as a skilled healer and an efficient administrator.[3] Like the trained nurses who succeeded her, she was expected to bring a vocational devotion to her work, to always put her patients' needs before her own and to ensure that the institution ran smoothly for the medical attendants.

Agnes Cowan was born in 1839 in Moffat, Scotland, the seventh and youngest child of John Cowan and Elizabeth Hastie (*Evening Telegram*, 10 Feb, 1984). Her family emigrated to Newfoundland in 1840, when John came to help his dying brother on his farm in the west end of St. John's. Arriving with some capital, the Cowans prospered in Newfoundland. John successfully farmed this initial holding and upon his death, Agnes' brother Robert expanded the family's fortunes by tenant farming a 365 acre farm known as "Brookfield", and his sons and a grandson later bought that property (Murray, 2002). With only this very sketchy knowledge of her background then, we cannot be sure why Agnes, and her sister before her, chose to leave home to live and work in the difficult conditions at the hospital. Were the new immigrants struggling to support all their children in their first few years in the town? Forestell and Chisholm have pointed out that most working women in St. John's in the nineteenth and early twentieth centuries went to work to relieve their families of another mouth to feed or to help support the rest of their family (Forestell and Chisholm, 1988). Was this the case with the Cowan sisters?

It is impossible to discuss Agnes' career without making reference to her eldest sister Janet, who was twenty years her senior. In 1859, when she was twenty years old Agnes joined her sister who was already living and working at the old St. John's Hospital at Riverhead in the west end of the town (J.H.A. 1867). The two sisters would spend the rest of Janet's life together, working at the hospital and living in the institution's basement. When Janet was appointed matron in 1860, Agnes was listed in the surgeons' reports as 'sub-matron' (Nevitt, 1978, 8-9). Unfortunately, nothing is known about Janet Cowan's life before her appointment. She was twenty when the family moved to Newfoundland and another nineteen years would pass before she took her sister to join her at the hospital. Agnes' training as both a nurse and administrator was gained under the tutelage of her older sister and it would be useful to know what, if any, education or experience Janet had before she went to work at the hospital. It is likely that Agnes Cowan had some basic schooling before joining her sister. In an 1864 report on conditions at the hospital, the visiting surgeons complained of the illiteracy of most of the nurses, fearing that misread instructions might endanger patients (J.H.A. 1865). This complaint clearly did not apply to the matron. While it is unknown how much formal education Agnes received, she was certainly able to read and write.

In the years immediately following her family's move to Newfoundland, Janet was likely occupied helping out at the farm and sharing in the care of her six younger siblings. By the late 1850s, the children had grown and those not essential to the running of the farm would have sought ways to support themselves, and possibly to advance the family's fortune. This was possibly the incentive for Janet to find a position for herself and her younger sister. Whatever their reason for entering the institution, the Cowan sisters would spend the rest of their lives in service to the St. John's Hospital and its successor, the General Hospital. Neither married, they lived at the hospitals, and they were on constant call to their patients.

Janet Cowan died in 1865 and less than one year later Agnes was appointed matron (Nevitt, 1978, 9). At only 26 years of age, Agnes was now responsible for much of the day to day running of the institution as well as the supervision of the domestic staff consisting of 6 nurses, 2 washerwomen, 2 cooks and a messenger. These new duties were, of course, added to her own demanding nursing responsibilities. As there was no resident physician at the hospital until the late 1880s the matron was on call day and night (J.H.A. 1867).

Agnes took over at the Riverhead Hospital in the midst of a controversy about the future of the building. Visiting surgeons constantly complained that the old building was unsafe and unhealthy. Wards were crowded, the structure was unsound and the water unfit for drinking. The servants' quarters in the basement were so cold and damp that the doctor's report for 1864 complained that the matron (Janet) as well as several nurses were consequently suffering from rheumatism and other diseases (J.H.A. 1864). Indeed, tuberculosis, one of these "other diseases", eventually resulted in the deaths of both Cowan sisters.

In 1866, the Newfoundland House of Assembly, after several years of pressure, finally appointed a committee to enquire into conditions at the hospital. This committee report, presented in April 1867, sheds some light on conditions faced by Agnes Cowan as well as some commentary on her performance (J.H.A., 1867). All testimony unanimously condemned the building but, with one exception, praised the staff for an exemplary job under unacceptable conditions. The one exception was the conclusion by an Anglican clergyman, James Kelly, who had been a visiting clergyman at the hospital for three months. He contended that the sanitary deficiencies were not strictly the result of unavoidable problems with the building. He shifted more of the blame to the domestic staff, particularly the matron. While acknowledging that he always found her "anxious to attend to any suggestions I made her," he went on to complain that she was too young and inexperienced for the job. He ignored the fact that even at 27, Agnes was already a seven-year veteran nurse/administrator at the institution. Kelly and the two other visiting clergymen were questioned together. The other two quickly leapt to Cowan's defence claiming they had never seen any indication of lack of cleanliness. The Reverend Moses Harvey, a well-known Presbyterian minister who had visited the hospital for 14 years, was particularly vehement in denying Kelly's charge. Harvey asserted that whatever her age, Agnes' intelligence and experience qualified her for her office. In fact, he argued that her youth was an asset in a job demanding great physical stamina. Most of his praise, however, appeared to focus on her care for her patients.

> I consider the Matron to be a very conscientious person, extremely kind to her patients and attentive to their wants; one who never spares herself, or shirks from visiting the worst cases of infectious diseases.[4]

The other clergyman, another long-time visitor to the institution, concurred with Harvey that the matron was, "in all respects, suitable ..."

Such praise was to follow Agnes Cowan throughout her career. Two years after the enquiry, the physician's report for 1869 noted the zeal and loyalty of the staff in a year when the hospital, in addition to its usual patients, had to deal with 657 fever victims (J.H.A. 1870). Despite the 1867 report, the old facility had not been replaced and there were no separate quarters for these infectious cases. The increased work in the abysmal conditions took its toll on the nursing staff. Agnes saw three of her nurses come down with scarlet fever and one died of the disease

(J.H.A.1870). Cowan herself survived these last few years at the Riverhead hospital and in 1871 helped in the move to the more suitable location at the recently abandoned military hospital on Forest Road in the eastern part of town (Nevitt, 1978, 11). This building is the one generally referred to as the first "General Hospital" and Agnes Cowan was to remain as its matron until her death in 1893.

While the long hours and demanding work continued at the new facility, Cowan's living conditions were vastly improved. Her apartment in the building must have seemed luxurious after twelve years in a dark basement enduring the smell of stagnant water and rotting vegetables. Over the next twenty years, Agnes no longer faced questions regarding her competence. In 1890, the St. John's Lunatic Asylum was undergoing reform and for a three-month transitional period while a new matron was found, Agnes Cowan was seconded to that institution. In his report for that year, attending physician Dr. K. MacKenzie gratefully acknowledged her service, praising her administrative ability and giving her credit for improved conditions at the facility (J.H.A. 1891).

Late in 1892, Agnes Cowan became ill and in March, 1893 she died of tuberculosis. While consumption was rampant in Newfoundland at the time, it is likely that over a decade of living in a damp, cold basement had taken its toll on Agnes as it had her sister before her. Cowan's obituaries referred to her gentle strength and loving nature and she was praised for her dedication to an often thankless job (*Evening Herald*, 27 March, 1893). Her death coincided with the early years of attempts to transform the St. John's Hospital's image into that of a modern healing institution.[5] During Cowan's tenure at the Forest Road hospital, there was no hint of concern regarding her training or suitability as matron. Upon her death, however, it was clear that hospital administrators would replace her with a graduate of a recognized nursing school (Nevitt, 1978, 17). The new era in nursing was underway and had arrived in Newfoundland.

The public respect which would be given to Mary Southcott and other twentieth century nurses was no less obvious than that afforded Agnes Cowan. The latter's memorials were not limited to a few paragraphs in the local paper. A group of women calling themselves the Cowan Mission began a long tradition of public service in her honour. They started as a visiting committee to bring comfort to hospital patients, but in a few years they opened a home on the grounds of the General Hospital. This building was initially used as a convalescent home but by 1920 was being operated as a residence for destitute elderly women. The Cowan Mission continued in this form until the 1970s when the government expropriated their building in an expansion of the hospital. Like the woman they honoured, the leaders of the Cowan Mission proved good administrators and when they disbanded they made donations in Cowan's name to two medical institutions (PANL, P8/A/35). Another honour to the pioneering nurse came in 1984 when her name was attached to an addition at the new General Hospital, the Health Sciences Complex. This addition, a 57-bed hostel, provides rooms for rural families visiting sick relatives at the hospital (*Evening Telegram*, 31 Jan. 1984).

McPherson has pointed out that nursing has always held a special place in women's history. It was a job embedded with images of women's "natural" role as care-givers and nurturers (McPherson, 1996, 1). Studies of nursing have emphasized nurses' struggles for professional recognition in the face of these assumptions. Dominated by stories of the charismatic Nightingales who transformed the domestic work of the nineteenth century into the respectable trained vocation of the twentieth, this historiography has paid little attention to the women who proceeded these leaders. McPherson, however, urges historians to remember that, "for thousands of Canadian women (and some men) in the twentieth century, nursing was in the first instance a means of economic survival. It was work" (McPherson, 1996, 2). This reminder is just as important when looking at the experience of institutional nurses in the nineteenth century and allows for a recognition of the continuity of women's experience across the two centuries rather than stressing disjuncture.

Agnes Cowan is listed in the nineteenth century St. John's directories as a nurse and as matron at the St. John's Hospital, first at Riverhead and later at Forest Road. She spent her adult life in the institutions. Whether by choice or circumstances she built her life around her work and was widely praised as an efficient administrator and a caring and competent nurse. At the time of her death, she had savings of $1600 to leave her beneficiaries.[6] In short, she had built a career that had supported her, given her independence and security, and brought her community respect. These same benefits would continue to be sought by nurses and other working women in the twentieth century.

Abbreviations Used in References
J.H.A. Journal of the House of Assembly of Newfoundland
PANL Public Archives of Newfoundland and Labrador

Archival Sources
Evening Telegram (St. John's) 10 Feb, 1984 and 31 Jan. 1984.

Evening Herald (St. John's) 27 March, 1893.

Report on the St. John's Hospital. *Journals of the House of Assembly, Appendix*. 1865, 1868, 1870, 1891.

Evidence Taken by the Select Committee on the St. John's Hospital. *Journal of the House of Assembly, Appendix*, 1867.

Records of the Cowan Mission. PANL P8/A/35.

Last Will and Testament of Agnes Cowan. March 1893. Probate Records, Supreme Court of Newfoundland and Labrador.

Notes
[1] Sarah Gamp was the fictional nurse/midwife caricatured in Charles Dickens' *Martin Chuzzlewit*. This slovenly, drunken character came to epitomize all that was wrong with hospital nursing in early nineteenth century England. Katherine Williams attributes this to the philanthropic movement which adopted the figure to illustrate the need for reform. (Williams, 1980)

[2] Williams warns that early studies in nursing history, dominated by nurses and hospital reformers have been greatly influenced by current occupational battles. In attempting to raise the status of nursing, for example, they have often been overly selective and inadequately critical in their selection of evidence.

[3] British, Canadian and American nursing histories tend to see the break between old untrained nurses and the "modern" "graduate" nurse as occurring in the mid-nineteenth century. Comparisons are then made between the early and late nineteenth century nurse. I generally discuss nineteenth versus twentieth century nurses because the St. John's Hospital did not come to depend on schooled nurses until after Cowan's death in 1893. The first school of nursing opened at the hospital in 1902 (White, 1992).

[4] Cowan was a devout Presbyterian, active in her church (Nevitt, 1976, 15). Reverend Harvey was an executor of Cowan's Will (Will of Agnes Cowan, 1893).

[5] For a discussion of this reform process in Canada and its links with the advent of training schools for nurses see Gagan and Gagan, 2002.

[6] Unfortunately little evidence exists regarding Cowan's salary after the 1860s. In that decade nurses made £14, the sub-matron £18 and the matron £34 12 (J.H.A. 1866). Later reports do not list salaries. Upon her death in 1893 Cowan left $1400 in Government Bonds and $200 on deposit at the Savings Bank. Initially the money was to go to her sister Betsy but upon her death, which occurred within weeks of Agnes', the money was directed to go to her nieces and nephews. (Last Will and Testament of Agnes Cowan, 1893, Probate Records, Supreme Court of Newfoundland and Labrador)

Effie's Landwash

Joanne Soper-Cook

WHENEVER SHE THINKS ABOUT THE FUTURE, she imagines herself in a white saltbox house high upon the cliffs above the landwash, all alone. She is never really sure *why* she imagines herself as being that way, but every time the image comes to her it's the same: the white saltbox house, its windows and their curtains, and the strong scent of sage growing near the front door. In this private kind of dream, it's always a windy summer day, and she's pinning laundry on the line. The laundry, like the house, is white. The grass is a verdurous, sharp green. Behind the house, beyond the convex swell of the land, she can see the sun-bright wave tops sparkling as they are dashed against the cliffs, hurtling themselves to death. Beyond the hill itself and beyond the portion of the waves that she can see, the ocean is roaring like a November gale. This is how she would like her life to be: austere, protected, surrounded by the ocean and the hills.

Of course, it isn't like that — life rarely follows any sort of wishing — there are no schemes. It's like looking at pictures of bathing suits in the Eaton's catalogue and imagining that a Newfoundland summer will look like that — that there will be the sun, and blazing heat, and sandy beaches. Mostly, she worries about money, because her husband Ches works for the Highways, and there's talk that there might be layoffs coming. She doesn't know what she will have to do if something like this happens, but she can imagine it very well. She will have to move away from here, leave their child in the care of Chester's mother, and go to St. John's to find work in a factory making sweet biscuits, rubber tires or bread. This wouldn't be quite so bad, except — there is her painting.

This is a secret no one knows, not even Ches. She has always been an artist, even in this place, where such pursuits are frowned upon, thought to be airy-fairy, not real. *What's real?* she wonders. She knows that only tangible things merit attention: the ability to bake a perfect partridgeberry pie, a talent for fine crochet or needlework. Painting — especially the kind of painting that Effie does — is regarded with suspicion. Effie paints the landscape in all its terrifying beauty. She doesn't want to lose this intense and personal view, this sense of paramount connection. When the child is asleep in the afternoons, Effie takes the pram and goes to the hills that overlook the landwash. She spreads her brushes out, carefully chooses one, steadies the flat canvas on her knees. She needs to capture the landscape as it is, before the water and the wind have changed it. She works quickly, sketching the contours of the hills, the muscular sea. While she works, she is immersed in it, immersed in the summer landscape. Often, there is a white saltbox house placed somewhere on the canvas. While the child sleeps beside her, dreaming infant dreams, Effie

191

inhabits the mystical landscape, the landwash of her dreams, and she is happier than she is anywhere else — happier than in her waking life. She never wants to live in any other space than this. Some part of her knows and instinctively rejects the world of matter and form, the world that would separate her from this thing that she loves above everything — more than her bones and skin and hair, more than the air that lines the pockets of her flesh.

But real events intrude, as they so often do, and one night Effie is setting the table for supper when Ches comes home and relays the inevitable: several of the men have been let go, and although his own job is still intact, there are more layoffs to come and nothing to say that he will not be next. He offers her this news in the same way he always does, as if expecting her to do something about it, leap up immediately and announce that she will sell as much Avon as it takes, or bake pies for the autumn fair, as many pies as anyone can stand. He expects her to say that she has just that moment been elected president of Ford, and she will make a million dollars. *Why don't you get a job,* he says, and Effie always thinks, I've got a job. I'm an artist.

She would never dare to say this out loud. She has experienced his temper, knows it far too well to try that sort of self-affirming stand. Many times throughout their scant married life, he has shouted his frustrations at her, demanded to know why she couldn't take a job in the fish plant like all the other women did, or go down to the beach to spread fish upon the flakes for some St. John's merchant. Other women did it, he told her, other women helped their husbands. He didn't understand that some kinds of help were not hers to offer, she couldn't sell herself that way, not unless things got truly desperate. If it came to that, if they were hungry and there was no way to make the groceries, feed the child — then she would. She was not so proud or selfish as to let catastrophe strike at them.

She escapes as often as she can to the cliffs above the landwash, carrying the canvas under her arm while one hand hoists the child, now grown enough to no longer need naps in the afternoon. She spreads a blanket on the grass and lets the child sit beside her while her hand moves rapidly across the blankness, sketching in the outlines of the landscape. She draws the hills, the abrupt drop of rock and tactile air, the sudden plunge into oblivion. The child plays as she does this, and Effie sketches with only part of her mind. The majority of her thoughts are taken up with the burden of her worries: Ches will be laid off, and Effie knows she is pregnant again. Pregnant — after she had secretly vowed that this one child would be her only offspring. She has known for several months now, even though she has not yet begun to show She will have to tell Ches very soon.

She wonders, as she sketches in the details of the landscape, whether she might do something about it. On her own she would have no idea, but surely there must be books that one could get, or some old women who could utter charms over it, banish it like putting away a wart. Just last night, as they were getting into bed, Ches said that Florence Tulk up to the dry goods store was looking for some help, and why didn't Effie go on up and put a word in for herself? Every time he suggests such things, Effie feels the bottom of her stomach contract into a fist-shape. A nameless fear claws its way up into her throat, paralyzing her. She can never speak to him, and if she did he wouldn't listen. She can never say, *I've already got a job. I'm an artist.* She could never get those words out of her mouth, could never push them past her lips, her clenched and desperate teeth. She wonders if this reluctance to expose herself to the mundane world is obstinacy or selfishness. She doesn't want to be selfish. She loves her husband. At night, when she is still awake, she leans over him and listens to the cadence of his breathing, measuring his respirations to her own. He does not know that he is cherished. He would laugh at Effie if if she tried to tell him. She feels this debt of love sometimes, lying there in bed between them, a formless presence. She feels it pressing down on her, this love she has, this otherness, this formality of souls. She feels that it might smother her. She feels that she is smothering already.

When Ches comes in for dinner, he is happy and smiling, and Effie feels a sense of calm. Perhaps he has found another job, something with better pay, that will negate the necessity of certain ruin and make them safe, as safe as houses. She is more attentive than usual, bringing extra bread, extra potatoes, stirring his tea for him. She can tell him about the baby now. She can show him all her pictures of the landwash. She can show him how she paints the same white saltbox house, over and over, as if dreaming it to life. She can confess the truth about the house, that it has appeared to her, a vision.

"I spoke to Flo, up to the dry goods store this morning." He is adding extra sugar to his tea. His face is bent. He cannot see her expression. "She's going to take on a woman to help out in the shop. I knowed you was interested."

Effie cannot feel her feet and hands. She thinks that she is holding a dish, but she can't be sure. It might be air or water that she's holding, or a stone.

"She said you can start the morrow morning. Mother said she'll look out to the youngster for ye." He is pleased with himself. She can discern something in his eyes, a surfeit of glee. He is not a bad man. She knows this and repeats it to herself, so that there will be no taint of guilt left after her, no trailing ribbon of shame like blood. He is her husband, and he loves her. He cannot know that he is doing her to death by inches. He doesn't even ask her what she thinks but goes on stirring up his tea and drinking it with every evidence of great enjoyment. Effie takes his plate away and scrapes it into the garbage, lays her own uneaten supper in the pantry. While he is playing with the child in the sitting room, she gathers up her brushes and a clean white canvas and goes out by the back door, climbing swiftly up the rise, until the house behind her is nearly lost to sight. There is a grassy hillock that she would sit upon, but this isn't what she wants now. She wanders up and down the ragged stretch of the land-wash, until she finds a crumbling cliff and an awful gorge open to the waves and the wind.

She begins as she has always done, laying strokes of blackness deep into the canvas. The wind is rising, dinning uproar into her bones, and she knows she must hurry, knows that she must finish quickly. She cannot see the ragged outlines of the coastline in the dark, and sight, especially, is necessary. She must fill her vision with the elemental taste of sea and stone. She must finish what she started.

She thinks she sees the house, the clapboard white and gleaming, the laundry flapping in the breeze, the rising wind. Her feet are bare, although she cannot remember kicking off her shoes, and the rain is pelting down, filling up her opened eyes. As soon as it is safe to leap, she does: falling faster than a stone, plummeting into the wash and flex of the sighing, reaching waves. She feels her body merging with the landscape, dissolving into nothing, rising up into the rain, evaporating. She is coming apart. She is weighted down with stones. She is a pocket full of sorrow.

To the People I Lost

It's only a dream. I wish I could wake up
and see your faces again.
When I lost you, I thought I was dreaming.
But it's not a dream
it's real.

You were all gone, and I'll never see you again.
I'll see you someday when I leave this world
but I'm not ready yet.
There is a lot to do here in this world
without drinking alcohol.
I'm trying very hard not to live the way you did.

Oh, I miss you all.
I'd better learn more
to not waste my life
like you did.

I see your faces in my dreams.
I talk to you in my dreams.
You talk to me in my dreams.
If only I could talk to you,
and tell you again not to drink,
you could listen.

I know you don't want to throw your life away
but something is controlling your life.
You're not strong enough,
you need someone beside you.
I know you can't do this alone.

You didn't make it.
It's too late now.
But I'm here.
I'm going to be strong.
I'll do it for you.

Marie Pokue lost her parents, four brothers and two sisters in an alcohol-related boating accident in 1979 when she was still a child.

Recollections

Louisa Flowers

INOLISIMAVUNGA QUEBECIMI. Atautsimik jâriKatillunga nolaukKugut Hebron, Labradorimut Kimutsikut. Sugusiutillunga ilonnatik Inuit aujatamât aullâKattalauttut iKalunniavimminut oganniaviminullu. Atâtaga ikajuKattalauttaga iKalunik salummasaitillugu siugaujaitillugulu. IKaluit pâllinut iliukKaKattalauttavut ilangani ullumi atautsimi 20-nik pâllinik tataiKattadluta, aijauniattilugit motavammut. Atâtaga iKaluluviniKattalauttuk. Pantialunga tatatsiasiaKattalauttuk iKalunut; KaKuttanut, aupalângajunut aupaluttanullu, aupalunningit kisimi aullaiKattadlugit. Anânaga panitseKattalauttuk KaKunninginik. Taikua taijaujut pitsik. Unuttualunik pitsiliuKattalauttuk aulaiKattadlugit kavamaup niuvigvinganut atautsik 10 cents-iutillugu.

1959-ami Inuit nogiaKalimmata Hebronimit Nainimut nolaukKugut tamânilu angutittâlaukKunga. Aujami Hebronimut utiKattalaukKugut iKalunniagiattudluta. Motavammi suliaKattet uKaniadlutik Hebroni Kaningiluadlaningani iKalunik aitsikatagvigigianga taimaimmat 1961-ami pigiasidluta OkKami iKalunniaKattanialidluta.

OkKak Kaninginilik 70-mailigalamik Nainiup tachâni; nainanillu sitondinik ingiggatausok motakkut. Tuvaituammat motavaillu tikituammata, July 1-imigalak aullâKattalaukKugut aullâsimanialidluta takKenik maggonik. Aujanâdlugu tupimmik illuKaKattavugut. Namminik tupiliuKattalaugaluattunga tupitsajaKaluKattagunnaimat pisiKattalikKugut sanagesimajunik. Aujaulauttuk sâtsiudluta OkKalialaukKugut. Uvallu angutigalu, atatautsik innivut maggolu ingutavuk, atautsilu innima iKalunniaKatinga.

Senanigalak tupiKaKattalaukKuk OkKami inuluviniKaKattadluni iKalunniajunik. Mânna ilangit nuluaKagunnaitut umiaKagatillu, unun-ningillu laisansiminik aullaisimalittuit. Taimaidlutik takpaungaKattagunnaitut. Aujaulauttuk atautsituinnamik tupiKalaukKuk, uvagutuinnait, taimaigaluattilugu tujummilautsimangi-lagut. Aullâvittini isumajâgutitsaKangilak, suliatsaKatsainnadlunilu. Ilangani kingomaKattagaluadluta ilattinik ikittukulogatta, taimaigaluattilugu utigumaKattangilanga. Isumaga atuppat sikukasânninganut aullâvimmiKattagajakKunga Nainiup silatâni nunaKagiak aliagidla-gakku, salumadlamat.

Ullâkut makiKattavunga fimfimi. Ullâsiutiliugegama ilakka tupâKattajakka. Ullâsiutitugetuagamik nulualiaKattajut paitillunga igadlunga, iKutuidlunga, pitsiliudlunga ubvalu tupimmik tuappingaid-jâtidlunga. Ilangani utsuliliuKattavunga puijiup utsunganik Crisco Oil-iKadlunga. Taimâk pigiamik sungiusimalikKunga taimâllu pigiak piugimmagijaga. Puijiup utsunga sunatuinnanut atuttausok, tâvatuak nutâtsajaugialik utsuliliugiamut. Akutsianik putjusedlutit utsuk atuinnagutiKattajait. Utsuk kikiatsajammut ukkusimmut tittisiagikKâdlugu akutsiat iganialidlugu utsumi.

PuijisiuKattavugut aKumigokkut. Ilonnasiangit puijiup piKutingit piuliKattajakka. Kisinga ulumik atudlunga KisiligiKattajaga. KisiligikKâdlugu iKutuKattajaga Kisik ubvautialummik atudlunga, Artic Power-imik - taikua piujullaget Kisinik iKutuigutigigiangit. Initsevimut ilidlugu silami panitsinialidlugu. Kisinga piujullagik pualuliugiamut (silapigunik) Kamiliugiamullu. Anânaga KajaliuKattalauttuk Kisijanik. KisiligikKâdlugu mikKuijadlugu mitsunialidlugu kilikittuagulautillugu.

Atâtaga KajaKaKattalauttuk angijualummik usisomik tamattinik uvannik angajuatsuganilu. Sunatuinnanik usiKattalauttuk Kajamigut - sanauganik, sukaranik, ilanganilu pinasuaKattadluni Kajamigut. Atautsik atâtamma Kajagilauttanga akuninitanik piuliumatsivimmejuk tamâni Nainimi.

Ilisimavunga Kisiligigiamik asinginilu omajugalait Kisinginik salummasaigiamik kamiliugiamillu anânakkukanit, ilinniatitsilaukKungalu tâkkuninga aggânitsak ilinniavimi. Upingasâmi sugusinik suvailfanik aulâKatiKalaukKugut Nainiup kangidluanut. Woggenik maggonik aullâsimadluta ilinniatilauttavut Kanuk aullâsimagvimi piKattamangâtta, ilinniatidlugit Kanuk panittunik Kijuttagiamik, pinasuagiamik Kanullu tumisiugiamik omajunik.

Motavak tikigaimmat aullâsimavittinut ilattinik Nainimejunik tujuiKattavugut puijiviniluvininnik, piluattumik tujudlugit InutuKait. Tujotivut idlivinut sikulinnut iliKattajavut sujugasuangimut. Motavait uvattinik pajutsainajut sikunik/milanik. Tâvatuak ilangani onaKialigaimmat akuniungituk sikuvut auKattajut piKalujatsiugiaKanialidluta pejaigvigiKattadlugit iKalutta sujugekkutitsanginnik.

OkKaliagiak iKaluit tasinit anigajâlittilugit aliagitsuajaga. Tiningalimmat aulsagatsaluvinik, taimailigaimmatalu silakKijadluta aulsaKattavugut. Anginingit aulaigatsautillugit piuliKattajavut mikiningit pitsiliuKattadlugit. Ilangani unuttualommata motavak nigiunnatinnagu ilonnatik pitsiliuKattajakka.

Pitsiliugiamik ililaukKunga anânaganit mikijodlunga. Sauninga pedlugu niKijanga agguKattajavut panisagaigasuamut. IKaluk mikijoppat savimmut Kupittausok niaKunganit pigiasidlutit, sauninga petuinnadlugu panitsinialidlugu siKinigâjumi. Angijunik pitsiliugama nânga peKattajaga nânga utsomat. Sauningit pejakKâdlugit niKijanga aggudlugu salummasadlugit Kangattadlugit panitsinialidlugit siKinigâjumi. SiKinigâtsiamat anugitâdlunilu woggimi atautsimi panisot. Taimâtsainak pimmijut tuttuvinet puijivinellu, nikkuliuKattavunga puijivininnik tuttuvininnilu. Tuttuvinimmik nikkuliugama nukinga pejaKattajaga, taimâtsainalu puijiviuniup utsunga pejaKattamidlugu.

NiKijanga sâttuagulautillugu aviukKaKattajaga. Ilangit idjunitsanik
sanaKattajut, sâttunik sanaKattavunga panisagaigasuamut. Kijummut
Kangattadlugit mumiKattadlugit panitsiKattajakka. Ujagait Kânganut
siammadlugit panitsijausongummijut siKinigâttumi.
Kamagijautsainagialet igunasongumata kamagijautsianginamik. Nikkuit
piujullaget nutaungitunikKâgatik. Nutâtsajaujojâsot takKinik sâtsinik
ailangitumi nilatâttumegamik Kuatsevimmilonnet.
   IKaluit tasinut utigaimmata panaigiasiKattavugut Nainimut utigiamut.
Ilonnasiatik atusimajavut aujanâdlugu salummasagiaKaKaKattajavut,
angiKautigiaKaKattagattigit. Ilonnatik nuluavut salummasadlugit uja-
gani panitsiKattajavut, panimmata idlivinut iliukKaKattadlugit.
   Nunak salummasaKattajavut. Ititsaliudluta sanet sauKattajavut utigut-
ta nunajavut salumagasuamut. Annugâvut ilonnatik iKutuKattajakka
ilonnatillu piKutivut atusimajavut salummasadlugit piuliukKadlugit.
NiKijatsatinik katitsuiKattavugut angiKaKâgata - timmianik, tuttuvinin-
nik, iKalunik. Salummasadlugit idlivinut pokKadlugit
angiKautiKattajavut tikigatta Kuatsevimmoniadlugit.
   Nainimut utisimaligatta nunivagiaKattavunga, uvilutsiugiaKattadlunga
aulsaKattadlungalu ogâtsunik. Ogâtsuit ogaujâkasâttut.
PitsiliuKattajakka. NiKijaKaKattavugut Kuatsevittini nâmmatunik
upingasâmunut, upingasâmi aulsagialiaKiKattadluta sikukkut. Skidoo-
kut aulsagiaKattavugut Nainiup kangidluanut aulsangugatta
aKiggisiuKattadluta ubvalu puijisiudluta nillisiudlutalu.

I was born in Quebec. When I was only one year old we moved all the
way from over there to Hebron in Labrador on dog team. When I was
growing up everybody used to go up north to go fishing in the summer-
time. I used to help my father clean the fish and salt them. We used to
put the fish in barrels — sometimes about 20 barrels in one day — and
the collector boat would pick them up. My father used to get a lot of fish.
His boat used to be full of char, white and pink and red ones, but they
wanted only red char. My mother always managed to dry the white ones
and pink ones. *Pitsik* is what you calls them. She used to make lots of pitsik and sell it to the government store, ten cents for one.
In 1959, when all the people had to move from Hebron, we moved to
Nain and I married there. We used to go back to Hebron in the summer-
time to go fishing. Then the people on the collector boat said that Hebron
is too far, so in 1961 we started to go to Okak.
Okak is about 70 miles north of Nain — nine hours to go up on the
boat. As soon as the ice breaks up and the collector boat comes, around
July 1, we go up north and stay there two months. We live in a tent all
summer. I used to make my own tent, but there is none of that kind of
material here now so we have to bring an already made one. This summer
six of us went up to Okak. There was me and my husband, one son, and

two grandchildren, and one person that was fishing with my son.

There used to be about 10 tents around Okak and a lot of people fishing there. Now some of them got no nets and no boat, most of them sold their licence. That's why they don't go up anymore. This summer there was one tent, just us, but we're never bored. Up there you don't think about nothing, always something to do. Sometimes it's lonely because there's only a few of us, but I don't want to come back. I would stay until almost freezing, I suppose because I like being outside of Nain. It's so fresh and clean.

In the morning, I wake up at five. I cook breakfast and I wake them up. Soon as they finish breakfast they go off to see the nets and I will stay home and cook dinner or wash clothes, make *pitsik*, or clean the tent. Sometimes I make donuts using seal fat oil — seal fat for my Crisco Oil. I'm used to it and I love it. Seal fat is used for everything, but it has to be fresh seal fat to make oil. You rise the dough and start cutting up the seal fat to put in the pot. You boil the fat in the iron pot and you just put the donuts in.

We look for seals in the speedboat. I save everything off the seal. I clean the sealskin with my ulu — the knife I use to scrape off the oil. Then I wash the skin in detergent — Arctic Power I use — real good for sealskin. I put it in a frame and hang it outside to dry. The sealskin is really good for mitts and boots. My mother used to sew the sealskins to make the kayak; clean them first, take the hair off, and sew it very neat. My father used to have this big, big kayak and me and my sister could fit inside. He would get everything with the kayak — flour and sugar, and sometimes he used to hunt for animals by kayak. One of the kayaks belong to my father is in the museum here in Nain.

I learned how to clean the sealskin and furs and make sealskin boots from my parents, and I was teaching that two years ago in the school. In the springtime we had to take 12 students up to Nain Bay for two weeks and teach them how to be outside Nain, how to pick the dry wood, hunt for animals, and look for the tracks.

When the collector boat comes, we send a lot of seal meat to Nain to share with other people, mostly the old people. We put it in the fish boxes in a lot of ice so it won't spoil. The collector boat always takes ice to us. But sometimes it's really hot and the ice melts, so we look around to see icebergs and we take little pieces and cut it up and put it in with the fish.

I like going up to Okak when the char is coming out from the lake. When it's low tide there's a lot of fish for rodding, so just for fun we go rodding. We save the big ones for selling and I make *pitsik* out of the small fish. Sometimes when there's a whole lot of fish and the collector boat is not coming for a few days I make pitsik out of them.

I learned to make the *pitsik* from my mother when I was small. You cut the meat off, then take the meat and cut little lines across it so it will dry faster. If the fish is small you take the knife and from the head you cut it down the middle, take the bones out, clean it, and dry it in the sun. If I make *pitsik* with big fish I cut the stomach away because the stomach part is very oily. Then I take the bones out, cut the lines, clean it, and hang it up until it dries in the sun. If it's very sunny and kind of windy, it can dry in one week. Same way with the caribou meat and the seal meat, I make *nikkuk* out of them. You take all the big muscles off the caribou meat and you take the fat off the seal meat. You cut the meat really thin. Some people make thick ones, but I make mine thin to dry fast. I hang it up on the stick and turn it over and over until it's dry. You can put them on top of the rocks and turn them over in the sun. You have to watch it all the time because it can stink. The *nikkuk* is really good when it is fresh. It can stay fresh about six months if you keep it in a cold place or in the freezer.

When all the fish is gone up in the lake, we start getting ready to come back to Nain. We have to clean every single thing we used all summer because we have to take everything back home. We clean all the nets and put them on the rocks to dry. When they're dry, we put them in boxes to come home.

We clean the land. We dig the ground and put all the garbage into the ground so when we come back next year it's going to be nice and clean. I wash the clothes and everything that we used for fishing by hand, and fix all of our stuff nice and neat. We gather some food — ducks, caribou, and char. We clean them and put them in the fish box and when we come back home I put them in the freezer.

Back in Nain I go berry picking and mussel picking and rock cod fishing. They are like codfish, but a little bit different. I make *pitsik* out of them. We have enough food in the freezer until spring comes. Then in the springtime we usually start ice fishing. We go up in Nain Bay on skidoo and when we're tired of fishing, we look for partridge or we go outside to look for seals and goose.

Letters and Diaries

R HODA DAWSON (1897-1992) was born in Chiswick, England, the daughter of distinguished artists. She trained as an artist in England, and, in 1930, set sail for Newfoundland to work with Sir Wilfred Grenfell in the Village Industrial Department in St. Anthony. For two or three years she taught crafts and designed rag rugs for local women to hook for the Grenfell Mission. The figurative designs she produced for Grenfell's audience were in sharp contrast to her own fondness for sophisticated, abstract patterns. In 1931, Rhoda began painting on the coast of Labrador near Battle Harbour and Red Bay. She wintered with the Chard family at Ailik near Makkovik in 1932, and documented her visits to other families and communities through diaries, photographs, watercolour paintings, and sketches. She also wrote many letters home to family and friends in England, as here to her friend Margaret Sclanders Kilpatrick. Her letters reflect both her appreciation of, and curiosity about, the new culture in which she found herself, and the imposition of her own cultural values and expectations on the people and community life she experienced.[1]

Makkovik
Labrador
Mar 28, 1932

Dear Margaret,
    Today is Easter Monday, and the last day of the Easter gathering here. Church, church, church, ever since Palm Sunday, but I was away for half of it and some how one does not tire of it, it is so sincere. If it would amuse you to hear about it and about the way we get about here, read on. I never felt sure I may not bore you, my news and my journeys are so small, my letters must sound like the Labrador men talking, all about dogs and harness and dog food and little small journeys that take all day. The way my Easter pilgrimage began was like this. There's a Newfoundland trader called Jo Chard, who lives and trades out at Ailik, 8 miles from here, on a cape out to sea. He said they might go to Hopedale for Easter, and I might go too. And his young driver said *he* didn't want to stop in Hopedale for a week, but he might go on 150 miles to Nain and take me. So I thought it sounded good, and I want to go to Nain, and I wanted a change, so I decided to make a go of it and call at Island Harbour as well. It is 25 miles to Island Harbour and across ice most of the way. It was a lovely day, and I have at last got suitable clothes, and I borrowed the missionary's sleeping bag. I feel it rather a delicate matter to borrow a gentleman's sleeping bag but he didn't seem to mind in the least, and we put it in a mail bag that was lying around. I had on, over my ordinary winter clothes and your skiing trousers — my sealskin pants,

long blanket stockings over the knee, boots with embroidered deerskin feet and furry sealskin legs, and various socks inside; a long blanket dickie with the hood edged with white hare fur, and a brown duxback dickie over, its hood edged with black fur, blanket and sealskin mitts, and sun spectacles and a motor helmet. And I was really comfortable. I got a lift as far as Big Bight, where Stanley Evans lives. This is Stanley. He has the longest nose on the Labrador and he can only use one hand for driving because he has to hang on to his nose with the other to keep it from frost bite.

There's a sort of queer relationship between Stanley's nose and the peak of Stanley's hood. He has a really dear little fat wife. Stanley took me on from Big Bight, glad of the excuse to go to Island Harbour and see his mother. Lizzie came a little ways on the komatic, then she kissed Stanley and bounced off and ran back home looking like a little fat fairy.

Island Harbour is a pretty place at the end of a bay and the people there are rather superior and know it, and all of Scotch descent. There are two houses, one very old where two families live. Uncle Ernie Lyall and Aunt Sis, and in the other is dear old Uncle Charles McNeil the father of the foreman at St. Anthony. Uncle Charles and I got on very well, I liked to talk to him about St. Anthony and he liked to talk to me about the King and Queen and all the dear Princesses. I stayed there sleeping on the parlour sofa in the sleeping bag (at his son's house) for 3 days and then George who looks like the photographs of my uncle in his teens and is really the sweetest and most thoughtful youth, took me to Ailik. It is 17 miles across the ice all the way. We started at 11 and reached Ailik at 4:30. It was a lovely day, but the snow was deep and soft and the dogs could hardly get along. All the way we kept on thinking about the deer meat Mrs. Chard would probably have cooked. And George insisted on my sharing his piece of cake. We were hungry when at last the land was near us. It always seems slow traveling over ice towards distant land. And at Ailik we found no deer meat, but partridge, almost better still. We also found Jo Chard sick, so they could not start for Hopedale the next day. George stayed overnight, traded a white fox skin for Uncle Charles and went back the

next day. Saturday was mail day in Makkovik and the Chards sent over for their mail but the March bags are always empty. I was the only one who got anything. However we heard the Makkovik news. A few people had gone there for Palm Sunday and the HBC man from Hopedale had come up, with 23 dogs, travelling by night. The "going" was shocking.

Sunday was a lovely day and I lay in bed and listened to Jo, who had nearly recovered, reading family prayers. I always have my meals alone in the parlour as the kitchen is considered too rough. And I must say I appreciate it, although it seems unsociable. So I got up when I liked. The sun shone in at the top of the window between the legs of a dog who was standing in the snow which is nearly up to the roof. And we wasted that love-ly day partly because they didn't much like to travel on Sunday and partly because Mrs. Chard was afraid for Jo, and then Sunday night the glass fell and the wind blew and the next day was a blizzard. The snow drifted up round the windows so quick we had to go out several times to dig it away or we should have been in darkness. The boys could not go out to their chores, and all day long literally and without stopping except for meals, Jo Chard read poetry aloud to a visiting boy, and I could hear him through the door …

"Then up spake brave 'Oratius'…"

Tuesday was fine and in the morning Jo's voice outside called the Missus to see the funny sky. I went with her and it was the oddest sight. The air was full of fine snow and the sun was shining. Round the sun was a halo apparently vertical, and overhead and passing through the sun a great white ring on a horizontal plane. At the points of intersection at either side of the sun glowed 2 false suns. At the top of the sun's halo lay a segment of a rainbow. 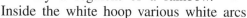Inside the white hoop various white arcs showed dimly, and below the whole thing were two rainbows, near the horizon, like this only overhead. I've read about one in Byrd's South Polar Expedition. It stayed nearly all day.

Mr. Chard said we should go that night and we sat sewing hard at new dresses and finishing touches for Easter, had a big supper of deer's meat and went to bed early. We got up about 12 and had breakfast, everyone very excited and foolish, Mrs. Chard singing hymns and Mr. Chard rather

Rhoda Dawson (r) with Birdie (L) and Nell in Labrador c.1930. CNSA, Coll-198, 6.20.044

dubious. We left Sam behind to keep house, and at last the komatic was loaded and they drove me back here again. It was rather an anti-climax when I returned to the mission house at dinner time as they thought I was in Nain by that time. But I'm glad I've been here for Easter because I know the people and it is nice to see all the relatives come in from all round.

There was a confirmation on Thursday afternoon. It was most affecting. The candidates sat up in a row and had to answer a lot of questions and Mr. Lenz said afterwards they did it very badly; but considering that one of them can't read or write and the others can only just read and write, and that they only get the chance to come to church about twice a year, I think it was wonderful. All the women were sniffing in the congregation and suddenly I saw poor Uncle Wilson Shephard mopping his how and wiping his eyes on the candidate's bench, and that did for me and I wept for the rest of the service. Alice has looked quite rapturous in church since then, in a wonderful new blue and red head shawl, and even poor Uncle Wilson looks more settled.

Uncle Wilson's family are lodging in the mission work-shop, and Aunt Susan came in one day when I

204

was having a late breakfast, so I had to offer her coffee. She contrived to strike my coffee some other time, as well, but this morning by some mistake I was up bright and early and when Aunt Susan popped her little witch like face round my door I had had breakfast an hour before. So she stayed a decent time and withdrew in good order but without her coffee. I did my washing before church. Mrs. Lenz rather horrified begged me not to hang it up on the mission line by the church, but after all it *was* Monday. So I hung it up in the kitchen and just then George came in. (Every house is an open house in Labrador). So I had to spin out the handkerchiefs and other innocuous pieces and leave my underwear in the rinsing pail till he chose to go; dear George, he wanted to buy all my chisels. I refused to part with them but I have promised him my beautiful Woolworth brace and bits which I shall sell him at a handsome profit. Then was church and I was in good time for once. Yesterday I was late and grabbed an Eskimo hymnbook as I went in so I had to share with an old old crone who looks as if she came from Mile End.

In the afternoon at 3 o'clock the entire village and the visitors, except for the tiniest babies and one or two sick folk and their attendants, went to the church for the "Love Feast". The Moravians always sit to sing, here, and we just sat and sang one hymn after another while the elders handed round cups of cool very sweet tea and hardtack. Every now and then a child was carried out and babies whimpered but mostly they were very good. Little Mr. Lenz, very straight and precise, sat at the table (like the altar) singing away and drinking his tea. Out of the window we could see blue sky and black fir trees, and the ice of the bay stretching to the horizon. The old ladies in their head shawls and dickies and the girls in wooly caps and coats and the men with clean handkerchiefs tied round their necks, all singing the "Church's One Foundation" and drinking lukewarm tea — it is a great sight. Some of them wear little net caps.

The boys play football in the snow with more heartiness than skill, all day from 7:30 till dark, except when they are in church. The HBC young man, who was once a boy scout, tries to teach them the rudiments but they won't bother to do it properly. John Thomas Cove was goal keeper for the visitors.

Everybody got into a big group mostly on the sloping roof of my house for Mr. Lenz to take a photograph. Then we all went a-visiting and I managed to coax dear old Aunt Ellen Morgan to let me take her photograph. She has a wunnerful big nose and she won't be took as a rule. I stayed and talked to various sporty old ladies who had all been nearly as good as men in their prime ("I can't think what's got the girls now-a-days. Sure, they can't do the things *we* did") and then I came back to a rather solitary tea. I must say it is lonely sometimes.

There are fine Northern Lights tonight and the dogs are howling at them. Must be 150 dogs in the village with all the visiting teams.

Sunday April 3

I meant to go on about Easter. The Love Feast was the climax, on Monday. All through Easter Week and on Good Friday and Sunday they have a reading in church of the happenings of the day in the bible story. It is rather impressive. Mr. Lenz reads very well, and at solemn or important points he makes them sing a suitable hymn. He has the most remarkable sense of fitness. He is a very good gardener, and he handles his simple congregation with the same love and care as he handles his boxes of seedlings.

On Easter morning we were called at 5:30 and went to church in a snowstorm, and afterwards all walked through the woods to the open space among the spruce where the graveyard was buried deep below 6 feet of snow. There was no sign even of the palings. It looked rather fine — men and women in white dickies singing hymns, the parson as well, black trees and snow falling. The men had stamped the snow hard the day before with snowshoes. I think it is a German custom to go to the graveyard. We came back home rather sleepy and I met Mr. Lenz in the passage taking off his dickie and shaking off the snow; he burst out "I do love that service, to stand over the graves singing hymns of victory." He really is so happy.

The back of the winter is broken now, as they say. The time simply flies when you live by the work of the seasons. It has been 10 degrees above Freezing all day once or twice and I could paint outside again. The weather was awful all through March and there's been more snow than they've had for years, but each warm day makes it go again and my windows are quite clear now. The birds are beginning to sing.

I often dream about European food. Everything is getting used up now. Mrs. Lenz is at her last sack of potatoes, today we missed our Sunday eggs for the first time, there's no cheese, onions are spoiling and growing out. I've had plenty of fresh meat, and here I get real butter, but I suppose it's the monotony of deer meat, partridge, seal meat, or tinned molasses pork and beans, or salt fish. They are the staple for most meals unless the people are poor, then it's loaf and tea. However, they are beginning to fish through holes in the ice for rock cod. In St. Anthony they'll be getting trout. Soon, it will be time to go home, back to St Anthony. I don't want to go back to England yet. I don't mind if never see London again, except for the family being there. I'm just getting into this place and my work.

I must have wasted a lot of time, I've nothing much to show for 6 months. And I'm happier than I've been since I grew up, except for not having any of my friends here.

I have Aunt Harriet and Uncle Wilson coming to tea this afternoon (Andrea's father and mother), after church. Aunt Harriet will be wearing her church cap underneath her bright new Tyroles head-shawl, and her best black plush coat. She's awfully like my grandmother especially with the church cap. She's a darling.

Love to all of you, and tell me what the baby's name is.

RD

Notes

[1] CNSA, Collection 198, 5.02.001; Obituary, *The Guardian*, 31 March, 1992 and *The Independent*, 2 April, 1992; P. Neary, " "Wry Comment": Rhoda Dawson's Cartoon of Newfoundland Society, 1936," in *Newfoundland Studies 8*, 1 (1992).

Thank you to Richard and Susan Wallington, London, England, for their assistance in the transcription of this letter.

Home Economics

We daughters of hard working
fathers and mothers all took home
economics as if we hadn't better
things to study at school. Cooking.
Potatoes, of all things, chopped and mashed
or halved and broiled in their skins,
those that grew anywhere and did
all along the fences, potatoes with eyes
and dirty skins stored and sprouting in cellars.
Turf ground into our fingers
when we scrubbed and sliced and peeled,
colanders steaming above the sinks.

There was sewing too, for the daughters
of fishermen and lumberjacks
and rosy cheeked shop keepers
and truck drivers, and itinerant evangelists
and iron ore miners, and mothers at home.
Also quilt blocking, tatting, ironing, pins
in a smocked bodice, purple gingham, appliqué,
a crooked running stitch.

And cleaning, our hair hidden in kerchiefs,
rubber gloves, mops with bleach, silver polish,
as if we owned silver or ever considered it.

She Seeketh Wool: Newfoundland Women's Use of Handknitting[1]

L. Lynda Harling Stalker

She seeketh wool, and flax, and worketh willingly with her hands.

—Proverbs: 31, 13

KNITTING, LIKE OTHER TEXTILE CRAFTS, HAS LONG BEEN women's work. Textile work, particularly when done by hand, is repetitive work perceived as compatible with childcare (Barber, 1994). It presents little danger to children, and interruptions are easily tolerated. It is a part of a woman's "highest calling" to provide her family with a safe and nurturing environment, where she is industrious in carrying out her work in the face of social changes. This perception echoes the tenets of maternal feminism, as developed into a theoretical perspective and political movement in the late 19th and 20th centuries. "Women themselves … identified their sex with a maternal role. A re-invigorated motherhood, the natural occupation for virtually all women, could serve as a buttress against all the destabilizing elements in Canada" (Strong-Boag, 1986, 181). What society needs to do, according to maternal feminists, is recognize and give merit to the contributions women make to their families and communities in their capacities as mothers and caregivers.

In Newfoundland, knitting is one of women's traditional domestic chores. Women knit mainly mitts, socks, and caps. Garments that tend to wear out quickly, they were once cheaper to knit than to buy. The Newfoundland grey sock became famous during World War I. Soldiers from different countries would often approach Newfoundland soldiers to ask for the socks which the Women's Patriotic Association worked endlessly to supply: "[T]he grey military sock assumed the status of icon during the Great War ... a proud symbol of distaff work in the public service" (Duley, 1994, 31). Recognition of the contributions Newfoundland women made to the war effort supported their efforts to gain the right to vote, which they achieved in 1925. The political element of maternal feminism was successful in establishing that "women's work was as difficult in its own way as men's, and political equality was a natural consequence" (Duley, 1994, 51). This historical example illustrates the use of "women's work" work to deal with social instability and change.

Knitting as "women's work" has survived many more periods of instability, including the major changes experienced in Newfoundland throughout the 1990s, the legacy of the 1992 cod moratorium that virtually shut down the industry that had shaped Newfoundland's economy and culture. Both harvesters and plant workers found themselves suddenly out of work; year-round unemployment increased, as did outmigra-

209

tion. The economic focus shifted to the development of other industries, including offshore oil, information technology and crab and shrimp fisheries. At the end of the 1990s, the Canadian media reported that Newfoundland had the fastest growing economy in the country; however, many people living in the outports would disagree. As anyone who listens to radio call-in shows knows, many people in rural areas feel that the capital city of St. John's is the only place benefiting from this growth. This is the context in which my research occurred.

As a handknitter, I have long been interested in what role this traditional craft plays in the lives of the women who engage in it on an ongoing basis. I am also interested in how people arrange their lives and work in regions with peripheral economies. I set out to talk to 19 rural Newfoundland women who habitually knit to explore what meaning handknitting has for them. From the information I gathered, I found that they use knitting as a means to deal with the abundant social and economic changes Newfoundland experienced in the 1990s.

Methodology

In pursuit of actionist research for this study[2], I conducted detailed semi-structured personal interviews with knitters in their homes during the summer of 1999. These knitters all worked for NONIA, a not-for-profit organization, on a piece-rate basis. All the women were over 30, and more than half were over 50. All were married or widowed, and only four had children under 18 living at home. At the time of the interviews, none were employed outside their homes.

By conducting interviews in the knitters' homes, I had the opportunity to see the environment within which the knitters worked and the items they made. Semi-structured interviews allowed the knitters to be heard in their own words. Furthermore, as a knitter myself, I was able to have a better understanding of how one knits, as well as an appreciation for what draws people to knitting. This allowed the knitters to use jargon that a non-knitter might not understand and provided common ground between the knitters and the researcher.

This social actionist approach allows research to focus not only on actions, but also on reasons for actions. It provided me with an opportunity to gain an understanding of the motivations and meanings knitting have for Newfoundland women. Campbell maintains that "motivation and meaning must be studied together — as they actually interact in real life" (1998, 88). By allowing the knitters to provide their own thoughts and interpretations on the knitting they do, one can come to understand why they knit for NONIA and why knitting is important to them.

Meaning of Handknitting – Appropriate Way to Fill Time

Society and culture set out what is an appropriate way for us to use our time. In Newfoundland in the 1990s, many people found they had time on their hands, especially with the cod moratorium. Some of the women had been working in the fishery and had lost their jobs because of the moratorium. They were not able to find other work because there were few employment opportunities. Older women also had more time to fill as they no longer had children, and in some cases spouses, to care for. Knitting provided an acceptable way to use this time.

Mrs. Parsons[3] described how she takes her knitting when she goes to meetings or even riding in the car:

> If I go out to a meeting, I sometimes take my knitting with me. [What type of meetings?] Any meetings: church meetings, recreation meetings, I'm involved in recreation. If I figure it's going to be a lengthy meeting and I have something that needs to get done, I'll take it with me. If I'm going in the car, I always have something to take in the car with me. I don't drive so I knit. I take it to pass the time. When you're driving, there isn't much to look at. When you go through the community I might look at the flowers.

Mrs. Parsons feels that she has to have her knitting to make sure she does not waste *any* time. Knitting prevents the possibility of her time being wasted during long discussions at meetings, which may not be fruitful. Taking her knitting with her in the car ensures that every moment of time is filled. Instead of being a passive passenger, Mrs. Parsons is active with her knitting.

This preoccupation with making sure that time is not wasted at meetings or driving is a common thread among the knitters. Mrs. Budgell said, "I go to a church group here and if I feel like knitting I take it. [Do people say anything?] Yeah, sometimes, but I say I'm not doing anything else." Mrs. Budgell needs to be sure that her time is fully occupied. There are times during a meeting when she does not contribute to the discussions; by knitting, Mrs. Budgell believes she is passing the time to its utmost capacity. Knitting ensures that she is an active agent during a social activity where she might otherwise be perceived at some moments to be passive vis-à-vis others — for example, listening to other people talking.

Mrs. Penney also needs to take knitting with her when she goes to meetings. "I can't imagine myself doing nothing," she said. "It's so relaxing. I don't go to a meeting if I don't got me knitting." This is not only a case of wanting to be sure that time is not wasted; it is also a way to alleviate any tension that might arise at a meeting. Knitting becomes Mrs. Penney's prevention mechanism against agitation; as she says, knitting relaxes her.

Knitting in the car, while being driven, is prevalent among the knitters.

To pass the five- to ten-minute trips to the grocery store, Mrs. Tucker said: "I take it [knitting] when I go grocery shopping. My husband drives and I knits. Sometimes I tell him to turn around and go back because I forgot something [knitting]. He knows what it is [her knitting]." Being a passenger means that you are not doing anything, so the time needs to be filled — knitting does that.

Knitting is also taken on holidays in case there is time not being used. Mrs. Parsons said, "I was in Halifax for ten days, and I took a bag of knitting." Mrs. Murphy goes further than this. She talked about her preparations for a trip to Ontario to visit her daughter

> See them two boxes there? That's full of wool. So now I'm going up to Ontario and I'm going to take them with me. What I'm going to do is put them in the mail ... This lot I'm doin' here is 36 skeins of wool ... What I'm doin' is I take some out to take with me because I'll get there before they do.

These comments demonstrate the amount of planning and foresight that Mrs. Murphy puts into ensuring that she has yarn to knit with in Ontario. She wants to be sure that she will not be sitting idle when her daughter is at work and her grandchildren are in school. By mailing wool and taking some on the plane with her, Mrs. Murphy is guarding herself against having time that needs filling or passing, time during which she would not know what to do with herself.

While the women depend on knitting to pass their time, they are also constantly searching for new patterns, the challenge, of something new to knit. This search permeates virtually every aspect of their lives — from being in church to being on vacation. As Mrs. Parsons said:

> It [knitting] was something that I set my sights on, that I want to do. If I saw a strange pattern, I had to try it. I've gone to church, now when my boys were in cadets; I remember there was a beautiful pattern of a sweater on the lady in front of me. And I got out a bulletin and a pen from my purse and I wrote the pattern down in church! I wanted to do that pattern bad.

This anecdote shows how the knitters are always looking for new patterns, and are even willing to violate norms, in this case writing in church, in order to get something new to challenge them.

Mrs. Budgell tells of a similar incident. She recounts an event that happened to her while on summer holidays:

> I find myself, if we're traveling, we were in Ottawa for two weeks, I watch what people have on. We were down at the market, the outdoor

market, and this man passed me with a sweater on. I found myself watching him. My son said, 'What are you looking at him for?' I found myself looking at his sweater!

In this account, Mrs. Budgell's attention is easily diverted from her surroundings to the point where it is noticeable to those around her. The preoccupation with knitting and, more specifically, noticing challenging new patterns, can invade times when the knitters are involved in other pursuits.

Knitting is seen by some as an activity that will safeguard against empty time when they are older, a sedentary activity that can be done at any age. Some of the younger knitters believe that by knowing how to knit they have an activity they can do for the rest of their lives. Mrs. O'Neill said this when asked if children should learn to knit:

I think at some point in their lives they're going to want to knit, when they get older. If they get something wrong with them and they can't do anything else, unless there's something wrong with their hands. That's what I'm afraid of, that's all I'm afraid of. I checks every day; I would rather break my leg before I break my arm.

Knitting is so ingrained into how the women deal with the temporal experiences of managing their lives that they cannot envision any other activities that would replace it. Mrs. Walsh says, "I don't like reading because I'm not using my fingers. If I gets crippled in my fingers it's just as well I die. I just can't sit down without my pair of needles." Mrs. Walsh cannot conceptualize her life without knitting. Knitters not only rely on knitting as a means to pass time, but also identify with the activity to the point of not being able to imagine life without the bodily ability to knit. For these women, knitting is *vital* to the preservation and maintenance of self.

Knitting is also incorporated into how *other* people perceive how these women pass the time, particularly their children. Two of the older knitters, Mrs. Brown and Mrs. Hickey, recounted that their children have said that they will be placing yarn and knitting needles in their caskets. Mrs. Hickey reported that her children said, "Mom, we'll have to put some wool and knittin' needles down in the box with you 'cause you always got it in your hands." Mrs. Brown's daughter told her she will have to put "wool and needles in the casket" when Mrs. Brown dies. These offers make a statement about how the bodies will finally and conclusively be shown socially. They are identity markers of important aspects of the knitters' selves. Knitting is so strongly associated with these women that the maternal image their children have includes the craft — even in the afterlife.

213

Knitting as a Link Between Generations

Knitting can also be a connector between women of different generations. With every stitch that is knit a physical link with a mother, mother-in-law, or daughter is created. An activity that can be passed on from one person to the next is a way of establishing traditions. As Theophano (2002) shows with cookbooks and Parker (1984) with embroidery, these "womanly" activities are ways women have historically developed and maintained connections between mothers and daughters.

Throughout Mrs. Budgell's interview, she spoke fondly of her mother. Knitting quickly brings to mind the many hours Mrs. Budgell's mother knit. She described how, through her mother's knitting, she now has ingrained ideas about what is appropriate behaviour for Sundays:

> I grew up in a home where you weren't allowed to knit on Sunday. I still can't. I knit on every other day. [Was that because knitting was seen as work?] I think so. My mother would never knit on Sunday. On Saturday night, her knitting was put aside until Monday morning. I saw her Sunday night after twelve o'clock get up and knit mitts for Dad that they had to have that day. She would not do knitting on Sunday. You know that was passed on to me. There is no real religious reason why; it was just tradition. I never take my knitting out on Sunday. I still put it aside even though I don't see it as work. I don't do it. The boys would think it very strange if they saw me knit on Sundays. It's just tradition, it is.

Even though Mrs. Budgell does not conceptualize knitting as work, like her mother did, she is compelled by the teachings of her mother not to knit on Sundays. Not knitting on Sundays is a "tradition" that her mother instilled in her, and even 40 years later Mrs. Budgell cannot break it. In this instance, *not* knitting actually becomes the connection between mother and knitter.

Mothers-in-law are also remembered when discussing knitting. Mrs. Ryan talks about the time she learned to knit just after getting married:

> She [her mother-in-law] only had the one son, so when I came to live here, after just having the one child, and having another woman coming in to live, there was a lot of tension; well, not a lot but a difference of opinions. She did things one way, and I would do things another. So I guess her being able to teach me something, it probably made her feel good as well.

Knitting became a common ground for Mrs. Ryan and her mother-in-law. It was an activity that they could share outside the tensions of jointly running a household. By teaching knitting, the mother-in-law demonstrated that she was able to share a talent she had that Mrs. Ryan did not have. It allowed the mother-in-law to maintain a sense of self-worth in her own household in spite of the new member. Knitting provided a mechanism to alleviate some of the strains put on them in this living arrangement.

Mrs. Morgan described how the inter-generational connection continues with her own daughter:

> My daughter, we only got the one daughter and she's in Ontario, and she knits. And she says when hockey games are on, and she's knitting, it reminds her of when she was a child, because the hockey games were always on at our house. And I was always knitting. And she said, 'Saturday nights I can see you in the rocking chair knitting and Dad watching the hockey game.'

In this instance, knitting at a particular time is a connection between the mother and daughter. As the daughter knits, she remembers her parents doing the same activity. It connects the generations over time and space. The knitting is not only being done years later in time, but also in a different geographical location. Knitting transcends time and space to provide a link between generations of women.

Knitting as a Part of the Identity of an Outport Female

When the women in this study identify themselves, it is in terms of whether they are housewives, mothers, or occasionally as retired fish plant workers. They would not identify themselves as knitters in the first instance. This being said, however, it became apparent that knitting is intrinsic to their concept of what it is to be a woman, a mother, and a wife in rural Newfoundland. Greenhill and Tye (1993) point out that this is not unusual. They state that traditions and folkways are means for socializing people into what are considered to be gender-appropriate activities and expectations. While the women claimed that being female was not the motivation for why they knit, it is apparent that gender determines who gets exposed to knitting and to whom the craft is passed on. Mrs. Budgell illustrated this well in her comments:

> If I had girls I would have taught them to knit. I should have taught the boys to knit. [Did the boys ever seem interested in knitting?] The youngest one, yes. Many times he would sit by me knitting and he'd say, 'Mom, I'd love to learn to knit.' And silly-like I'd probably say, 'Ach, you don't want to knit.' Now I know a person in particular, a man whose mother taught them to knit. He knits his own socks. It was just silly of me not to think of it, but I just never did. [Why is that?] I don't know. I probably thought they had no need for it. [Do

you think knitting is for girls?] I think for me it was. The boys were always off doing something else. I don't think there's anything wrong with a man learning to knit. I know a man that knits, several men that knit. They don't as much but they can do it. At one time, you depended on your mother or wife to knit.

We see here that Mrs. Budgell intuitively perceives boys as "always off doing something else." By discussing this, she sees that she has had this gender stereotype of how boys and girls should spend their time. Further, knitting is perceived as an activity that women do to care for their families.

The women I interviewed clearly viewed knitting as appropriate to — if not expected of — women: women should knit. Mrs. Morgan reflected this viewpoint when she described a neighbour:

Now I had a friend up the road, and she had 11 children, and she didn't knit a stitch. I said, ' "Well, how can you manage with their mitts and socks for the winter?" ' She said, ' "The way I looks at it, if I don't know how to do it I haven't got to do it." ' And you know neighbours and that around used to knit mitts and socks for her youngsters. So I could see her point.

Mrs. Morgan believes that her friend was not meeting the expectations the community has of a mother. The other women in the community felt compelled to ensure that the children had what they needed, handknit socks, and mitts. The mother has not used her time to supply her children with the items sanctioned by her peers.

Pocius (1979) discusses how, after Confederation, many Newfoundland women stopped doing many textile crafts, as they believed that by doing crafts they would be seen as "backwards." Store-bought items were seen as more desirable because you do not have to make them yourself. This attitude continues to some degree today. Mrs. Budgell reported: "I get women who say, 'I don't even want to knit' 'cause they say it's from the bay. You know I came from the bay and so what? I love to do it." There is the perception that one would be less sophisticated, less urban, if one knit. Women should have other things to do with their time and no need to knit. People can now easily drive to a town that has a department store to buy all they need. Knitting may have acquired negative connotations — not "modern" or "progressive" — but the women I interviewed turned it into a reaffirmation of how they identify themselves — as outport Newfoundland women.

This idea that women are the knitters was reiterated when the women talked about what can be described as the "elusive male knitter." Many mentioned a man in their community who knows how to knit and do other textile work. Like Mrs. Morgan, they tell of men who can knit their own socks. They would often qualify the male knitters like Mrs. Penney does: "I know there's one fellow here; he does all kinds of crochet work. My dear, *just like a woman*" (emphasis added). When men knit, their work is compared to an arbitrary standard of how well a woman could do the work.

Conclusion

This article demonstrates how in a changing society rural Newfoundland women use knitting to cope with change and create a sense of continuity. The women in this study use a traditional form of women's work to deal with contemporary societal shifts. In essence, we see maternal feminism exemplified — traditional women's work used as a buffer to instability. It is not surprising that knitting is used this way; it is an activity that has long been central to women's work in Newfoundland. Initially a part of women's contribution to the household, providing the clothing needed for men to work on the sea and in the woods, it is work that is no longer required but still done. With necessity removed, the meaning of knitting does not centre on the objects made; the activity takes on much more personal and social meanings.

First of all, knitting provides security against empty time in one's life and an appropriate way to fill it, whether the emptiness arises out of lack of employment opportunities, age, or other factors. For the participants in this research, knitting is also an expression of what it means to be female. Like the women in Leonard's (1994) study, knitting is seen as is part of their "natural" abilities. It is an activity reserved for women. If a man does decide to knit, his work is always judged on how it resembles a woman's knitting — "he knits as goods as a woman." Knitting is also a physical manifestation of the links between generations of Newfoundland women. It is a skill passed on from mother to daughter. And when the mother has passed away, the daughter remembers the times spent learning from her mother. It is a perpetuation of a line of knitters, providing continuity from one generation to the next that can act as a cushion against destabilizing social change.

Knitting permeates through the knitters' lives, often paramount in their thoughts when they are engaged in other activities. It is part of the knitters' identities, their relationships with family, and their understandings of what activities are parts of outport Newfoundland life. For the women in my study, handknitting exemplifies what it means to be a Newfoundland woman — one who uses her time wisely and appropriately, a skilled and caring woman. How well this fits the tenets of maternal feminism.

Notes
[1] I wish to thank the J.R. Smallwood Centre and the Dr. Anna C.

Templeton estate for their financial support of this research. I would also like to thank Dr. Doug House and Dr. Judith Adler for their supervision on this project.

[2] For a more detailed discussion on the methods used in this research, please see my MA thesis *Wool and needles in my casket: Knitting as habit among rural Newfoundland women (2000)*.

[3] The names of the participants have been changed to ensure anonymity and confidentiality. The title "Mrs." is used as it is what each of the participants used themselves, and the last names were chosen randomly as common Newfoundland names.

Eighty Year Old Woman Hauls Slabs of Wood

Marian Frances White

The fog has lifted
we can see out the bay
wanna go for a drive, just for an hour, I plea
a drive—after lunch—she scolds,
and me with no work done yet today

I point past the kitchen window
clothes hang uniformly on the line,
to the spotless floor,
to dinner plates washed, drip drying
I suppose we can, she concedes,
we'll take your father's truck

Up the Bay, we drive down back roads
and talk of lives gone, homes boarded up
lace curtains, threadbare in windows
chimneys missing bricks
bottomless boats in decaying heaps of hay

Further along mother eyes a mound of wood pallets
stacked beside an abandoned fish meal plant
they're good slabs for kindling, she says,
if Ted were with me we'd stop for a load
I suppose that's too much for you,
you with your good clothes on

This is her challenge

I gear down, turn around
Drive through the gate marked:
>   *Private Wharf:*
>   *No Unauthorized Vehicles*
>   *Beyond This Point*
Drive on through, she indicates with her finger
straight ahead, never mind the sign
no one will bother us
and she's right, no one does

The pallets are heavy after winter and two days rain
she lifts each with certainty
I follow her rhythm, avoid tripping and nails,

until the truck is filled to capacity
a long, knotted rope secures the load

Driving down the Bay road
she sees me glance in the mirror
you needn't worry about that load holdin'
Ted usually has it blocked up to the roof of the cab
you're lucky, we got away with a small load

Drive up the back lane, she suggests,
children will soon be out of school
I back the truck to the high point of land
beyond *his* driveway and *her* flower garden
the earth is soft, wheels dig in
we'll have to unload it from here, she says undaunted
an hour later, pleased with the effort, we go inside

Mother adds wood to the fire, boils the kettle, pours tea
if you weren't going back to town, she says
as she spreads bakeapple jam over homemade bread
I'd say to go for another load
but I know you got some poetry thing to attend
my, it's a fine day now, the sky is clearing
I hate to think of all that wood lying up there, rotting
....don't get me wrong,
I know a second load would be too much on you

This is her second challenge

We finish tea and the last heel of bread
get back in the cab
this time with proper clothes for the task
rubberized gloves and thick-soled boots
as tough as nails

A young woman walks her dog down the lane
stops to inquire about father in hospital
eighty looks good on you, she says
what are you doing with yourself these days
mother folds her feet to hide work boots,
nothing much, making lots of jam, she waves good-bye
I hope we don't meet her on the way back, she sputters,
I can hide the boots, but not a fine load of slabs

This time we load wood high to the level of the cab
knot the rope securely for the return ride
this time I drive pass the driveway and flower bed
find the rhythm to unload her slabs

I love doing this, she says,
this isn't work, it's pleasure
the fresh air, the exercise
why did you say you were going back to town?

A women's poetry reading
March 8th every year

Sure wood is a poem, she laughs,
you can call this one
eighty year old woman
hauls a load of wood *or*
she's as tough as nails, and be sure to say
there's a line in every slab

"Out of Date in a Good Many Respects": Newfoundland's Fight for Judicial Separation and Divorce in the 1940s[1]

Sara Flaherty

THE 1940S WAS A DECADE FULL OF CHANGE AND uncertainty in Newfoundland. Economic depression and government corruption led to the suspension of Responsible Government in 1934 and the appointment of a six man Commission Government, responsible for administering the affairs of the dominion. At the outset, no one knew how long the Commission would govern. The economic recovery was quicker than anticipated and largely precipitated by events beyond the control of the well-meaning commissioners. The poverty of the 1930s turned to prosperity in the 1940s as World War II gave the world-wide economy a shot in the arm. In Newfoundland, the war brought a period of unprecedented wages and employment to the recently bankrupt island. Britain leased territory in its colony to the governments of Canada and the United States. Bases were constructed at St. John, Argentia, and Stephenville where thousands of servicemen were to be trained. Many local men left the fishery, at least temporarily, to assist in building these bases and then upon completion many women found employment as domestics.

The histories of other nations show that social problems often increase at times of war, and in this way, Newfoundland was no exception. There were frequent reports of liaisons between local women and Canadian and American men, not all of whom were free to pursue such dalliances. The increase in illegitimacy rates and reports of adultery attracted the attention of the general public, military officials, religious leaders, and the state (Benoit, 1995; Neary, 1998). Increasingly, individuals whose husbands or wives had been unfaithful were appealing to the Commission Government to consider legal remedies such as judicial separation and divorce, both of which Newfoundland lacked. Such requests evoked a polite amount of sympathy from the commissioners, but they were unwilling to change existing policies, recognizing that they would face the wrath of the various denominations if they attempted to bring Newfoundland's marriage legislation in line with that of Britain.[2] As the war came to an end, the commissioners acknowledged that the demands for change had not gone away and that the passage of time would serve only to exacerbate the problem.

The purpose of this essay is to explore briefly the anomalous situation that developed in Newfoundland whereby married couples were unable to legally separate or divorce until the middle of the twentieth century. This essay will demonstrate that the desire for legislation to allow for separation and divorce was apparent for decades and that couples were willing to find ways to contravene the law. It will also focus on the decision handed down by Supreme Court Justice Brian Dunfield in the case of *Hounsell v Hounsell* in 1948. Dunfield's careful examination of Newfoundland's legal history revealed that the Newfoundland courts actually had the jurisdiction to grant judicial separations as early as the first Judicature Act in 1791. Despite a century and a half time lag in using this power, Dunfield saw it as available to Winnifred Hounsell and to other similarly compromised individuals.

Records from the late 18th century have indicated that the conservatism which would grow to dominate Newfoundland was not inherent. Willeen Keough's research into the court records at Ferryland turned up seven separation cases between 1750 and 1860. In all but one of those cases, wives initiated the proceedings. In addition to being granted the separations they sought, these women retained custody of the children and were awarded child support. One particular case interested Keough and legal historian, Christopher English. In January 1791, Thomas Hanahan was given 36 lashes and sent to jail for beating and attempting to suffocate his child. Thomas had also threatened to kill his wife when she intervened. It was noted at his trial that the plaintiff, Margaret Hanahan, wished to be separated from her husband. Thomas Hanahan was ordered to leave the district, and English and Keough noted that with the banishment, the court had, in effect, ordered a separation, if not a divorce. Keough's view was that the informal marital regime at the local level allowed Margaret to move into an informal family arrangement (Keough, 2001, 592). While Keough acknowledged that Newfoundland lacked jurisdiction on matrimonial causes until the late 1940s, these kinds of cases indicate that it had de facto jurisdiction long before that date.

Judicial separation, also known as *divorce a mensa et thoro*, literally means separation from bed and board. At the Council of Trent in 1563, the Roman Catholic Church proclaimed that a consummated marriage was indissoluble. It recognized, however, that one spouse may commit offences against the other that were so serious that the couple could no longer live together. *Divorce a mensa et thoro* was introduced, allowing spouses to separate under ecclesiastical law, while remaining husband and wife. Neither individual was free to marry again as long as the other was living. While legal separation became part of the ecclesiastical law of England, no statutory provisions on divorce were passed by the British Parliament, (Bissett-Johnson and Day, 1986, 2). Absolute divorce could only be obtained through a Private Act of Parliament until 1857. A costly venture, it was available to wealthy men and no women. Even when the issue of reforming divorce law came about in the mid-1850s, many members of the English Parliament were unwilling to make access available to both sexes, asserting that keeping divorce in the hands of men would protect women. They also argued that divorce was a way to punish an adulterous wife and to assure a man of the legitimacy of his off-spring (Shanley, 1989, 36). Further to this, they speculated that changes to divorce or matrimonial property legislation would undermine the authority of husbands and would contribute to the moral decline of English society, sentiments that were echoed by the established church, the Church of England, (Holcombe, 1983, 18). While English women were granted the right to seek divorce with the Matrimonial Causes Act of 1857, they remained in a subordinate position. Men needed to prove only adultery by their wives, but women had to prove adultery aggravated by cruelty or desertion. Divorce laws in England would not be equalized until 1923.[3]

Christopher English (1990) has noted the impracticality of transplanting British law intact to Newfoundland, calling the law that was established a unique amalgam, the result of local adaptations to the dictates of imperial policy tempered by the local realities of isolation, an inhospitable climate and a non-agricultural landscape (91). Jerry Bannister (1999), pointed out that the family did not become the dominant social unit in Newfoundland until the late eighteenth century, largely due to the fact that women made up less than a third of the total population.[4] As the female population grew, settlement was seen as being of a more permanent nature, and the courts were increasingly called upon to offer protection to women. It seems, however, that this protection came at the cost of limiting some of the freedoms women in Newfoundland had previously enjoyed. This view has been supported by Keough's research, as well as that of Trudi Johnson. Johnson's (1999) examination of matrimonial property law in Newfoundland has shown that women in 18th and 19th century Newfoundland maintained much more control over their property, retaining it in their name after marriage and passing it on in their wills to those they deemed deserving. It appears to have been a much more egalitarian system than in England where married women retained very few rights over property.

The family was not the dominant social unit until the late 18th century, nor was religion firmly rooted in Newfoundland until an even later period. John Fitzgerald (1997) has credited Bishop Fleming with firmly establishing the Roman Catholic Church as a force in Newfoundland religious, political, and temporal affairs in the 1830's. The absence of a strong religious element until this period may go a long way toward explaining the lenient attitude of the courts as exemplified in the Hanahan case. In her research on the Ferryland area, Keough noted the high incidence of informal and common law marriages. She wrote that while these unions were largely accepted by the local population they raised the ire of Thomas Ewer, the Roman Catholic priest at Ferryland (Keough, 2001, 570). By the 1830s, it was obvious that Newfoundland was a settled colony requiring the same institutions and regulations as other colonies within the empire. Perhaps with an increasing female population and a more thorough understanding of the cost of illegitimate children[5] and single mothers on the government, the marriage bond took on an even greater importance.

The economics of the fishery may have also played a factor. Sean Cadigan (1991) argued that as the fishery moved from a seasonal to a resident one, the family became the dominant unit of production. Women took on the role of the shore crew, responsible for the drying of fish on flakes. Cadigan demonstrated that while women were indispensable in the production of cod, they were still subject to patriarchal domination and were not recognized as formal partners in the trade. Cadigan's research indicated that this patriarchal domination occasionally took on a more physical form. Spousal abuse was fairly common and daughters were also not immune to the violence. He went on to argue that the basic struggle for survival required solidarity within the household, despite the threat of male violence (Cadigan, 1991, 221).

In the era before marriage was closely regulated, some separations were permitted by magistrates, however, as the population grew and Newfoundland became a settled colony, this changed. The implications must have been felt immediately, but for the purposes of this essay, we are going to look ahead to the first half of the 20th century. In that era the records of government offer a glimpse of the suffering, desperation and outrage that was felt by some of the Newfoundlanders who wished to disentangle themselves from violent and adulterous spouses. The correspondence showed a clear desire for reform on the part of the affected individuals and a reluctance to tamper with the laws by the commissioners who governed the colony. The fact that reform was close at hand but to come from a source other than the government has made the enquiry into this era that much more fascinating.

In 1916, Newfoundland's minister of justice Richard Squires noted the difficulty in interfering in the marital relationship. While a woman could go before a magistrate in the event of abuse by her husband, such a husband could make the home very unpleasant for her. Squires' words were in response to a request asking him to outline the rights and options available to an abused woman. Squires concluded that although unreasonable and unjust, when a woman marries a man she has to put up with what she is getting and that it is only under very exceptional circumstances, which involve cruelty, lack of support or abnormally unreasonably behaviour, that the courts will interfere with husband and wife (Squires to Bowring, 10 March, 1916). Squires was well versed in the inadequacies of the law to protect wives yet he accepted it as a matter of fact and encouraged the friend who wrote on the woman's behalf to do the same.

Lacking a legal remedy, some couples separated informally. Census records from the early 20th century feature individuals listed as separated from their spouse. One example would be Charles Gushue and his wife Lily, residents of Brigus. The 1921 census lists them as a married couple residing with their children in the southside of that town (1921 nominal census, 12). Fourteen years later, the couple was living apart and listed as divorced (1935 nominal census, 31). It seems however that the couple had separated without seeking the consent of the courts. In 1937, Charles Gushue again entered the public record, this time as the result of his death from a fall. At an enquiry into the accident, testimony taken from his stepbrother Robert Gushue indicated that Charles had resided with him for the past eleven years. Robert went on to say that Charles was married during that time but living apart from his family. The home Charles and Lily had shared belonged to her prior to their marriage and she continued to reside there (GN 5/3/B/1, Box 12, 41- 57). The 1945 census indicates that another divorced individual was living in Brigus, a woman by the name of Evelyn Morgan. A second reference to Mrs. Morgan and her marital status can be found in the records of the Newfoundland Department of Public Welfare in 1949. She was at that time seeking a pension after years of working as a domestic servant at Government House. The records noted that she had one daughter dependent on her for support and that Mrs. Morgan was separated from her husband (GN 37/1 O.A.P. 272, File 7961).

These individuals were not free to marry again. However, evidence indicates that some Newfoundlanders were able to divorce and remarry although these were exceptional cases in which private wealth enabled them to leave Newfoundland to take advantage of foreign divorce laws. In researching the issue of divorces by Newfoundland residents in 1944, the Commission Government found evidence of two cases. The first, from 1936, involved a man who obtained a divorce on the grounds of infidelity. His wife had left him for another man with whom she had moved to South Africa. Several years later, the husband also went there and obtained a divorce. The second case involved a member of the local elite who had married an American woman. After just a year or two of marriage, she returned to the United States, citing differences of temperament. She later obtained a divorce, although the Commission was unaware of the grounds. Her former husband later married again (GN 38, Box S 4-1-4, File 5). Correspondence from the Commission indicated that they were unsure if these individuals should be considered bigamous upon their return to Newfoundland.

The Commission Government was interested in these cases because they were facing a number of requests for divorces or the enactment of divorce legislation. During the early 1940s, several people wrote to the Commission wondering why Newfoundland was without the power to legally separate unhappy couples or allow them to divorce. These requests, received so closely together, indicate a growing desire for a review of the situation. It forced the Commission to evaluate its position and take a stand. Mrs. George W. B. Ayre made it clear that she was not seeking a response from the government so that she could obtain a divorce (GN 38, Box S 4-1-4, File 5). She simply wanted to know why Newfoundlanders should be forced to stay in unhappy marriages. The Dominions Secretary had informed her that a divorce law would be impractical in Newfoundland. Mrs. Ayre was unable to comprehend why this was the case and contacted the governor for an explanation. Divorce, she asserted, would be an act of mercy for some individuals. Why ruin their lives by keeping them joined to those they no longer cared for? She asked if this unwillingness to move with the times was due to the influence of the Roman Catholic Church, forcing Newfoundlanders to seek out foreign divorce laws was a disgrace to the country. In a second letter, she attacked the medical, legal, and religious leaders of the island for not doing more to force the issue. She was sure that they were aware of the hardship endured because of the absence of divorce legislation, yet they chose to remain silent. She had dire warnings that until the government took some progressive steps, Newfoundland would remain a backward island, incapable of governing itself.

A second woman who joined in the campaign was not as personally disinterested, stating outright that her appeal to Commission Government was directed by her misery as a wife. She wrote that she had been placed in a very difficult position, which only a divorce law could remedy. Correspondence between members of the Commission indicated that her husband was a known adulterer and although they were sympathetic towards her plight, they felt that the timing was not right to tackle the issue of divorce. Citing that the Commission Government was prohibited from passing legislation dealing with divorce without having first obtained the consent of the Secretary of State, they opted not to act (GN 38, Box S 4-1-4, File 5).

Within three years, the Commission Government was subjected to a renewed flurry of requests seeking divorce. By now the situation was considered more serious and the individuals worthy of sympathy and action. By 1942, over ten thousand Newfoundland men and women were serving overseas (Neary, 1988, 118). While they faced the terror of war, the lives some of them had left behind were compromised. In 1944, the Commission was contacted by a gunner in the Royal Artillery. Overseas since 1940, the man identified as Gunner Feltham, learned in December 1943 that his wife was living with an American serviceman and that she was pregnant. Several months later, she wrote to inform him that she had given birth to twins and wanted a divorce so that she could marry their father. Feltham contacted the Commission Government to determine if it would be possible to officially end their marriage (GN 13/1/B 105A, File 5). On the heels of that first request arrived another plea from an able seaman in the Royal Navy who had been informed of his wife's adultery. The Commission recognized that it would likely face a barrage of such requests.

Again, the Commission Government professed sympathy towards the plight of the two men overseas but remained reluctant to alter the status quo. In a confidential memorandum Lewis Emerson, commissioner for justice and defense, wrote that "it is my opinion that the Commission Government should not depart from the traditional policy on this subject." He felt certain that the Commission was not in a position to impose a divorce law, fearing the wrath of a large number of people of all denominations (GN 13/1/B 105A, File 5). He went on to assume that a very large portion of the population would oppose the introduction of any form of divorce law. Emerson felt that the issue would best be settled not by the Commission but when Representative or Responsible Government returned to Newfoundland. He went on to write that he could foresee the time approaching when some method for obtaining divorce may have to be provided, particularly in cases of infidelity.

Right up to March 1947, when the lawyer for a Scottish war bride wrote seeking a divorce for his client, the Commission refused to deviate from existing policy. In fact, all the institutions that played a key role in shaping Newfoundland's development as a colony seemed to favour keeping the marriage bond intact. The churches, the government and the legal community — the elites, the powerful — resisted any change in spite of a surge of cases which demonstrated the need for legislation to deal with marital discord. What were Newfoundlanders to do when marriages had irretrievably broken down?

Justice Brian Dunfield took the responsibility for this monumental decision off the shoulders of the Commission and placed it in the courts. In 1948, he was one of three justices of the Supreme Court of Newfoundland, a position he had held for nearly a decade. In that year, Dunfield was asked to consider whether the courts could hear cases involving judicial separation and maintenance. As Dunfield noted, this was the first time in living memory that the court had grappled with that issue head on. The case involved Winnifred Hounsell and her husband, Thomas. Mrs. Hounsell, the plaintiff, said that Thomas Hounsell had expelled her from their home and refused to give her the necessary maintenance for her support. Details about the events leading up to hearing are few as the only information readily available on the case is found in the Dunfield's 1997 *Newfoundland Law Reports (Hounsell v Hounsell)*.

Before the case could proceed, counsel for Mr. Hounsell argued that the Supreme Court of Newfoundland did not have the jurisdiction to award maintenance or alimony as it lacked the jurisdiction of the ecclesiastical courts of England. Eric Cook, K.C., contended that this power had resided with the ecclesiastical courts when the Newfoundland Supreme

Court received its charter in 1791. Cook went on to claim that even if the Court did have jurisdiction, the wife did not have to be awarded maintenance. She had the right to pledge her husband's credit for necessities, and that was all. Cook's arguments led to the request for a preliminary hearing before the Supreme Court on points of law.

It is Dunfield's judgement that we examine now. Dunfield saw Cook's issues as falling under four headings: Do we have the jurisdiction formerly held by the English ecclesiastical courts? If so, did these Courts award maintenance to wives out of their husband's estates? Could we have inherited this jurisdiction from any other sources of law? If we have the jurisdiction, from where did we get it — through statute or charter or by virtue of being a settled British colony and inheriting those laws (*Newfoundland Law Reports*, 312-313)? In answering these questions, Dunfield considered the first charters that referred to Newfoundland, the development of the fishing admiral system, the surrogate courts, and the Supreme Court. He clarified the powers that were arrived at through each development and statute. He found that Newfoundland, because it was a settled and not a conquered colony, inherited the laws of England. Dunfield noted that by 1791, there was in Newfoundland a small but established colony of definitely British character (*Newfoundland Law Reports*, 324). He disagreed with Eric Cook's argument that the ecclesiastical law of England did not necessarily pass to a settled colony. Dunfield believed that the Church Courts had jurisdiction over some things not expressly connected to church doctrine. These were matters of everyday concern, such as probate and marital causes, including nullity of marriage and *divorce a mensa et thoro*, with alimony. Dunfield argued that the law of common things administered by the ecclesiastical courts was part of the law of England, not the Church as such; and indeed after the assumption of the headship of the Church by the sovereign, under Henry VIII, even the governing law of the Church may be said to be the King's law (*Newfoundland Law Reports*, 331). To lend support to his assessment, Dunfield put forward the views of several English legal theorists, men who also felt that the common law embraced all the ancient and approved customs of England.

The common law was firmly established in Newfoundland with the Judicature Act of 1791 and its powers were further increased by the subsequent Acts of 1792, 1809 and 1824. An Ecclesiastical Courts Commission in England in 1932 moved the powers of matrimonial causes for separation and nullity of marriage away from the ecclesiastical courts, stating that those were purely questions of civil rights. This, however, had no effect on establishing where the Supreme Court stood on the issue in 1948. When Newfoundland was granted Representative Government in 1832, its own legislature became responsible for adopting the laws it wanted. Any changes to the ecclesiastical or common law of

England that Newfoundland had been vested with prior to 1832 were not automatically adopted. While the legislature followed the lead of Britain in most regards, it chose not to adopt any of the changes to the laws relating to separation or divorce, such as the Matrimonial Causes Act of 1857. Jurisdiction over these issues still lay with the same body that had that authority when Representative Government was granted. In 1832, that institution was the Supreme Court of Newfoundland.

The Judicature Act of 1791 gave Newfoundlanders a court with a very general jurisdiction. The 1792 Judicature Act expanded upon those powers and the authority to judge all cases of a civil or criminal nature, based on the laws of England at that time. Again, Dunfield pointed to the general nature of the Supreme Court powers. Although Dunfield saw jurisdiction over judicial separations as covered under the 1791 Act, he pointed to 1824 Act as giving the Supreme Court the means of dealing with all legal problems arising locally. The ability to hear cases of *divorce a mensa et thoro* was one power he saw the court as absolutely possessing (*Newfoundland Law Reports*, 329).

Dunfield held that cases involving judicial separation could be decided by the Supreme Court of Newfoundland. He continued his examination of the law to determine a wife's right to alimony following the granting of a separation. On this issue, Dunfield also ruled against Mr. Cook. Delving into precedent-setting cases in England and Canada, Dunfield stated that marriage is a contract and that a key principle of this contract is that a man support his wife. This obligation did not end with judicial separation (*Newfoundland Law Reports*, 338). In discussing that aspect of *Hounsell v Hounsell*, Dunfield mentioned the changes to the status of women that had taken place since Newfoundland won Representative Government in 1832. Dunfield asserted that husbands no longer had coercive powers over their wives and that the position of women in relation to the law needed to be refined on a number of points. Dunfield stoically concluded his examination of matrimonial issues by saying "our law is out of date in a good many respects" (*Newfoundland Law Reports*, 338).

Dunfield's careful analysis of Newfoundland legal history enabled him to clarify a particularly thorny area of family law in Newfoundland. By verifying that the Judicature Acts supplied the Supreme Court of Newfoundland with the power to rule on cases of judicial separation, Dunfield had marshalled in a new era in Newfoundland legal development. The court finally recognized that when marriages broke down they had the authority to separate couples, freeing them from having to reside together and affording women the right to maintenance. As this essay has shown, the movement for change had been afoot for some time, yet the government, churches, and legal community had maintained a unified front in the face of growing demands for reform. The fear of moral decline and radical social change were powerful forces that had led to some dramatic fence sitting, only broken by the intellectual rigour of Dunfield's judgement.

Even after the court's authority to hear cases for judicial separation had been affirmed, Newfoundland still lacked legislation allowing for divorce, due to the efforts of the various religious denominations, most notably the Roman Catholic Church. During the Confederation debates of 1948, the Catholic Church took a strong stand against union with Canada, fearful that it would bring a decline in morality and Christian values. The Catholic Church under Roche was very much aware that Newfoundland did not have the same level of illegitimacy or marital separations as its neighbours, the Maritime Provinces of Canada. It wanted it to stay that way. The Church fought hard to ensure that Newfoundland would not have to adopt divorce legislation in order to fit in with the rest of Canada. In the terms of union that were set down, Newfoundland secured the right to keep its denominational education system and as each of the provinces was responsible for its own policy on divorce, it did not have to alter its course dramatically. Yet, there was one major change. From 31 March, 1949, residents of Newfoundland would be able to secure divorce through an act of the Senate of Canada. This was the same method employed in Quebec. A difficult and time consuming process, it was undertaken 115 times in the years prior to the 1968 Divorce Act which provided one divorce law for the entire nation (Cullum and Baird, 1993, 151).

Again, we must return to the Supreme Court ambivalence regarding its authority to hear judicial separation cases. No conclusive answers can be offered as to why the court hesitated to assert its jurisdiction, only a review of speculations aired earlier. Was it due to the innate conservatism of the local churches? A by-product of the family-oriented fishery? Born of a desire by the elites to keep families together to preserve social order? Feminist historians have examined the relationship between matrimonial law and the subordination of women. Is it possible to explain the issue of judicial separation in those terms? Causation can seldom be pinned down to a single factor, particularly in cases where attitudes and responses are being considered. The safest conclusion to draw is that an amalgam of factors contributed to the longtime political and judicial failure of Newfoundland to exercise a jurisdiction over judicial separation, a juris-diction that had been at the discretion of the Supreme Court since 1791.

Archival Sources
British Statutes
(1791) 31 Geo. III, c. 29: *An Act for Establishing a Court of Civil Jurisdiction in the Island of Newfoundland for a Limited Time.*

(1792) 32 Geo. III, c. 46: *An Act for Establishing Courts of Judicature in the Island of Newfoundland and the Islands Adjacent.*

(1809) 49 Geo. III, c. 27: *An Act for Establishing Courts of Judicature in the Islands of Newfoundland and the Islands Adjacent; and for re-annexing part of the coast of Labrador and the Islands lying on the said coast to the Government of Newfoundland.*

(1824) 5 Geo. IV, c. 67: *An Act for the Better Administration of Justice in Newfoundland, and for other purposes.*

Government Records, Provincial Archives of Newfoundland and Labrador

GN 5/3/B/1. Department of Justice and Defense, Magisterial Court, Northern Circuit, Minutes.

GN 38/S/4/1/4. Department of Justice and Defense, Administrative Section.

GN 13/1/B. Department of Justice and Defense.

GN 37/1. Department of Public Welfare.

1921 Nominal Census, Port de Grave District, Community of Brigus.

1935 Nominal Census, Port de Grave District, Community of Brigus.

1945 Nominal Census, Port de Grave District, Community of Brigus.

Manuscript Collection

The Papers of Sir Richard Squires, Coll-250. Centre for Newfoundland Studies Archives, Memorial University of Newfoundland.

Notes

[1] This essay is based on research carried out for the completion of my Master of Arts degree in 2001 and 2002. Out of that same research I have co-authored a short essay with Christopher English entitled "What is to be Done for Failed Marriages?". It appeared in the Spring 2003 publication of *Newfoundland Studies*.

[2] The Commission had attempted to reform the denominational education system but its efforts were opposed by the churches. Separation and divorce would also arouse the hostility of the religious leaders and many of their followers.

[3] Dorothy M. Stetson noted that in the years following World War I Parliament adopted three statutes which reformed divorce and matrimonial property laws. The first of the three, the Matrimonial Causes Act of 1923, made the grounds for divorce the same for both men and women. For more on this please see *A Woman's Issue: The Politics of Family Law Reform in England.*

[4] According to the figures Bannister (1999) offered, women made up 15% of the population in 1750, 21% in 1775 and 38% in 1795. Please see p. 332 of *The Custom of the Country: Justice and the Colonial State in Eighteenth Century Newfoundland.*

[5] The first legislation relating to the maintenance of illegitimate children in Newfoundland was enacted in 1834. In 1865, the maintenance of illegitimate children, deserted wives and children, and aged children was incorporated into one act.

Mat

Mary Dalton

Some of them could go fast as the wind–
Nell now–and she was a great hand at it,
Scrolls and squares and dogs and roses
And one time a red punt on the water.
And then the scrubbing–
Dragging mats down to the cove in summer.
We beat them against the beach rocks,
And the salt water gave back their colour.
And come Christmas
Out we went mummering,
Out in the fools, happy as kings.
Mat rags sewed into our clothes.

Narrowing the Gaps? Gender, Employment and Incomes on the Bonavista Peninsula, Newfoundland, 1951-1996[1]

Peter Sinclair

A BOUT 1950, NEWFOUNDLAND'S BONAVISTA Peninsula featured a household fishing economy with a radical sexual division of
labour. Over the next 50 years, social transformation took place with the
incorporation of this area into an industrial capitalist economy and the
Canadian welfare state. In this paper, I explore the labour market experience of Bonavista women living in a local environment deeply penetrat-
ed by national and global developments. In particular, I argue that women
remained in a disadvantaged position in most respects, but their labour
force participation increased, becoming more like that of men. However,
there was no equivalent closing of the gap in incomes, except among the
young.

The paper explains different life outcomes of women and men in a way
that avoids implying excessive determination by the social structure.
However, it is impossible to account for what happened in Bonavista
without awareness of the impact of broad forces of development, including globalization, which defined limits for local action. Globalization is
essentially a process through which the activities of people everywhere
become more tightly interconnected and interdependent. Considering
only Newfoundland and its fisheries, it is clear that local people's lives
were thrown into crisis on several occasions in the late twentieth century
as a result of their dependence on depleted fish resources that were caught
by vessels from elsewhere in Canada and from many other countries (e.g.,
Hutchings and Myers, 1995; Sinclair, 1987).

Neis and Williams (1997, and this volume) have analysed the ecological and social issues in rural Newfoundland as local manifestations of
processes that were global in dimension. This paper is more finely
focussed on the Bonavista Peninsula. In taking a longer time period, it is
possible to identify some positive aspects for women and some compres-
sion of differences between the women of this rural periphery and those
of mainstream Canada.

Bonavista had always been part of an international economy built
around the export of fish, and people survived by combining what they
could purchase from selling fish with a substantial amount of subsistence
production. In that globalization focuses on inclusiveness and integration, it is not a new process; rather it is an older one that now operates at
a faster pace, more comprehensively and with greater visibility.
Capitalism has been a powerful force of globalization. In Bonavista, the
extension of capitalism to a position of dominance in the fishery radical-

ly changed life in important respects, which makes the area an excellent location to investigate processes of restructuring on the peripheries of contemporary capitalist societies. This is but one of many cases in which fish and local communities are both at risk (Otterstat and Symes, 1996).

Is there still space for local action? What difference does capitalist development make to the ways that people maintain themselves and their households? Do women benefit in the sense of participating more equally with men in the labour market and in social life more generally? I did not expect that economic inequality between women and men would vanish, but perhaps differences would be reduced as the expansion of wage labour in the fishery drew women from their homes into the labour market. Did the gaps separating men and women become narrower? Although a full analysis would cover the household division of labour and the informal sector, this paper is limited to paid employment, incomes and occupational segregation. Apart from secondary data, the analysis is based on two main sources from Memorial University's eco-research program. This study included a general social survey of all people 16 and older in 320 randomly selected households that produced 619 interviews. In addition to the survey, 45 detailed life history interviews were conducted separately in 1995 by the project's field researchers. I will use several of these interviews to complement the survey material.

Bonavista before Industrialization

Economic life on the Bonavista Peninsula in about 1950 was essentially non-industrial in form, based on household labour. Cod were fished with hand-lines, traps and baited hooks, depending on the season. Crews were normally composed of related men, often from the same household, while women frequently participated in processing fish on shore and laying them to dry on the flakes (wooden stages at the edge of the water) or rocks. Dried fish would then be sold to a local merchant, but rarely for cash prior to confederation. Early in the twentieth century, the fishery was more capital intensive in that local schooners sailed to Labrador where fish were taken close to shore, salted, and then returned to the island for final processing. By 1950, the Labrador fishery was almost exhausted, draggers had not yet appeared, and the fishery was more clearly a household activity than at any other time.

One of our respondents, reflecting on his youth in Keels in the 1930s, provides a useful description of the household fishery, which absorbed the men from childhood. The division of labour was quite flexible, being influenced by the household's age and sex composition in relation to the tasks of fishing and domestic production. "We was taken out of school when we was 12 year old and put in a boat. In those times, see, you had to." Jack worked on his father's boat, part of a crew of five that also included an uncle and neighbour. "I was hand-lining, see. And I never got no part of the cod trap at all. Whatever I caught myself I owns." However, Jack would buy what his mother asked him to at the store, once he had been paid. Normally his father had an account that was paid off in the Fall, when supplies ("winter scrub") would also be purchased. To reach that stage, the fish would have to be dried and that was a key part of his mother's labour.

After the drying process had been successfully completed, two or three times a year they would make the two hour boat trip to Bonavista town where his father dealt with the old firm of Templeman's. These were occasions for special treats from "old man Templeman's" bag of "knick-knacks." Little cash remained after the accounts were settled, and most people engaged in extensive subsistence production to supplement fish sales or exchanges. "Everyone reared their own animals, see, kill them in the Fall of the year." Horses, goats, pigs and sheep were kept. His family also maintained extensive gardens and all members shared in this work. Rabbits and other animals were hunted. With two brothers and four sisters, Jack found himself part of an extensive producing and consuming household in which he also had indoor work. For example, his mother would "… card the wool and I used to help her spin it on the big spinning wheel. I had to do all that. Mother and them would be out on the flake, right." Although this is only one case, it usefully prevents us from subscribing to a view of the sexual division of labour that is overly rigid. Some boundaries (e.g., the reservation of fish-catching for men) were rarely crossed, but practical adjustments to the "rules" for women and men did take place.

This said, the 1951 census indicates an extremely low proportion of women working for pay (only 8.1 percent of those 14 and over were employed) in contrast with men (64.7 percent employed). Three-quarters of the women were recorded as keeping house, but this should not be taken as evidence that they had no involvement in the *production* of food, clothes and fish. Such labour, as evidenced in the Keels household, was unpaid and unrecorded. It is likely that scarcely any married women were employed outside the household. This was to change.

How dominating were local men around the middle of the twentieth century? Some authors (e.g., Antler, 1981) claim that women in rural Newfoundland had equal power with men because they were so important for the economic survival of the household. Their tasks included processing dried cod, which was the principal source of goods or income, depending on time and place. Women were considered in control of their sphere of action. Their independence and importance were never greater than on the numerous occasions when husbands were away for weeks or months, fishing in Labrador or working in the woods. Others (e.g., Firestone, 1967) point out that men worked less hard, were served first by women, took the key economic decisions, inherited fishing places and property, and generally expected their women to move to their home village.

For the Bonavista area, Murray's (1979) study of her home village illustrates a male-centred view of the period in which women performed important labour, but with tight limits on what they could do. There was little questioning of what life could be; so mothers brought up their daughters to fill the same roles as themselves. Some men valued the contribution of women's labour, even to the point of recognizing it as "more than 50 percent." And no doubt there was variation in the degree to which both men and women attempted to impose their own wishes on the patterning of their lives. Yet, it was difficult for a woman to live any other way than as the domestic labourer for a fisher unless she was part of the small educated elite or was able to move away. Moving away to anything but domestic or unskilled labour was unlikely for people with minimal levels of education.

The limitations on women and also the possibility of resisting them are well illustrated by Susan. When Susan reflected on her life as a young married woman in the early 1940s, she recounted how angry she felt when, after living with her in-laws for two years, her husband and brother purchased a house that she had not even seen until she moved there. "So I kind of felt a bit rebellious about that, that they could do things like that. And I vowed and declared, first chance I get, I was going to be out it." Seven years after moving to the home she had never seen, Susan's husband moved to Toronto because the Labrador schooner fishery was providing a poor living. A few months later she followed with their children.

Although her story of powerlessness with respect to where she lived is evidence of male domination, it also shows its limits because this domination was not accepted as legitimate, and change was possible. It was certainly not easy to escape from the limitations of available occupations and marriage. Growing up, most people had no examples that suggested something different to them. Although Susan believed changes had indeed taken place, she described the women of her youth as being uninterested in taking any action, not even voting when that became possible. Why not? " 'Cause it didn't matter ... It was a man's world." It is no longer as difficult to be different as it was for Susan, although equality is not at hand.

Industrial Capitalism, the Fishery and Local Society

After 1950, industrial capitalism and the welfare state became the dominant formal economic forces (Ommer and Sinclair, 1999). At Confederation, the provincial government's push towards an industrial fishery coincided with the objectives of Canada's federal government. By the early 1970s, the dominant fisheries technology had shifted to mobile trawls, large steel draggers and factory processing of the more diversified frozen groundfish industry. At the same time, commercial forestry, and thus the prospects for winter wage-labour by inshore fishers, contracted.

Industrialization of the fisheries had several key effects. First, the fishery became more socially fragmented as outport people adapted in different ways to the pressures for change. A large number persisted with an inshore fishery aided directly by state income support and capital infusions, as well as indirectly by the paid labour of other household members in fish plants and service industries. Increasingly, however, small-scale fishers found it hard to survive when the federal government limited movement from one species to another and industrial technologies pressured the cod stocks.

Bonavista saw the first experiments in Newfoundland (in the early 1950s) with fisher-owned decked vessels, "longliners," that were capable of going well offshore and used more productive gear. With a labour force less than ten percent of the small boat sector, these vessels accounted for about one-third of the province's cod catch by the 1970s. On the Bonavista Peninsula, however, they were much less important than the deep-sea trawlers owned by Fishery Products (later FPI) that supplied Catalina's modern processing plant, the second largest on the island. Established in 1957, this plant for frozen groundfish became a year-round operation based on trawlers in 1973. Following the expansion of Canadian cod landings after extended jurisdiction (1977), the plant's capacity was doubled in 1980 (Porter, 1990, 208). In Bonavista, the old cold storage plant continued to function as an inshore-midshore seasonal cod plant, to which a crab processing line was added.

The emergence of wage-labour was the second major change in the fishery. This involved the substitution of wage labour for self-employment in fish catching and the transformation of women's seasonal unpaid labour in "making fish" into full-time, sometimes full-year employment in the plants. The Catalina plant functioned year-round and employed over 1,000 people after 1980. Apart from its significance for work experience, a critical consequence of wage-work was that outport people became increasingly dependent on cash income to combine with their well developed informal sector of subsistence production and inter-household cooperation. Another important impact was that it became more difficult to meet outport people's expectations in the late twentieth century by relying on past formal and informal economic practices. Education levels rose and mass media brought knowledge of the consumption patterns of mainland North America into most households, so that few were satisfied with the deprivations that earlier generations endured, even if some regretted a perceived decline in cooperation and sharing that characterized pre-industrial life. In an area where incomes were usually low, the desire for more consumer goods probably drew some women into wage labour when the opportunity arose. Thus industrial capitalism changed the culture as well as economic relationships in the old outports.

A useful way to appreciate the extent of change involved is to examine the structure of occupations. Table 1, which compares occupational distributions for men and women between 1961 and 1991 shows quite different profiles, not only in that women were much less engaged in primary production (fishing), but also in their predominance in routine white collar work (clerical, sales and service). The most significant change evident in this table is the major expansion of women's participation in paid work as a whole, which will be amplified below. Over time, it became more common for women to fill blue collar jobs, mostly in fish plants, where they approached men in number. The key point is that occupational gender-typing remained widespread, even more so than would be evident from either the census or the survey. For example, semi-structured interviews indicate that women and men, listed as engaged in processing, actually worked at different jobs in the fish plants, for the most part. The decline in the percentage of employed women in managerial and professional employment is somewhat misleading because it masks the growth in absolute numbers of women in these categories. Clearly total employment for women increased at a faster pace in the less prestigious occupations.

Table 1: Occupational Groups by Gender, Bonavista Bay-Trinity North, 1961-1991

	1961		1991	
Number	*Men*	*Women*	*Men*	Women
Managerial & admin.	392	206	635	375
Professional	332	232	930	1,135
Routine white collar	647	564	1,500	4,115
Primary	2,201	10	1,620	270
Blue Collar	3,368	41	5,360	1,560
Total	6,940	1,053	10,045	7,455
Percent of All Occupations				
Managerial & admin.	5.6	19.6	6.3	5.0
Professional	4.8	22.0	9.3	15.2
Routine white collar	9.3	53.6	14.9	55.2
Primary	31.7	0.9	16.1	3.6
Blue Collar	48.5	3.9	53.4	20.9

Participation in the Paid Labour Force Since 1950

We should expect that Bonavista-Trinity women would figure more prominently in the formal labour force as the labour market expanded around an industrial capitalist fishery. Indeed, Figure 1 captures the radical shift that took place all over Canada as women's labour force involvement rose close to that of men, which changed little over the 45 years from 1951 to 1996. The male-female difference was reduced by about three-quarters. Also noteworthy is the strong geographical dimension to labour force participation — both women and men changed at roughly similar rates so that Bonavista-Trinity consistently lagged Newfoundland which remained below Canada as a whole. (Figure 1)

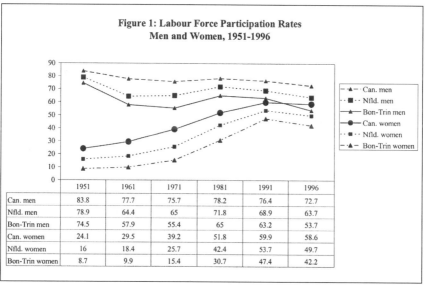

Figure 1: Labour Force Participation Rates
Men and Women, 1951-1996

	1951	1961	1971	1981	1991	1996
Can. men	83.8	77.7	75.7	78.2	76.4	72.7
Nfld. men	78.9	64.4	65	71.8	68.9	63.7
Bon-Trin men	74.5	57.9	55.4	65	63.2	53.7
Can. women	24.1	29.5	39.2	51.8	59.9	58.6
Nfld. women	16	18.4	25.7	42.4	53.7	49.7
Bon-Trin women	8.7	9.9	15.4	30.7	47.4	42.2

Unemployment rates tell a different story. After 1970, unemployment for Canadian men and women remained under 10 percent at the census dates, whereas sharp increases were evident in Newfoundland as a whole and in Bonavista-Trinity, where they peaked at just over 40 percent in 1991 (Census of Canada, various years). Thus, being in the labour force did not necessarily mean having a job for most of the year. Focusing more narrowly on the Bonavista Peninsula in the 1990s, the level of employment presents a bleak picture — opportunity for paid work was clearly limited compared with many other parts of the country. In 1996, the overall employment to population rate of 25.2 was less than half that for the rest of Canada. In part, this reflects the decline of fisheries employment after the moratorium of 1992. A low labour force participation rate of 43.7 was accompanied by an extremely high unemployment rate of 41.8 (Statistics Canada, no date). In the eco-research survey, conducted in the fall and early winter, when seasonal employment would normally drop away, only 21.5 percent of the sample was employed.

Were women or men more likely to be included among the employed minority? Overall, the project survey showed no significant difference, but some indication that men over 50 and women under 30 were more likely to report employment than women and men in the respective age groups. This evidence is consistent with the 1996 census, which provides labour force information for those under 25 in the same geographical area. Although only 16 percent of young women were employed, they still fared better than young men (12 percent employed). However, men 25 and over had a higher employment rate (33 percent) than women (22 percent). Thus, both sources suggest that young women were actually employed more often than young men, which is true also for Canada as a whole.

Women's higher participation in the paid labour force arose because of changes in the local economy that provided new opportunities, but it is partly a product of their own action to create better conditions by directly challenging barriers in the work place. Karen provides an excellent illustration. Middle aged and divorced at the time of the interview, Karen was an independent woman who had experienced a life of great emotional stress. Rather than be limited to packing, which was low status women's work in the Bonavista FPI plant, Karen asked to join the weighers. She established herself a reputation as highly efficient, able to do the work of two normal weighers. After becoming proficient on some new weighing equipment, she felt able to do anything a man could do. Breaking down the barrier in the fish plant had a physical component as well:

> Before, it was two separate rooms. The women were in one side and the men was in the other room, and everything would come through little holes in the wall, come through on conveyor belts. So we never had no contact with the men at all until someone finally decided 'this wall needs to be knocked down' and made more convenient. So, when the walls got knocked down all the inhibitions that the women had, you know, from the men, started to give way. So anyhow, the women didn't mind if they wore their jeans and wore the jackets like the men did. The women started givin' up the white bibs and wore the cap like the men. You know, the paper caps. So then they said, 'Well, maybe the women can do it.' And then I set it all off.

When the wall came down, interaction with men increased and women felt more comfortable behaving like the men, first in dress and later in work. Up to then, only men had been employed at cutting out the bones, but several women felt they could do this work just as well:

At that time I was already in the union and so I wanted to see if I could de-bone a fish like the men could. And so I went to the foreman and we had a little meeting about it. He said, 'Okay, if you want to try your hand at de-boning a fish, fine. Go ahead.' Then there was another couple of girls got brave and wanted to do it as well. So anyway, we went out there and they found that the women was just as fast, and even better boners than the men, because we didn't leave as many bones in the fish.

Once it was evident that women could do "men's" work, inequality in pay had to be sorted out as well. Initially, some women were allowed to work at de-boning, but received much less than the men, who were actually slower at the job. Faced with this pay equity challenge, management agreed to adjust rates provided that the women passed the official de-boning test. As many men had not taken the test, this led to wholesale testing for speed and quality.

And they had timing set out for how long it takes you to do this one particular pan of fish and everybody was given their pan of fish. I was going right to town ... the men, they didn't know what they were at. I mean they lost on their yield. They lost on their defaults that they were supposed to have, like bones. The time was up and fish was still left in their pan, not gettin' all done. And here am I, I've got mine all done. The girls got theirs done. Some of the men, yes. And anyway, now you had to get the quality control guys in. Now they had to be all checked, you know. Came back, I had the fastest time and the cleanest fish ... I was the fastest on the plant that did the timings, that did the test and they had no choice [but] to give us the rate of pay.

This appeared to be the end of any automatic or systematic segregation in the plant's manual labour force: "After that, women started trying their hand at other things. Whenever a job came up, man's job came up, women would apply for it and women would get it and prove to be just as good as the men." Karen's story is one full of determination and change, as this working class woman took action to reconstruct her own work role and contribute significantly to the experience of other women by opening up new possibilities.

Incomes

Although labour force participation was fairly evenly distributed among younger men and women, this does not mean that their incomes were equal. In this respect there has been much less progress for women than might be expected from rising labour market participation. By 1996 women's mean employment and total incomes were still only about 55 percent of what men received (Census of Canada, 1996). Women's total personal incomes were more heavily skewed towards the low end of the distribution (Figure 2).

In Bonavista town, the median income for women was $11,760, which

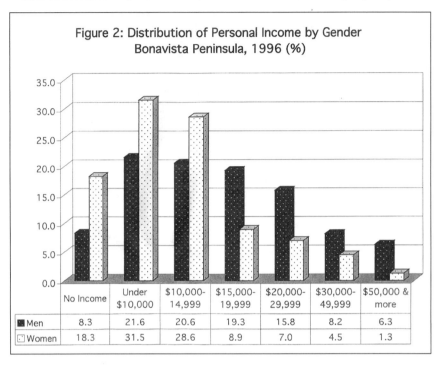

Figure 2: Distribution of Personal Income by Gender
Bonavista Peninsula, 1996 (%)

	No Income	Under $10,000	$10,000-14,999	$15,000-19,999	$20,000-29,999	$30,000-49,999	$50,000 & more
Men	8.3	21.6	20.6	19.3	15.8	8.2	6.3
Women	18.3	31.5	28.6	8.9	7.0	4.5	1.3

was 78.5 percent of that for men. Considering only income that is directly connected to employment, the position of women was clearly inferior (Table 2). Except in the town of Bonavista, full-year, full-time workers earned from 60 to 70 percent of men in the same labour market status. In comparison, women in Newfoundland were less unequal with respect to employment income. Part-year or part-time female workers, who were much more common than full-time workers in the study area, fared worse as they earned slightly less than half the income of their male counterparts (Table 2).

In our 1994 sample, women received on average 65 percent of both men's total and earned incomes. We might expect younger women to be less disadvantaged than older women simply because they are more likely to be in the labour force. Therefore, the relationship between income and gender was examined separately for three age groups (Table 3). There is evidence of a fairly strong relationship among older people for total income (i.e., women had significantly lower incomes than men in this age group). Among those between 30 and 50, the income differences for

Table 2: Persons with Employment Income by Employment Status and Gender, 1996						
Area	*Gender*	*Employment Status*				
		Full-year, Full-time		*Part-year or Part-time*		
		Number	*Average employment income*	*Number*	*Average employment income*	
Newfoundland	Men	56,850	$40,064	76,110	$15,153	
	Women	43,220	$26,353	65,520	$8,568	
	W. as % of M.	76.0	65.8	86.1	56.5	
Bonavista-Trinity North	Men	2,895	$36,876	6,615	$15,083	
	Women	2,200	$22,889	5,015	$7,305	
	W. as % of M.	76.0	62.1	75.8	48.4	
Bonavista town	Men	220	$28,088	625	$17,441	
	Women	200	$26,719	510	$8,560	
	W. as % of M.	90.9	95.1	81.6	49.1	

Source: Census of Canada 1996: <www.statcan.estat2.ca>

women and men were not significant, and there was no hint of a difference among those under 30. For employment incomes, the pattern was similar. It is possible that greater inequalities of income by gender will emerge if the young women unmarried in1994 should marry and reduce their labour force participation.

In Bonavista, if we look only at the 1990s, we see local people at a moment in a long process of constructing or structuring social life. However, the past enters the present as the source of taken-for-granted assumptions and because past actions impact on the distribution of resources today. Until recently, it is likely that most women's acceptance of their traditional role in the household made it difficult for them to participate equally with men. I have demonstrated that women's overall participation in the economy of the area became more like that of men, although it was certainly not the same; and women, the young excepted, remained well behind in terms of income.

I have also shown that the gendered character of economic relationships still leaves space for women actively to change their roles. The cases of Karen and Susan do not prove that the Bonavista-Trinity area was once patriarchal and is now close to being gender-neutral in economic life. Other women, following more conventional life paths, could have been

Table 3: Annual Total Income of Men and Women by Age,
Bonavista Peninsula, 1994

Age	Annual Personal Income	Percent of Gender		Chi-sq p.	eta
		Men	*Women*		
Under 30	<$1,000	30.4	26.7	0.831	0.01
(N=116)	$1,000-6,999 30.4	40.0	(NS)		
	$7,000-14,999	23.2	18.3		
	$15,000-24,999	8.9	6.7		
	$25,000 & over	7.1	8.3		
30-49	<$1,000	5.7	9.3	0.000	0.311
(N=185)	$1,000-6,999 4.5	22.7			
	$7,000-14,999	36.4	44.3		
	$15,000-24,999	31.8	15.5		
	$25,000 & over	21.6	8.2		
50 & over	<$1,000	1.5	15.9	0.000	0.422
(N=153)	$1,000-6,999 6.2	21.6			
	$7,000-14,999	50.8	52.3		
	$15,000-24,999	27.7	6.8		
	$25,000 & over	13.8	3.4		

selected from this research to give a different impression. The point I wish to stress is that some women could resist dominant ideas and take action that contributed to a new structuring. This is encouraging in a situation where global forces appear to threaten and even eliminate the possibility of local action that makes a difference. Women are narrowing the gaps.

Notes

[1] Lynn Downton in Catalina, Theresa Heath in Port Rexton, and Heather Squires in Bonavista conducted the field research and collected the life history interviews which provide an important base for this paper. Angela Watson assisted with the general social survey. This paper is part of the interdisciplinary research program, Sustainability in a Changing Cold Ocean Coastal Environment, funded by Environment Canada through Canada's three academic research councils. Thanks to Marilyn Porter, Peter Baehr and *Atlantis* reviewers for comments on earlier drafts.

A Brace of Rabbits

Robin McGrath

The ladies of the Women's Institute,
Knitting and tatting in hand,
Plan a pot-luck supper for the seniors
To celebrate Valentine's Day.
Slowly around the circle they go,
Volunteering a menu to suit
Loose dentures, aging palates, poor digestion:
Jello salads, tuna casserole, bread rolls,
A cloying army of cakes and desserts.

"I'll be coming in from the country," says one woman.
"What can I bring from *there*?"
"A brace of rabbits," answers another.
They all laugh, clicking their knitting needles,
And settle for tea bags and Carnation milk
Which she can buy at a convenience store.

But the pungent thought of a brace of rabbits
Hangs in the musty air of the Sunshine Club
And in their minds the women skin the pair,
Peeling the fur off over the rabbits' heads
Like pulling sweaters off their children,
And each knows the feel and smell
Of rabbit guts being drawn,
Kidneys fondly separated and set aside,
Limbs disjointed and severed for the pot,
The hot, rich smell of cooking meat,
Fir boughs and nights in the woods,
Before children and Jello salads
Subdued the wild hunger in their hearts.

The Wounded Gift: Meanings of Community Under TAGS

Sharon Taylor

IN THIS PAPER, I EXAMINE THE SOCIAL CONSTRUCTION of meanings of community, their origins, and how those meanings interact with each other to shape people's experiences within, and expectations of, their communities. The concept "community" is employed in everyday life, the media, academic work, government documents and elsewhere, however, little research has focused on the social construction of meanings of community, and the relationship between those meanings and the experience of community members. Here, I unravel multiple meanings of community used in the late 1990s by research participants from Comorra, an inshore fishing community on the Avalon Peninsula. I explore how the sudden closure in 1992 of a key industry, the northern cod fishery, upon which Comorra had depended for centuries, influenced research participants' sense of that community in the years following the closure.

The first government response to the 1992 Cod moratorium was a two-tiered assistance program called the Northern Cod Adjustment and Rehabilitation Program (NCARP), with higher funding for those who chose training outside the fishing industry. NCARP was terminated in May 1994 and replaced with The Atlantic Ground Fish Strategy (TAGS), a labour market adjustment program for individuals experiencing economic distress from the fisheries crisis. The main purpose of TAGS was to encourage recipients to find careers outside the fishery.

Fishing families in Comorra have a shared sense of community, but as would be expected with creative social actors with different life stories, their meanings of community also diverge somewhat. A central element of their shared meaning of community is a sense of history, a key part of which is a shared sense of past and present oppression. The construction of fishery people and their lives in documents of the federal government adjustment program differs from their own constructions, particularly as these relate to meanings of community. Looking at these documents from the standpoints of fishery people reveals their ideological character, a character the people of Comorra recognized, and saw as a continuation of the oppression that had always shaped their community. Their shared meanings of community also demonstrated continued resistance to "the wounded gift" as one person called TAGS. She said that TAGS was seen as "a gift to fishing communities from Canada, well if that's what they think, its one that is killing us."

Consistent with sociologist Dorothy Smith's line of fault argument (1987, 49-60), my research begins with the lives of local people and their experience of the everyday. For the people of Comorra, personal knowledge of daily events situates them on one side of a line of fault that separates them from the apparently neutral bureaucratic domain of a government where knowledge of the world is created with a view to administering it. Government ideologies inform policy intended to regulate and control events in local settings. As I demonstrate elsewhere (Taylor, 2001), management of the fishery crisis was informed by an ideology about the fishery that treated it as the domain of individuals, separate from community and family life. This ideology allowed government to design programs for individuals rather than families and communities. This gulf between policy and everyday experience contributes to the formation of a line of fault between what people know based on their everyday experiences and the government policies. My work shows that participants are aware of how their lives are ordered to support interests other than their own, and the implications of this for their daily life. In addition, lines of fault between experiences of community life and government policy are mediated by gender. We see the continued capacity of government to perpetuate the hierarchy of social privileges into, and through, crisis, despite challenges and acts of resistance.

Charting Lines of Fault: Meanings of Community Under TAGS

Individualism, as an ideology (Smith, 1990), assumes that individuals are able to shape their lives through will and determination, and that any failure to do so is personal failure (Briskin, 1990). My textual analysis of TAGS literature reveals that support for individual fishers and plant workers was equated with support for family and community. TAGS particularly emphasized individual fishers, neglecting their connection to other fishers, and to groups or individuals other than fishers within the community.

Community divisions in Comorra were partly a result of TAGS ideological frame of individualism. Interviews revealed the impact within people's every day lives of the ideology of individualism that organized TAGS program. Some people saw TAGS as having created tension and conflict in the community by privileging one group of individuals. One research participant, Colleen, quotes her mother, Sara as saying, "... it was like the plant workers were second class citizens ..."; Bridget, another participant, says, "... TAGS is only for those that got paid." Sara and Bridget both fought for benefits, and both were angry about lack of community support for their efforts. Rory, a male participant, felt TAGS isolated fishers from the rest of the community, and that TAGS bureaucrats blamed them for creating the crisis in the first place: "[N]ot totally, but mostly, the fishermen are blamed for what's happened." Rory encapsulates a belief of many that TAGS had a hidden agenda to "get rid of places like this," because the inshore fishery was not "going ahead anymore," and there would be "nobody here." Bridget also comments on the consequences of

TAGS' ideological frame of individualism when she speaks of words "spoken that tear people apart" and "getting everybody wore out." A female plant worker's observations show how TAGS contributed to inconsistencies and inequities, and created tensions in families and the community.

Some of it is the way they decides who gets what, and it doesn't seem to be consistent, like, you know, some people worked on the plant for a long time, and somebody else was on the boat for less time; so how come if they are using time as a guide, then the one is on TAGS and the other not? Then you got men who fished for years, and now they're told they don't make ... (qualify for benefits) ... because they didn't earn enough. You know, it got to get to people. I think we got to stick together and try to work it out.

Participants were fearful of fallout from TAGS, as well as people's response to TAGS. People of Comorra feared that because some had lied about their fishery participation in order to receive benefits, they themselves might be forced to lie or to expose the lies. This would lead to permanent rifts in the community. A female plant worker expressed this concern.

There is animosity brought about by TAGS, no question ... You don't have to look too far. It causes problems in families. Then some people have lied for other people about their fishing, you know. People knows about it so that creates tension for everybody because what if they start asking questions.

Others, like Bridget and Sara, felt unsupported by their community in their battle for benefits. Both plant workers and fishers who were denied benefits felt like this. One fisher said,

I wish we all got along better that's all. Not that there's fighting or scratching or anything, but, you know, people are distant ... afraid to speak out, afraid that they are the next one's going to lose TAGS. So the only one who wins out of this is government. Divide and conquer.

These comments show the rupture in social relations and support caused by TAGS' ideology of individualism. This rupture hampered participants' ability to collectively challenge TAGS, and left individuals vulnerable to the dictates of the ruling group. Other researchers have identified similar divisions, and comparable consequences for collective action, in other Newfoundland communities (Williams, 1996; Woodrow, 1996; Sinclair, Squires, Heath and Downton, 1999).

Many participants linked TAGS and its management to the federal government's unacknowledged resettlement agenda. Writer bell hooks (1990, 218) and others have affirmed this naming process as part of throwing off "the colonizer mentality." Participants showed in the interviews that they had examined TAGS, and uncovered its many impacts on their everyday life. They were all angry about TAGS, but with paradoxical results. While TAGS ideology of individualism divided people from one another, shared anger at covert resettlement policies brought people together, reinforcing the meaning of community shared among them. One woman commented,

> The community has been put through a lot with TAGS. No doubt about it. In some ways there have been a lot of changes. But you know in other ways they are the same. People still look out for each other. They still have good times together. We got through hard times here before. With the grace of God we'll get through this.

One male fisher exemplified resistance to the ideology of individualism inherent in TAGS when he emphasized differences between life in the community and in St. John's, strengthening the boundary of belonging to the community in opposition to outsiders, including the researcher.

> We are the working class here and wherever we went, that's who we are. There's no getting away from that. I got no problem with being working class here. We owns our own home, we got a few bills but we're not beholden to anybody. So we are pretty free here in a way. We are freer here than you crowd in St. John's, you got more things out there but you got more people with their hands in your wallets too. I know people got big expenses here but most of us got small boats here so you haven't got the banks after you the way they are after the fellers with the big boats. And things have changed, no doubt but then again you can always find somebody to give you a hand with the boat or whatever. I think we need one another now more than we are used to, we were getting away from that. But I think people are realizing that they have to get back to the kind of life our parents had.

While participants show an awareness of the ideology of individualism in TAGS, the interviews also revealed its paradoxical impact. This individualist ideology allowed some to participate, but excluded others, resulting in internal divisions.

TAGS and the Social Regulation and Oppression of Women and Men

Under TAGS, social regulation of women and men occurred, and participants grew to understand this as oppressive. TAGS was a sharply gendered program, however, regulating men and women in different ways (Taylor, 2001; Robbins, 1997; Williams, 1996). Social regulation contributed to the marginalization and economic vulnerability of women, while paradoxically raising consciousness about oppression among both men and women. My research documents participants' consciousness of this oppression and ongoing struggle with it.

Men and women of Comorra were familiar with social regulation of their lives by government and by the church. The struggle is both similar and different for men and women, and both are angry about oppression from external forces. Rory talks about how people in his community were regulated in the past, saying, "we had to have politicians from outside for years, from a wealthy family. Not anymore. We can speak for ourselves." He acknowledges that, "it just goes to show how people are led down the garden path by the powers that be ... we are not as bad as then ... we know the difference ... but it still happens." Paradoxically, while Rory is angry at TAGS for exacerbating conflict in his community, he also describes changes in his self-perception as a result of TAGS. He sees himself less as a "strong" man, accepting himself as a man who cries.

Men cried, some of them for the first time. You wouldn't supposed to cry ... I still don't as much as I want to ... that's the way it is. I know it's all right, but it's hard to do ... you are the man, you are supposed to be strong ... you also have feelings, a lot of people don't know how to cope with all we have been going through.

Bridget also sees being "strong" as essential to men's self-perception. She says,

Men have to think they're stronger ... that's the way, I suppose, they were taught ... the way of teaching and learning through the years ... they think they shouldn't cry.

Rory learned to deal with the hurt and uncertainty created in the community by the fishing crisis and TAGS, observing that some people tried to cope by living as if nothing had changed. He believes that being more conscious of feelings is difficult for men, but that it has been transformative for him. This was supported by other participants. Bridget understood that women and men coped differently with the situation.

"Women's struggles" were more complex and conflicted than those facing men. On the one hand, they wished to belong to their community and

252

fight for its survival. On the other, they saw TAGS upholding men's interests over their own. While Bridget, Colleen and Sara were angry about
the impact of TAGS on their community, they are also angry about their
differential treatment under TAGS. Bridget was aware of a profound rupture between TAGS policy and propaganda which claimed to support both
genders, and she also knew of the denial of women's historical attachment
to the fishery. She advocates collective action, but implies that action that
has already taken place has focused on taking care of the men. Frazer and
Lacey (1993) argue that social policy for communities generally supports
a gendered division of labour, sexual subordination and silencing of
women. While Bridget shows a sense of having a life (Cole, 1991, 40),
she is still angry about the situation of women. She sees herself and other
women as victims, particularly in relation to definitions of their work,

> TAGS is only for those that got paid. There's not much we can do
> about that now. Perhaps if we got up in arms about it in the begin-
> ning but we didn't. Most people figured we were lucky to get any-
> thing the way things were going. Fishing is like farming ... It's a fam-
> ily enterprise.

Bridget, like many participants, references the critical role of unpaid
work in historical meanings of everyday community life for both genders.
"Hard work" is empowering because it is equated with independence,
self-reliance and self-respect for themselves and each other. She notes,
"if you did something, like help on the wharf, something you could stand
back and be proud of, that's work, paid or not." Thus, hard work, paid or
unpaid, was established as a meaning of community for both women and
men. While Bridget did not create a gender division for most "hard"
work, she indicated that women carry additional burdens of work, including care for both children and men. Her own life shows that women are
burdened by the additional work of caregiving for their stressed men.
While not angry about this responsibility, Bridget acknowledges that it is
a gendered expectation, linked to the expectation that as a woman, she
should be more patient.

The exclusion of women's work under TAGS alienated women from the
creation and organization of everyday community life. Smith (1990)
argues alienation contributes to maintaining the ruling apparatus as long
as it remains unchallenged. Bridget understands the need to challenge the
practice of TAGS in relation to women's work. She sees the practice as
different from the organization of her experience of everyday community
life when she says "that's our way, not theirs." She is reluctant to challenge these practices at this point, however, as though to do so might
undermine the "we" of everyday community life. Bridget demonstrates a
sense of belonging to the community when she expresses anger about per-

ceptions of TAGS held by policy makers and people outside of the community. She identifies with TAGS recipients as a group, and is angry at the lack of understanding by the Canadian public and HRDC about recipients and their lives.

> The way the people across the country sees it, we don't want to work. We "got it made" with TAGS coming in and everybody home looking out the window. Well, we are hard working people here. People at HRD act like they are doing you a big favour, like people use to be with the welfare officer years ago. We worked hard for what we get. We work hard just to stay alive. Not many extras around here.

Other female participants in the study show the same conflicts as Bridget. They spoke of anger at their treatment under TAGS, arguing this is how government has consistently treated women in the fishery. They feel their contribution to the fishing industry has been overlooked historically, and that the ruling group perpetuates the perception that women's work in the fishing industry is somehow fraudulent. As one woman plant worker says,

> There is some people never fished a day in their life and gets top dollar. And some who fished from the time they were youngsters who can't get a cent. Plant workers don't count with this crowd. You have to be in a boat ... own it too. Well, there are others like myself ... left out in the cold. Well, ever since the moratorium started, it's been one thing after another ... no end in sight. People who used to get on best kind are at each other's throats ... so everybody is staying clear of each other. I probably got too big a mouth ... but I have to say what's on my mind. There's people what never went on the boats in their lives getting, and others who been in the fishery, maybe not on boats, and nobody cares.

While there was a general feeling of unfairness related to TAGS eligibility, most participants avoided addressing specifics. Concern about deepening community conflict, and people "being at each other's throats" may explain this reluctance. Many participants from Comorra faced significant social costs if they challenged the status quo. Their comments to me, as an interviewer asking about TAGS, were both shaped and hindered by this community silencing. As this comment shows, women's frustration with their oppression was most often directed at outsiders and institutions.

> You hardly sees a woman in the pictures they show, let alone at the fish ... not ladylike, I guess. And the men ... they shows the old clothes, so that's their idea of fishing. We're proud of the way we all kept it going, but they don't show that.

In my previous work, textual analysis of government documents shows that TAGS supported a patriarchal ideological frame by reinforcing the image of the fishery as a male domain, granting social power to men (Taylor, 2001). In contast, the women and men I interviewed spoke passionately about the contributions of women's work to their fishing industry and fishing community. Research showed, however, that women no longer engaged in many of the activities associated with being "good" women, selflessly making "sacrifices" for family and community in the past. While idealizing these historical images and seeing themselves as different, women interviewed saw gender roles as having changed, and themselves as moving away from this older regulation of their everyday lives. As one woman says, "... good women ... they looked after the old people, the priest, the church, everybody. But nobody wants to live like that today. That's not living. I just wish we got along better, that's all."

Female participants do seek to retain some characteristics of "good" women: they continue to support their community's church, quietly supervise and take care of vulnerable people in the community. They also see themselves as loyal to their husbands, families and communities. One woman pointed out that being good was still the central message for young girls: " 'Be a good girl'... the main thing is to look after your husband and children." Consequently, talking to a researcher such as myself, could be "not safe" for a "good" woman. Some women acknowledged distress over their treatment under TAGS, but did not want to speak if it would jeopardize their husband's eligibility for TAGS. This may be a realistic response to their family's economic vulnerability, rather than behaviour regulated by gendered social expectations. As one woman said, "This is not the place to talk about it ... there's too much going on."

Both women and men were concerned about the results of my research, who would be reading it, and the consequences for their community. This unease was related to people's uncertainty about who was making decisions about them. During my research, people often talked in their homes about the lack of public support for TAGS, and the probability that it would be cut back or closed. While men and women were anxious, women were more concerned because, as females, they received less support from TAGS, and were more likely to be dropped from the program. For women like Bridget and Sara, this emerged as a point of rupture because they could not trust the state to support them through the crisis. Smith (1987) argues that the ruling group depends upon the silence of those excluded from the creation of ruling relations. Fearing reprisals for self-expression, women consistently asked me to exclude their angry comments about their treatment under TAGS. They did not want to be identified as troublemakers by Human Resources and Development Canada (HRDC), as it could result in a future backlash. Women appear torn between perceived duty to family and community, and the need to speak of their own oppression.

Ironically, TAGS training appeared to be more acceptable for women than for men within the community. More women than men participated in training outside the fishing industry. Male participants, like Colleen's father, were stressed about returning to school and being "tied to a desk like a youngster." One man was "never much for school," and going back would "take some doing." Most men also resisted training because TAGS policy implied that male participants would have to abandon the fishing industry after training, meaning a significant loss of investment in boats and gear. Men were offered training to work in mines, which would be "the end of the fishery for them," but one male participant doing the geology course saw himself as having no choice.

> It's a good course. I like doing it. I don't want to leave my family no more than any other man but that's the way of it. You got bills to pay and youngsters to look after and TAGS is not going to last forever and that's a fact. And the fish is not looking good from the signs of it. So you do what got to be done.

Women, in contrast, took courses such as accounting and computer programming. These assisted the family enterprise, and did not jeopardize fishing licences since few women held them. Several female participants were taking courses at a private college in their community and were generally positive about them, feeling, as one female student says,

> Great to get up in the morning and get out of the house, away from everything. I was scared to death when we first went in but they had good people there, put you right at ease. We are all alike so that's good. But what a good time we had, all of us together. And I come home and did my homework with the children. They were some proud of me. I surprised myself at the marks I got.

Women also worried about succeeding in school, as others in the community took a keen interest in their progress. "They all wanted to know how you were doing. When you did okay you didn't mind but it was hard when you didn't do so well." The training undertaken by Sara strengthened her, and other female participants involved in training also felt empowered. This encouraged some to leave the community to find work.

Thus, people of Comorra showed that they were able to resist TAGS' agenda, and in fact, employ it to strengthen their sense of community. While TAGS served to maintain the invisibility of women's role in the fishery, it also provided an avenue of empowerment for women through training programs. Moreover, participants strengthened the boundaries of community and overcame divisions by directing their anger and frustration at TAGS, treating it as the opposition to community.

TAGS Neglect of Social Relations and Informal Support Systems

Shared meanings of community, such as support during crisis and shared experience of oppression and survival, are the basis for a sense of belonging to community. As their stories indicate, Colleen, Bridget and Rory move freely between the impact of the fisheries crisis and government response, and its impact on themselves, their families and their community. A point of rupture for each of them was the secrecy, deceit and conflict that TAGS policy promoted in the family and community relationships from which participants normally drew support. For example, the relationship between Colleen's parents was disrupted by the discrepancy in the policy between fishers and plant workers. Resulting tension in their home created a vacuum in the children's social lives. Colleen withdrew from her family and community, saying, "I just want to get away from here." For young people like Colleen, leaving home becomes less stressful than staying. Low expectations for their own and their families' futures in Comorra contributed to high levels of stress in homes and in the community in general. Canning notes this also contributes to both poverty and lower educational achievement for young people (1996, 40). Williams (1998), in her report on the impact of economic change on young people, suggests there are not enough counselling and treatment services for young people experiencing high levels of stress due to the economic and social changes in communities.

The out-migration of young people and families worries older people in particular; they are afraid that their social supports are being eroded. Historically, elders in their declining years counted on younger families to assist them in remaining in their homes and community. Elders indicate that out-migration will mean that many of them will have to move to senior citizens' facilities that are located away from their community. The community as a whole feels the loss of young people's energy, as workers lament the lack of available youth and young adults to help with jobs such as pulling up boats, babysitting or eldercare.

My research points to participants' awareness of TAGS contribution to meanings of community, meanings that are drawn from internal and external connections, including social support and social relations, history and cultural representation, and agency. Textual analysis of TAGS demonstrates that the designers of TAGS assumed those affected by the policy lacked insight. This negative view of human agency creates a rupture in everyday community life. People cannot participate fully in a process that assumes they are powerless and unaware of ruling relations.

Colleen, Bridget and Rory worried about their families and their community, showing compassion for those losing their traditional work and for those without real choices for the future. Colleen watched social supports she had known for most of childhood collapse around her, and the effect is apparent in her urgency to leave home. The needs and concerns

257

of young people such as Colleen were not addressed by TAGS. Participants were frustrated that support was available for their own training, but not for their children. As one male fisher said, "It's not fair. I can't be expected to be taking up space from the young fellow over there. He's just starting out and I'm about ready to give it up. What's the sense?" Neis (1998) agrees that TAGS ignored the impact of the fisheries crisis on the upcoming generation.

Some participants hope to heal the strain and conflict in the community. As a female plant worker and mother says, people of Comorra don't think "we can go back to what we was ... we got to move past where we are some way or another. They say time heals all things. We just have to wait." Others see this hope as a desire to reclaim the past. The past is often idealized, and present, everyday community life is coloured by the reflected prestige of this idealized past community life. According to both Cohen (1982) and Cole (1991), this idealization of a commonly experienced past is a powerful mechanism for creation and maintenance of a sense of community. Some participants believe that "ideal" or "traditional" everyday community life changed because TAGS broke down social relations in the community which had emerged from an ideal past. Other participants welcomed some of these changes, such as in the sacrificial role of women, and the involvement of male partners in homemaking and child care activities.

Comorra has a shared historical meaning as a fishing community. The TAGS objective of moving people out of the fishery was experienced as a rupture in this shared meaning. The fear of breaking connection to the past makes it difficult to envision a future, thus alienating a community from its own future. As a male fisher said, "... this is a changing time for the community. Perhaps the worst time in the history because we always had a future. Now we don't."

Lines of Fault, Resistance and Belonging

Research participants show that TAGS contributed to lines of fault in everyday community life. Less obvious are the links between these lines of fault, resistance to TAGS, and the resulting reinforcement of community meanings. While TAGS created lines of fault in the lives of participants, these fault lines also strengthened boundaries of belonging to community.

Belonging means more than "... merely having been born in a place" (Cohen, 1982, 21). In his work in Shetland, Cohen saw that people of Whalsay demonstrated "belonging" to their Island community by setting boundaries, including a public face or mask created for the outside world (1986, 13). Boundary symbolizes belonging in at least two ways: how a community is seen by outsiders, and how the community itself both experiences and gives internal meaning to community. Cohen (1986) argues that while boundaries "condense symbolically their bearers' social theories of similarity and difference," they are also inherently oppositional, so "almost any matter of perceived difference between a community and the outside world can be rendered symbolically as a resource for its boundary" (17). He says that community members use opposition from outside to enhance their boundaries and strengthen belonging, as, "members of a community can make virtually anything grist to the symbolic mill of cultural distance" (1986, 17). Cole (1991) demonstrates this use of opposition by showing how the *pescadores* in one Portugese community constructed a positive social identity through a "culture of opposition" to the *lavradores,* with whom they shared common origins and distant kinship, but not a common socioeconomic status. While Cohen's observations focus on men for the most part, and Cole's focus mainly on women, both show that external opposition strengthens belonging. They also recognize the agency of community members, for recognizing the activity and creativity of social agency is vital to understanding the power and complexity of the meanings assigned to everyday community life.

My research shows that community response to TAGS in Comorra follows a similar pattern to that suggested by both Cohen and Cole. TAGS was used by some participants to construct boundaries to strengthen their mask for outsiders, as well as to enhance internal boundaries. Both women and men described themselves as belonging to a collective of sufferers experiencing negative attitudes towards them as a TAGS-dependent community. This negative opposition was seen as external to the community as, "[the media] make it sound like we don't want to work, don't know how to work." Some women and men employed TAGS to construct gender relations within the community, and many struggled with ruptures in meanings of community created by the inherent contradictions of TAGS program. Almost all participants demonstrated a critical social analysis of their experience under TAGS, both by understanding the contradictions it created, and by strengthening boundaries. In this critical social analysis, participants made connections between their personal experiences and the social and material conditions engendering these experiences. This is what bell hooks calls "a critical understanding of the concrete material reality that lays the groundwork for personal experience" (1988, 108). Participants articulated their own theories about what was happening to them and their community. My research was not instrumental in their discernment of TAGS as constructed by the ruling group for their own advantage, or in the ways participants used TAGS to construct boundaries. Rather, my work reveals participants to be interpretive and communicative actors.

The Comorra study shows that meanings of community can be gendered as well. The gender analysis employed here allows for "critical standpoints," in which meanings of community emerge differently for women and for men. For example, while the female participants identified with the experiences of male oppression in relation to TAGS, the male participants generally did not address the collective experiences of women. However, the men were often concerned for individual women. This gender difference is also evident in the tendency for women to talk about taking, or failing to take, collective action, while men adopted a more individual sense of responsibility for lack of action against TAGS.

Some meanings of community were not gendered. For example, both women and men describe ruptures in meanings of community created by TAGS that reduced community cohesion. Considerable tension resulted from differential treatment in terms of benefits and eligibility under the TAGS program. This is consistent with the research of Sinclair, Downton, Heath and Squires (1999) in which people in Bonavista saw themselves as less cohesive and more individualistic than in the past. In the early days of the moratorium, Solberg (1997) found that people on the Bonavista Peninsula were satisfied with their communities, despite tensions related to the cod moratorium. Canning (1997) indicated that high levels of stress, social anxiety, and weakened social support were not present during the early years of the moratorium, but warned that adverse effects might increase over time.

In conclusion, I suggest that meanings of everyday community life in Comorra were linked to, and ruptured by, TAGS in many significant ways. In my research study, participants showed an awareness of a profound rupture between TAGS' stated objective of stabilizing community and their own experiences of TAGS in everyday community life. The established forms of resistance in everyday community life were mediated by the practices of TAGS which consistently threatened to assist people out of the fishery, and therefore, out of their communities. Women, in particular, were marginalized as a group, since TAGS ideology saw the fishery as primarily a male-dominated industry, and ignored gender difference in fisheries work, women's histories, and current needs and roles in everyday community life. Women's historical identity as "good" wives and mothers had served as a mechanism of social regulation within community life in the past. TAGS ideological practices reinforced this perception, and women have been further marginalized by TAGS policy. The consequent reality for these women is that the "good" behaviour expected of them has made it difficult to challenge TAGS policy, to some extent silencing them about their own marginalization. Other social realities include their families' and communities' economic dependency on TAGS, and the historical invisibility of women in the fishery. These realities make women very vulnerable. The combined realities of male privilege, economic hardship and dependency, all reinforced by TAGS, serve to disempower women.

No room existed within TAGS for discussing other responses to the crisis. Under TAGS, downsizing the fishery was normalized as the removal of people from the fishery, therefore threatening the existence of communities. All the while, TAGS policy acknowledged this possibility. Thus, TAGS ideology and practice created frustration and dissonance within community life. Paradoxically, however, my research shows participants used TAGS to strengthen their sense of belonging to community by relating to each other as a community of sufferers, misunderstood and oppressed by TAGS and its practices. In their conversations, the people of Comorra made visible the hidden agendas of TAGS and its practices in order to resist its influence over the future of their community. In doing so, they demonstrated their understanding of, and resistance to, the ordering of their lives by TAGS. They resisted TAGS in ways which strengthened community, such as choosing whether to participate in training programs, or using training programs to encourage children to leave the industry and their communities. In other words, people of Comorra demonstrated that they are indeed interpretive and communicators actors who daily resist and challenge the "wounded gift."

Green Pepper

Sue Sinclair

Glossy as a photograph, the bent
circumference catching
the light on its rim. Like a car's
dented fender, the owner desperate
to assess the damage, unable
to say, like the sun, *it can't
be helped.*

Conspicuous and irregular
all its life, born
with its eyes shut tight,
as though there really were a collision
it was trying to avoid. But it hasn't
happened yet—there is only
the impact of light: it has never

been in love, never drifted apart,
never fantasized about another
fragrant vegetable, never
been flattered, never been denied,
never wanted more than it has.
A life governed by absence:

the gleam of white
on its hollow body.

Guns and Lovers

(an excerpt from *Finishing School,* a novel in-progress)

Helen Fogwill Porter

IKNEW THINGS WERE TOO QUIET LATELY. Mike went up to Lorraine's the other night, supposed to be pickin up Jason to take him out to supper. Jason was really lookin forward to it, too. He loves the chips over to Ches's. Anyway, Mike walked in the door and told Lorraine she had to come back to him or he'd kill himself. Then he hauled a sawed-off shotgun out of a Woolworth's bag and pointed it at his head. Well, Jason started shoutin and Ashley began to screech. Eileen had sense enough to tell the two of em to run next door to Mrs. Bastow's. Jason didn't want to leave first but Mike told him to go on with Ashley, then said if Lorraine moved he was gonna pull the trigger. Mrs. Bastow called the police — what else could she do — and the next thing they were all there with their sirens and their riot gear. Some of the cops loves that kinda stuff, gives em a chance to show off and get their guns out. They had the loudspeakers blarin. The whole Circle knew what was goin on. After about half an hour Mike gave up, thank God, and went with the police. He spent the night in the lockup.

Lorraine told me after that she kept cool while Mike was there with the gun but after the cops took him she went right to pieces. How much more can that girl take? A policewoman stayed with her for a while. She was the one phoned me. When Lorraine calmed down a bit the constable went next door and told Mrs. Bastow to bring the youngsters home. Ashley was okay but Jason was right upset, askin where his father was and would he have to go to jail? He was mad with Lorraine, too, said she should never have left Mike. Poor kid, he's all mixed up.

As soon as I found out I went up to Lorraine's and the next thing I knew Heather was there too, and Fred. Heather heard about it on the radio and figured it was Mike. They didn't give out the name. And, of course, Fred got it all on the Police Band. Fred was really good with Jason, took him to the store and bought him hockey cards and chips. I hope he keeps in touch.

The next morning Mike had to appear in court. I was afraid Lorraine would drop the charges but she didn't. A couple of women from Kirby House went down to Atlantic Place with her. She told me after that Mike looked so pitiful she felt like givin in. Mom used to get like that with Dad. I don't think she ever took him to court, unless she did it while I was in the States. The judge put Mike under a bond not to go near Lorraine. A Salvation Army office — Major Hall — got all to do with him.

I don't know if the bond'll do any good or not. If Mike feels like goin up there again, a bond is not gonna stop him. Lorraine can't even enjoy her nice new house. If Mike wanted to hold on to her so much, why didn't he treat her better? He been makin her life hell for years and now he expects her to pity him. I'm glad she stuck to her guns. Only trouble is, Mike is the one with the guns. One of the policemen told Lorraine the gun he had with him that night wasn't even loaded.

He says he can't live without her. A funny way he got of showin it most of the time. He'll sook up to his mother now, I spose, and she'll baby him like she always does. "If Lorraine never left him this wouldn't of happened." I can hear her now.

Lorraine is pickin her head again. That's a habit she got. The doctor told her stress causes it. If that's the case, it's a wonder she haven't got her scalp picked away. Young Ashley does it, too, sometimes. Our family are full of habits. I always jiggles my foot when I'm sittin down and Patsy used to rub her skirt. When she was in school she rubbed her uniform skirt right through. Fred looks up at the ceiling all the time and moves stuff around on the table, pepper and salt shakers and that. And Shirley and Heather and I all count stairs — especially in places I've never been in before. I thought I was the only one did that until I mentioned it one day and the two of them told me they does it, too. Heather said sometimes she counts them in French, for a change. I can't remember enough French to do that.

There's a youngster with Tourette's Syndrome that comes in to work to get her hair cut. Poor thing, she finds it really hard to keep still. They get tics. If she feels like kicking a chair she got to do it. And you should hear the language out of her. She curses and swears and comes out with the dirtiest words you ever heard. Words you wouldn't even expect her to know. Her mother told me it's all part of the illness. She's not as bad as she used to be since she got on the right medication. She's a sweet-lookin youngster, smart too. Jean says most people with Tourette's are really intelligent. She picks up a lot in that student assistant job. She told me about a nun who got it.

Jean would love to be a teacher. She'd make a good one, too, but she haven't got the education for it. I'm sure she's just as good with the crowd over to I.J. as them two trained teachers over there. Jean got the real knack. Mom always said that about nurses, you either had the knack or you didn't. When I was in hospital for my hysterectomy there was some difference in the nurses on the floor. Some were stiff and strict, more interested in makin sure the rules were kept than anything else. There was an old woman in the room with me — Mrs. Summers, she was ninety-odd–and she was hardly eatin anything off her tray. If the tray was still there when her daughter came in, she'd feed her mother, and Mrs. Summers would eat a nice bit. One evening when the daughter was feedin her the head nurse came in, and didn't she get mad. "Mrs Summers is capable of feeding herself," she said in her high-falutin voice. "I was only trying to help," the daughter said. For sure the nurses got no time to do it; they're run off their feet. Think she'd be glad to get a bit of help.

One lovely little nursing assistant was on nights. Tammy, her name was. From the Battery. Even her smile would make you feel better. And when she gave you a backrub it seemed like she really wanted to do it. She'd always have a little chat, too. She was the same with everyone. Mrs. Summers loved her.

She died after, Mrs. Summers. I saw it in the paper. She was a lucky old woman, her family thought the world of her. When she was in the room with me was the first time she was ever in hospital; had all her children home. No wonder she felt strange. Her daughter and her sons and her grandchildren came in nearly every day. There was even a couple of great-grandchildren used to come sometimes.

I phoned Lorraine tonight and she said she haven't heard a peep out of Mike since. Course it's only been a few days. The policewoman who was up there that night rang yesterday to tell her they're arranging counseling for Jason, and for Ashley too if she wants to go. It's Jason Lorraine worries about the most.

The police force is some different than it used to be. When poor Mrs. Holwell over on Barter's Hill used to call the police they wouldn't even come half the time. And her husband tore the place apart every payday. I'll never forget that In Memoriam verse they put in the paper when she was dead a year. Talkin about her cleanin and shinin stuff in the House of the Lord. Poor soul needed a rest more than anything, where no one could get at her. Heather says the Constabulary got their consciousness raised now, especially since they got women in the force. First when they let women in, I thought they were crazy but most everything I hears about em is good.

I had a letter from Lloyd today, a note really. He don't write me very often, phones once in a while. I daresay he got a woman in Yellowknife. He did want me to go with him; I had my chance. I'm glad I didn't though. It's so far away. Why would I leave my family and move there? Mollie says I woulda gone if I really loved him but I don't know. I don't want to live anywhere except St. John's. A real townie, I guess. A trip now and then would be nice, especially this time of the year when it's so mausy here. I haven't been off the island since I came back from Iowa.

Jean asked me if I wanted to spend a weekend in their cabin up on the Witless Bay Line sometime. They goes up most every weekend, even wintertime. It was nice of her to ask me but I really wouldn't be bothered. I likes modern conveniences — the bathroom, the washer, the dryer, the heat. And I like to be able to go downtown when I feels like it, or into the Mall. Sometimes when I'm depressed, like I been a lot this winter between Tom and Marie and Lorraine and all the rest of it, I'll get ready and take the bus into the Avalon Mall or the Village. I'll always meet a few people I know, sometimes sit down with one of em for a snack. It's so nice and bright in there, and everything so clean. And it don't matter what the weather is like. One night I even went to a movie by myself. I never did that in the nighttime before in my life. I saw *Driving Miss Daisy*. One of the women into work told me it was good, and it was. I'd hate to be barred away up in the country. I never liked the country, anyhow. That's half the reason I hated Iowa so much; we were so far from anywhere. If we had lived in a city there, and if we were to ourselves, I probably never woulda come home.

I never felt the same about Lloyd as I did about Gary. And Lloyd didn't turn me on like Tom did. He was a good man, though, and he'd do anything for me. His first wife left him because he drank but he was all over that by the time I met him, went to an AA meeting every night. He still liked goin to clubs but he'd drink Pepsi or coffee. I met him up to the LeMarchant Club; that's mostly for people our age. He asked me to dance one night when I was there with Mollie; they were playing *Could I Have This Dance for the Rest of My Life?* Anne Murray. It wasn't long after he lost his son in a car accident in Saskatchewan. He didn't have much to do with his two boys after the divorce; they stayed with their mother. But on David's last trip home Lloyd and him went around the bay to see Lloyd's father. He was glad about that.

Funny, isn't it, how you're attracted to some men and not to others? There was nothing wrong with Lloyd and sex with him was okay. But never more than that. He could be kind of boring, too, never had much to talk about. I'd like to have him for a friend forever. But he wants more than that. I hope he got a nice woman for himself, to keep him warm up there in the north.

He wrote to tell me he ran into my cousin Alec in Yellowknife. Said he looks just like Fred. I didn't even know where Alec was to, haven't seen him since Aunt Pearl died. Lloyd wanted to come home for Christmas but it's so expensive, no cheap flights that time of the year. He's hopin to come the summer. Maybe he'll be here the same time as Gary. If this was a movie, I'd probably be bouncin back and forth from Tom to Lloyd to Gary. But this is real life.

Herb got his mind made up to move down to Glenbrook when he gets out of the Miller Centre. I didn't even know he had his application in. He musta got the social worker to fill it out for him. It depends on how soon he can get a bed, of course. They probably got a long waiting list. But at least he's reconciled to go. I thought you'd have to drag him out of that house. Praps he's finally accepted that Mom is gone and she won't be coming back.

Mollie's Uncle Roy is over to St. Clare's, in Palliative Care. She phoned yesterday to tell me; she knows I always thought the world of him. Poor old fella, maybe he was lyin on the couch for a reason. She wants me to go up to see him with her. I never been up there, and I got a real dread of the place. It must be awful to know that when you goes in there you're never gonna come out, except in a box, and that you'll just get worse and worse. Mollie says it's right homey up there, though, and they have visitors all the time. They don't get any treatments, just morphine and that to ease the pain. Herb wouldn't let Mom go up there. He looked after her home. Not every man would do that, or every woman either. No one ever told her she wouldn't get better. All the same, I'm sure she knew, even though she didn't say anything about it to us.

Does anyone ever get better in Palliative Care, I wonder? I never heard talk of it. I'd love to hear about someone who did. Those doctors are not always right. Anyway, I should really go up with Mollie. Uncle Roy was askin for me, she said. He got lung cancer, smoked all his life. That's probably what I'll end up with if I don't give up the cigarettes. I been smokin so long it probably wouldn't matter if I did give them up now. Bev's father is ninety-one and still smokin. Mom used to say you'd never go till your time was come. She never said it after she got sick, though.

Adolescent Sexual Decision-Making in Newfoundland and Labrador[1]

Annette Johns, Karene Tweedie and Kathy Watkins

IT IS WIDELY KNOWN THAT ADOLESCENTS ARE AT RISK for unplanned pregnancies, sexually transmitted infections, and relationship violence. We also know from clinical experience that adolescents are engaging in sexual activity at a much younger age. Yet, there has been limited inquiry into the knowledge, attitudes and behaviors of adolescents concerning sexual decision-making in Newfoundland and Labrador. In addition, there is currently no sexual health framework or strategy to guide sexual health programming and service delivery in this province. A greater understanding of how adolescents make decisions regarding their sexual health is needed if health care providers, educators and governments are to develop appropriate and effective programs, services and policies to meet the sexual health needs of adolescents as they grow and develop. This study was initiated to explore some of the influential factors affecting adolescent sexual decision-making and to give adolescents a voice in talking about these issues.

This research study was conducted with adolescent females and males in 2001-2002 in each of the six provincial health care regions, which included St. John's, Eastern, Central, Western, Grenfell and Labrador. The purpose of the study was to explore adolescent sexual decision-making and the factors that influence sexual decisions in Newfoundland and Labrador. Two further long-term goals were to create awareness and understanding of the sexual health needs of adolescents throughout the province, and to create an advocacy network for the action needed to meet those needs by exploring the experiences of adolescents.

A total of 86 grade 10 adolescents, 54 females and 32 males, participated in the study. Ten same-sex focus groups were conducted with the idea that such groups might encourage adolescent participants to speak more freely. The study participants were recruited through random selection of high schools in each health care region.

We also used a questionnaire to obtain data from professionals who work with adolescents including physicians, pharmacists, teachers, guidance counselors, social workers, clergy, and community health nurses. However, this article only presents the findings from the focus group discussions with the adolescents. These findings provide much needed evidence to further advocate for the development of an effective provincial strategy to promote informed and healthy adolescent sexual decision-making in Newfoundland and Labrador.

Reflections from the Voices of Adolescents

The findings were categorized into several subject areas, including the meanings of sexual activity, healthy and unhealthy sexual decision-making, perceptions of healthy and unhealthy relationships, and the factors influencing adolescent sexual decision-making. As well, adolescent perceptions of gender roles, attitudes towards lesbian, bisexual, gay and transgendered (LBGT) persons and access to sexual health information, services and support were explored.

Most of the adolescent males and females in the study defined sex primarily by the physical aspects, such as vaginal and anal sex, touching and masturbation. In several of the focus groups, adolescents reported that oral sex was not considered to be as significant an activity as sexual intercourse. One female commented, "Well, when you talk about oral sex, you don't mean it as sex. No one really takes it as that."

The majority of participants in our study regarded pregnancy as the number one risk of unprotected sexual intercourse, followed by sexually transmitted infections. One participant said, "the first thing that you think is, 'Oh, I'm not pregnant', then I wonder if I have any diseases." On the other hand, some of the males identified HIV as the "worst thing that could happen to a person." However, some of the adolescents did not perceive HIV as being a significant issue in their communities. They experienced a false sense of security in rural areas, believing that they were not at risk for contracting sexually transmitted infections. When asked if they were concerned about these infections, one female stated: "Not around here. Usually you know before, if you are going out with someone, they should tell you."

The majority of the adolescent participants stated that the media influenced their sexual decision-making and that over the past few years the media has promoted a more casual view of sex. As one participant stated:

Yeah, 'cause in all the teen shows, like Dawson's Creek, people are sleeping around all over the place. It gets portrayed as the normal thing to happen and that's what it is going to be like.

Peer pressure emerged as a significant factor in influencing adolescent sexual decision-making. In a heterosexual relationship, females were more likely to feel pressure from their partners to have sex and to concede to the pressure in order to maintain the relationship. Several participants reported a distinct "rite of passage" when entering high school that puts pressure on adolescents to become sexually active. Participants also reflected on the young age at which adolescents are beginning to engage in sexual activity, at times as young as 12 or 13 years.

The majority of adolescents in this study reported that the use of alcohol and/or drugs influenced sexual decision-making. However, there were varying opinions of the degree to which alcohol and/or drug use influenced sexual decision-making. One male participant referred to alcohol as "liquid confidence." In fact, many of the adolescents reported that they were still able to make informed/healthy sexual decisions while under the influence of alcohol.

Overall, participants indicated that negative attitudes towards lesbian, bisexual, gay and transgendered persons prevailed in their communities. Some felt that these attitudes stemmed from family values and experiences. One participant explained:

> When I was a little girl I saw my Mom and Dad together. I see my sister and a boyfriend. I never had the experience of people of the same sex having a relationship ... I grew up all my life thinking that a man should marry a woman.

The majority of the study participants reported that there was minimal education about LBGT issues in schools.

The majority of the adolescents also reported limited access to sexual health information, services and supports in their communities. Lack of trust and a perceived lack of confidentiality in health care professionals and educators further limited access to sexual health services. Friends were identified as the primary source of sexual health information because they were trusted, and adolescents felt comfortable talking to one another.

The findings from this study reflect many of the complex issues and factors that influence adolescent sexual decision-making. As we analyzed these findings, several themes emerged including adolescents' searching for trust and confidentiality, their fear of being judged, discrepant gender attitudes towards sex, their seeking of power and control, their taking risks but seeking security, and empowerment through communication.

Searching for Trust and Confidentiality

The adolescent females and males in the study expressed the need for trust and confidentiality when accessing sexual health information and services. They wanted to have trust in the professional they were seeing, and be assured of confidentiality. However, there was the perception among the majority of the adolescents that they could not trust teachers, guidance counselors, nurses, pharmacists or doctors in their communities to keep their personal information confidential. For example, participants made the following comments: "I don't trust my doctor" and "No! We wouldn't know if we could trust them [health care providers]."

Many participants indicated that they wouldn't seek out supportive services in their community fearing that their parents would find out they were contemplating sexual activity or were already sexually active. Many adolescents reported that this fear was even greater in rural communities where everyone knows everyone else. The lack of trust and perceived lack of confidentiality led to unhealthy decisions such as not using condoms for fear of being seen buying them, not using birth control, and not talking with a physician or counselor about their sexual health. As one participant stated:

> That's another thing. We're a small community. You don't want to go into the store. You go in and buy a condom at the drugstore, guaranteed that someone in there is going to know your parents, right?

Fear of their parents finding out was one of the main concerns for the majority of adolescents. As one female reported: "It makes you think twice 'cause you're just afraid that your parents are gonna find out." Another female stated:

> No, we really don't know the guidance counselor so we feel uncomfortable walking in to say, 'I would like to know more about sex.' Personally, I would feel uncomfortable doing it, especially around here where the guidance counselor knows your boyfriend and knows you. Maybe the guidance counselor is a good friend of my boyfriend's mother. You're afraid that, oh my God, if I think about sex she will go and tell his mother because where it is a small community, everyone talks to everybody.

Fear of Being Judged

Much of the data indicated that adolescents in the study were afraid of being judged negatively by their peers, parents, health care professionals, and residents of their community. The participants felt that living in a small community made them more susceptible to these judgments. The perceptions were that they would be judged as being sexually promiscuous if they were seen buying condoms, accessing the nurse in their community or seeing the guidance counselor in school. One female adolescent stated that there was a fear that professionals would judge them negatively:

> If I felt that I did something wrong, it is not that I wouldn't care what people thought, but I think she [guidance counselor] may think I'm a slut. I would be worried of what she thinks.

The adolescents were concerned that if they got pregnant or contracted a sexually transmitted infection they would be labeled as "bad" or "skanky."[2] Participants reported that the ideas of "stud" vs. "skanky" were real issues for them and they identified this as having an impact on decision-making. For example, the males reported they would feel uncomfortable asking their partners about previous sexual partners and risk of infections, out of fear that their female partners would feel offended and think they were being labeled as "slutty". As one male participant stated:

> If you ask a girl do she have anything, she'd definitely slap ya ... 'cause then she'd think that you thinks she got something.

There was also the fear that they didn't want to be seen as being different from their peers or be considered "losers." This was reflected in the comments made about LBGT persons as well. For example, one male participant indicated that he didn't want to be alone with someone who was gay for fear of being "hit on" and then being labeled as gay. This was more of an issue for the males than for the females.

Fear of judgment about sexual performance was also identified as an issue and many respondents felt that sessions on how to please your partner should be covered in sexual health education. Many of the males expressed that if they didn't perform well sexually, they would be made fun of by their friends and partner.

Discrepant Gender Attitudes Towards Sex

The adolescents indicated attitude discrepancies between males and females regarding sexual activity that influence their sexual decision-making. For example, the females emphasized the importance of the emotional aspects of a sexual relationship and reported "sex is more special for girls." They suggested females think more about the decision to become sexually active than males do, and that females reflect on the emotional aspects of the relationship and feelings of closeness with their partner. In contrast, males focused on the physical act of sex and were more concerned about sexual performance than were the females. One female stated:

> Guys just want to have sex. Girls will think about a lot more stuff. They think of the consequences. If I'm going to get pregnant, should I do this? I'd say, well I can get pregnant. Females want it more special than guys. Guys don't care if it is in the back seat of a truck. Sex is more special to girls.

The data indicated a double standard for males and females in relation to sexual activity. Both groups reported a stereotypical pattern of greater acceptance of male sexual activity and multiple partners; males were considered "studs" whereas females were perceived as "sluts" in the same circumstances. Even among their own peer groups, females view other females that have sex with multiple partners as "players" or "skanks."

Females in the study also felt they had greater responsibilities in sexual decision-making. These included ensuring that they don't get pregnant, protecting their reputation, and maintaining the relationship. One female stated:

It is more risky for us, like for pregnancy and stuff. It is not like a decision for us. The guys like to do it with whomever and whenever, but for us it is to do it when we are ready. What happens when something happens? They [males] get diseases too but pregnancy is the first thing that you think of.

When considering sexual decisions, the females placed emphasis on their reputation and how others viewed them. They felt that males did not have to protect their reputation nearly as much as females when faced with a sexual decision. When asked to explain their thoughts on teenage pregnancy, females indicated a fear of losing respect from their parents, teachers, and peers, particularly if they dropped out of school.

Male students also agreed that males and females view sexual relationships differently. One male stated:

They say for guys sex is always something special to do. Girls see it as a commitment. It is different for guys. Guys think sex is cool and you gotta do it.

The males reported that when making a sexual decision, females had a more difficult decision to make because of the risk of an unplanned pregnancy, as they would be the ones to "carry the baby" and live with this "burden." Males perceived that females wanted sex to be perfect with "romance and candles." Although the majority of males in this study stressed that love, honesty, trust and being with the person for a long period of time were important in terms of sexual decision-making, they felt that females had the final say in the decision to have sexual intercourse. According to one male participant, "They [girls] decide, guys give the pressure."

Seeking Power and Control

In striving for independence, adolescents are seeking power and control in their lives in general, and in this study, they indicated that they need power and control in their sexual decision-making. Acquiring power and control in making informed and healthy decisions is related to several factors, including education, access to information and services, self-esteem, confidence and a positive body image. These are some of the tools the adolescents require to develop power and control in their sexual decision-making.

The adolescent participants regarded self-esteem as a major factor influencing their sexual decision-making. The males reported that having high self-esteem was important in terms of making the right decision. One male stated:

> If you have lower self-esteem you'll probably do what your partner says. You regret making your decision. But with high self-esteem you say, 'No'. You probably feel you never made a mistake.

According to a female participant:

> If you don't have self-esteem ... you're more vulnerable to consent to sexual activity even when you don't want to. You don't think a lot of yourself so you think this is my only chance or something. No one will like me if I don't try to fit in.

The adolescent females and males recognized the importance of self-esteem and wanted it addressed in sexual health education. They also made many recommendations regarding sexual health education that reflected the idea that knowledge is power. They recommended that education should:

Begin earlier and continue throughout the school years. "The longer you are informed, the better decisions you make."

Be taught by someone well versed in the subject, who can provide current information, and is comfortable with the topic.

Be taught in mixed classes. One female participant stated: "I think it should always be together because guys need to know just as much about girls. The guy needs to know about birth control methods and what to be aware of and pregnancy too. They need to be informed just as much as we do and it should be together."

Address emotional aspects, relationship issues and the development of effective communication skills.

Be practical in its approach. One female remarked, "What would you do if you got into a situation that you thought you were pregnant? What would you do after that? What about the morning after pill? Go to what doctor? What do I ask? What do I do?"

Be receptive to their input. As one female participant stated, "It's for our benefit. That's why we should have something to say about it."

The study participants also want improved access to information and services, such as ready access to condoms, affordable birth control, confidential health services, and onsite resources in their schools. They felt it was important to have someone trustworthy at school with whom they could talk about sexual decision-making and indicated that guidance counselor services need to be promoted. As one female explained, "I know most of us know she [guidance counselor] can be trusted, but some people don't even have a clue of her name. If she was more out there it would help."

On one hand, the adolescents are seeking power and control through education, ready access to services, and improved self-esteem, but on the other, they struggle with feelings of powerlessness. In this study, participants reported that the media has an influence on participants' self-perception, self-esteem and body image. Although many of the adolescents challenged the messages about sex and portrayal of adolescents in the media, they felt they lacked the power to do anything about it.

They [media] make you feel like you are all alone. Like you're not good enough for anyone ... like it seems like you have to do it [sex] just to be in with the times ... 'Cause everybody's doing it, you have to do it to fit in.

They [media] ruins it for all of us. They make us have a bad rep [reputation]. They [parents] think we're all having sex and we're all doing drugs.

Peer pressure was also extremely influential. For example, participants stated,

But if you're insecure and like, your friends are having sex — you're like, Oh God, I have to do this to fit in ... if you care about what other people think you are going to give in to peer pressure every time.

One male indicated that some of his male peers viewed sex as a competitive game. He stated:

A group of guys will say, OK, you have sex with her, you get eight points in your name. They have points on a certain one. Like level threes [grade 12 students], if you have sex with a level three you're a five, but if you have sex with a grade nine you are a twenty points.

For adolescents, attaining power and control in their sexual decision-making can be a struggle involving opposing forces: some are internal and part of normal adolescent development; others are external, such as the media and peer pressure. These forces can be very influential. Overall, as adolescents strive for independence they have an increasing need for power and control.

Taking Risks But Seeking Security

Risk taking is a normal part of adolescent emotional and sexual development. The data in this study indicate that while youth take risks, they also need a sense of security in relation to sexual decision-making. Adolescents often engage in risky behaviors and have feelings of invincibility, but they need some reassurance of safety and security as well. Even though many of the youth in this study were aware of the risks and consequences associated with risk taking and sexual decision-making, they still felt that "nothing bad will happen" to them. One female stated:

> I think they [adolescents] think it can't happen to them and I think a lot of people around here think that way, like, 'Oh I can't get AIDS'. I'm not a loser.

A male participant stated:

> They [youth] really don't take time to find out the consequences. But mainly because they think they are young now and it won't happen to them. Yeah, they don't think much because it doesn't even come to their minds to start thinking of that. As soon as the button comes undone you don't have very much time to think.

Peer pressure has a significant influence on adolescent risk taking behavior. Many participants reported being pressured to have sex "to fit in" and sex was even considered a rite of passage for beginning high school. One female adolescent commented:

> From the grade 9 girls that came up here [high school] last year, I'd say maybe 85-90% lost their virginity to a level three guy, one you would never, ever expect … like the biggest goody-goodies ever, who would never … They just did it to fit in, just to come to high school.

Despite indulging in risk taking behavior, the adolescents indicated that they were seeking a sense of security in their sexual decision-making. This security is sought from a variety of sources, but friends, in particular, are regarded as providing security, trust and comfort for each other. Participants stated:

Your friend is gonna understand cause they know exactly what it is like." "Wise girls always go with their friends to ensure that no one harms or rapes them.

At our age, we go out drinking with a group of friends and nothing probably will happen because you are with people you know and we are close with. But once you get older, you are going to parties with a lot of people you don't know.

Unfortunately, there was sometimes evidence of a false sense of security. One group of female participants felt that you could not contract a sexually transmitted infection or HIV in a small, rural community because as one participant stated: "You know where they [males] grew up and their family." They believed their friends would tell them if the person they were dating had an infection.

Most of the study participants reported that they would like to be able to talk to their parents about sex but there were comfort issues. One participant stated:

It's not that I don't feel comfortable. It's just that they [parents] don't feel comfortable. If I had to go up and talk to them, they'd bawl and ground me.

As well, most of the females and males said they would like to see more parental involvement in sexual health education and have parents that are comfortable addressing this subject. One female adolescent suggested that there should be a course for adolescents and parents to help them communicate better about sexual health and teenage issues. She stated:

Well, if they had people who could come and explain to them in health groups and sessions with parents and teenagers, it might give our parents a clearer idea of what teenagers are going through.

The adolescents desire accurate information in order to make informed sexual decisions and have the knowledge and resources to deal with consequences such as pregnancy or infection. As one female commented: "experiment when you have the information." The participants also want educators and health care professionals to help facilitate their sexual decision-making needs, and they want the security of knowing that confidentiality will be maintained. These adolescents are seeking a sense of security in their sexual decision-making, but are not always finding it.

Empowerment Through Communication
The adolescents identified open and effective communication as a com-

ponent of a healthy relationship and perceived it as empowering. For example, adolescents were empowered in their decision-making by having good communication with their partner regarding sexual issues such as using birth control, practicing safer sex and pleasing each other. Two participants said:

> You sit down and talk to each other about how you feel about each other. That's healthy. You need to communicate.

> Make sure the two people engaging in the sexual act understands each other, each person's wants, needs, desires and things like that and being comfortable with the person so you can say 'no.'

Effective communication skills can also enable adolescents to access information and services. Also, one female participant stressed the need for educators to use proper terminology when providing sex education. She explained:

> Instead of saying penis, they [educators] will say 'you know when a guy and a girl get together right.' To a grade 5 [student], they don't know. They think they're talking about a boy who is their friend and they get confused.

Another participant identified the need for sexual health information to be communicated in a comprehensive manner to facilitate informed sexual decision-making. One participant stated:

> They [adolescents] are going to suffer the consequences 'cause they're going to find out the hard way. 'Cause they're going to find out one way or another, so it's just as well that somebody tell them.

Interactions with health professionals and educators may be enhanced through effective communication, and may produce improved outcomes in terms of informed sexual decision-making. This, in turn, may help facilitate trust and allay concerns about a lack of confidentiality, and it may also facilitate the development of confidence and healthy self-esteem.

More Similarities Than Differences: Conclusions

This chapter has focused on the findings from our focus group discussions with adolescent females and males across Newfoundland and Labrador. Although the survey findings from the professionals have not been discussed here, we did compare them with the focus group discussions. The results were interesting and rather surprising, as we expected many divergent viewpoints with perhaps some similarities. The comparisons yielded many more similarities than differences, however. The professionals and adolescents shared similar ideas and concerns about the factors influencing adolescent sexual decision-making such as drug and alcohol use, peer pressure, self-esteem, education, access to services, and the media. They also identified similar recommendations regarding adolescent sexual health education and service planning and delivery. This included the need for improved access to sexual health information and services, improvements in the school curriculum to enhance sexual health education, educating adolescents at an earlier age, peer education, professional education, coordinated sexual health services, and parental involvement.

On the question of access to sex education and services, the professionals and adolescents diverged in opinion. The survey data indicated most professionals believed adolescents have ready access to sex education and services, whereas the majority of adolescents reported that, for them, such access was very limited. Adolescents want access to services that are confidential, non-judgmental and youth friendly. In addition, because these programs are for them, they would also like to have input into how they are developed and implemented.

It is encouraging that, according to the survey, professionals that work with adolescents are "on the same wavelength" in discussions around the factors influencing adolescent sexual decision-making and what is needed to address these issues. This suggests that improving education and services to more effectively address adolescent sexual decision-making might be readily accomplished.

In conclusion, parents, educators, health care professionals, community workers, and government must work together in collaboration with adolescents to ensure that education and service provision meets the sexual health needs of adolescents in Newfoundland and Labrador.

Notes

[1] The authors would like to thank Gail Lush, formerly with the Women's Health Network Newfoundland and Labrador (WHNNL), who was involved in the research study. This was a joint project between Planned Parenthood Newfoundland and Labrador and the WHNNL. The authors also gratefully acknowledge the financial contribution provided by Status of Women Canada.

This article is based on the research report entitled "Adolescent Sexual Decision-Making in Newfoundland and Labrador." The full report can be found on-line at www.nlsexualhealthcentre.org or by contacting the Newfoundland and Labrador Sexual Health Centre.

[2] The term skanky is a variation of the word slut, and is a common word used by adolescents to signify that a person is sexually promiscuous.

Fire Water

Christine (Kisitinis) Poker

I am an Innu
I have
Everything that anyone wants
Trees and wind
Healthy air to breathe
Dawn and sunset
The soft voices
Of the animals that live with us
The country is my life

Everything changed when I saw
My father grab my mother by the hair
Call her a name I did not know was hers
Wear a face he did not have in the morning
Show hatred and anger in his eyes

I looked at his lips
Saw spit drip from his mouth
Knew then he had been drinking
The fire water

Bars, Booze and Sexual Violence: Young St. John's Women Speak[1]

Donna Malone
With Support from:
Victim Services, Department of Justice
The Violence Prevention Initiative, Government of NL

VIOLENCE AFFECTS WOMEN OF ALL AGES and backgrounds in Newfoundland and Labrador. Sexual violence happens in our homes, in our workplaces and in our communities. Bars have traditionally had the reputation as gathering places where people go to have a few drinks, socialize, lose their inhibitions and, perhaps, "meet someone". However, bars can be dangerous places, particularly for women.

Women's groups and anti-violence activists have worked hard to discredit social acceptance of the myth that alcohol is the reason for men's violence against women. While alcohol may exacerbate a violent situation, the underlying cause of violence is the abuse of power and control, usually by those who are most powerful in our society. Very seldom has this discussion of alcohol and violence focused on bars. It is important to examine the environment of bars in St. John's as some have suggested they are becoming increasingly sexualized, with seemingly few controls in place to ensure the safety of their patrons. This environment poses serious safety concerns for women. Campaigns against date rape drugs have drawn attention to the issue of women's safety in bars. These campaigns have emphasized women's responsibility in taking precautions against those who may want to slip something in their drink. But women's education alone will not solve the problem of sexual violence in bars. Bars profit from society's acceptance of women's inequality through the condoning of sexual violence and therefore have an important role to play.

In this first stage of the *Bars, Booze and Sexual Violence* project, we explored young women's experiences in downtown St. John's bars, their perceptions or experience of sexual violence, and their opinions of the environment of downtown bars. Second, we examined the degree to which the specific nature of the St. John's bar environment increases the risk of women experiencing sexual violence.[2]

People and Places

The bars most frequented by participants include, but are not limited to, Bender's, Turkey Joe's, Junctions, McMurdo's, Merlin's, Rob Roy, The Cornerstone, Sam Shades, Brewskies, Peddler's, Lottie's, The Sundance, Club Etomik, and the Breezeway. Others mentioned less often were O'Reilly's, The Edge, Calio's, and Peter Easton's Pub. A common thread among most of these bars is their target market of young people. Participants reported "going downtown" between five times weekly and once monthly. Several noted that they go downtown more frequently in the summer time, in particular to those bars with outside patios. While a few women reported going downtown alone, most indicated they go with one friend or a group of friends.

Why "Go Downtown?"

Some participants in the study spoke of how they go downtown to socialize, relax from a busy week, and enjoy the music. Other women said they go downtown to drink or to meet new people, either friends or a potential new romantic interest.

A lot of girls go to pick up guys. Six months ago I was going downtown to get drunk and find myself a man ... and sure enough I found myself a man.

I love going, I love being able to talk to everybody that I can run into that I know, I love the opportunity to be able to dress up in stuff that I can't normally wear during the week. I am also single and it is always going to be something that is there. I go and look at guys who are also dressed up for one day of the week and say 'Hey'.

The Down Side of Downtown

However, what should be a positive experience for women is sometimes unpleasant, challenging and disturbing. By far the greatest number of responses centered on the chaotic and dirty physical environment, the unpleasant atmosphere of violence and excessive drinking and the highly sexualized environment built upon our society's and men's sexist attitudes towards women.

Some women said they feel they have the right to express their sexuality in bars and that men have the same right. However, they described the dominant bar environment as unhealthy. They spoke of male bar patrons' sexual objectification of them and of other women. Men of all ages are perpetrators of sexual harassment, however, young male bonding and competition for the attention of women commonly plays out as overly aggressive, violent behaviour. Alcohol is used by men as an instrument of control over women and as an excuse to be explicitly sexist in their language and actions.

The way guys act when they are loaded ... they have no respect ... they think women are objects and they can go do anything they want.

They go down there to pick up girls ... if they buy you drinks and get you drunk they think they can take you home, a lot of them do.

Two participants pointed out that not all men downtown have similar sexist attitudes towards women.

I met my boyfriend on George Street and I have been going out with him on and off for 5 years.

Women can be just as bad as guys. Some girls go looking for relationships, some guys go looking for relationships, some girls go looking for sex, some guys go looking for sex.

However, bars intentionally create a sexualized environment, and some participants suggested this contributes to bar patrons engaging in sex inside the bars and near bar premises.

They even have the Rhino Room at Merlin's. There is like one big dance floor and coffee tables and a couch here, couch there, and the bar and then you go up 4 stairs and there is like 2 beds and 2 pool tables. Two Queen size beds with leopard prints all over the wall, and mirrors and that. People go up there to make out for sure. There is a bouncer there ... you wouldn't go up there to have sex or anything. You go up there to sit and be quiet and talk, and, like stroke hair.

Outside in the alleys. By Junctions, you can go behind and go to the Zone. Oh, that alley is ridiculous. Somebody told me he walked by and some missus was giving head to some guy. How degrading, man, imagine a bunch of people see you getting out with a guy.

This sexualized environment also dictates what is socially acceptable dress for women in St. John's bars.

I always feel like I have to dress up just so. If I go to the Breezeway I can wear jeans and sneakers and I feel like myself and I feel comfortable but if you go downtown you gotta dress up and you're always thinking, like 'oh, god they are looking at me'.

The atmosphere is sexual. You wouldn't go downtown in splash pants and sneakers and a sweatshirt, even though that is what you are most comfortable in. You wouldn't wear your Sunday church clothes. You got a downtown wardrobe. Tank tops and tight pants, makeup and your hair is done. I always dress up. You are probably more comfy in something else, but you wear that anyway.

Sexual Contests

Women in our study group said that sexual contests are used by bar owners to lure patrons to the establishments. Designed to draw heterosexual men to their bars, these contests include the wet t-shirt contest, funnel contest, sexiest underwear contest, blind date contest, and various others. In a radio interview, a local female bar manager said there is stiff competition among bars to attract and keep clients and that these contests are "creative" ways to do this. Deb offered an overview of these contests, and Lara shared her experience of participating in a wet t-shirt contest.

Then there is all this lovely, wet t-shirt, get the stick in the whole game. Who can get a condom on quickest, fake orgasm, put a condom on the toilet plunger. Vibrator races. They have a lot of contests, the worse one I find is the wet t-shirt contest ... A lot more gets wet than your t-shirt and a lot more comes off than your t-shirt. Women have stripped to nothing or underwear. And the whole thing happens after bar specials from 9 to 11 with the contest at 12 or 1 when everybody is wasted. A friend of mine, we got loaded and she got into it and we had to get her out of it. The bar specials started at 9 and it was a ladies' night. So women got cheaper drinks. I was wasted too, but I am just not into that. It was terrible. It was terrible. This bar had some pretty big prizes.

I was in the wet t-shirt contest, I won a bar tab. I was definitely glad I did once, but it is not something I would do twice. The experience was weird. I made a friend out of it. The girl who got up with me ... it was a definite experience and it was good, but, like, the crowd, they are crazy ... I wasn't doing it because I wanted to attract some guy in the corner or offend that group over there, it was just like a dare thing, and its just more of a memory, like you're gonna kick yourself after.

On the other hand, Elaine stopped going to one of her favourite bar because of the wet t-shirt contest.

That drove me out of Junctions on Wednesday nights, 'cause me and my friends were hard core Wednesday nighters. I went away for 2 weeks, it's Wednesday night, we go, and all of a sudden there are naked girls, and there are a lot of skeety guys. I couldn't see anything cause the guys were literally hanging off the rafters up on the deck ... And then my friend said, 'oh my god, she is taking her shirt off.' The same girl who had won the week before was back — returning champion and she decided she was going to make it easier to disrobe. What she had done was make a slit in the top of her shirt so she didn't have to work at ripping it of ... it was easier to rip off. Because what they do at Junctions is provide you with a shirt because they are so considerate. They are like 'Oh, don't tear your own shirt, tear ours.' You didn't plan on it, and now you are drunk, we've got a t-shirt for you.

The women were asked whether or not they felt women were pressured into participating in the contests. Some women said male bar patrons and staff expect and coerce women to participate.

You get into this thing, you are really drunk and the crowd is going wild. They are egging you on, they are saying all these things. You go a bit further than you would sober.

However, other women in our study pointed out that entering the contest is a woman's choice.

Most of the time you sign up for it, you sign the little sheet, you have the choice of whether you do it or not. But most people want to do it for the bar tab. Twenty-five dollars, that's 25 beer. To show your boobs.

Young people with limited incomes have few choices about which bars they go to. Particular bars target the young and/or student market.

It is very, very cheap. You can't afford to pay $4 bucks a beer. You could be drinking for free.

A few participants in the study felt that there was no harm in such sexualized contests, pointing to "wet boxer shorts" contests for men. But Joan argued that wet boxer shorts contests did not parallel wet t-shirt contests for women.

What I don't think is fair, is that when they have the wet t-shirt contest they have the guys up there in boxers contest. And that is supposed to be the equivalent. I think it is absolutely ridiculous, how is a guy up there with boxer shorts down to his knees equivalent to a woman with her breasts flying in the wind? Wet and visible for everyone. It was in response to women's concerns about it … it is not equivalent, it is not even close.

Many women felt the contests create a dangerous environment for women downtown. Some said these contests help to perpetuate negative societal attitudes about women in general.

They are trying to draw people in. And then once you are in there, the clientele it attracts, the males, they hit on you more. Like they have a right to hit on you. Females provided for you. Or they feel like they have a right. If you are wearing a short skirt. Or if you are in the wet t-shirt contest. Females are provided for them. Automatically you are fair game. You were up there and stripped, you are coming home with me and strip. That is the mentality. That is what I think these things cause, these sexual contests.

This exploitation can have negative repercussions for women both inside and outside of bars.

Obviously the men don't make the women get up there and do it, they do it on their own for personal reasons or for the tab. So then you have all these guys who are like, excited. They think this is great. So they leave the bar and say me and my friend are walking down the road and we have no idea — we weren't even at the same bar, we weren't anywhere near it — so all of sudden they are all fired up from looking at naked women. So even though we were not there, we had no part of it, it's almost like, we are kind of victims of what they have done. I'm not saying it's the women's fault or men's fault, but it the whole societal thing. When they leave that bar, what is in their heads about what they are allowed to do.

Dawn talked insightfully about how bar owners capitalize on the fact that wet t-shirt contests are a "cultural phenomenon" in our society.

I think there is this whole aura or mystique type thing built around wet t-shirts. For lack of a better term, it is a cultural phenomenon. You don't hear of guys getting their boxers wet. It's not equivalent in that way. But you have this whole build-up to women and wet t-shirts. Well we all know what happens when girls are in college and they get wet t-shirts, it's a big party. Girls have a little more sense. Guys are more like 'Tits, yah!' They just freak out when there is a set of tits in their face. They lose their minds. It's about what society is saying is acceptable. I mean look at TV, look at videos. Women are totally exploited in my opinion in pop culture big time. Society is saying this is OK. When it comes down to what happens in the bars, it is just a much bigger problem. Things like date rape.

Sexual Violence and Bars

We asked a broad question about whether the women in the study, or other women they knew, felt unsafe in a situation arising in a bar context. This broad question prompted many stories of women's experiences of

286

sexual violence, including intimidation, sexual harassment, and sexual assault within and in the close environment of bars.

> I was broke up with my boyfriend about 2 weeks and we went downtown to Brewskies and I was dancin' with this fella and he cut between both of us and said 'That's my girlfriend', and I was like 'No, now, we are broke up, so, come on.' And he was there tellin' all his friends, 'Don't go near her, don't go near her that's my girlfriend, that's my girlfriend.' And not one fella would come and dance with me. I had to like, go get a bouncer to tell him to stay away from me. The fellas were afraid of what would happen. He is really a jealous type, like, you don't understand, he is really nasty for that.

Several women described incidents of verbal insults, pressure to remove clothing, and having men follow them.

> We were in the bathroom at the Battery Hotel. Georgie had this camera and me and two other girls was gonna strip. I was shaking, I was scared, I said 'No, no'. So I just I hauled down my pants, showed them my thong and my tattoo. I was so loaded, I was embarrassed when I did it and I will never ever do it again, because when I seen myself do it I was like 'Oh, my god.' That's not me, I'm not like that. And Georgie went around showing everybody. It was on video, and I would never do that again.

> Me and my friend went down ... and there were these 2 guys chasing us around. They weren't doing anything, they weren't touching us or anything, but everywhere we went they were there. And they would kind of like corner us and they'd talk and we'd be like, well we have to go to the bathroom and we would run away. It is hard to do what you want when you have a guy or two guys trailing behind you all the time. We weren't interested in them, it is not like we were trying to hook up with them. So that is annoying, when you got someone bugging you.

In keeping with statistics on sexual assault, many of the incidents women described were perpetrated by men they knew, or with whom they were acquainted.

> I was hanging out with someone I've known for almost a year. And he asked if I wanted to back to his house and have some drinks ... And he and his buddy tried to rape me in his room ... and I called a cab.

It is also more difficult to deal with the betrayal of trust when someone you know well carries out the assault.

I think a lot of people think that if they are with people they know that they are more safe. The way Newfoundland is you know so many people and a lot of us grew up in little tiny places where everybody is friends since you were kids. I heard about this girl, and she was really, really drunk and this guy she has known since she was a little girl said, 'Well I'll take you home cause you are really drunk.' So he took her home. She passed out along the way when they were walking down the street and he dragged her and put her in the truck and went to take her home. She started to come to, what brought her to was the sound of a horn. When she came to she realized it was her forehead up against the horn making the noise and he was behind her sexually assaulting her.

I would go out drinking with myself and like eight guys in a field. Yah, that is a smart move, in a field, in the woods, at someone's house. I didn't care. I thought, nothing would happen to me, these are my friends. Until the night I woke up and one of my best friend's hands was up my shirt.

Lisa pointed out how women and men are differently affected by sexual violence.

It's more unsafe for women ... I went down one night, it was the end of term. I had been stressed out all week, tired, not eating enough, I didn't even have that much to drink. I got completely tanked to the point where I got kicked out of the bar. All my friends, they had all left me, I was there by myself. I had blackouts that night. I still don't remember everything that happened. Anyone, some guy who is out on the prowl, looking for someone vulnerable, he could have picked me up, took me home and did what ever he wanted to me and I never would have known.

Participants described many incidents of sexual harassment by older men, of their fathers' generation. This harassment was particularly disturbing for some. While sexual attention from young men is sometimes flattering to some young women, attention from older men is threatening.

I had a guy follow me one time. He followed me right around the bar, shaking my hand saying 'Hi, what's your name ... he was like 50 and he was buying me drinks ... I didn't know it was him buying me drinks, I thought it was a young guy. He said 'I bought you all those

288

drinks and you won't even talk to me.'

Yah, older men come up to the bar and probably put their hand on your ass and pretend that they don't mean it ... 'Oh, excuse me', they say. Mostly it's older men who do that, brush up against you.

I don't like drunk old men, I find I have a phobia of old people downtown anyway. They kind of freak me out. It's like if someone my dad's age is hitting on me, that is pretty gross.

Women's Response to Sexual Violence

Our participants described a number of ways in which they deal with the sexual violence they experience downtown. Some women feel that to go downtown means to expect, and accept, the "boys will be boys" adage, while also developing resilience to violence through finely tuned strategies and communication skills. Other women denounced the abuse by men and emphasized the societal barriers to naming and confronting sexual violence in bars. So some women confront their harassers, yelling "Get your hands off me!," while others deflect unwanted male attention by lying, telling them they are lesbians or saying, "Look, my boyfriend is over there."

Some women felt it was a woman's responsibility to keep herself safe by dressing "appropriately" downtown. They felt that if a woman wears revealing clothing, she is responsible for unwanted sexual attention and perhaps assault, suggesting that the problem lies in the women's poor decision-making rather than in men's attitudes.

They will have a lot of guys wanting to take them home, but they are not gonna get respect by dressing like that.

However, some of the younger women expressed anger and loathing — "lateral hostility" — for other women whose actions they perceived to attract negative male attention. Their hostile use of words like "slut" and "whore" can be seen as an act of self-contempt, striving to distance these women from themselves and improve their own status vis-a-vis men on the bar scene.

I know a girl, she is after taking at least 10-15 guys home with her. Friday, Saturday night she will end up taking 2 cab loads of people back to her house, and ends up at one of their houses. She is a big whore, basically. She remembers it, but she will say she don't but she will. She will say bits and pieces of it. She laughs about it, she's lost a lot of friends over it. They don't want to hang around with her because of how she gets on downtown. She makes me look like a big slut downtown and I am not a slut downtown, I am not a slut. I don't want to be associated with her.

While such "lateral hostility" against other young women serves to perpetuate the sexual subordination of women and limit the development of understanding and solidarity among them, there are other, more positive opinions about the link between dress and sexuality.

> There are certain messages that certain people don't really get, like just because I have a condom, doesn't mean I want to have sex, just because I am wearing a tight shirt, doesn't mean ... when I go out, I wear clothes that are tight because I feel comfortable, I like how I look in those things. And guys can look all they want, as long as they don't feel that just because I am wearing that, that they have the right to have a hand session with it.

A key problem for our participants was how to communicate when dealing with sexual advances from men. Some expressed difficulty in saying "no" in the face of potential danger, and frustration with men who do not take "no" for an answer, saying,

> He is being flattering and a lot of girls don't know how to get out of it ... Once you start talking to him it is really difficult to all of a sudden put up a guard.

Self-awareness and assertiveness are crucial communication skills for women downtown.

> You know what the assumption is gonna be if you are dressed a certain way. You gotta know how to be un-approached ... if someone comes up to you and you know initially that you don't want them near you. You should be able to know right away how to get out of that situation. 'Cause there are a lot of people who don't know how to get out of it. Awareness. Self-awareness. How to give off signals, maybe not so much verbal, appropriate signals that you don't want to be near this person. Assertiveness. How to go about doing that. Be educated.

Dealing with unwanted sexual advances is much more difficult for very young women, as they don't yet "know the ropes" and are lacking in skills required to navigate downtown culture. Three women said they didn't confront unwanted sexual advances out of fear of reprisal, that men "... might flip out and go after you ..." or that "... they would try something on me ..."

Ellen and Brenda shared strategies that they and their friends have developed to help each other be safe — including a "big buddy system."

> We cab it together home, whoever is last out of the cab has to call the others as soon as they get in. We try to stay awake waiting for the phone call. If one if us goes missing, everyone is out looking. One of my friends disappeared one night and we all got pretty freaked out. We did find her, she was OK.

Barriers to Reporting Sexual Violence in Bars

Generally speaking, less than 1 in 7 women report violent incidents to the police (CRIAW website, 2005). That rate may be lower in the highly sexualized, violent context of bars, especially where women perceive that it was "their fault" that they were assaulted — because she flirted with the guy, or he was drunk and didn't know what he was doing. There is also high tolerance for sexual harassment and violence in bars, which forces women to accept behaviour that they would otherwise reject.

> It has happened to me lots of times — well, a few times. Someone will grab your breasts or your crotch, or your ass. Those times I try to pass it off. I have heard of guys coming up and saying 'Can I touch your tits?' And you say 'No.' And they have done it. That happened to one of my girlfriends. And she just ignored it. She said 'you big jerk', but didn't bring it to anyone's attention. It might be fear or maybe even shame — you are guilty by being there. What were you doing there, you went downtown and you deserved it. Like if someone touches my ass in a crowded bar. If I try to bring up assault charges I'd feel stupid going to the RNC or something. 'Well, I can identify the guy.' 'What did he do?' 'Well, he touched my ass in a crowded bar.'

> There is also the whole thing of assuming you are going to be laughed at ... But if you are walking down the hallway at school and someone grabs you, it is more likely to be taken seriously. It is not like I was in a line at Kentucky Fried Chicken and someone grabbed my crotch. There is way more tolerance for this shit in bars. There is a lot that does not get reported because it is a bar.

Too often young women do not understand what does, and what does not, constitute consent.

> I have heard of cases worse than that — like sex, intercourse is taking place. And the woman has said no, and it's happening anyway.

She says, well, I guess I wasn't clear enough, I didn't get through to him. I was loaded. I went home with him, and I brought condoms. There is the big thing — like the NO Means NO, which is a great campaign ... The girl goes home with a guy, she is incredibly loaded, he is incredibly loaded, she has sex with him. She wakes up in the morning and he is inside her going at it again. Is that considered date rape? A lot of people don't get those times when it is not OK.

Women's Ideas for Change

We asked the participants how the second phase of *Bars, Booze and Sexual Violence* might address the problem of sexual violence downtown. Frances and others suggested education for young men and women is needed, however,

It is not just about downtown, it is everywhere. Everything is about sex at our age, everywhere you go. I just think something has to be changed. I don't know how, I would like to think that something could be done — it might have to be bigger than the bars.

Ramona suggested society's attitude toward violence against women has to change.

A lot of people think if you are drinking it is your own fault, or if you dress a certain way it is your own fault. That is asking for it. You should be able to feel attractive without putting yourself in danger. There are people who wouldn't feel so bad for a woman if she was raped while she was drunk and had a short skirt on than she was walking home from work and got attacked in an alley. Lots of people out there think like that. Attitudes like that have to be changed.

Gina argued that exposing the problem of the acceptance of sexual violence in bars is required.

There has got to be a way to get other people to start talking about it. If we do not have our own stance on what is right and what is wrong, how do we expect to get our message out ... There are a lot of barriers out there. You can go to bars and talk to the people there, but you wouldn't be allowed into the bars.

Conclusions

All these responses show young women thinking about, and addressing, the problem of violence in bars as part of the much larger problem of violence against women and sexist attitudes in society at large.

Every six minutes there is a sexual assault committed in Canada and

90% of the victims are female (Newfoundland and Labrador Sexual Assault Crisis and Prevention Centre, n.d). More than half of the women under the age of 16 in Canada have experienced some form of unwanted sexual attention (Statistics Canada, 1993; Tremblay, 1999).[3] Sexual violence in bars will not stop by encouraging young women to develop "survival strategies" alone. Violence against women will remain a pervasive problem until the patriarchal ordering of our society and its underlying attitudes of gender inequality change. Men commit acts of sexual violence because there has yet to be a strong enough message against it.

Members of the Regional Coordinating Coalition Against Violence are deeply disturbed by the contents of this report and are determined to take action to improve the safety of bars for young women. A first step is to discuss this issue with representatives from the Liquor Corporation, bar owners, the RCMP, the RNC, taxi drivers, municipal councillors, and community violence prevention organizations. We recommend that the City of St. John's institute standardized policies and procedures for bars dealing with the safety of bar patrons, including protocol and training for bar staff in recognizing and responding to violence against women. A minimum pricing by-law for bars should take effect immediately and bars must discontinue marketing practices designed to exploit women and to create a highly sexualized environment. Police officers on downtown duty must be trained in the dynamics of violence against women. Finally, community and school gender-based violence prevention initiatives for young men and women should emphasize the role of alcohol and date rape drugs in violence against women.

Notes

[1] This is an excerpt from a project report entitled, *Bars, Booze and Sexual Violence: Young St. John's Women Speak* completed in June 2001. It was produced in co-operation with the Regional Coordinating Coalition Against Violence and the Victim Services Regional Advisory Committee, with support from Victim Services, Department of Justice and The Violence Prevention Initiative, Government of Newfoundland and Labrador. The second phase, called *Bars, Booze and Sexual Violence: Moving Masculinities* written by Jay Goulding was completed in March 2003. Phase III, *A Workshop Guide for Violence Free Communities: Involving Men and Boys*, developed by Jay Goulding, assisted by the Provincial Advisory Council on the Status of Women, was published in October 2004. Financial Support for these phases was provided by the Government of Canada's National Crime Prevention Strategy and in-kind support was provided by The Regional Coordinating Coalition Against Violence, the Royal Newfoundland Constabulary and The Provincial Advisory Council on the Status of Women.

See the project website for downloading documents: http://www.coalitionagainstviolence.ca.

[2] The two criteria for participation were that women be under 30 years of age and that they have experienced the downtown bar "scene" to an average or above average degree. Focus group recruitment posters were placed in approximately 50 locations at community organizations, educational institutions, and downtown businesses. One focus group was held at Memorial University while three were held in the community. Two groups were held in collaboration with community agencies serving the youth population. Focus group size ranged from 2 to 12. A total of 30 women between the ages of 17 to 24 participated. Women were attending high school, university, or some other form of education, or were working, while still others were neither working nor attending school at the time.

[3] It is recognized that the data used in the Tremblay report are under-representative of actual incidence rates. The figures for Tremblay's research were derived from the 1998 *Revised Uniform Crime Reporting Survey* of the CCJS. Only 169 police forces in 6 provinces participated in this survey, and the data represents only 46% of crimes committed in 1998. It is important to note that in 1993, four times the number of cases of spousal violence against women were reported by the Violence Against Women Survey, than by the police (*Revised Uniform Crime Reporting Survey.*)

Women and the Military — Can They Ever Mix?

Brenda Kitchen

Man should be trained for war and woman for the recreation of the warrior: all else is folly.

—Friedrich Nietzsche, 1883

WOMEN HAVE BEEN INVOLVED in Canada's military for longer than most people realize. Their roles expanded in 1971 after the Department of National Defence (DND) reviewed the recommendations made by the Royal Commission on the Status of Women. In 1987, DND created an office to study the impact of employing women in combat units and in 1989 all restrictions on female participation, with the exception of submarine service, were lifted. The goal was the full integration of women by 1999. The Minister's Advisory Board on Gender Integration was mandated to monitor progress. Initiatives were put in place to create awareness of gender issues and to eliminate discriminatory practices and attitudes. But how has this official acceptance actually manifested itself? Can women ever feel truly accepted in the military or is there something fundamental about soldiering that is inherently sexist and anti-women?

In 1988, I became a member of the Royal Canadian Army Cadets because my hometown — Robinson's, Newfoundland — lacked activities for youth. I had a wonderful and memorable cadet career; I met new people, earned money, and had the opportunity to travel. I received two awards: for Outstanding and Most Disciplined cadet. Both featured a cadet standing tall and proud — a male cadet. Such reminders that I was part of something profoundly male were pervasive as I continued my involvement in the military. My experiences led me to focus my research on the experiences of women in the military and the ways in which the male ethos continues to affect women members.

In this article I explore two manifestations of the way in which the male ethos is both deeply embedded in the military and acts to discriminate and discourage women soldiers: sexist language and violence against women. The site of my research was the Royal Newfoundland Regiment (RNR). This regiment has a unique history as the oldest military unit in North America. It also has special meaning for the people of Newfoundland and Labrador, many of whom have had a relative or friend serve in the unit.[1]

Traditionally women have been assigned very specific roles by the military: as moral support on the home front, and as victims or providers of sexual services. If women can be made to "play the role of wives, daughters, mothers, and 'sweethearts,' waving their men off to war, writing them letters of encouragement and devotion in the field, reminding them that women's and children's safety depends on men's bravery, *then* women can be an invaluable resource to commanders" (Enloe, 1988, 5). Women's role as rape victim is often a structured part of military policy. "Rape during armed conflict is a socially constructed experience, that is produced by a series of deliberate policy decisions, and that is therefore neither inevitable nor unchangeable" (Moser & Clark, 2001, 56). Military commanders have often provided prostitutes in an attempt to maintain morale. It is clear that sexuality and militarism are intertwined. Further, it seems that "each time a military establishment reasserts its 'masculine' identity, it is inclined to do so by purging or marginalizing women, and it does this by insinuating that women are essentially whores" (Enloe, 1988, 19). As women try to construct their identity as soldiers and warriors, they have to confront these traditional roles. Women are now formally in the military, but the institution remains predominantly male, in command structure, hierarchy, culture, and recruitment. Its culture continues to remind us of the polarity between the masculine and the feminine — the idea that men and women are fundamentally different.

Knowing Your Place

Language and terminology are used in the military to ensure that women "know their place," as evident in even the milder uses of non-inclusive sexist language I encountered. One respondent, Gregory, talking about the use of the exclusive term "rifleman," said that he wanted "to do the right thing and use the proper words." He, "asked the Warrant Officer and he said that it was a military term and that you're not offending anyone by using it." Is it offensive? Why say rifleman? Are there other words that can be substituted? The term "infanteer" is used in place of infantryman, so could rifleman easily be changed to rifle or rifleperson? The continued use of "rifleman" symbolically excludes women. Some male soldiers believe it is worthwhile to change the terminology. Jonah said, "I don't call them b'ys, I like troops ... I'll say, come on troops. I don't say b'ys or treat them any different." Tracy told me about a lesson she attended where the instructor was "up in front of the classroom and he said something like infantryman and then he made a big point to say something like, infantry persons ... excuse me. It wasn't to be politically correct, but it was to be an asshole." It would not have been difficult for the instructor to simply say infanteers. His choice of words immediately turned that classroom into an uncomfortable place for the women students and created unnecessary tension and division for everyone present.

Is this language use really trivial or "no big thing" as some of my respondents suggested? We can argue that resistance to the use of inclusive terminology demonstrates its importance. The terminology reflects the male image of the institution, and the failure to change it is a refusal

296

to fully accept women in the military.

Language is also used to insult and degrade troops. Pamela referred to statements such as "'the females didn't make it' as putting down every single female that has really tried and made it." As a researcher, I went out into the field with soldiers and experienced this for myself. As part of one exercise, we went on a seven-kilometre march with 35-40-pound rucksacks on our backs. As we climbed a hill, a male Master Corporal, then a female and a male soldier fell out of line. The female soldier returned to the hike without her rucksack. An officer went quickly up the hill, red-faced and angry and barking at us, "Five metres, five fucking metres apart!" He then turned around and yelled, "Come on ladies," to the entire platoon. I did a double take. Three people, two men and one woman had fallen out. I was distressed and insulted. The officer's attempt to motivate the soldiers was to insult them by calling them women. When I spoke to him, he did not remember the incident but said that he was angry at the troop's performance, and that was his way to motivate them to do better.

The Oxford Dictionary defines being "manly" or "masculine" as having qualities traditionally associated with men, such as courage or strength. To be "womanly" or "feminine" means to have qualities traditionally associated with women, especially delicacy and prettiness. In the dichotomy between "manly" and "womanly," the qualities the military requires, particularly of its infantry, are associated with men and non-desirable qualities are associated with women. To describe a man using traditionally feminine qualities is therefore insulting. Calling these soldiers "ladies" was an attempt to insult the men's masculinity and to challenge them to do better. But what did it do to the women soldiers among them?

Tracy discussed another incident involving sexist and sexually suggestive language.

Overnight on our indoc [indoctrination] course we had a mock attack by the instructors. We had the arctic tent all set up and instructors attacked and we all had to get out. This guy, when everyone was supposed to run out, he decided that he was going to turn off the lantern and get back in his sleeping bag and go back to sleep ... So the instructor was right to freak out ... So, anyway, he came back and realized what happened and he said 'If you don't get out of that tent I am going to kick you in the cunt.' That was very sexist and degrading. Why did he say that? There were a lot more appropriate things to say, even kick you in the ass. Anyway, he could have taken him up on charges.

To threaten to kick a man in his non-existent female genitalia is a double threat: the threat of violence, and the threat to the soldier's masculinity. We do not know what impact this had on the male soldier in question, but we do know what Tracy felt. She was disgusted with "that word, cunt." She "hates it," it is "the stupidest word ever," it is "disgusting," and it is "dirty and slut and whore all in one word." The use of this kind of language not only insults the target of the comment, but also others who are listening. It brings down morale and erodes respect.

Masculinity, Power and Sex

Despite the Canadian Forces' formal efforts to integrate women, the experience war provides "is presented as an exclusively male experience and a masculinity defined in terms of being tough and selfless, having courage, guts and endurance, a lack of squeamishness, a high resistance to pain and discomfort and tight control in emotional matters" (Beynon, 2002, 67). Men see that their success depends on initiative, assertiveness (if not aggressiveness), and persistence. The male body should reflect this by being strong and tough. The ways in which men dress, walk and talk all mirror these expectations. In acting out this masculinity, men find common ground that brings them closer together. This version of masculinity equates manhood with power, but to have power, one must have domain over something or someone. When playing out this role includes the pursuit of females, men not only exercise their power over women, but also receive approval from other men that brings them even closer together. Manhood and "masculinism is celebrated through 'buddydom' and relationships between men" (Beynon, 2002, 17). When one respondent, Oliver, was asked about soldiers' pursuit of females, he acknowledged that, "there's a guy mentality, ... when you go to a bar and pick up and do that [have sex with women]. Now some guys think that's perfectly okay. If they spend six weeks around guys then it starts to rub off on them and they just go with it." The "guy mentality" Oliver refers to pervades the training grounds where men and women are supposed to interact as comrades.

Military men live almost exclusively among other men and are constantly subjected to pressures to conform to standards of "masculine" behaviour, standards amplified in the military where men are trained to be more aggressive, more male and, consequently, more sexually aggressive. Women in the military are placed in an intolerable contradictory position. On the one hand they are expected to become soldiers, traditionally framed as demonstrating "male" characteristics; on the other, they are expected to look and act like stereotypical women. Part of the traditional — and sexist — understanding of the relationships between men and women is that a man who sleeps around and has multiple sex partners is a "man's man" or more masculine. Men engaging in promiscuous sex are viewed as powerful; women who do the same are viewed in a derogatory manner. Gregory maintained that "the way it is, if a girl sleeps with more then one guy then she's loose ... and if a guy does it, it's like yeah, way to go, you're the man."

Central to this image of maleness is the belief in sex as power; sex with women equates to power over women. "Locker room" talk presents men as always interested in and ready for sex, even in the trenches. Such talk reinforces male bonding; at the same time, it maintains power over women, undermining their confidence as soldiers and reminding them of their vulnerability. Erin described a female recruit who was in a trench with a soldier who "kept hitting on her. And he kept it up. It got so bad that she left the trench. She took her weapon, she took her kit and she got up and she went to the next trench over." Erin went on to say that during section attacks the same male soldier would "be standing there staring at your ass and making comments." How could this female recruit conduct herself as a soldier while fighting off the advances of her comrade? How could she view herself as an equal when her trench partner saw her as nothing more than a sexual object?

Male bonding and the hierarchies men create among themselves and the ways they express their sexuality with each other have repercussions for women even though women are not directly involved (Hester, 1992, 14). When I asked Tracy what it felt like to hear overtly sexual conversations among male soldiers, she responded:

I don't know what I am doing here. They are nothing but a bunch of sexist pigs ... But what they talk about is so disgusting and demeaning. It is about doing somebody. They don't care that I am here. They have no concern that I would feel whatever about it. I don't think you need to watch every word you say but sometimes the conversation is so disgusting that they shouldn't be talking about it whether I was there or not there.

In the past, the absence of women soldiers permitted men to act without inhibition. Now women are in the trenches next to them, as comrades, yet sexist attitudes prevail. Women are pushed away if they engage in sex, but they are equally pushed away if they do not. Rebecca said:

You couldn't win. I found the guys, if you didn't put out they hated you because you were like, you ain't getting nothing off her. Or if you did put out you were a ground sheet and don't talk to her. So either way, this is what I find with women in the infantry, it sucks to be a woman for that reason.

Regimental Ground Sheet

A term that surfaced in conversations with both men and women was "regimental ground sheet." Its original meaning is a piece of equipment issued to a soldier to put between the ground and sleeping bag and/or air mattress. As the term kept emerging in interviews, however, it clearly meant something else. When I inquired about this, Gregory explained:

> What I heard has only been addressed to a female. I haven't heard it addressed to a male. Basically, she would lie down for anyone, any-one can have a go at her ... she was like the platoon whore, a company whore ... girls slept around and they like, banged guys in the army, they were part of the routine and banged guys, or guys were banging them, whatever you call it.

"Regimental ground sheet" applies to women only, and men's use of the term reinforces their power over women: "power manifests itself in many forms of harassment of women, such as sexual gestures, innuendos, jokes and remarks which remind women of their vulnerability and subordinate status as sex objects" (Hester, 1984, 14).

For women who "sleep around" the consequence is to be viewed, as Rebecca said, as "a dirty crack, whore, skank." Women are unable to claim the power that men acquire by behaving in the same way. If women could gain status in this manner, it would mean that they would have power over their objects, men. The persistent sexual comments reported to me highlight how military culture serves to maintain control over women as they seek equality in a new and alien environment.

There is also a persistent stereotype that many military women are "loose" or promiscuous. As Oliver pointed out, "yes, you do get girls who go away on their QL2[2] and become ground sheets. Like whores. They will screw anything with legs ... Some girls go from ... they take innocence and throw it out the window and become whore-ish. That's what happened, they take up the guy mentality." Perhaps these women are trying to fit into the regime by becoming more male, more masculine; perhaps they really feel that this is liberation.

Some women I interviewed held beliefs similar to the men's. Samantha agreed that, "women in the military, 90 per cent are not good. When I met some of the girls in the other battalion, there was a girl who was there banging everybody." Erin said, "I try to keep my distance from other women because I want to know if they are there to try or ... I mean, I knew of a girl who just joined up for the guys and when it got to the point where she had to do push-ups and ruck marches she got out. So it is hard to know why the women are there. Is she there for the guys?" Tracy echoed this sentiment: "there were other girls who slept around the whole time. I can understand why they were in."

The persistence of the double standard not only draws boundaries between men and women. It erodes the solidarity between female soldiers, especially when women, like men, assume that other women are entering the military to access a new dating pool.

Some female respondents also believed that sex was used as a tool to gain promotion. Denise said, "You're a girl and you only got where you are because you slept your way there, which is what a lot of girls do. But I know that some girls have done it and that's how they got promoted." Erin agreed that "there are girls like that who try to advance their careers by sleeping with the key people." The negative backlash against successful female soldiers from both men and other women is a cause of frustration and further obstacles to integration. Tracy was offered a course and "this guy wasn't anything to me but he said, 'Yeah, well, we know how she got that.' " It is assumed that a woman's ability is not enough to gain her promotion or a seat in a sought-after course. Even if some women are using sex as a kind of countervailing power, it is a limited power and one that further serves men's interests.

If women are to find a genuine place in the military, knowledgeable, proactive and efficient leadership is required. When one respondent was questioned about the relationships that develop between those in charge and recruits, she discussed an incident where "these Sergeants and Master Corporals got these girls drunk ... and they were just recruits and they took off to a hotel and they did their thing." This kind of behaviour is frowned on at the official level, but still takes place frequently, with negative effects on unit cohesion and devastating effects for the women involved.

Erin discussed the implications of the development of personal relationships and perceptions of favouritism: "because the instructor favours her and is dating her or whatever, she is getting special treatment." Another respondent said, "the way the instructors interact with them [female recruits] will probably be a little more joking with the girl than with the guy. You know a little more lenient with the girl than the guy and depending on the girl, if she's attractive ... you know like flirting or whatever, you know, it's there." Erin said, "how can you respect your instructor when he's got this fling going on with one of the girls?"

Another respondent discussed her confusion following an incident at a local bar while on a course, "we went out to a bar and one guy had me in the corner trying to get his hands up my shirt. He was like ... you know ... my staff and I'm a troop and he's not supposed to be like that ... so this other Master Corporal came over and rescued me ... lo and behold we were in the cab and he had his arm around me and was trying to kiss me." Those in leadership positions tend to be trusted by those under their command. It is their responsibility to create an atmosphere that is professional and welcoming to women. It is unfortunate that some misuse their power and are poor examples of leadership.

Beyond Inappropriate

The construction and use of male sexuality through rape, sexual murder, sexual harassment in the street, at home and at work, sexual abuse of children, obscene telephone calls and so on, intimidates and controls women. In the military, this extreme form of male sexuality reveals itself when male soldiers openly discuss sexual conquests that include sexual misconduct[3], constituting a form of sexual harassment. Some instances I heard about were not only intimidating, but illegal.

> I was in there trying to sleep and the guys were talking about sex ... they started making a list of everyone they've done, names included and all the stuff that they've seen. There was five or six guys that were talking and what they were talking about literally made me sick inside. I never felt this way before in my entire life ... I don't know ... it didn't have anything to do with me ... it was about different women and it made me so sick inside I thought that I was going to have to get up and get my kit and talk to the guys outside and say take me home. I'm getting out of here; I don't care what you do to me. (One) was talking about how him and this girl was making out and he would ... they were out behind the mall or something ... and he would pull her shirt up over her head and make out with her and the other guys would come out and see her tits, or feel them and she didn't know. The one that really got to me was ... this guy was talking about how he used to make his girlfriend get naked on the bed and four of his friends used to come in and do whatever they wanted to her and she used to be crying. And that's what got me. She didn't want to do it and he used to make her.

It is appalling that this conversation would occur in a military context when male and female soldiers are sleeping under the same shelter. While harassment policies are in place, they are unable to challenge deeply ingrained mores of the military culture. The impact of that conversation on one woman soldier is clear. She was offended and her inferior status was reasserted. Meanwhile, she was expected to work the following day with the soldiers who had just discussed women as sexual objects. At the same time, the men involved in the conversation were bonding and the behaviour of the chief offender was rewarded with friendship.

> Well, everyone was laughing. They thought it was hilarious. Not everyone, but these five or six guys. They were saying what they did and the other guy would pipe in, yeah, well, I did this ... Like I said, when you're a minority with all men you're going to hear stuff. But I mean, this stuff was to the extreme. But it really got to me. I don't know how to approach it. I never got up out of bed. I was ... think-

ing that they were going to talk about me, I was listening to hear if they were going to bring up my name because they were talking about everybody. The company ground sheets. But they never. I don't know if they thought I was there and that I might be awake. I don't know.

While some topics of conversation might seem permissible even if inappropriate, the conversation cited here clearly crossed a line. One respondent asserted that there was "a line, and you can allow certain degrees, there's like a gray area and you can let it go." However, this discussion was about sexual assault, a chargeable offense under the law. As an act of sexual violence against women, rape "is the ultimate expression of a patriarchal order, a crime that epitomizes women's oppressed status by proclaiming, in the loudest possible voice, the most degrading truths about women that a hostile world has to offer" (Cahill, 2001, 2).

The violent act of rape has been historically connected with the military. Enloe argues that, "it may be there are aspects of the military institution and ideology which greatly increase the pressure on militarized men to 'perform' sexually, whether they have a sexual 'need' or emotional feelings or not" and that these aspects include the pressures "to conform to the standards of 'masculine' behaviour" (Enloe, 1998, 35). It may also be a result of the need to be a part of a "family", in this case, the unit or platoon. A soldier can "only earn buddies by proving he is a 'man,' that he isn't squeamish in the face of violence and rape is seen as a violent act" (Enloe, 1998, 36).

In the tent my respondent shared, men boasted of their manhood and sexual conquests to gain the approval of other men. The discussion rendered masculinity all-powerful. It is the kind of talk that induces in women a "timid and careful" response to men (Coveney, 1984, 19). The respondent, usually an outspoken woman, could not find her voice in that situation. Another respondent discussed a similar incident that a fellow soldier told her about:

I know this girl who was working one summer and there were all these regular force guys around her. She was out one day when it started to rain, so they all got inside this tank together to stay dry. She didn't feel weird at first because she was the only female in this little tank with five other guys. But then it got weird. The b'ys were talking and the only person she knew was the driver and they were sitting down in this confined space. 'It wasn't like I could get out and walk away. They started to talk about rape. They were saying, Now this is a perfect place now that we could rape someone. You could tie her hands over there and her ankle here and her other ankle there ... and we could all bang fuck her and no one would know because they would never hear her scream and we all got an alibi because we could all pick up for each other. And no one would ever know.' She said, 'I never felt so uncomfortable in my life. I was just sitting there and I wasn't saying anything, but I was super uncomfortable, I just got out and stood in the rain. I didn't know what else to do'. The driver said to her after, 'don't mind them, they're assholes'. She said she didn't know how to deal with it.

Major Adams-Roy discusses sexual harassment in *Harassment in the Canadian Forces: Results of the 1998 Survey*. Military personnel reported that sexual teasing, jokes and remarks were common, with 86% reporting examples. Fifty-six percent reported sexually suggestive body language and 53% reported sexual talk creating an intimidating environment. One respondent reported actual or attempted rape (1999, 17). A survey of personnel undergoing initial training in Spring 1998, including personnel attending the Royal Military College (RMC), confirmed these results (1999, 44).

Fighting the Obstacles

There are men who support the integration of women into the military. They choose to see women as soldiers, and not as sexual objects to be conquered. When I asked one of these men about the obstacles created by sexual harassment, he commented that he was "sure that there are ignorant fucks that don't know any better. You got to get over those people, ignore them, and keep your mind focused on being a good soldier and doing your job. Regardless of who you are. That's what is important. Things are never easy so learn to drive on and dig in and be tough." Such soldiers have to work hard to overcome the sexist behaviour of the majority.

In spite of the obstacles, women are persisting in their efforts to integrate into the military. My research showed women beginning to construct their own culture. The women soldiers I talked to were focused and dedicated to their personal goals. Pamela observed that "when I put on the uniform, I feel that I am somebody, somebody different, but I feel that I can do anything, that I can take on anyone." They also have a clear loyalty to the Royal Newfoundland Regiment. Alison said, "It's historic too. The Regiment played a big part in world wars. So, as for being a Newfoundlander, being involved in the Regiment means a lot." The skills they learn promote a sense of self-respect. Rebecca affirmed this when she said, "the more I did, the prouder I got. I was proud to be a woman and I was proud to do it. I mean we were doing section attacks and my friends were home flipping burgers." There are other ways in which women can forge their independence within military culture. An example is the way women come together during physical training. Alison: "if one of us did a pull-up it was a big deal, we would be clapping and stuff," illustrating that "groups [that] lack power collectively, define their positions and use their informal relations to adapt to or resist powerlessness" (Anderson, 1993, 132).

Conclusion

My research demonstrated many ways in which the existing military culture hinders women's integration. Despite all the difficulties women face, many persevere and find it a positive experience, and increasing numbers of male soldiers are welcoming them.

To enter any organization one must be prepared to obey rules and regulations. But the military is unique. It requires one to obey orders without question and, in times of war, to be prepared to take a human life. To accomplish this, basic training deconstructs recruits and rebuilds them as soldiers. Soldiers must be ready to put themselves in harm's way, to battle not only the enemy but the elements, and most importantly, themselves. One result of the history and mandate of the military is that a pervasive male culture has evolved that creates obstacles for women. To overcome them, men and women will need to respect each other as soldiers, as team members. As long as women are viewed as sexual objects rather than soldiers, they will never become the full members of the military that they aspire to become.

Notes

[1] Newfoundland soldiers were among the first to answer the call for Commonwealth troops in 1914. At that time they were known as the Newfoundland Regiment, and their first actions were in Egypt and Gallipoli. The Regiment is the only unit in Canada with the battle honor, Gallipoli. After serving in Turkey, the Regiment was moved to France with the rest of the 29th Division for the battle of Somme. On July 1st 1916, the worst single day of casualties in British Army history, the Regiment suffered the highest percent of casualties, losing all but 68 of its 802 soldiers. The Regiment rebuilt itself and was back in action within a few months. The unit fought in the battle of Cambrai, where tanks were used for the first time and was honored with the title "Royal," for its action in this encounter. The Regiment disbanded in 1919; however, on October 24th, 1949, authority was granted by King George VI to revive The Royal Newfoundland Regiment as a reserve unit of the Canadian Army.

[2] This abbreviation means Qualification Level 2, Basic Recruit Training.

[3] Sexual misconduct includes, (but is not limited to) actual or attempted rape or sexual assault (Adams-Roy, 1998, 9).

305

Letters and Diaries

FRANCES CLUETT (1883-1969) was born in Belleoram, Fortune Bay, Newfoundland and taught school prior to WWI. In 1916, at the age of 33, she left home to join the Volunteer Aid Detachment of St. John Ambulance and then the British Expeditionary Force in France during WWI. Her letters to her sister Lillian, her mother Matilda and other family and friends document her life as a nurse, a curious visitor to a new country and culture, and as a reflective observer of war. During her time in France, her cousin Vince was killed in action and some of her letters reflect the pain of his loss. When she returned to Newfoundland in November 1920 from her final posting in Constantinople, Fanny attended Normal School in St. John's and went on to teach primary school in Belleoram. She also ran a small general store, played the organ in church, and was called upon frequently to tend those who were ill. While many of her letters reflect the joy of life and curiosity she seems to have possessed, here Fanny tries to explain the horrors of war and the pressures of nursing wounded, maimed and dying soldiers in France.[1]

10 General Hospital
31/3/18

Easter Sunday Morning

Dear Mother,
I am going to Church at 11:15 a.m., for I am so terribly tired. We are awfully busy, nearly killed since this last rush! If this war does not soon end there won't be a man living on the face of the earth. It is brutal, it is cold-blooded murder; it is hell upon earth. Ah! If you could only see and go through what we do Mother, it is enough to drive one mad.
I am on night duty in the compound. I shall never forget these days. Convoys are coming in all night long; patients are vacating in the midst of it. I have four wards with a little help once in a while; if this rush continues, some of us will give out altogether.
I came back from "leave" five nights ago; arriving at Rouen 8 p.m. Matron sent me on night duty at 10 p.m. same night. Oh! My head was so heavy from travelling; had been on train two days, the second night on train I did not sleep at all, it was so cold.
From the train I went on duty at 10 p.m. I did not stop a minute until 8 a.m. next morning, except to have a cup of tea at 12 p.m.
I say again this war is simply horrible. What a blessing some of these boy's mothers do not see their husbands and sons.
Sometimes an orderly comes through to help me a little bit. I have to

Francis Cluett and friend (L), c. 1920. CNSA, Coll-174, 5.02.167

wait on the patients such as giving them drinks, the bedpans, then perhaps the stretcher bearer comes in for a man to go to the theatre to have his wounds opened, or his hand off, whatever the case may be. Well! If he is a helpless patient, I've got to try to do the best I can to get him on the stretcher or run for an orderly, or look for Sister to help. Then when he is taken away, his bed has to be made into an operation bed ready for him again; just as you finish that, in comes the stretcher bearers for another one; by the time he is ready to go, the other one is brought back, then put on his bed, a vomiting basin given him, and watched at intervals for vomiting, haemorrhages, etc. Then probably we are warned by the Sergeant that a convoy is going out at such a time to England. He names the patients in each ward who are going; I have then to prepare for travelling. I tell you Mother it's nothing easy to dress a helpless patient, pulling vests, shirts, cardigan, jacket, drawers, pants; sometimes you can only get one leg in the drawers, and only one sleeve of the jacket. Then one must see that everything as regards their papers go with them. These papers indicate when they are taken sick, to what hospital they are sent, his name, regiment, rank, where wounded, etc; essential papers.

Well, while getting them ready for the stretcher bearers to take them to the reception tent before getting in the travelling boat, perhaps a convoy has just come down from the line; in they come stretcher after stretcher. Oh my! Their clothes have to be cut off, shirts, pants and everything; such a state of blood and mud. They are then bathed and one has to handle them very, very carefully, especially if he is shot in the head. No head

307

case is allowed to sit up at all. Some of them can't see at all, all smashed to pieces; one poor, young boy, lying day after day with eyes bandaged. Think of them, blind for life and so young.

I have been so tired towards morning that I could scarcely walk; the bottoms of my feet are like boils. My first ward on night duty this year was C1. Just as we had one washed and shrouded, ready to be taken to the mortuary, I was sent to go to another ward to help Sister prepare another for the mortuary. Next evening I was told to watch a man until his last breath went. I never thought Mother that I would do what I have done. I went behind the screen and stayed with him until he died. Oh the pitiful sights, the worn faces. One man asked just before he died when he could see his mother.

Next night in the midst of our rush, I was sent to special a man. He was wounded in the buttock, left arm and abdomen. His arm was in "Thomas" splint, that is, bound on steel rods. The poor thing was raving at times. We were giving him a saline injection, but gave it up. He died about 7 p.m. When I came on duty this morning, one of our patients was slowly fading. You cannot realize Mother what we go through.

I have been to church. Both going and coming I saw them taking the stretchers with the Union Jack on them. You know what that means.

It is now 1 a.m. I must go to bed as we get up, are rather called, at 6:30 a.m.

One of the patients was telling me about this last push when the Germans drove them back. He said you could see them coming, as fast as you knock one down another took his place. There was no end to them. At last they had to retire. The Germans are getting the best of it. Out of one of the boy's battalion, only 9 came back; they tell us it is murder. Of course, we get it right from the persons who are engaged in the battle and not from the papers. Another said he just went with his company to dig a trench. They were not fighting men, but found when they had finished they had to hold the line. And he said he was no good at all, not able to do anything of the kind. One old man got knocked about a bit; he couldn't run, he said, like the younger ones. Poor old chap must have lain in the cold quite a while, he is so wheezy. The Germans nearly encircled them.

To hear the draughts go up the line every evening singing and cheering, band playing; Sister said yesterday it made her blood run cold. They go up never to return, except to come maimed for life. I don't think I have written like this before Mother, which plainly says things are much worse.

Paris was shelled from the Germans 75-mile gun. As we came through one street there the chauffeur showed us where the bombs had been dropped. Sister Coneys came through Paris; one shell dropped 20 yards from their ambulance. She was down south when I was there, but I left a few days before. I went into two churches while in Paris. Perhaps it might have been one of these that was shelled.

The Casualty Clearing Stations are bombed. We have nearly twenty sisters who had to leave for their life, saved nothing, only what they wore. Shells flying everywhere. They say at one place there are 6000 wounded Tommies waiting to be sent somewhere, walking about in horrid conditions. Of course, if these C.C.s had not been bombed, we would not have been so busy. This is now like a Casualty Clearing Station. Boys are dying for want of attention. They cannot be attended to before being sent down here; wounds lying so long of course must kill them. It is horrible Mother.

Goodbye. Nothing would induce me to give it up Mother.

Fannie

Notes
[1] CNSA Coll-174, 2.01.003.

The Dear Domestic World: Washing Up

Roberta Buchanan

My mother stands at the sink;
her choleric hands in suds
rattle the cutlery
knock the plates together.
I am drying that particular knife:
sharp point, long blade spotted with black—
I long to plunge it in her rigid back
right between her disapproving shoulders.
      (What if she turns round? I wouldn't dare!
      Those icy blue eyes always
      flash-freeze my rebellion.)
I wipe the spotted blade carefully,
I place it discretely in the drawer.

Tomorrow this scene will be repeated.

Sexism Goes Underground in the 21st Century

Lori Yetman

IN A CLASSROOM TODAY, A YOUNG MALE GRADUATE student, a lab instructor in the school of engineering, said that women and gays were "spoiled", that in their efforts to be sensitive, men were doing the work of women and gays in engineering, that women and gays were adversely impacting men's productivity. A young woman supports his perspective, adding that she sees women using "cute behavior" to get ahead at work. In another classroom, a young male student asks whether it is okay to have sex with a woman when she's unconscious. In yet another, a young man defends the jokes he tells, arguing that sexist, racist, and homophobic jokes are acceptable here — "the women don't say anything, we're all white, and there are no queers." *You've got to be able to tell a joke.* A woman I hardly know confides that she was low-balled on her salary; that compared to other male managers, she is underpaid and without what she describes as a "female entourage" of assistants to open her mail, answer her phone, do her photocopying or schedule her day. I hear almost identical stories from other women.

These are the stories I hear everyday. I am a Sexual Harassment Advisor. I am careful not to share the stories that are told behind the closed doors of my office, at least not in this context. But I can share those stories and perspectives that are told to me when I speak publicly … or when I just walk across campus. People tell me things … too much sometimes. I frequently return to my office or home feeling done in … tired … angry. Why haven't I become immune to it, cynical? (*I keep waiting for that moment*) Why does it still create that adrenaline rush, that knot in my stomach? (*Why won't it disappear?*) Why do I feel like crying the moment I'm alone? Why do I still get so frustrated? Why can't I sleep? Maybe because I had hoped things were getting better … and I've discovered that they're getting worse …

When I enter a classroom for the first time, either as someone who has been invited to educate students about inclusive learning environments, or as a teacher of Women's Studies, I know that my first goal will be to convince the audience of my relevance and the relevance of what I am there to teach. If I were discussing geography, history, physics, or classical sociological theory, I would not have to argue relevance. I would not have to argue the relevance of what I do if I were anything else but this. There is a pervasive misconception that all is all right now — that we have accomplished the "feminist mission": equality. The misconception only lasts for so long — at least among the female students. Once they are provided with the language to articulate and describe their daily encounters with these previously unnamed or uncharacterized behaviors, words, conversations, looks, experiences, feelings, they talk … and they talk about

311

sexism. (*Just consider what I'm saying here ... didn't Betty Friedan do this in 1963?*)

Sexism in the 21st century seems worse to me. First, it is so systemic, so embedded within our social structures, within our psyches, it is the norm. As a norm, of course, it is permissible. Those in power know, however, that human rights legislation exists that "discourages" sexism, that "prohibits" sex discrimination, that "promotes" equity. I can't help but wonder if, in response to that legislation, sexism has gone underground. Over the past 20 years, for example, I hear the word less. When the word is spoken in a mainstream context, I have seen people react physically to it — wincing. I think that many people have learned to curtail blatant expressions of sexist attitudes. And ... that is not necessarily a good thing. That means that you may not be prepared for the inevitable impact that sexist attitudes have on behavior. That means that if you experience sexism, you may not be able to identify it, name it. It isn't talked about — and why would it be? *The problem has been fixed, remember?*

In my introductory Women's Studies class, students can choose to write two out of four essays on sex, masculinity, heterosexism, or sexual harassment. In these reports, the students are asked to relate the assigned readings to their personal experiences and/or observations. Initially, there are several objections to one of the choices — we can't write about our observations of sexual harassment, we've never seen nor experienced it. I let this go. I ask them to wait until later in term to make that determination. Several weeks later, I invite my theatre group to perform an educational play about issues pertaining to gender and sexual harassment — it consists of dramatizations of discrimination and harassment as experienced by students. After the presentation, the entire class decides to write the report. I read 35 accounts of their daily experiences with sexism, sexual harassment, and, in some cases, sexual assault. Most of it happened in their schools, most of it was condoned by school authorities, all of it was unnamed. It was perceived to be an inevitable, normal component of their everyday lives as women (Larkin, 1994).

As a sexual harassment advisor, as a teacher, as a woman, I know that sexual harassment — or any other form of gendered violence — would not exist without all of the little hurts that come before it — the permissible sexism. I know that my students would not have been able to anticipate daily sexism and sexual harassment if they had not had been exposed to it, gradually, everyday, without anyone in any position of authority intervening. Yet, as a sexual harassment advisor, it's the little things I'm supposed to ignore or not to consider as *formal complaints*. The one time touch. The one time remark. The one time look. The one time request. The one time sexist word, conversation, behaviour or gesture that is directed by one man, towards one woman at a time, at different time intervals in different places. (As one man in a position of authority argued, this is not serious.) *But ... I can't ignore the little things. Maybe it's because I'm a good housekeeper. If you ignore those small tasks — like cleaning behind the toilet or the fridge — what was once a minor task becomes insurmountable ... huge ... requiring an entire weekend to accomplish. Mildew. Mold. Cat fur. Dust. All of it just accumulating ...*

These are the things that do not constitute sexual harassment — at least according to human rights legislation and institutional policies. According to these definitions, sexual harassment is unwanted conduct of a sexual or romantic nature that is either repetitious or serious. To be considered harassment, the perpetrator ought reasonably to have known that the conduct was unwelcome and/or unwanted. In a society in which sexism is a permissible prejudice — and its consequence, sexist discrimination, is systemic, it is exactly that which I am supposed to ignore that leads to sexual harassment. It is exactly that which I am supposed to ignore that the power structures fail to see — it is invisible. If not invisible, then perceived as having little impact or consequence. So, I ask myself, how can I do my job? It's like spring cleaning without a bucket.

Although most educational institutions and workplaces have policies that prohibit sexual harassment, their operational definitions of sexual harassment are not based on the real experiences of women within a sexist society. According to human rights legislation and most institutional definitions of sexual harassment, it is imperative that the target of the problematic behavior conveys that it is unwanted. Human rights legislators state that they *do* recognize the power imbalances that often prevent someone from expressing that a behavior is unwelcome — so, they suggest that harassers "ought to have reasonably known" and then state that in lieu of a direct "no", harassers ought to pick up on other cues: body language, reluctance to comply, hesitations, failure to participate, etc. Yet ... what happens when sexism is the norm? What happens when not only the alleged perpetrator of the harassment believes his actions to be normal or acceptable, but the body responsible for dealing with the complaint — or, more importantly, the complainant herself — believes this too? What if she is so accustomed to sexist behavior or a sexist environment that despite her discomfort, she believes that she must comply or participate in that which makes her work and learning environment intimidating and inappropriately sexualized/sexist/racist/ homophobic? What if? What if she has never known an environment that is *not* sexist? What if she seeks my advice because she is merely feeling "uncomfortable" — or if she is suddenly unable to cope with everyday (*unnamed*) sexism because it has escalated? She finds out during the consultation that she is experiencing a chilly climate or sexual harassment. Her inability to identify the behaviors as anything but a "norm" has meant that she has never conveyed to the perpetrators that it is "unwelcome" and "unwanted" — because she is the minority. In such a sexist environment, neither the complainant nor respondent identify their behavior as inappropriate, as sexist. In such an environment, it is very likely that this sexism was blatant — yet also invisible to those in positions of authority who fail to recognize it as inappropriate and who thus also fail to lead by example.

And what about the issue of gender role socialization? Do operational definitions of sexual harassment consider that? It should now be common knowledge that as women we are still socialized and still expected to be nice, to not express anger, to avoid hurting feelings — we are still very much defined as the caretakers, the nurturers — whether we are actually mothering in the home, managing an office, or teaching within a university setting. Just ask female professors about their course evaluations and how their periodic failure to conform to feminine gender norms impacts their scores — particularly as it relates to nurturing behaviors. Often, girls are still not encouraged to develop assertiveness skills. Consider female socialization within the context of some isolated, rural communities in Newfoundland. Female students leave their homes and come to St. John's to go to university. They are told that they are welcome at university, that the institution will meet their needs through its employees and its services. They have been socialized not to question authority; they have been socialized to believe that they should defer to those with education and prestige. Then they find themselves experiencing behaviors that make them increasingly uncomfortable — and the person making them feel uncomfortable is an employee of this great institution of higher learning. What do they do? Policies suggest that they confront the perpetrator. Let them know upfront that their behavior is unwanted or inappropriate. Some policies actually suggest that this is the first step — and that this step must be taken before any other formal forms of intervention can be used. But, seriously, what is the likelihood? What is the likelihood that a young woman, whose socialization did not include assertive skill training, or whose education did not include "sexual harassment awareness", will confront a man whose education, age, and experience exceeds hers? What are the chances that she will clearly convey in her interactions with this man that his behaviors are unwanted, unwelcome. And ... given that women's and men's perceptions of what is considered inappropriate or sexual harassment are different, what are the chances that he will even concur with her assessment of his behaviors? For example, I recently participated in an alternative dispute-training workshop: mediation is one procedure for resolving sexual harassment complaints used by most Canadian universities. The training consisted of role-plays in which the trainees assumed either the role of mediator or the roles of the disputants to learn how to resolve conflict. In one such role-play, I was assigned the role of the male respondent of a sexual harassment complaint. The behaviors that I was alleged to have engaged in were repeatedly asking my younger, female assistant for dates, staring at her breasts, spontaneously massaging her shoulders, holding her elbow as she walked and placing my hand on her lower back. Another female played the role of the complainant while a male played the role of mediator. After the fictitious mediation ended, we were permitted 30 minutes to de-brief. The man who played the role of mediator did not perceive my behaviors as sexual harassment, arguing that the complainant failed to be direct when the respondent asked her out (*she said she was busy*), the touching was "normal" (*I do this all of the time*), and the staring at her chest ... (*well, that sometimes cannot be helped.*) The other woman and I made eye contact, making an unspoken agreement to turn this into a teachable moment. We explained that the complainant had been afraid to be direct — that because the subject of her complaint was her boss, she perceived herself at risk of losing her job if she said "no". We also explained that women sometimes try to be nice in how they reject advances; we try to avoid hurting someone. We also asserted that staring at a woman's chest *can* be helped. Men are not compelled to stare at our breasts through some kind of biological imperative. To illustrate my points, I told a story of a young man I had interviewed for a job. It was summer, I was wearing a t-shirt, the air-conditioning had been on in my office. The young man's eyes stayed on my chest for the entire interview. He didn't get the job. The man who had played the role of the mediator exclaimed, "*Why didn't you put your jacket on?*" It was at that point I realized (*again*) how frightening this all is. If sexism is the norm, if the behaviors that hurt women are perceived as normal, how can women achieve justice through current human rights legislation or through internal sexual harassment policies? The entire process is going to depend on all of the players "seeing" sexism as abnormal: those doing the mediating, the investigating; those on the commissions established to hear these complaints; those behind the judicial bench; and those making the final decisions about whether harassment occurred or not.

Another component of the definition of sexual harassment within human rights legislation and most institutional policies is the characterization of the offending behavior as "sexual". Leering, grabbing, sexual innuendoes, and propositions for dates or sexual favors are cited as examples of what constitutes sexual. In 1989, the Supreme Court of Canada ruled that sexual harassment is sex discrimination. In *Janzen v. Platy Enterprises Ltd.* (1989), the Court found that "the key fact in the case was that it was only female employees who ran the risk of being sexually harassed. The women were subject to a disadvantage because of being women; no male employee in these circumstances would have been subject to the same disadvantage". I am neither questioning nor disputing the Supreme Court's judgment in this case. What I am questioning is the distinction between "sexual" and "sexist". To be sexually harassed because one is a woman is sexist, discriminatory — as the court decided. It is sex discrimination. But not all unwanted, repetitious or serious *sexist* behavior is considered sexual harassment. Is this distinction useful? Is it grounded in women's experience of sexist-based harassment? If the cause of sexual harassment is sexism — sexist stereotypes and attitudes that lead to sexist behaviors — does it make sense to differentiate between sexist and sexual? From my perspective, as one who is on the front lines, as one who is designated to hear individuals' concerns, reports, questions or complaints of sexual harassment, does it make sense for me to tell a woman: *I'm sorry but this set of behaviors is sexist, not sexual — you will have to be referred to another person in charge of another policy. Yes, you have experienced gender-based put-downs. Yes, you have not been taken seriously because you are a woman. Yes, this has created a hostile learning environment. However, you were not leered at, grabbed or propositioned — so, you will have to go elsewhere.*

To me, the consequences of sexist attitudes — sexist, discriminatory behaviors — exist on a continuum. As women, we are exposed to acts, images, words, behaviours, and attitudes that demean, devalue and objectify us. Yet, sometimes, maybe most often, these acts, images, and words seem so commonplace, so insignificant, that we ignore them. We tell ourselves that in the context of our busy days of studying, working, parenting, struggling to make ends meet, and living ... that the joke, the remark, the image, the attitude, the act, the lesser pay, the small-acts of discrimination, the almost-harassment, just isn't worth confronting or doing anything about. We tell ourselves that it's an isolated thing, no harm intended, especially when it's not directed at us, when it's just something we observe from a distance, or overhear, when it's happening to someone else. We move on, too busy, too harried to put *yesterday's* little hurt in the context of *today's* little hurt. We fail to realize that its effect is cumulative, that by ignoring what we find hurtful, offensive, disrespectful, and demeaning today, will only get worse tomorrow.

Personally, I cannot differentiate between sexual behaviour that is sexist and non-sexual behavior that is sexist. If I can't, how can those women who come to me for help? For example, gender stereotypes about women include their designation as sexual objects. As sexual objects, women's identity in our society is very much related to appearance. Appearance is identity. We live in a society where women are valued for being attractive and young. Many of us struggle to conform to this norm, this expectation — we buy the appropriate clothing, workout regularly, purchase cosmetics, and maintain our hair. We come to work. We go to a board meeting. The meeting is male dominated. We walk in. The men stare. One of them says, "You look great". Unlike anyone else in that room, our appearance has been deemed relevant when, in fact, it has nothing to do with our performance, our competence. Let's just say, for the sake of argument, that this happens quite frequently. Would this be considered "conduct of a sexual nature" or just simple sexism, or nothing, just a compliment? Is sexism ever non-sexual, given the fact that women are often treated according to gender role stereotypes that define them primarily as sexual objects? Try telling women who are experiencing sexist-based harassment, or who are exposed to daily sexist attitudes, the fine line between sexual vs. non-sexual sexism. Try telling them in a way that makes sense. You can't. Because it doesn't make sense.

The final component of most definitions of sexual harassment is "repetitious or serious." In other words, whether something can be considered sexual harassment depends on one of two things — whether there was a pattern of behavior of "little hurts" that eventually escalated into "big hurts" or just one incident that could be considered a "big hurt". How does one assess whether a "hurt" is little or big? Well, apparently this depends on how the "reasonable person" assesses the behavior. Would a reasonable person be hurt by this behavior? Would a reasonable person consider this behavior as objectionable or offensive? Let's examine the situation of a female student who enters her professor's office to get help with a term paper. During the consultation, held during office hours, the student sees a pornographic screensaver appear on the professor's computer, presently inactive because they are talking. He notices that she has suddenly become speechless. He notices that her facial expression connotes surprise. He moves his mouse to make the screensaver disappear and resumes his commentary. She invents an excuse to leave his office and hurries out. She doesn't get the help she needs and it is unlikely that she will return to his office. Sexual harassment? Again, who knows? Did the professor engage in other behaviors that might be considered inappropriate? No. Were there other objectionable images in his office? No. Did he talk to her in a paternalistic, condescending, sexist fashion? No. Just the screensaver. Not repetitious. No pattern of behavior. So…was it serious? What would the "reasonable person" say? From the student's perspective, she went to his office to get help. Because of the pornographic images that appeared on her professor's computer, she felt too uncomfortable to get that help. For her now, this is serious. It has serious implications. What if she does not fulfill the term paper requirements because of her inability to get help? Is she being reasonable or unreasonable in her assessment of the situation as objectionable, as offensive? Most policies would suggest that the student confront this professor, convey her discomfort. It might be suggested that a reasonable person would. But who is this reasonable person? What if the standard being used to determine "reason" is the white, heterosexual, urban male who says, "anyone with any degree of assertiveness skills would have been able to tell this professor that he was crazy to have these images on his computer?" What if the standard being used to determine "reason" is a

317

sexist norm? What if the standard being used to determine reason does not include the perspective of a 19-year old female, who in this case, was from an isolated community of 300 where the teacher, the pastor, and the local doctor are considered the authorities on everything simply because they went to university?

Sexual harassment and issues pertaining to sexual harassment are often examined and decided within a society that still fails to recognize the faces of everyday sexism; a society in which sexism is still permissible; a society in which gender is still reluctantly problematized or considered; a society in which those in positions of authority refer their subordinates to sexual harassment awareness training, never realizing (or caring?) that their level of knowledge about the issue and its causes and consequences may be less than those that they mandate to be trained. I keep thinking back to the advertisement for my job — the ad to which I responded by submitting an eventually successful application. The qualifications mandated were "considerable experience in counseling ... graduation from a 4-year college or university with a degree in clinical psychology, counseling, social work, or a similar field ... preferably supplemented by Master's level course work in a related area ..." The required qualifications did not include "degree in women's studies or specialization in gender studies". Yet, it seems so obvious to me that knowledge about gender — advanced knowledge through advanced degrees — would be a necessary prerequisite for any position that entails determining whether something constitutes sexual harassment, especially when women are the majority of complainants and men the majority of respondents. The problem of sexual harassment is inextricably related to the social construction of gender.

I am doing my job in a gendered context. Gender is socially constructed within our society in such a way that it benefits some and oppresses others. Gender, as it interacts with social class, age, ability, race/ethnicity, or sexual orientation can create multiple layers of oppression — a matrix of domination. I thus see myself not primarily an educator about sexual harassment but about this matrix of domination.

I'm a sexual harassment advisor. I couldn't resist using the housekeeping metaphor to describe what I do. Because it is like housework. Never-ending. And, unless others are helping by picking up for themselves (by reflecting on their belief systems and how they influence their behaviors) or by offering to assume responsibility for some of the tasks (by confronting sexism when they see it), the areas that I've cleaned of sexism through "awareness" training, stays free of sexism for just a few days, and then it needs to be repeated. I cannot do this work alone. Like a household with many children and only one spouse contributing to reproductive work, I need help. I need those in power to contribute by leading through example, by reinforcing what I do. I need them to act on each of the little hurts, those one-time occurrences that do not constitute harassment because I firmly believe that if we let the little things go — these minute indicators of major systemic sexism — then sexual harassment is inevitable. Misogynist attitudes, sexism, still permissible prejudices, will inevitably become real acts of (still permissible) discrimination. Does this make me an extremist? An unreasonable person? Maybe … But I don't think so. It's so bloody obvious to me. I just don't understand why I sometimes feel I'm the only one who sees.

Co-operation and Conflict in Rape Crisis Work St. John's, Newfoundland and Labrador, 1977-1989[1]

Lynn Hartery

IN THE LATE 1960S, THE WOMEN'S MOVEMENT in North America turned its attention to the issue of rape. Women who had been sexually assaulted began speaking out. Analysis and literature examining rape as a widespread social issue increased. Society grappled with the idea that "normal" men rape women, and that women were often raped by men they knew, as opposed to strangers. With this anti-rape movement came more knowledge about the prevalence of rape, and the societal attitudes that permitted the sexual abuse of women and also discouraged them from speaking about their experiences were challenged. Examination of legal and social services revealed inadequate laws and services to assist and protect women from rape. The anti-rape movement identified two main strategies to deal with this inequality and injustice towards women: first, to work towards the revision or rewriting of rape laws and, second, to change societal attitudes that reflected and reinforced laws and myths surrounding rape (Kasinsky, 1978, 159). These goals were to be met while assisting rape victims in the short term, and eliminating rape from society in the long term.

By the early 1970s, the anti-rape movement in Canada began to unite around the concept and formation of rape crisis centres which would have the dual purpose of providing support to rape victims and pressuring governmental and other public agencies for changes that would lessen the negative impact on the victim of reporting the offence. Centres developed around the framework of service provision, by women, for women, that was unavailable from traditional counselling or aid agencies. The centres aimed to provide a non-judgmental and supportive listener who understood the societal underpinnings of violence against women and could offer information about the process of seeking medical attention or legal advice.

Twenty-five community-based rape crisis centres were established in Canada between 1975 and 1978. In Newfoundland and Labrador, a rape crisis committee emerged from the work of the Newfoundland Status of Women Council (NSWC), established in St. John's in November, 1972 in response to the 1970 Report of the Royal Commission on the Status of Women.[2] The NSWC set up a Women's Centre in downtown St. John's and organized active committees to address different social issues.[3] Rape, or violence against women, was added to the NSWC agenda in June, 1977 when Diane Duggan, a member of the NSWC, advanced the rape crisis cause and organized the committee that later became the Rape

Crisis Centre.[4]

Here I examine the changing relationship between the NSWC and the RCC as the latter moved toward being an autonomous organization working within the walls of the Women's Centre. Part of the story of the St. John's Rape Crisis Centre from 1977 to 1989 is that of a struggle for recognition and public awareness of rape as a serious issue; another part is the fight for material and human resources to do the job. Woven through the daily work of both organizations is the on-going tension between two groups as differences in approach and opinions about rape crisis intervention became apparent.

Getting Organized: the St. John's Rape Crisis Centre

The idea of setting up a rape crisis service in St. John's stemmed from a 1977 visit by Joanie Vance, the Co-ordinator for the National Association for Rape Crisis Centres, established at a national conference in 1975.[5] Members of the Newfoundland Status of Women Council were cautious about whether they could offer an effective rape crisis service. Already reliant on volunteer hours, NSWC members were uncertain about taking on another project demanding more commitment and time. Diane Duggan took the lead, investigating the feasibility of a rape crisis service, and gathering information on current service provision. In November 1977, the rape crisis committee was struck with Diane Duggan as coordinator.

Duggan became the "face" of the Rape Crisis Centre and her name synonymous with it. As colleague Wendy Williams notes, from the beginning, "Diane was the person who was willing to take on the issue of rape. Everybody was busy doing their thing and Diane's thing was rape crisis." Other volunteers named Duggan as the leader, the decision-maker, the one who took the most responsibility, and the one volunteers and community members called upon if they needed advice, information or simply to talk. This description of a strong, dominant individual as a leader challenges the collective, non-hierarchical structure the RCC described as its form (Rape Crisis Centre, *How We Work Together*, n.d.). However, Williams suggests that the RCC could never be a collective, because Duggan invested so much in the RCC that there was never equal power among the volunteers. Beth Lacey agreed, saying "... people didn't feel they had Diane's knowledge ... her history, her strength and her courage, so while they tried to act as a collective, there was no question Diane was the leader." Duggan remained co-ordinator of the RCC, officially or unofficially, for the next twelve years. Documentary evidence and interviews suggest that contestations over ideology, material resources and power existed in the relationship between the NSWC and the RCC. Struggles for recognition of the serious nature of rape in Newfoundland society, for space and money to operate the crisis telephone line, and for control over the workings of RCC separate from NSWC, consumed time, energy and volunteers.

In 1978, the rape crisis group was still technically a "committee" of the NSWC, even though the organization was referred to as the Rape Crisis "Centre" by all involved. Like other Rape Crisis Centres across Canada, offering anonymous and confidential emergency counseling and support to rape victims through a crisis telephone line was seen as vital to the work of the RCC in St. John's. This approach is based on a model of peer support and the belief that assisting other women is working to end the common oppression of women, in all its forms.

Keeping the RCC afloat was not an easy task: volunteers did the work and small donations were used to keep the crisis line operating. At the Women's Centre, a tiny, rent-free office in the back of the house became the "rape crisis centre," and was a site for information storage, to do paperwork and whatever else constituted the growing rape crisis work. This included keeping Logbooks where RCC members noted concerns, requests for information, activities and meeting notes. These books provided a key medium of exchange and communication between the RCC and the NSWC. Initially mail for the RCC was received and opened by the NSWC staff, however this approach was significantly altered in the coming years. The RCC remained relatively underfunded in this period, choosing to not apply for, or being unsuccessful in their application to, provincial or federal government funding to accomplish its work. Small yearly municipal funding grants, public and private donations were accepted to keep the crisis line open. Day-to-day office expenses formed an in-kind donation from the NSWC.

RCC meetings, held in the Women's Centre after business hours, provided a chance for the volunteers to talk about their work and share information, and work on their own consciousness-raising process. They also discussed current events relevant to their work such as rape charges, court cases and media attention. Coverage of the work of the RCC in the local media gradually led to community awareness of the RCC and its services, resulting in requests for public presentations on sexual assault and child sexual abuse.

During early 1978, the RCC and NSWC worked hard to promote attitude change, raise public awareness about rape and help rape victims. The groups countered newspaper articles suggesting "Women's Lib" promoted rape; wrote press releases on rape laws; met with national rape crisis centres; worked with the RCMP and the Royal Newfoundland Constabulary (RNC) to increase police awareness; and supported rape victims at the police station. As the RCC increased its public profile, some donations came in: the Avalon Band Citizen Radio donated $100.00 and the RCC received $1000.00 from St. John's City Council to pay for the separate 24-hour crisis line established in July 1978.

Despite (or because of) this intense work together, and perhaps the forthcoming official opening of the Women's Centre in June, tensions within the NSWC increased and a "Day of Discussion" was held in late May 1978. At this meeting, NSWC members noted that although the projects of the RCC — rape crisis centre, an information and meeting place and feminist library — were needed, "... they did not provide an overall focus or goal for the entire organization to become involved in" (Women's Centre Opens, *Evening Telegram*, 2; NSWC Minutes, 27 May, 1978). Rape crisis work was to be only one of the goals of the NSWC.

In June the official opening of the Women's Centre was held and, in July, the rape crisis telephone line was established. Then, in August, the implicit split in focus and work of the NSWC and the RCC noted at the Day of Discussion became more apparent. Duggan wrote in the daily Logbook that,

from now on the RCC mail will be handled separately [from the NSWC] — in its own mail book. Whoever gets the mail should put it to one side unopened. There is also a Logbook [specifically] for the RCC ..." (NSWC Logbook, 2 August 1978).

This request explicitly separates the work of the NSWC and the Women's Centre from RCC, as now, the RCC mail was likely opened only by members of the RCC. The establishment of a dedicated rape crisis telephone line, coupled with the discrete physical space — the back office — in the Women's Centre, were factors establishing the RCC as a separate entity from the NSCW. The request to have independent mail and record handling further established the boundaries and solidified the unofficial separation of the two organizations. The work of the RCC and the NSWC appears to be running on parallel tracks by the end of 1978.

To maintain the RCC crisis telephone line, volunteers were essential. In the fall of 1978, the RCC organized the first rape crisis training session open to women from beyond the borders of the NSWC. The 30 hours of training, drawing on community resources and information from other rape crisis centres, included consciousness raising about the prevalence of violence against women, discussions of confidentiality and group process at RCC, dealing with crisis, suicide and crank calls, and the police, judicial and hospital procedures for victims of assault. The number of volunteers fluctuated over the years – between 2 and 12 – and the length of time they volunteered varied considerably. Some volunteers left during training because they felt overwhelmed by the information about sexual assault (Doyle, 2001). In Fall 1978, thirteen women participated in the training session and became the first group of Rape Crisis Centre volunteers.

Affiliated But Autonomous

The Rape Crisis Centre activities of 1979 focused on the public visibility, operation of the RCC and staffing the crisis line located in the Women's Centre. The NSWC daily Logbooks record efforts at public awareness through education, conference presentations, television and radio interviews and connections in the community. Information-gathering from different agencies, including health care professions, police, and justice officials continued. The RCC was active on the national scene as well, joining the Association of Canadian Rape Crisis Centres in 1978 and contributing to the drafting of the national constitution that year. However, the crisis line remained the mainstay of the organization, and volunteers took "shifts" of a day or two carrying a beeper that alerted the carrier when someone telephoned for assistance.

The Logbooks also record continuing tensions between the RCC and the NSWC. Early in 1979, Duggan's entries in the NSCW Logbooks show frustration with the NSWC. Communication and control over the RCC appear: one entry reveals concern that she had not been received a message left for her; another points to privacy and safety issues and urges that this be "the final request for people not to leave the back office [RCC] unlocked" (NSWC Logbooks, 14 January 1979). Aside from her obvious frustration at these occurrences, it is interesting that Diane chose to communicate her frustrations through the Logbooks. All members of the NSWC would get the message of her concern, since all could read the Logbooks. Writing it in this way was a very public way of communicating.

Notes in the Logbooks from, or about, the RCC become rare after this, and nothing appears in the NSWC Meeting Minutes for a full eight months — between January and September 1979. This means that the NSWC did not record any discussions about the RCC, nor did the RCC (essentially Duggan) maintain communication by making notes in the Logbook. If the Logbook served as a way for members to keep in touch when they didn't physically see each other, had the communication stopped? Or was there ongoing contact and related discussions that were not officially documented? Over the ensuing months, an unidentified woman acted as "liaison" between the NSWC and the RCC, which further indicates organizational problems.

Finally, in October, the RCC sought clarification from the NSWC about the relationship between the two groups, specifically whether the members of the RCC needed to bring correspondence, action plans, and decisions to the NSWC executive for approval, as this would be "postponing action" in some cases. NSWC noted in its monthly meeting that:

What must be brought before the [NSWC] executive is not day-to-day business, but the responsibilites of the executive in terms of time, money, personnel, news releases, public announcements and requests for further funding, requests for feminst services, labor, etc. This will be taken back to the Centre and discussed [by the NSWC] (NSWC Minutes, October 1979).

In effect, the NSWC were stating that operational control of the Rape Crisis Centre was to be in the hands of NSWC, rather than the RCC volunteers. The language used by the NSWC when referring to the RCC — "they" — also signals a sense of separation, or less overlap, between the two groups (NSWC Minutes, October 1979).

The relationship and obligations of the organizations to each other was the first order of business for the 5 November meeting. The RCC proposal that it would be "affiliated but autonomous," meant that the RCC would be self-governing, although it would continue to make monthly reports to the NSWC. Contrary to the statement put forth by the NSWC, the RCC proposed that it would not wait for approval from NSWC to issue press releases or seek funding. At this meeting, the members of NSWC agreed that the

rape crisis centre is neither a standing committee nor a project of the NSWC and that the two organizations are affiliated: the affiliation is by consent of both groups. Therefore the rape crisis centre is autonomous in its operation (NSWC Minutes, 5 November 1979).

Guidelines were established for the separate operation of the organizations, as they still shared physical space in the Women's Centre. For example, the RCC would use its own letterhead, maintain its own locked and confidential filing cabinets, and Women's Centre personnel would not answer the rape crisis telephone, as they had not been trained to deal specifically with rape crisis calls. However, the back room was now to be shared, with priority given to emergencies, counselling and RCC work, as well as other business, including NSWC. A motion to this effect was passed during the meeting (NSWC Minutes, 5 November 1979). This marked the recognition that the St. John's Rape Crisis Centre was an organization in itself, although it continued to work out of the small back office of the Women's Centre for the next twelve years.

Conflict and Co-operation: the RCC and NSWC in the 1980s

The 1980s mark a period of fluctuation in the relationship between the RCC and the NSWC Women's Centre. There is no mention of the RCC or its work in the Logbooks of 1981 or 1982. Examination of the NSWC minutes, however, reveals the relationship between the organizations, though less intense, was maintained. Some communication related to administrative concerns persisted, and the Women's Centre continued to be used as "home base" by the RCC.

As there are no documents from the RCC itself, we are left to speculate how the early 1980s played out for the group. From my interviews with former RCC and NSWC members, it is clear that the RCC volunteer effort was constantly in flux. In the months following the recruiting and training session for new RCC volunteers, there were sufficient numbers of volunteers, but they slowly dwindled until only a few core members remained. Indeed, by 1983, the RCC had only two volunteers, Diane Duggan and Mary Doyle. Doyle began her volunteer work with RCC in 1978, but the turnover of volunteers was so rapid that of the early group with whom she trained, Doyle was the only one still active in RCC after the first year. She made significant contacts with other Canadian Rape Crisis Centres and was aware of national rape crisis work. A teacher, Mary left the RCC in the late 1980s. This fluctuation in volunteers made sustaining the crisis line difficult.

With few volunteers and significant financial problems, the crisis line was disconnected in 1983 because of unpaid bills (NSWC Minutes, 7 February 1983). The RCC approached the NSWC to help reconnect the phone, and plans were made for a discussion with Diane Duggan about how the NSWC could help (NSWC Minutes, 2 April 1984). Records show the NSWC questioned why there were only two volunteers, and they sought reassurance that a volunteer training session would soon be held.

Six months later, a training session was arranged for the two new co-ordinators of the Women's Centre, as a temporary measure. An agreement was made that the Women's Centre co-ordinators, one of whom was Beth Lacey[6], handle rape crisis calls from 9:00 a.m. to 5:00 p.m., or during working hours, to relieve the stress faced by Doyle and Duggan, the two RCC volunteers. After working hours, calls were forwarded to the home numbers of the two volunteers. While this was an interim solution until a training session was organized, the Women's Centre Co-ordinators continued to field rape information calls, and handled the crisis line during their work hours throughout 1984 and 1985.

Increased co-operation during this time may signal renewed interest in working together on the issue of rape. Beth Lacey saw rape crisis line work as draining for those involved, an attitude which no doubt influenced her decision to actively support and assist the RCC by answering calls during work hours. NSWC members also worked with RCC to give presentations in schools, and over the summer the groups organized the first *Take Back the Night March* in St. John's for the fall of 1984. The organizational partnership continued for the *Take Back the Night March* in Fall 1985.

This collaboration marked a rare period of close cooperation between the RCC's two volunteers and the NSWC. However, mail for the RCC continued to come into the Women's Centre and was picked up by one of the volunteers, so the distinction of who was RCC and who was not remained, despite the cooperative effort. Beth Lacey described the relationship between the RCC and the Women's Centre as "symbiotic," suggesting that the work of the RCC took a lot of pressure off the Women's Centre. In turn, access to support and services such as photocopying, telephone line and office space was provided by the Women's Centre. The NSWC noted that, "... things seemed to be going better. Their answering machine has been hooked up" (NSWC Minutes, 29 September 1986). This machine, on the RCC line, provided the number of the Women's Centre for calls during work hours.

In early 1987, Ann Donovan, a member of the NSWC, volunteeered to help RCC with interviewing and training of new volunteers to be held in February. By January 27, however, Donovan declared she had "had it" with the RCC training, feeling she had done most of the work. A motion was put forward, and unanimously supported, that the NSWC strike a committee to take over responsibility for working with the RCC, beyond helping out with training. There was unanimous approval and plans were made to discuss this with Duggan (NSWC Minutes, 27 January 1987).

In this fraught atmosphere, a meeting took place in early February between four members of the NSWC and three RCC volunteers. How a third volunteer was recruited is not documented. However, it is possible that this was a former NSWC volunteer who had taken the training. The agenda for this meeting was extensive, covering training of new volunteers, repayment of money loaned to the RCC by NSWC, and a proposal that NSWC become part of RCC (NSWC Minutes, 9 February 1987).

The financial discussion in particular was difficult. The Women's Centre sought repayment of $1500.00 loaned to the RCC in 1985, and requested receipts from *Take Back the Night* expenses or monies raised by the RCC. Duggan reported that some of the money borrowed from the NSWC had been lent to another Women's Centre, who now could not repay it. She refused to divulge the amount loaned or to whom, and a lack of record keeping by the RCC made further inquiry impossible. In response, the NSWC suggested they would reduce the outstanding loan by $500.00 if the remaining monies from *Take Back the Night March* were turned over. Duggan noted that approximately $750.00 remained from the March. As with the Minutes of most organizations, those of the NSWC often conceal, or only hint at, more than they reveal, and "private" meetings often have no recorded minutes. Thus the NSWC refer only to a "very emotional" private meeting (NSWC Minutes, 9 February 1987), and the contents of this discussion remain obscure.

The NSWC also proposed that it be considered part of the Rape Crisis Centre. Once again, this issue was not resolved and few details are recorded. The NSWC minutes indicate only that such a working relationship was not acceptable (NSWC Minutes, 9 February 1987), however it is not clear why this proposal was unacceptable, or to whom. A report of this meeting, written by members of the NSWC, suggested Duggan's approach was more obstructive than cooperative. She refused to give information to the NSWC and she hedged on, then declined, the proposal that the NSWC become members of the RCC, thus potentially increasing a much-needed volunteer base. In the months following, the NSWC objected to the way the RCC recruited volunteers, specifically that they were being interviewed for suitability on the crisis line. There was further correspondence between the organizations, including written communication from Diane Duggan voicing concerns with the NSWC and RCC liaison. Finally, in March 1987, the NSWC resolved to set up their own 24-hour rape crisis service because members felt "the needs of women in this community are not being met" (NSWC Minutes, 2 March 1987). Later that month, Ann Donovan suggested the use of a mediator to attempt resolution of the problems between the NSWC and the RCC (NSWC Minutes, 16 March 1987). Duggan replied and the NSWC drafted a response, but as with other vital correspondence, records are silent on the exact content of these exchanges (NSWC Minutes, 30 March 1987).

The meeting of 28 April indicates a hard-nosed approach being taken by the NSWC: letters demanded payment of outstanding photocopy bills; NSWC decision deadlines were set for offering their own rape crisis service; expectations of a separate NSWC meeting and final decisions regarding the RCC appear. The NSWC decision deadline for offering a rape crisis service was one the members wanted brought to the NSWC AGM (NSWC Minutes, 28 April 1987). In June and July plans were made to gather information to support Women's Centre staff in offering rape crisis counseling. By mid-August, however, there was some resolution to the tension between the organizations. Duggan reported a 24-hour rape crisis line, serviced by an agency that would forward all calls to RCC volunteers, was being installed at the Women's Centre (NSWC Minutes, 3 August; 17 August and 31 August 1987). Whether the idea of the NSWC setting up their own rape crisis service spurred Duggan into action, or whether circumstances changed allowing the establishment of the line is not clear. Perhaps in light of these changes, the possibility of a liaison person working between the organizations was broached again by the NSWC (NSWC Minutes, 13 October 1987).

In the Logbooks and NSWC minutes of 1988, the Rape Crisis Centre is cited fairly consistently. Meetings are held in the Women's Centre, speakers on the subject of rape are organized. An understanding of some kind was reached, for the NSWC's request for another training session to produce a pool of RCC volunteers was met and the 24-hour crisis line was operating. Both of these developments lessened the presence of the RCC in the personal lives of the few volunteers who were taking calls at home, and who had had only themselves and two Women's Centre co-ordinators to handle the rape crisis work.

In the summer of 1988, the NSWC employed three regular staff and five summer students. With an additional two summer students hired by RCC, the Women's Centre space became untenable and tensions rose again. RCC lacked space for its students and NSWC staff complained they were being "strained beyond capacity" at the Women's Centre. This development seemed to mark another period of progressively less com- munication between NSWC and the RCC, specifically Diane Duggan. Ultimately, the NSWC staff decided to use the back office, and offered to help the RCC find new space for the RCC workers to meet with clients during the day (NSWC Minutes, 2 and 16 February, 7 and 21 June 1988).

This period of discord coincides with the time Duggan started docu- menting her struggles with depression. In early June, an RCC volunteer expressed her concerns about the relationship between the two organiza- tions. Identifying herself as "someone personally concerned" and not a representative of the RCC, the volunteer suggested a meeting between the NSWC and the RCC. However, the RCC declined to meet with the NSWC until later in the Fall, citing an overworked schedule, and not wanting to engage in a committee of both the NSWC and RCC. Such a meeting would be considered again in the Fall (NSWC Minutes 7 and 21 June 1988). Then, early in 1989, the RCC requested a further loan of $300.00 to pay their telephone bill, to which the NSWC agreed (NSWC Minutes, 1 February 1989). Clearly, lack of financial resources continued to plague the RCC and its volunteers.

On April 27, 1989 Diane Duggan committed suicide after many months of severe depression. The personal effects of crisis counselling for a dozen years are difficult to measure, so it is impossible to tell how much of this contributed to her depression and death. Knowing that the Rape Crisis Centre was a reality because of Diane Duggan's efforts, Beth Lacey observed that Duggan "... didn't trust anyone to feel as committed to it as she did." None of the women interviewed for my larger thesis project challenged the work, time and energy Duggan contributed to the RCC, or her committment to the women who called the crisis line.

After Diane Duggan's death the NSWC continued the rape crisis work and Pat Balsom took over as chair of the RCC committee. Doubtless, Duggan's death had a major impact on the RCC workers. The two RCC current volunteers were "exhausted" and the answering service had been suspended. While a 24-hour service could not be offered, the Women's Centre co-ordinators once again answered the phone during work hours, and agreed to call a meeting to organize volunteers for the crisis line, at least until another training session could be organized in the fall (NSWC Minutes, 27 June 1989). Two more women volunteered to help out, and a beeper or paging system for the crisis line was instituted by July. This allowed the volunteers more freedom when they were on call and was less expensive to operate. Soon fourteen volunteer counsellors were available to respond to the crisis line calls (NSWC Minutes, 11 July and 25 July 1989). A new evening training program of ten to twelve weeks for Rape Crisis Centre volunteers was held in October 1989. Ironically, after years of struggling with little or no funding, the RCC received $13,000.00 from the annual Monte Carlo Night run by Memorial University of Newfoundland medical students (NSWC Minutes, 17 October, 1989; 27 November 1989). The work of the RCC carried on.

Conclusion

Within two years of its establishment as a committee of the NSWC, the Rape Crisis Centre sought an organizational structure and status independent of the NSWC. In the decade 1980-1990 volunteers came and went, with few remaining involved for extended periods of time. Diane Duggan, who continued to be involved until her death in 1989, led the RCC and was, at times, one of only two volunteers.

The relationship between the RCC and the NSWC was often fraught with tensions. Both Mary Doyle and Beth Lacey refer to periods when the relationship between the two groups was "not very good" and when there "was not much trust between the RCC and the Women's Centre." While the focus of concern at a given moment varied over the years, this lack of trust on both sides weakened the relationship between the organizations. The RCC refused full NSWC participation in rape crisis work, while the NSWC in turn believed the RCC was not always meeting the needs of the women it purported to serve. Two major factors that influenced the ability of the RCC to meet their goals were the fluctuating number of volunteers and a lack of stable funding, which resulted in the crisis line being disabled for significant periods of time. In turn, these developments were cause for concern on the part of the NSWC, along with the fact that there were no records kept by the RCC.

The two organizations clashed on process as well. The NSWC was government funded, while the RCC was not. The NSWC, therefore, had hired staff and an executive, which constituted a hierarchical organization. The RCC struggled to operate as a collective, without a "coordinator," and with minimal funding, accountable only to the women it served. Whether this was a salient point in the tensions between the organizations is unclear. Also, the question of whether the RCC outright rejected the idea of government funding or, just did not succeed is receiving government funding may depend on the period and the people involved. Finally, the NSWC disagreed with the RCC approach to volunteer recruitment procedures. The relationship, rather than being symbiotic, as Beth Lacey described, appears more unbalanced: the RCC relied on the NSWC for help (financial and otherwise), and yet refused to allow the NSWC to be an active part of the Rape Crisis Centre.

Tensions between the organizations stemmed from the NSWC's concern that the RCC was not accountable to anyone for the work being done, and possibly concern that Diane Duggan was reluctant to bring anyone else into the RCC. Documented exchanges between the organizations focus on the NSWC request that new volunteers be brought in, if they were to help the RCC get through difficulties such as paying bills. Their reasons are not explicitly stated or documented, but NSWC members may have felt torn between supporting the idea of a Rape Crisis Centre, but not supporting the manner in which this particular RCC had developed. This view is most evident in the decision of the NSWC to offer its own rape crisis service.

The St. John's Rape Crisis Centre represents one of the best outcomes of the feminist movement in important ways. It was a service provided by women, for women, to deal with violence against them. It was an organization rooted in feminist principles, building from the Newfoundland Status of Women Council and branching out to offer more services. In reality though, how well did the RCC fit the NSWC ideals? Did the structure and operation of the RCC also represent exclusion? Was the lack of volunteers due to a lack of interest or because potential volunteers were screened out by the women running the RCC? Once recruited, were the demands placed on volunteers too great, resulting in exhaustion and over-work, leading to their resignations? Williams pointed out that this was one of the worst things about the women's movement of the time — the expectation that you give everything to the cause, which can be seen as a form of exploitation in itself. How beneficial was it to the RCC to divide the women of the NSWC into "RCC people" and others, in terms of answering the phone and opening the mail?

Was the St. John's RCC successful in its work? Have rape crisis centres in general been successful? As early as 1977, Lorene Clark wrote that the impact of rape, and the subsequent turmoil with reporting, was considerably lessened by the establishment and work of rape crisis centres (13). The St. John's Rape Crisis Centre, with all its difficulties and conflicts, likely mirrors the development of similar centres that attempt to fulfill an ambitious and worthy ideal with few resources to support it. And what of the women served by the RCC? The opinions of women who used the services might well reveal new information and perspectives. Perhaps we would then understand more about how the RCC affected or shaped their process of dealing with a sexual assault. There is no doubt that the volunteers were dedicated to helping individual women through a very traumatic experience. The St. John's Rape Crisis Centre, through its very existence, acknowledged and publicized the problem of rape and brought attention to the sexual abuse of women and children. It has played a key role in educating the public, and social agencies, about the pervasiveness and lasting effects of sexual violence against women.

Archival Sources

NSWC Logbooks 1972-1989. Newfoundland Status of Women Council. Status of Women Council, St. John's Women's Centre.

NSWC Minutes 1972-1989. Newfoundland Status of Women Council. Status of Women Council, St. John's Women's Centre. MG 1004, Provincial Archives of Newfoundland and Labrador (PANL).

Notes

[1] This article is drawn from my unpublished Master's thesis (2002), *Radical Feminism in Action?: A Historical Look at the St. John's Rape Crisis Centre and Its Volunteers (1977-1990)*, undertaken in the Women's Studies Program, Memorial University of Newfoundland.

[2] The NSWC changed its name to the St. John's Status of Women Council in 1984 to more accurately reflect its membership and focus, and to acknowledge other Status of Women Councils that were established in the province.

[3] For a broader examination of the women's movement in Newfoundland and Labrador, see Sharon Gray Pope and Jane Burnham, "Change Within and Without: The Modern Women's Movement in Newfoundland and Labrador" in L. Kealey (ed.) *Pursuing Equality: Historical Perspectives on Women in Newfoundland and Labrador*. St. John's: ISER Books, 1993.

[4] The RCC is currently named the Newfoundland and Labrador Sexual Assault Crisis and Prevention Centre Inc.

[5] This organization later became known as the Canadian Association of Sexual Assault Centres (CASAC). It still exists today. For more information, see the CASAC website: http//:www.casac.ca

[6] Beth Lacey served as Co-ordinator of the Women's Centre from 1983 to 1987.

Bob

Roberta Buchanan

Fifteen is the perfect age
the curve of the lip
small waist
not yet thickening
a thin line of down on the upper lip
eagerly shaved!
What's the hurry, Bob?
Age will come too soon
The bags beneath the eyes
the loosening teeth
wrinkles, white hair

A Suitable Woman

Joanne Soper-Cook

ELIZABETH HAS BEEN AWAY AT COLLEGE, studying to he a veterinarian. She wants to live on the trackless barrens, somewhere far away from here, tending sheep and cattle, living in a cottage with stout walls and thick old windows, the kettle on the hob. She has come home for the weekend, long enough to visit with her mother and to pose for this photograph in the back yard of their family home in Harbour Grace. The grass has grown up in her absence; it is nearing the end of August now, time for Elizabeth to return to study. Before she boards the Sunday morning bus to university, she will change into a pair of her dead brother's overalls, don a pair of rubber goat hoots, and mow the yard one final time. The push mower is old, and its rusty blades hack and stutter at the grass. But Elizabeth is stubborn, and besides, she likes the exercise. It will help her in the future, she thinks. It will strengthen her for what is to come.

Her mother, so glad that Elizabeth has been home, cannot hear to speak of her daughter's imminent departure. As the weekend winds itself into a warp and weft of things unsaid, she busies herself in the kitchen, preparing little cakes and loaves of bread for Elizabeth to take with her on the bus. She hurries from the counter to the cupboards, from the cupboards to the pantry, and from there to the oven's opened mouth. Tears drop into the dough as she kneads, her muscular arms squeezing, shaping the loaves, and she wipes her tears in the hem of her apron, while Elizabeth's mower cuts narrow paths in the surfeit of grass. Eventually, Elizabeth thinks, she will have to tell her mother. Eventually, there will have to be a reckoning, not unlike confession, where she will tell her mother everything. She has privately murmured over this decision all weekend, enumerating the reasons, and she has decided to tell her mother when they get to the bus. She will have to. She cannot bear the burden of the secret any longer. If she doesn't speak this truth out loud, then it will burst her frame wide open. She feels it pulsing underneath her breastbone, waiting.

Elizabeth's mother has something to tell as well — something that cannot wait, something that will not be put off, something that must he spoken. Many times she has tried to frame it in a letter to her daughter, addressed to the veterinary college, and many times she has laid the crumpled paper carefully among the oven's burning coals. It isn't speculation any longer: there is the doctor's evidence, the months of bloodied undergarments smelling curiously of yeast and rust, a melancholic bottom note of rot. This must be spoken. It cannot he allowed to lie between them, filling up their familiar spaces.

Elizabeth finishes the mowing and goes into the house, leaving her boots just outside the door. She is acutely conscious of the sentiments of trespass and rinses her hands at the garden tap. The margins of her fingernails are stained deep green, the blood of August. Soon, the stubble fields upon the hillsides will turn brown and dry, crackling in the watery sunlight. Summer will die quietly and quickly, a blown-out candle.

Their evening meal is simple: soup that her mother has made, slices cut from a fresh loaf of bread, some cheese. The daylight dies quickly behind the curtains; there is silence save for the ticking of a clock in the back room somewhere, hidden in the house. Elizabeth tries to drink the tea that her mother has made, but it has long since gone cold, and the chill of it constricts her throat.

"Mummy, there's something you should know." She tries to speak calmly and clearly, as she was taught at school, many years ago — many years ago, before her father went to sea and never came back, before her mother finally abandoned all hope of grandchildren. Yes, the older woman has seen all this, and she knows what Elizabeth will say.

"Say what's on your mind, child." Her mother busies herself with clearing away the supper things, rinsing dishes at the sink, emptying cold tea into the drain. Elizabeth hates the dying daylight, the stain of darkness that slowly tints the sky She feels as if she were dissolving, being swallowed by this exquisite misery of truth. Night creatures, rising from the yard's truncated grass, begin a plainsong underneath the kitchen windows.

"Mummy, when you were a girl, did you ever have a special friend?" The words are hard to say, and yet Elizabeth knows she must say them before the evening draws too dark a curtain. "One very special girlfriend, that you loved more than ever you could a sister?"

Her mother takes the teapot between her palms, her face sketched blank, without expression. "Why, yes," she says at last, "there was a girl I knew from Bonavista — her name was Louise. She married an American."

She cannot possibly understand, Elizabeth thinks. In the gloaming, her grass-green fingernails appear bloody. "Not like that exactly, Mummy."

"I know what you mean!" Her mother sets the teapot on the sideboard with a thump. "You think I've never seen those mannish women with their hair cut off? When your father was alive, we went on holiday down to Florida. I saw two of them, walking on the street. Dressed like men, they were."

"It isn't like that!" Elizabeth cries, distressed. "Amelia and I have planned to make our lives together!"

She thinks her mother's sudden sharp intake of breath is a reaction to the confession she has made. If they permitted themselves to be demonstrative with familial affection, perhaps Elizabeth might go to her mother's side, clasp the older woman's work-weary hands in hers. Such action is of course impossible. It cannot be done. And so Elizabeth waits until her mother has gone upstairs, and then she slips into her dead brother's anorak and boots, and with the house key in her pocket, goes guiltily out into the August twilight.

The local pub is close by, only a few moments' walk, and she takes a table gratefully. She orders whisky and takes it with just a little water. She remembers Amelia's scorn for her lifelong habit of sherry and Amelia's insistence upon good whisky in their shared lodgings. A sharp and tensile loneliness assails her, and she goes out to the telephone, listening breathlessly to the disjointed ringing. "I've told my mother everything," she says. She wants Amelia to know the sacrifices she has made. She wonders if it might have been accomplished some other way. Perhaps it is wrong to tell, just as it is wrong to keep silent. She longs for the morning when the bus will take her once again into the familiar landscape of home. She cannot bear to he here any longer. She cannot bear the silences or the wordless hum of night creatures underneath the kitchen window. She cannot bear her mother's expression of silent rebuke.

"Behave yourself and study hard." Elizabeth's mother does not get out of the car; Elizabeth takes her suitcase out of the trunk herself. There is much more she wants to say and cannot: the silence is a chasm, an abyss too large to breach. She waves as Elizabeth steps aboard the bus. She waves until the bus is lost to sight, as the familiar hills and furrows of the land dissolve and blur. The yard and all its echoes are still waiting, and there is the teapot and the kitchen. The stubble fields are warm as August dies into September. There are no letters. There is nothing, after all.

Steady Goods

Carol Hobbs

Cabbage pickles
with bright mustard and black beads of pepper.
Considering also the beets, I stand in the pantry
while something famous happens outside.
My brother has climbed the ladder one story to the roof.
His running gait shakes the shelves and jars.
He leaps and flies, following the geese, south.
And in the brief silence
before the groan, I take
a silver rod of herring from its brine.

Everyone pities our mother,
commends her longsuffering and good sense
and speed in brushing him off –
Stand up! Walk!
Mothers speak in this biblical way.

And in the known world, I am
lost among steady goods, the labeled bottles –
the preserved *moose, seal* (oily and black as loam),
jams in amber and garnet *bakeapple partidgeberry damson*
a white rabbit in its perfect cardigan of fur,
hanged by the wire snare.

The Stylist

Lisa Moore

THE STYLIST STANDS BEHIND YOU AND LEANS IN. She scrunches your hair in her fists, testing bounce. She lifts it to the sides like wings, tugging her fingers through the snags.

She says, What's the idea here?

The idea is I want to look good.

You want a change, she says. Your husband left you. Your husband left you. Your husband left you.

Uncross your legs, she says. You adjust your posture. She spreads her hands on your shoulders, meets your eyes in the mirror.

Now listen, you'll have to sit up straight.

You have hunched since competitive diving at the Aquarena when you were twelve and grew breasts. Your bathing suit, the frosty green of the old Ford. The green of leaves covered with short silver hair, lucent grapes. You wore this bathing suit every day after school. The chlorine wearing the lycra thin, fading the sheen. When the bathing suit was wet your nipples were visible. The colour of your nipples.

You hunch your shoulders. You aren't like the older girls whose breasts are a fact.

Your breasts are tender, a rumour, the beginning of a long story, a page-turner. It's the worst when you're speaking with your coach. The bathing suit transparent as the skin of a grape you peel with your teeth.

The lineup for the ladder is the worst. Long enough for the warm lights to make the beads of water on your arms creep to a standstill, chlorine tingles your skin. Under the water nobody can see your nipples. Diving practice enchants you. You fall asleep as soon as you get home. Asleep before the soaps, drooling on the cushion. Over your fried eggs and beans, the ketchup screaming on the white plate.

This is what the table looks like: placemats with illustrations of a fox hunt. Red riding jackets, top hats, hounds. A silver water pitcher, greasy with condensation. An ashtray with a smoking cigarette. Your father's empty chair. His placemat, without the cutlery. Your mother is likely to cry. She cries every night. Sometimes while watching the news, sometimes over supper. These are her specialties: sweet-and-sour ribs with tears, spaghetti with tears, steak, baked potato, tears. Mom, hold the tears.

This is what you see out the window: hideous icicles, a row of fangs. You dream you kiss your coach.

A kiss so ripe and desperate, nothing else will ever come close.

He kisses you and cups his hand under your chin and one of your front teeth drops into his open palm. Blood seeps from the fleshy hole. You know at once it isn't a baby tooth. Now you must go through life like this. Icicles crash from the eaves.

338

In the morning you run your tongue and run your tongue. Your mother and you live in the mouth of winter, waterlogged. The sky is a ravenous mink, the spruce trees raking its wet fur underbelly. You have become enchanted. Your coach lifting weights in the chrome gym, wiping his glistening neck with a white towel, rolling his shoulders, sweat in his eyelashes. He lies on his back, a leg on either side of the black vinyl bench. The leg of his shorts gapes and you see the white perforated cotton inside and the bulge of his penis, pubic hair. You have never seen. This is something else. Something else again. When he stands up the foggy print of his sweat in the vinyl, his spine, his shoulder blades like the wings of a dragonfly. Rank gym, feet, the iron smell of clanking weights, chlorine, boiling hotdogs from the hot air vent, the tangy liniment. The slap of his hand against his wet neck. The smell of his liniment. Like laundry dried in the wind and licorice, coniferous.

How fickle the water is. You slip in from a great height and the blush in your cheeks cools. The water unzippers your new-girl body, your breasts, the hunch. The water peels you. The saddest thing you've ever seen is the back of your father's green Ford raising clouds of dust that make the alders unshiny. The saddest thing is that Ford turning the corner.

Or the pool rises up in a fist and mangles your face.

A month ago you blackened both your eyes. They swelled shut. Two plums sitting neat. Sockets like eggcups. A blow so stunning it seemed ordained. The fangs snapped shut. Mink savaging the hind leg of a cloud. Your mother kneeling near your head on the concrete.

Next we'll see the macaroni, she says.

You vomit chlorine and macaroni. Where has she come from? She was supposed to be at work. How long have you been out? She would have had to come across the city. The back of her hand on your cheek. She would have had to know without being told.

But here you are again, toes curled over the edge of the ten-metre board. It's warm up here because you're near the lights. You're in the rafters. Far away, at the other end of the Aquarena, an aerobics class.

Your coach could turn on the bubbles. No matter what, it will be okay if he turns on the bubbles, which cost money, which aren't allowed at the Nationals, which make the water as welcoming as whipped cream.

He wants to see a triple.

You want the bubbles but you don't ask. You are in love, the black Trans Am with a flame that bursts over the hood, the megaphone. He's sitting in a canvas chair by the side of the pool and he's wearing black flip-flops with red plastic flowers. He speaks to you.

Shoulders, he says. Although it's a megaphone, his tone sounds bedroomy. He calls you by your last name.

Fo*cus* Malone.

It's strange, but you are very good at diving. You are the youngest on the provincial team. You will go to the Nationals. You have come to suspect you can do absolutely anything. It's intoxicating, this glimmer of your will. The pool crunches your ribs like a nutcracker, the board nicks your shin, unspooling a ribbon of blood in the water, a love tap on the left shoulder so you can't lift your arm.

Or the pool plays dead. It doesn't matter, you keep doing it. Doing begets doing. You could go on like this forever.

You unhunch. It's a magic trick, the triple. The action doesn't happen until it's over. It happens in the future and you catch up. A triple is déjà vu. Trusting the untrustable.

The key: give yourself over/over/over.

The stylist reams a finger around your cape collar, loosening. Takes a steel comb, flicks it against her hipbone. You are thirty-four and you've been to a stylist a handful of times. Maybe six, not ten.

She says, That length is doing nothing for you.

She whips your swivel chair: slur of mirror, porcelain, chrome, fluorescent nettles stick themselves to the glass. Droning hair dryers, running water, phones.

The stylists talk. A mazey, elliptical daisy chain of talk. They adhere to nothing. Vacation packages, electric toothbrushes, blind dates. (He's got to be kidding: *coffee*. Going for coffee equals *death*. Night skiing, spritzers, bowling, sea-kayaking, I'm like, Okay. Let's *go*. But coffee? He's kidding, right?) They are the experts on every topic. Hair is a mild distraction. Hair happens.

She flicks the steel comb and it whirs near her hip. She's drawing a conclusion.

Your hair: upkeep, damage, regrowth, definition, product, lifestyle, frost, frizz, product, streaks, foils, body, cut. Where you're a small person. Where you've got a round face.

Outside, the storm slows traffic like a narcotic. You haven't seen a winter like this since. The equipment is breaking down. Bring in the army, they're saying. At night the snowplows crash into the drifts and stagger backward like dazed prizefighters. The windshields have bushy eyebrows. Cars stuck on the hills, smoking tires, engines squealing like dolphins. You haven't seen anything like this since you were a kid. You and your mother, the icicles, the lake catching over, the wind circling the glassy trees like a wet finger tracing a crystal rim. Her sleeping pills, the alarm clock blaring near her ear. Stumbling from your room at dawn to wake her so she can drive you to diving practice. The smell of chlorine in your skin always, your hair.

You like your driveway to be scraped down to the pavement since your husband left you. You get out there early every Saturday morning. The children watch from the living-room window. Your little daughter taps the glass. She waves. Your son puts his lips against the glass in a big gummy kiss.

The hospital room zings. Your husband says he wants a smoke. His forehead is gleaming, his eyebrows raised. He's feral, acute with stillness. His hazel eyes, flecks of rust, hair white as a fresh sheet of paper. He's socking one fist gently into his open palm.

You breathe. The minute hand reverberates each time it moves, a *twang*. You wait, wait for it, wait. The minute hand moves. Your mother lays an icy towel on your forehead. A drop of water moves down your temple and into your ear. The moving drop is exquisite in every way. The contraction recedes. The nurse is driving a spaceship in her sleep. She's gripping the arms of the chair, leaning slightly forward, snoring.

Go have your smoke, you say. Nothing's happening yet.

But it starts to happen while he's in the parking lot. He tells you later about his moment: how he will never be the same. He's standing on a slab of concrete near a loading entrance at the back of the hospital. The door is tied open with a piece of rubber tubing. The smell of cold food, sausage, powdered egg, the churning of dishwashers, spilled cutlery. It's a foggy night and he can smell the harbour and something bitter, pigeon shit. He's bewildered, hardly able to remember how he got where he is.

When he goes back to your hospital room his son's head is visible, becomes visible with each contraction and disappears again. It's the most awesome, unlovely, soul-quaking thing he has ever seen. He cups one of your heels in his hand, your mother holds your other heel. The baby is mauve coloured, smeared darkly with guck, and crying.

Your hair will be by Suzanne.

They're single or have just eloped, the stylists, young or staving off age with fashion, trend. The best one-room apartments in the city.

Do you have children, Suzanne?

Nope. No. Thank. You.

And you don't ever?

You got that right. Kids are so ex*pen*sive. Why would you?

Suzanne knows what she doesn't want. Sometimes desire is forged by the process of elimination. Your husband wanted golfing and hockey, a new tent, to celebrate his Native heritage (hitherto unmentioned during seven years of marriage), to become a theologian, to hunt seals. (There's a white mask the Inuit hunter holds to his face while approaching the seal basking at the edge of an ice floe. Everything is white, the hunter's white furs, the ice, the air. When he lifts the white mask he's obliterated. Your husband, the empty landscape, your husband, the empty landscape.) You prefer oblique dreams but you are too tired to manufacture the oblique. He wanted to be a vegetarian. (There are foods you can't face anymore. Basil you can't eat because of him. Even the smell of it.) To add on an apartment. (He got to keep the house through a conspiracy inspired by his mother.)

Then he realized what he didn't want. To be married anymore. To you. And now he's with Rayleen, an airhead.

The idea is to look good, you tell the stylist. That's the idea.

Things the stylists insist upon: a fireplace, a cappuccino maker. Toronto once a year, loyalty, techno music. A stuffed toy.

What's going on out there?

Suzanne: Still snowing.

The streets have become impossibly narrow. Snowbanks muscling the cars like ululating throats. The stylists win dance contests. Drink B52s, martinis.

You are here to learn how to become vulnerable again. How to give yourself over. They like a nice glass, fruit. They like their drinks to be blue, orange slices; they tip flamboyantly. There's a big, decaying city in their past. Havana, maybe. Venice. They have no past.

The stylist absolutely insists upon silence at certain hours. Watching the February snow make the sky listless, the slob ice on the harbour lifting in swells so gentle it seems the couch moves beneath them. Hand-knit socks. Original art. Brand names: Le Chateau, Swatch, Paderno. To watch the dusk settle. Soap operas. The primacy of their cats.

Suzanne has one item in her fridge: dehydrated miniature crabs. She can see the whole city from her window in the Battery.

Your mother has been begging you for years to get your hair streaked. You have breakfast together and she puts down her fork.

Enough, your mother says. She leans over the table and touches your cheek with the back of her hand. You have been going with the salt over the eggs. You stop. And you go and go and go with the salt. Then you toss it across the kitchen.

You have made everything soft for him, like whipped cream.

There he is in the La-Z-Boy, hungover, misty-eyed. I made a mistake, he says, I fucked someone.

Enough, you say.

Your mother cannot understand, nor will she accept, that you don't want streaks. You had no money in law school. Sometimes you were hungry. You left home, and your mother had to shovel. Sleeping pills. It got dark so early. There aren't even streetlights out that way. Her asthma. She'd have to walk through waist-deep snow and stop to use her inhaler. Icicles glinting. Leaks in the roof. You hear her smoke over the phone. A pause while she smokes. You hear the whir of the microwave, the bell. You hear the ice in her glass of scotch. You hear the icicles dripping outside. You hear her crying. What will make you stop crying, Mom?

She says, Have you thought about streaks?

Your husband wants to be an actor. He wants to give up his career as a bank manager. He wants a break from the kids. He wants the kids in his arms. He wants to go bankrupt, be a filmmaker. He has begun to identify with the clients whose assets he's been forced to seize. They aren't such bad guys.

The stylist takes a pair of scissors from the jar of blue liquid. Snaps them twice, flicking drops.

Suzanne's hair is short, stucco-like in texture, blond with ironic roots. Black-framed glasses. The bones of her hips pressing the red plastic jeans. Her shirt is clingy, reveals her belly button, a piercing. There are two kinds of hair, you've been told. The long and wispy: fuck-me hair. The short and androgynous: fuck-you hair.

You don't have the money now nor you will ever have the money to get your hair done every four months, which is how often you must in order to keep the roots from showing. You hate them. You will not incur the extra expense just now when your bastard prick of a husband, who has run up every jointly owned credit card, who has spent the nest egg saved to help your mother retire early and not have to wade through snowbanks with her inhaler. The bastard prick has a spending disorder, in fact, hitherto unmentioned, and has left you with half his debt, which is the law, and is seeing an airhead, and you can't trust him to come up his half of the. You won't incur the extra expense for anything because you had to buy a new house and a second-hand car, the engine of which is tied together with dental floss.

Suzanne says, You're thinking colour.

Yes I am.

You need colour.

Yes I do.

I'm thinking streaks.

So am I.

When you are in your ninth month with Adrian, a youth hurls his chair across the courtroom at you. You see one metal leg blur past your temple. You've prosecuted this kid several times. Perhaps five. His sister also. Almost all the girls who appear in youth court are named Amanda. They are named after Rachel's daughter on the discontinued soap opera *Another World*. Most of the boys are named Cory. The boy leaps onto a table and is striding across the backs of the fixed seating. The judge has a button on his desk for moments like these. He presses the button, his black robes puff with air, and the safety door clicks quietly closed behind him. You can see him in the small square window of the door peering out to watch the action.

You think: Judge Burke has saved himself. You are taken up with a giddiness. Judge Burke strikes you as humorously prissy. You are trembling with a fit of suppressed giggles. But as the boy gets closer, your initial feeling about judge Burke changes. You realize his decision to save himself and leave you, along with the handful of spectators, three security guards, three more youth also scheduled to appear before him this morning — Judge Burke's decision is a sound one. Certain men, given the appropriate circumstances, will behave with decisive and thorough self-centredness that smacks of sound judgement. Burke is elderly, completely unable to defend himself against a physical attack. Batty, even. His pronouncements are usually unsound. You often have to say, Judge Burke, I can see you're angry because your face is getting red, and I can tell by the tone of your voice that you are upset because you are speaking very loudly, but I feel I have to continue. You say things like this for the benefit of the court stenographer so the records will reflect Judge Burke's demeanour, should he come to the batty conclusion that he should charge you with contempt. Right now Judge Burke is nowhere to be seen. Right now a young man named Cory is going to kill you just before you give birth to your son, Adrian. As far as you know there have never been any Adrians on *Another World*. The youth is leaping, you have a contraction that doubles you, the security guards have him, water pours down your legs.

The male stylists are openly gay, mavericks, blithe, built. But it's the women who interest you. The women are beautiful, or look beautiful, stubbornly independent, current, childless. They enter and win lip-sync and wet T-shirt contests. At home in airports. Their families make allowances. They don't shovel. At Christmas they are the most extravagant, most deflated by the aftermath of unwrapped presents. They are the babies in the family. They're allowed to pick at the turkey. Suzanne brings you to the porcelain sink with the scoop for the neck. You lean back, close your eyes. You are determined to enjoy this.

She says, You don't have to hold your neck like that.

You have been holding your neck. You let your neck go loose. You are submitting. You let go. The salon falls away. Your scalp is a grass fire. You would kiss something if you could, or drift to sleep. The long, greying hair is such a weight. The hose makes you tingle all over. A hot, delicate raking. She's raking you to the surface of yourself. She drops the hose. Squirts a thread of viscous cherry over your scalp and begins with her fingers. She lets her nails graze. No one has touched you like this since your husband left. You almost kiss the snow white inside of Suzanne's wrist.

You are alone. It's your husband's night with the kids. Since your husband left, you have been falling asleep early in the evening. You haven't bought a TV. You got to keep the CD player but you only have a handful of CDs. You have listened to Cat Stevens's *Greatest Hits* so often you can. At first you kept the radio on all the time. A cheap radio in every room. Then you got tired of the radio. You listen hard but there's nothing to hear.

A row of icicles falls from the eaves startling you so badly you almost. You don't turn on the lights. You see your neighbour across the street pull into his driveway, his headlights lighting up falling snow. He can't see you in your window because the lights are off. He has asked you over for a glass of wine. Once you awoke to the sound of him shovelling your driveway. He gets out of the car and the light over his porch comes on. He looks up into the sky. He's standing in his driveway with his hands in his pockets, his head tilted back. He stays that way. Your fridge cuts in. Nothing moves on the street for a long time, no cars, just the snow. Your neighbour goes inside and you are alone. You are very much alone.

Suzanne fits a rubber skullcap over your head. The skullcap is full of holes and she tugs strands of hair through each hole with a metal hook. It hurts so much you think you might cry. Then you do cry. Suzanne doesn't make a big deal of it. She's seen all this before. She keeps pulling your hair.

That's the price, she says. She paints your hair with a foaming chemical. It's an awful stink, poisonous and angry. It makes you feel exuberant.

Everyone has left the Aquarena because of the storm and your mother hasn't come. Your coach switches off all the lights. They make a thwack noise when they go off, and the frla-ments burn pink then blue. The pool is empty and has gone still. The pool is a chameleon and it has changed its skin so it resembles nothing more than a swimming pool. It has become invisible. Your thirteenth birthday is coming and very soon you will lose interest in diving. One day you can think of nothing else, you are haunted. The next day diving hardly exists. You can't remember anything about it. You let your mother sleep in.

The storm has closed roads. Where is your mother? Your coach drives you home. The Trans Am flies through white-outs. You lose the road. The flame on the hood swallowed by the mouth. You have been saying. Talking. Telling him. Your eyes two soft plums, and a soft plum in your throat. Your heart is aching, but your heart is your eyes and you have two and they are bruised and weeping. Your coach pulls over. You pull over into Lovers Lane together. The trees slap the windows, paw the roof. He cups his hand under your chin and he kisses you. He gently sucks a bright plum from your throat. He kisses and kisses. You have never. Nothing will ever be as wonderful as this. You give yourself over/over/over.

You want Suzanne to give you some advice before you leave, and she, does. She tells you that from now on you must use a round brush. She holds a mirror behind so you can see how sharp the cut is. You can see your neck. You don't recognize yourself from this angle. She's sprayed you and blown the whole thing dry so your hair feels as hard as a helmet. The blond is called ash and it glints like a tough metal.

The New Right, Gender and the Fisheries Crisis: Local and Global Dimensions

Barbara Neis and Susan Williams

The Atlantic Fisheries Crisis and the New Right Agenda

The effects of overfishing during the 1980s, perhaps heightened by oceanographic changes, forced fishery closures in Atlantic Canada in the 1990s (Hutchings and Myers, 1995). A moratorium on northern cod was imposed in 1992, and other closures followed in 1993. Overall, over 50,000 people working in the industry were affected. An estimated 47,000 others in fishery-dependent sectors such as trucking and retail sales also lost their livelihoods. The Canadian government set up adjustment programs costing over $2 billion. By late 1995, 39,778 people in the region had been accepted for these programs. Those indirectly dependent on the industry were not eligible. The closures affected entire communities and regions where groundfish was the economic mainstay. The crisis has been most acute in Newfoundland and Labrador, where over 35,000 fishery workers were laid off (Williams, 1996).

In Atlantic Canada, fish resources and harvesting are a federal responsibility, while processing is under provincial jurisdiction. The federal response to the fishery crisis has been consistent with the New Right agenda, and there has been little opposition to this approach from provincial governments. From the perspective of New Right politics, the origins of the fisheries crisis are to be found in "too many fishermen chasing too few fish." The excess of fishery workers is blamed on overly generous social programs and a failure of political will—in other words, too much democracy. From this perspective, state intervention in the economy caused unemployment by discouraging outmigration and inflating wages, and political pressure from unemployed and underemployed people prompted federal and provincial governments to use the fishery as an "employer of last resort." Generous unemployment insurance benefits interfered with the effective operation of the market and had a corrosive effect on the "traditional self-reliance" of rural communities (May and Hollett, 1995). The result was "overcapacity" in fishing and processing. The New Right solution to the problem of "too many fishermen chasing too few fish" is to cut social support programs, limit access to and eventually privatize fishery resources, and transfer responsibility for scientific research and management from government to the private sector. Reliance on market forces and a conservation ethic supposedly associated with property ownership will, it is argued, produce a smaller, sustainable and efficient industry (Fisheries Council of Canada, 1994).

New Right advocates overstate the extent of democratic decision-making within the fishing industry (Felt, Neis and McCay, 1999) and understate the contributions of government mismanagement, corporations and competitive capitalism. In the 1980s, the federal government consulted with the representatives of fishers and with industry, but fishers were fragmented between many different committees and women fishers and plantworkers in particular had little opportunity to influence policy (MacInnes and Davis, 1996). In 1977, with the extension of the 200-mile Exclusive Economic Zone, the federal government assumed responsibility for the recovery of depleted fish stocks. Their claim to this responsibility was based on a false set of techno-utopian beliefs about the marine ecosystem and the potential of science-based management. The outcome was consistent over-estimation of stock abundance resulting in overfishing (Finlayson, 1994).

In 1992, the federal government acknowledged the existence of a fisheries crisis that had been affecting the industry for several years. As the uncertainty of fishing incomes increased, so did reliance on unemployment insurance, particularly in small boat enterprises. When net income from these enterprises could no longer support multiple households, they tended to fragment and rely more on family members (including wives) as crew, bringing new entrants into the fishery (Larkin, 1990). This strategy helped them keep the fishing income and related unemployment insurance within the household. As competition for the resource increased, processors built more plants in new locations and operated existing plants for shorter periods, augmenting the excess capacity in the industry. As work became less certain, more household members had to find work to supplement incomes.

The New Right defines overcapacity almost exclusively in terms of the number of individuals and plants in the industry. This obscures the dramatic differences in catching and processing capacity in different sectors, and differences in the amount of fish required to sustain enterprises in the labour-intensive inshore sector as opposed to the capital- and energy-intensive midshore and offshore sectors. Sectors also varied in terms of the options available to them to respond to the deepening crisis. The inshore sector was experiencing lower landings of groundfish and increasing fishing costs as early as the mid-1980s in many areas (Blackwood, 1996; Neis et al., 1999). The mobile, corporate fishing sector and under 65 foot midshore fleet were also affected by resource decline but somewhat differently due to their high capital costs, and somewhat later as they had privileged access to certain high-value species and greater fishing capacity (Davis, 1991; Palmer, 1992). Processors were able to obtain more leverage over fish prices and wages by owning several plants in different communities, owning or controlling some large vessels, encouraging new entrants, and refusing to purchase catch only from *bona fide* fishers. Some used their control over access to UI to discourage unionization, keep wages and prices low, and subsidize their operations. This pattern was particularly strong in the seasonal inshore sector where female workers were concentrated in a narrow range of jobs directly dependent on supplies of fish. As a consequence, female fishers and processing workers appear to have experienced the greatest constraints when attempting to maintain their incomes and job security in the face of resource decline (Rowe, 1991).

New Right explanations and solutions also neglect the role of global factors in the development of the crisis in the Atlantic fishery. Overfishing occurred not only in this region, but throughout the North Atlantic, and in many other parts of the world. Like other resource-based industries, fisheries were sacrificing the incomes of future generations by overharvesting in the present and, in the process, depressing prices in international markets. Low prices probably increased the pressure on Atlantic fishers and companies to intensify production.

The New Right agenda obscures the issues of intergenerational equity and equity within the current generation that are fundamental to the development of sustainable fisheries (Boyce, 1995). It neglects the potential negative impacts of cuts to social programs and privatization of the resource on fishery communities and on the resource itself. A focus on the number of individuals in the industry, and the number of processing plants, draws our attention away from fundamental questions. For example, how much wealth would a well-managed fishery in this region be capable of producing? How can resources and the wealth they produce be sustained over generations? Where should that wealth end up? What would be the best way to harvest, process and market these resources? From the perspective of the New Right, the answer is simple: let the market decide. However, the market places no value on the preservation of natural resources, unpaid labour and social equity (Waring, 1988). It is thus not surprising that the New Right agenda is not good news for either women in the Atlantic fishing industry or fishery resources themselves. In the words of Marjorie Cohen:

> [w]omen have long recognized that when markets are left alone, and business is left to pursue profits any way it wants, things do not turn out well for us .... Our experience is that justice and fairness have to be imposed on the market: they cannot be left to chance (1991, 2).

Gendered Impacts of the Fisheries Crisis and "Adjustment Initiatives"

Before the closures, there were 15,000 women working in the Newfoundland and Labrador fishery, making up about one-third of its labour force. They were equally important in the fisheries of the Maritime provinces. In Newfoundland and Labrador, women held half of the processing jobs, working on fish lines, in clerical jobs and in plant management. About 12 percent of the province's fishers were women with full-time or part-time licences, working as crew members in family vessels or on their own. About 12,000 women lost jobs in the industry. The crisis also affected women doing unpaid work in their husbands' fishing enter-prises, such as bookkeeping, supplying and cooking for crews. Other women lost work in child care and the retail sector in fishery-dependent communities. In addition, outmigration and government cutbacks reduced the number of women employed in education, health and social services (Williams, 1996).

Women with children have borne much of the stress of the moratorium associated with loss of work, self-esteem, income and the capacity to plan for the future. They are often responsible for managing household accounts and, since the crisis, have had to manage with less money. In their role as tension managers, some feel that they cannot show their own distress because this would prove too much for other family members (Brookes, 1993). In offshore fishing households, women who were used to prolonged male absence and relative independence have experienced adjustment difficulties: "His frustration at not working and his loss of self-esteem combined with her frustration over the erosion of her auton-omy can lead to an unbearable tension between the couple" (Binkley, 1995, 93). None of these outcomes are evident in the system of account-ing that has guided government response. Patriarchal assumptions have informed relevant accounts. Media reports, cultural events and govern-ment reports related to the crisis have tended to highlight its significance for fishermen, fish companies and financially-strapped governments (Robbins, 1997; Robinson, 1995). Where women are mentioned in most mainstream sources, they are "revered as mothers, wives ... (but rarely] as co-workers" (Robinson 1995, 22).

In some analyses of the crisis, women have been indirectly blamed for the slow pace of industrialization in the inshore fishery and for the increase in fisheries-related employment in the 1980s. For example, offi-cial statistics show a greater participation by women in the fishery since the 1960s. This is seen as one indicator of Newfoundland's dependence on the fishery to bolster the economy and on UI to support an inflated labour force (Carter, 1993). However, the figures on increasing numbers of women working in the industry are misleading, because they would have excluded women who processed fish at the household level in the 1950s and 1960s. As women went to work in the formal sector for wages, they were counted as workers for the first time. This analysis also obscures the role of stock declines, limited employment alternatives and increases in the cost of living, all of which led to a greater reliance on UI and an influx of women and young people into the fishing industry. In addition, it overlooks the sexist state and corporate policies that limited women's involvement in the fishery until they were challenged in the

1970s and 1980s (McCay, 1988; Neis, 1993). As in other parts of Canada, a higher cost of living pushed women and older children to enter the paid labour force, and enjoyment of the work, as well as successful struggles to remove barriers to more equal participation, pulled women into plants and onto fishing vessels. Declining catches meant that fishing costs increased in relation to the volume and value of landings. This encouraged fishery-dependent households to look for ways to keep fishing incomes in the household, and to augment individual incomes with those of other family members.

Patriarchal assumptions have also played a role in shaping the adjustment mechanisms established in response to the fisheries crisis. Examination of the report of the *Task Force on Incomes and Adjustment in the Atlantic Fishery*, which provided a blueprint for government response, illustrates this point. This *Task Force* was established in 1992, to "advise on the continued supply of the resource, the future stability and profitability of the industry, the achievement of stable and adequate incomes for those who make a living in the fishery, and alternative training, employment and other adjustment possibilities" (1993,109). Women are explicitly mentioned in only one of the 42 recommendations of the *Task Force* report. In Recommendation 23, we are told:

> Women's role as the binding force in the fishing community will be essential to the adjustment process. Their participation in the process should be specifically recognized and planned in any adjustment program, using existing fisheries organizations wherever possible (1993, 102).

A brief section of the *Task Force* report acknowledged the existence of historical barriers to women's entry into fishing, but there were no recommendations for action to ensure that "adjustment" programs would not reinforce these barriers or create new ones.

The more than $2 billion price tag of adjustment programs providing income support to displaced fishery workers would appear to be inconsistent with the New Right commitment to state debt reduction and reduced state involvement in the economy. However, whereas fishery workers tended to define the bi-weekly benefits as compensation for lost income caused by government mismanagement of the fishery, the government defined them as part of a larger set of programs and policies to help fishery workers "adjust" to a downsized fishery through retraining, outmigration and early retirement. The government also defined the fishery crisis as affecting only certain individuals who could meet the specific eligibility criteria for its adjustment programs. These criteria did not attempt to mitigate the effects of a history of practices and programs that had limited women's independent access to fishery-generated wealth.

Women fishers have had greater difficulty qualifying for adjustment payments and programs because of male norms for what is considered fishing work, and because of the longer and more stable male involvement in fishing. Negative attitudes on the part of some fisheries officers and some male fishers may also have played a role (Williams, 1996). Because they were ineligible for government income support or training programs, those who had to adjust most quickly were the young people who had worked in the industry or had planned to, and those whose employment was indirectly dependent on the fishery, such as service sector workers. Many of these workers are women. Some have left their communities and those who remain may account for some of the growing number of Atlantic Canadians on social assistance.

Financial compensation for fishers and plant workers under "adjustment" programs was based on previous work patterns and income levels. The *Task Force* report acknowledged that women's average wage in fish processing had been lower than men's, but it made no recommendation to stop government from reproducing this inequity in its adjustment programs. Because benefits and eligibility for programs were based on "historical attachment" to the industry and pre-moratorium incomes, adjustment programs replicated the gendered income inequalities created by a history of male dominance within the industry. These were supported to some extent by sexist welfare state programs and fisheries management policies (Neis, 1993). Women received lower average compensation rates, and most were scheduled to be removed from the program earlier than men (Williams, 1996).[1]

Fishery workers who were eligible for adjustment programs were initially required to seek training or risk loss of benefits. They were led to believe that those who trained outside the fishery would not be able to return to the industry in the future. Women make up about 50 percent of the plant labour force in Newfoundland and Labrador, concentrated in low-wage jobs with limited chances to get ahead and with food-processing skills that are not easily transferable to other occupations. While training for work outside the fishery became the main emphasis of adjustment programs, there are few occupational alternatives in rural areas. Retraining for non-fishery jobs meant moving to cities to look for work, and people were reluctant to leave their communities and to abandon the industry that was the centre of their work and their communities. In addition, women are often tied to their communities by the needs of children, husbands, the elderly and the disabled who depend on them for care. Research describes middle generation women as "trapped" in their communities by the fishery crisis (Davis, 1995). They are caught in a "circular trap which revolves *through* the household," forcing them to "commit untold effort to ensuring the survival of the household, because without it, their position as women outside households or women in women-headed households would be, in most cases, economically pitiful" (Porter 1993, 148).

Women fishers and plant workers had little say in the design of re-training programs. Those on adjustment programs reported frustration with available training opportunities. They felt that they had little help in determining what kind of training would lead to successful employment or self-employment in their communities (Educational Planning, 1994; FFAW/CAW, 1994; Robbins, 1995). Not surprisingly, women have called for training to be linked to community economic development that is based, in part, on diversification around the fishery. Instead, many were steered into areas of training where the labour market is already saturated, often because it was the most convenient type of training to offer (Williams, 1996).

Changes to unemployment insurance regulations will also limit the educational and financial options of fishery households in the future. Although the unemployment insurance fund is currently running a multi-billion dollar surplus (partly because of the transfer of fishery workers to adjustment programs), the federal government introduced cuts and changes to unemployment insurance (UI, now Employment Insurance or EI) that target seasonal workers. A theory of UI dependency, which accuses seasonal workers, small-scale fishers, women and youth of over-using the program, combined with a public relations strategy emphasizing the high incomes of a few fishermen qualifying for UI, helped to create a climate for cuts and allowed the federal government to ignore regional opposition. It has been estimated that the UI reforms would remove $105 million a year from the Newfoundland and Labrador economy alone (*Union Advocate*, 1996, 8).

The UI reforms included increases in the period of time needed to qualify, reductions in the duration of benefits and access to training, and measures to penalize seasonal users of the program. Under the new regulations introduced in 1996, benefits are based on hours worked, instead of weeks, and the hours are divided over more weeks, including weeks with very few hours of work.

All applicants, but especially new entrants, will find it more difficult to qualify in future. Fishery workers who have not found enough work to qualify for UI and who have had to depend on the "adjustment" program, would be classified as new entrants to the labour force when their payments ended (Earl McCurdy, *CBC Fisheries Broadcast*, December 1996). Many would be forced to leave the region. Limited access to UI adds to the pressure on government to re-open fisheries. Higher eligibility requirements contribute to more intense competition for the limited work available.

Cuts and changes in eligibility criteria for UI and government-sponsored training affect women and men differently. The rules permitting fishermen's wives and children to qualify for UI — the "arm's length policy" — have been tightened. In the past, it was only necessary for women to be involved in catching fish, and to show that if the family member was not employed, someone else would be hired at the same wage and under the same conditions. It is now necessary to show that the family member is paid on a regular basis at a "reasonable" rate, and that she has a proper workspace in the home (Bay St. Lawrence Women's FishNet, 1996, 3; DesRoches and Lord, 1996, 11). Similar requirements to show "arms length" and earnings at a "reasonable" rate are restricting benefits paid to child care workers who are related to their employers. Moreover, women who do shore work for fishing enterprises, such as unloading and net mending, are still not eligible for fisher's UI because they are not in the boat.

New Right policies are not only limiting resources for the poor, but also shifting social responsibilities from the state to the family. Consistent with this is the introduction of a system of eligibility for some UI recipients based on household as opposed to individual incomes. On the positive side, households with incomes of $26,000 or less will be exempted from the frequent user penalties. But the use of household income as a determinant of benefits is a major departure for a government agency whose mandate has always been employment-related. In the future, cuts and penalties could be imposed on the basis of household income. If this happens, even small pay cheques from working wives could result in UI penalties, if these push household incomes above a ceiling. It could leave lower-income, seasonally-employed women plant workers and fishers ineligible for UI if their spouses are better paid. The household approach to income support assumes that women will have access to their husbands' incomes to meet the needs of their children and themselves, which may not be the case. Working wives and mothers will lose a crucial margin of independence and financial security under such a system and many households with low incomes will be poorer still in the future.

Gender bias can also be found within resource management initiatives associated with the fishery crisis. The strict criteria of adjustment programs have divided communities based on who was eligible and who was considered by authorities to be part of the "core" fishery. Access to fishing licenses is being limited through the introduction of a professionalization program and relatively strict criteria for defining membership in a "core" fishery. Few women fishers will be eligible for "core" status because of their relatively recent entry into fishing and because of their status as part-time license holders and crew members.[2] Nowhere do we hear a discussion of the need for an affirmative action program to ensure women have a place in the future "core" fishery and to ensure that "core" status does not increase women's economic dependence on their husbands.

Government initiatives are encouraging the concentration of harvesting and processing work in the hands of fewer workers and fewer communities, leaving others to seek economic development initiatives outside the fishery. The continued scarcity of groundfish, combined with overfishing of other species and cuts to benefits have contributed to growing support for a more limited fishery in the future. For example, support among fishers for dividing up the fishable resource into individual boat quotas (IQs) appears to be increasing.[3] Women fishers could lose more than men from initiatives to privatize ownership of fisheries resources. In Norway, when a system of IQs was introduced after a fisheries crisis in 1989, women ended up with only a small proportion of the resulting quotas, because fishing was culturally and economically a male preserve, and because women's flexible combination of shore and fishery work interfered with their eligibility for quotas (Munk-Madsen, 1996). Women fish plant workers will be profoundly affected by the process chosen for reducing the number of plants in the industry. However, no attempt has been made to ensure that they are well-represented in the decision-making processes concerning resource management and industry restructuring.

The fisheries crisis has made it easier for the federal government to pursue a decade-old agenda. In the words of John Crosbie, the federal Minister of Fisheries who announced the moratorium in 1992: "I felt and still feel it was the opportunity for the government to change the management of the fishery" (Blades, 1996). By limiting the funding for adjustment programs on the basis of fiscal restraint, by imposing individualistic eligibility criteria that ignore the household and community basis of the industry, and by cutting social programs, the federal government is gradually forcing many current and future fishery workers out of the industry and out of fishery communities altogether. The federal government has treated the crisis with short-term programs, when in reality, fish stocks in some areas are recovering slowly and some may never recover, threatening the displacement of future generations.

A context of broad Canadian acceptance of the need for fiscal restraint and the collapse of the major fish stocks have allowed the federal government to forge ahead with these New Right initiatives. Atlantic Canadian fishery workers have not, however, been entirely passive in their response. The exodus from the industry was slow in starting. The adjustment programs provided many with some financial security and people in fishing communities were reluctant to abandon substantial investments in homes, fishing gear and skills. Limited work with other species, high prices and, in the case of snow crab, apparent increases in abundance and wider access to this fishery helped some workers fill their empty days and supplement their adjustment income. Because their own employment *and* that of future generations was threatened, and because displaced youth were ineligible for support, some parents directed

354

resources to supporting the training and outmigration of their children, in the hope that they would find work elsewhere. In the Maritimes, where fisheries have been less severely affected, increased licensing fees have prompted widespread protests, including the occupation of DFO offices. In Newfoundland and Labrador, anger concerning the stock collapse and fears about the future have been channeled into protests about reductions in the adjustment "package" and changes to the UI program. Throughout the region, women from fishery communities have repeatedly supported attempts to limit the cuts, protect themselves and their families, and ensure the future of their communities.

As a result of this New Right program, more communities than necessary will die out. There will also be greater polarization than necessary within those communities that remain, as wealth becomes concentrated in fewer hands, and men and women, and parents and children compete for work and income (Davis, 1995; Neis 1993).[4] Failure to address the social justice issues at the heart of the fishery crisis will threaten the future of the resource and the industry itself (Boyce, 1995). There is a significant risk that groundfish stocks will never be allowed to recover to anything near their potential productivity. The displacement of fishery workers, and entire fishery communities, from parts of the Newfoundland and Labrador coast will open up these areas to corporate and individual control over new industrial development in the areas of tourism and aquaculture. Some increases in fisheries production are being achieved through aquaculture, but aquaculture also appears unlikely to employ large numbers of displaced fisheries workers. Its potential limited, particularly in northern areas, there are strong pressures towards a corporate-controlled high-tech form of aquaculture. The development of aquaculture is part of a global restructuring of fisheries in response to resource depletion and continued high demand for fish products that will not necessarily result in the concentration of fish production in the same areas that relied on wild fisheries.

Conclusion

The New Right agenda for solving the fisheries crisis, both local and global, does not address the root causes of this crisis. A management strategy of reducing the number of players and privatizing the resource simply results in a build-up of harvesting capacity in the higher-technology fleets that remain, many of which are owned or financed by fish corporations and need to maximize their catching efficiency in order to cover costs and meet profit targets.

Limited entry, licensing, quotas and other restrictions upon human access to resources will do little to check the Tragedy of Technology as it remorselessly imposes new techniques upon technologically-saturated fisheries. Redundant technologies do nothing but threaten stocks or add

355

to the expense of harvesting a finite resource and force more people out of the industry — denying ever-increasing numbers of people access to natural resources, making them redundant and breaking up communities (Fairlie et al, 1995, 67).

The New Right agenda attempts to leave the job of maximizing the health of remaining fish stocks, their resilience and their employment potential to the market. However, the rich have more votes in the market-place than the poor, and ecological sustainability cannot be achieved without the elimination of economic and political inequities, including the inequities between women and men (Boyce, 1996). Because the fisheries crisis is global, women of the North must work together with those of the South to resist the New Right agenda and stop the destruction of fishery resources, fishery households and fishery communities. Women are more than the glue of fishery communities. In Atlantic Canada, as elsewhere, they contribute directly to the fishery as workers, organizers and managers in fishery households, industries and communities. They have fishery knowledge and skills, and depend on the resources and industry for their livelihood. The household basis of fisheries in Atlantic Canada, Norway and many other parts of the world is well-documented. Women contribute financially and organizationally to these enterprises. However, the crisis restructuring programs, and the new approaches in fisheries science and management, are rarely scrutinized for their assumptions about women's place or their impacts on women's lives and their capacity to hold their communities together. If this is to change, the "[p]reservation of the coastal population and its culture must ... become part of fisheries management. Nor is it sufficient to focus exclusively on the fishermen; the entire household must be economically and socially sustainable. In this, women are seen to occupy a critical role" (Toril Pettersen, 1996, 247). Women's relationships to communities and to fishery resources are different from men's, and their perspectives and interests are also different, although by no means homogeneous. Greater participation by women in managing our treatment of marine areas and resources could help pave the way for a "counter-ecological revolution" in fisheries in which our wild resources remain public resources, are allowed to fully recover and, in conjunction with some forms of aquaculture, provide the basis for food security.[5]

Notes

[1] Because men who fished and who worked in plants were more likely than women fishery workers to qualify for the full period of benefits, the recent elimination of the last year of funding has, ironically, had the effect of reducing gender inequities in eligibility.

[2] Core fishers are defined as heads of fishing enterprises, with seven

years' full-time fishing experience, and with 75 percent of their earned income, or recent actual enterprise revenues of $20,000, from fishing. They are subject to "special eligibility criteria". Less than two percent of those meeting special eligibility criteria for fishers are women (Williams, 1996, 47).

3 Western industrial fisheries are generally managed using scientific stock assessments as a basis for establishing total allowable catches (TACS). In Atlantic Canada, in the 1980s, portions of these TACS were allocated to the big companies in the form of Enterprise Allocations and other portions were allocated to some of the larger, owner-operated fishing vessel owners in the form of individual quotas (IQs) (individual portions of the TAC) and ITQs, individual portions that fisher-owners have the right to sell.

4 Recent non-fishery job creation projects, such as the Hibernia oil project, have been harder for women to access because most involve traditional men's work in construction and mining. Those women who were able to access nontraditional jobs at Hibernia were subject to high levels of workplace harassment (Grzetic et al, 1996).

5 Thanks to Gabriele Dietrich for this suggestion that we need to organize a "counter ecological revolution."

I Followed My Heart

Nympha Byrne

No permanent courts exist in any of the coastal communities of Labrador, so a circuit court with a full slate of characters — a judge, a Crown prosecutor, RCMP and legal aid lawyers, along with all their props — travels periodically to these communities, much like a traveling road show. The court is held in English, a language many people speak barely or not at all, and interpreters are difficult to find. When someone agrees to translate, he or she is faced with many legal terms for which there are no Innu words or concepts. The Innu word for "police", for instance, is *kamakunuest* or the Man Who Locks People Up. The justice system is a foreign one that clashes deeply with Innu culture, and one that the Innu feel creates even more problems for individuals and their families. In December 1993, a group of women in Utshimassits (Davis Inlet), including Nympha, were fed up with what they saw happening in court and decided to take action. Their decision came from a simple belief that women can do anything when they set their minds to it — but it was an unimaginable act that shocked all of Canada.

I remember listening to the judge during the court session. The RCMP officers stood by the door. The families of the accused sat around and waited to hear how long their son or brother or husband would be locked up. There were some people in the lock-up in the trailer. They were waiting for their sentencing, waiting to be taken away out of the community. I didn't stay very long. I was too angry to listen to any more charges and sentences. These people don't understand us, I thought to myself. They don't understand our culture.

For years, I have watched non-Natives come in and out, and do what they want. They are not sensitive to our culture. Sometimes they would just throw the charges out, because they were too old. The court would often leave town before having heard all the cases, and people would forget about the charges by the time the court came around again.

I remember one time, not long before we threw out the court, a young man had been charged with assault. His girlfriend, who was his victim, was supposed to testify against him but she was very afraid. She couldn't speak English. I watched her and she looked so scared. She sat at the stand with her head down. There was no translator. She was six months pregnant. The judge was really hard on her. He didn't talk very nicely to her. He said he would wait as long as it took her to say something. He said if she didn't testify, he would just release her boyfriend. She still couldn't say anything. She was also afraid of his family. This often happens when a woman is assaulted. She won't press charges because she is afraid that the man's family will be really mad at her. They will harass her and talk behind her back. I tried to encourage her to say something. I was mad at the way the judge was handling the situation. I went to Katie Rich's office. She was the chief at the time. We talked about it and she said she knew this kind of thing was happening in court.

The circuit court came around again. This time I just stuck my head in there. I was still so angry. I didn't want to listen any more. Katie went and sat in while the people went forward with their charges. I was working with Social Services at the time. From my office window, I could see Katie walking back and forth to her office during break time and lunch. I could tell she was really angry. Then she called me on the phone. She was wondering what to do. I went to her office and she showed me a letter she had drafted. The letter was telling the judge to leave the community with his court. I barely read the letter and I signed it. My heart was telling me that something needed to be done. I knew the women had the strength, the heart, and the power to take action. There were maybe 15 or 20 other women who also signed the letter. Some of them were pretty nervous, but Katie told them they did not have to come with us to present the letter to the judge. It was their choice. Everyone decided to come along. Katie asked Innu constable Justine Noah Jack to accompany us, so she could keep the peace and so things wouldn't get out of hand.

We marched in while the court was in session. Katie led the way. I followed with Justine Noah Jack, and the rest of the women came behind. It was very exciting. We were not aggressive. We walked in quietly and peacefully. The room froze and everyone turned to look at us. The judge, the lawyers, and Crown prosecutor stared in disbelief. Katie just walked up to the judge. I remember looking at his face. Did he look frightened or was he surprised? I don't know how to describe it. The judge took the letter and read it. He didn't know what to say. He told us he had to make a phone call. He left the hall and headed for the RCMP trailer. He never came back. We waited for him. The people were sitting around looking and the men were laughing at us. They told us we were asking for trouble and we would land in jail. One of the women went over to the judge's table and sat in his chair. His papers still lay on the table. The RCMP were around the whole time, but when they saw the judge wasn't returning, they took his papers and recording equipment and left.

Finally, we adjourned the court and everyone walked out. I went back to my office to lock up. A lot of people were gathering outside the RCMP trailer. They started a bonfire to keep warm because it was very cold. People began shouting to the judge to leave town. Later that day, the charter came to fly the judge, the lawyers and the Crown prosecutor back to Goose Bay.

We took this action because, the way I see it, the courts have failed our people. When they throw people in jail, there are no programs to help them with their problems. What purpose does it serve for them to be in jail? When they return to the community after spending time in jail, they do the same thing all over again. Many people told me they couldn't believe we had thrown the judge out of the community. But for me, it was nothing. It was no big deal. When I saw the story on the media, it was such a big thing for the non-Innu society. But for me, it was just that I could see something was wrong and something had to be done about it. I had to do this for my people. Sometimes what I have seen is that my people let things go, instead of standing up for themselves. This time we had to take some action.

They didn't charge us right away. Katie, Justine and I were the only ones who were charged and it was a year and a half later before they came to arrest us and take us into custody. They never charged the other women. I guess because of our jobs, they thought the three of us were the ringleaders. In 1994, my family moved to Goose Bay and even when I was there, the RCMP never came to pick me up. I remember waiting, but they never came knocking on my door. There was talk about our charges. Katie would call me all the time to keep me informed on what was happening. We would wonder why they were taking so long to put us in jail. We would laugh about it. I felt like they could see the mistakes they had made in our community, and they must have been feeling guilty about it. They were realizing how little they knew about our culture with all their papers and their foreign laws. I had always had a lot of difficulty understanding their courts, all the big words they used that we have no translation for in our language.

Finally, in the spring of 1995, I was back in *Utshimassits* to collect stories for this book and it was then the RCMP took us into custody. Camille was very annoyed because we had a very small budget for this book and we hadn't finished the job. But all she could do was take pictures of us being hauled away. Many people from the community followed us to the plane to show their support. For a while, a couple of the men stood face to face between the blades of the propeller to keep the plane from leaving. In the end, the plane took off and they brought us to the lock-up in Goose Bay. Many people came to visit us: family members like my sister from *Utshimassits*, lawyers, leaders from the Innu Nation and the band council. Camille came to give me a hard time for abandoning her and to show her support.

We were given undertakings to sign, but Katie and I refused. Justine decided to sign. Katie and I were shipped to the Women's Correctional Centre in Stephenville, Newfoundland, until our court date. In all, we spent 10 days in jail. We were always having fun and laughing in there. We stayed up late in the night, talking and sharing stories. I felt like a caged animal. I knew why animals in zoos look so sad. I didn't feel like I belonged in that jail. I worried about my children — what were they thinking?

While we were still in the lock-up in Goose Bay, my youngest cried and said she wanted me home. She kept telling me that I hadn't done anything wrong and I shouldn't be in jail. They came to visit me to bring me fruit because the food they gave us was so greasy. My sister Judith and her husband also came. She looked so sad when I saw her face. "How could they lock you up?" she asked me. I described to her what our cell was like. We had two benches for beds, and Justine had a mat on the floor. The toilet was right out in the open in front of us in this small room. Those two kept smoking cigarettes. I didn't smoke and it was hard on my lungs. Then we left for Stephenville.

I hated the jail in Stephenville because of the barbed wire around the building. Then I really felt like a caged animal. When we first went in there, they strip-searched us everywhere. I felt invaded. They made us shower and took us to our separate cells. We were in solitary confinement for 24 hours. The next day, they put us in the same room again. We became friends with the other inmates. They couldn't believe we hadn't signed our undertakings. They said if they had been in our shoes, they would have signed right away. They kept asking us about throwing the judge out of the community. They were so amazed. They said they could never have done what we did. I ended up counseling a White woman. She was talking about her drinking problem and we shared our stories. We became friends. She said she really missed me after we left. Katie had her own buddies. I would hear them laughing in the smoking room.

When our trial date arrived, they took us to Deer Lake, where we caught a plane to go back to Goose Bay. A lot of supporters were waiting outside the Supreme Court when we arrived. The weather was down, so my mother and Katie's parents couldn't make it from *Utshimassits*. Both Katie and I had braided our hair. I remembered how one elder had once told me how my hair was my strength. We walked in to face the judge and he released us. We thought we would be sentenced to jail for sure. This felt like another victory. We went over to my house, drank tea and laughed about it. We were so saucy.

Feminism: Our Basis Of Unity: Premises, Principles and Practices[1]

Michelle A. Smith

A S WE ATTEMPT TO DEFINE THE MANDATE AND DIRECTION of our equality-seeking and anti-violence work, we continue to look for our common ground. The logical place to look for this is in our mutual understanding of feminism and the women's movement. Whether we are aware of it or not, or whether we describe ourselves and our organizations as "feminist," the women's movement influences every effort we make in the pursuit of equality and inclusion.

There is no single way to describe feminism. For some women it is simply the way we live every day, seeing the world through our women's eyes from our women's experience. For others it means working quietly within relationships, communities and workplaces, insisting on a fair share for women and men. For others who consider themselves feminist activists, it is advocating for change within structures and institutions to create women-centred policies, practices and programs. What unites us as a movement is a desire to transform our communities, organizations and even the world into safe and equitable places.

The feminist movement includes women and girls of all ages, races, sexualities, abilities and classes from every corner of the world. We may be workers or volunteers, mothers or activists. Regardless of the roles we choose, we have in common a fundamental belief in women's social, legal, political, economic and cultural equality. As feminists, we respect each other's experience and background, celebrating our diversity and supporting each other in the choices we make. We are equally committed to deepening our individual and organizational understandings of the world around us, and questioning why we make the choices we do. It is this commitment that enables us to understand how our values and beliefs have been shaped and influenced by our life experiences, and how our thinking impacts upon the work and vision of our feminist organizations.

Feminism challenges us to critically and continuously examine our individual values and belief systems, and to consider the ways in which they have been formed and shaped over time. We need to become aware of our place in society and question those institutions, such as family, church, media, government, and education that affect and influence our choices and thinking as women. How we view women's roles and contributions, and perceive feminism and the women's movement, is very much informed by the structures around us. Feminism inspires us to view the world through a lens of women's experience, and to challenge each other on principles and practices that unintentionally carry the messages of marginalization and exclusion we have been taught from birth. This process enables us to work toward a common understanding of feminism within our individual efforts toward women's equality.

We may encounter many challenges associated with building and maintaining a healthy equality-seeking feminist organization. Lack of adequate funds is a constant struggle for many groups, as is balancing the delivery of community-based services and programs with advocacy and lobbying efforts. In addition, not everyone agrees with the work of feminist groups, and public opinion is not always in our favour. Patriarchal institutions that exclude or minimize the contributions of women are not generally supportive of policies and initiatives that seek to change the status quo. By challenging and upsetting existing power structures, feminists often experience some degree of opposition or backlash from those within traditional hierarchies. As we learn and grow, as individual women and as women's organizations, we must continuously re-examine our feminist principles and practices and gather our collective strength in our efforts toward equality and inclusion.

To deepen our common understanding of feminism, we must look beyond our current time and place. We need to learn about and honour the struggles and successes of the generations of feminists who came before us, and recognize that many of the rights and freedoms we have today are directly due to their efforts (e.g., the right to vote, own property, go to university). We also need to educate ourselves about the ongoing efforts of the women's movement today, and find ways of supporting and sharing within our common work. As feminists we have a global vision, and recognize that the issues facing women in other parts of the world are our issues as well. Peace, equality and justice for all: this is our feminist basis of unity.

Our Premises of Feminism

As a feminist equality-seeking organization, the Provincial Advisory Council on the Status of Women (PACSW) works from a feminist perspective in advocating for women's full and equal participation. Feminist premises ground us in our thinking and analysis, and provide our organization with a basis from which to operate. We accept that there are differences in perception and understanding of feminist principles, practices and processes. Through openness, communication and mutual respect, we are able to work with and challenge each other to help us grow — as individual women and as a women's collective dedicated to working for the social, legal, political, economic and cultural equality of women in Newfoundland and Labrador.

What unites us as members of an equality-seeking organization is our common understanding of the meaning of feminism to our group: our collective set of core values that inform the healthy and equitable practice of feminist principles. These values have been developed over two decades of work by women who served on the Board of the Provincial Advisory Council on the Status of Women. They form our feminist premises and inform our feminist practices.

Consider the common agreements that currently exist within your group. What are the values that unite you in your ongoing pursuit of equality and inclusion? In other words, what is your organization's feminist basis of unity? We invite you to look at the feminist premises that form the Provincial Advisory Council on the Status of Women Basis of Unity as a starting point for your discussions. Which premises do you recognize as similar to your existing values? Which premises represent values that are new or unfamiliar? Consider the meaning of each to you and your organization as you read through.

• To be a feminist is to assert our equal value as women in a society that too often undervalues our worth, contributions and experiences.

• To be a feminist is to challenge the inequities in power and privilege that exist because of sexism, classism, heterosexism, ageism, ableism, racism and all other forms of exclusion.

• To be a feminist is to question the institution of family as it is currently structured, and to challenge the roles and responsibilities of women and men in family care giving.

• To be a feminist is to be a strategist in challenging structures and institutions that are built upon male values and experience, and that limit women's equal participation.

• To be a feminist is to view the world through our women's eyes from our women's experience, and to see this lens as valuable and necessary in the pursuit of equality and inclusion.

• To be a feminist is to recognize, include and value women's different kinds of knowledge, including knowledge informed by personal experience and knowledge acquired through work and education.

• To be a feminist is to acknowledge that the world is not always a safe place for women to speak out about inequality. The strength that exists in the collective voice of women's organizations makes our challenges safer and more effective.

• To be a feminist is to take responsibility for learning about the issues that often seem to divide us (the environment, war, sexuality), and to create safe spaces to talk about our disagreements.

• To be a feminist is to challenge men to support our feminist agenda, and to support pro-feminist men who share our common agenda for peace, equality and justice.

• To be a feminist is to take pride in feminism as a movement for transforming the world into an equitable, peaceful and just place for women, men and children.

• To be a feminist is to examine our organization's principles, practices and processes to ensure that we are creating opportunities to include the perspectives of women whose voices have not been included (e.g., young women, seniors, lesbians, Aboriginal women).

• To be a feminist is to take our agenda for women's equality and inclusion into every meeting, regardless of the structured agenda.

• To be a feminist is to make every meeting a celebration, and every celebration a meeting: to continuously acknowledge both the challenges and joys of working for and with women.

13 Feminist Principles for Healthy Feminist Organizing

Feminist principles guide the work that we do within equality-seeking organizations, as well as the way that we do it. Taking the time to examine or revisit our feminist principles can assist in deepening our understanding of feminist practices and processes, and reconnecting with our feminist basis of unity. We have identified thirteen feminist principles that are informed by a diversity of women's backgrounds and experiences in feminist organizing: Accountability, Advocacy, Challenge and Conflict, Choice, Consultation, Diversity, Education and Mentoring, Equality and Inclusion, Evaluation, Joy and Celebration, Leadership, Power Sharing and finally, Safety.

This may be the first time you have considered these principles. You may also be very familiar with them, or have others of your own. Whether we are emerging organizations or new members of an established group, reflecting on our principles, practices and processes can assist in connecting the meaning of feminism to our equality-seeking mandate.

The Feminist Principle of Accountability

The feminist principle of accountability is necessary to building and maintaining healthy, active equality-seeking organizations. As feminists and feminist groups, we hold ourselves accountable to each other and to the global women's movement. This improves and strengthens our collective efforts toward peace, equality and justice.

The feminist principle of accountability means we hold ourselves responsible to the women we work for and with in our pursuit of equality and inclusion. We are accountable through our practice of feminist principles and our commitment to feminism as our basis of unity.

The Feminist Principle of Advocacy

The feminist principle of advocacy is central in our efforts toward an equitable and inclusive world for women and men. Through advocacy we apply our understanding and analysis of the issues affecting women as a call for improving our social, legal, political, economic and cultural status.

The feminist principle of advocacy means supporting or recommending a position or course of action that has been informed by women's experiences in our efforts to bring about equality and inclusion. Advocacy may take place through a variety of actions and strategies, ranging from demonstrations and protests to meetings and dialogue.

The Feminist Principle of Challenge and Conflict

The feminist principle of challenge and conflict is vital to feminist organizing. As feminists, we anticipate conflict as part of the learning and growing process in our work toward equality and inclusion. The feminist principle of challenge and conflict enables us to challenge our individual and collective understanding and work through conflict in a healthy way.

The feminist principle of challenge and conflict means that we accept conflict as inevitable while embracing challenge as the practice of calling into account, questioning, provoking thought, and reflecting. When we are committed to respectful ways of challenging and healthy conflict resolution processes, we deepen our individual and collective understanding.

The Feminist Principle of Choice

The feminist principle of choice is central to the mandate of equality-seeking organizations. It underlies both the work that we do and the way that we do it. Understanding the meaning of choice and how it informs our organization's work strengthens the collective women's movement.

The feminist principle of choice means that we respect, support and advocate for women's individual and collective right to make our own decisions about our bodies, our families, our jobs and our lives. The right to choose is integral to the feminist pursuit of social, legal, political, economic and cultural equality for women.

The Feminist Principle of Consultation

The feminist principle of consultation is necessary to building and maintaining connections to the women we work for and with in our equality-seeking organizations. Within the feminist movement, women and organizations work collaboratively to share information, ideas and strategies in our common efforts. By continuously consulting with others, we inform ourselves, our organizations and our communities about issues affecting women's social, legal, political, economic and cultural equality.

The feminist principle of consultation means working collaboratively, seeking guidance and sharing information to develop strategies and actions to advance women's equality.

The Feminist Principle of Diversity

The feminist principle of diversity is fundamental to healthy equality-seeking organizations. When we are inclusive and embrace a diversity of experiences and backgrounds, we increase our awareness and understanding of a broad range of issues affecting women, families and communities. This enables us to better represent the interests of the women we work both for and with in our pursuit of social, legal, political, economic and cultural equality.

The feminist principle of diversity means that we respect, accept and celebrate our individual and collective differences as women, including those based on age, race, culture, ability, sexuality, geography, religion, politics, class, education and image, among others.

The Feminist Principle of Education and Mentoring

The feminist principle of education and mentoring is crucial to the health of equality-seeking organizations. If we are to make real progress in our efforts toward equality, we must learn about the women who came before us, as well as the realities of women's lives today. The constant sharing of knowledge informed by women's experience is key to understanding our history and embracing the challenge of our work toward equality and social justice.

The feminist principle of education and mentoring means creating opportunities to guide, counsel, coach, tutor and teach each other. Constantly sharing our skills, knowledge, history and understanding makes our organizations healthier and more effective in our pursuit of equality and inclusion.

The Feminist Principle of Equality and Inclusion

The feminist principle of equality and inclusion is at the core of our equality-seeking work. As feminists, we acknowledge exclusion as the mechanism through which inequality is maintained. By applying the feminist principle of equality and inclusion to both the work and practices of our organizations, we reflect and strengthen our efforts toward women's social, legal, political, economic and cultural equality.

The feminist principle of equality and inclusion means, as feminist organizations, we apply a feminist analysis to policies, programs, practices, services and legislation to ensure they are inclusive of women and other marginalized groups. We advocate for equity practices to eliminate the barriers to inclusion, recognizing that inclusion leads to equality.

The Feminist Principle of Evaluation

The feminist principle of evaluation is necessary to the long-term effectiveness of equality-seeking organizations. Evaluation is one of the best ways to recognize and celebrate our individual and collective efforts within the women's movement. The feminist principle of evaluation can help identify our successes as well as our challenges in our ongoing efforts toward women's equality and inclusion.

The feminist principle of evaluation means taking the time to reflect upon whether we are achieving what we set out to do as well as how we are going about it. Evaluation presents an opportunity to examine the work that we do and the feminist principles, practices and processes that guide and inform this work.

The Feminist Principle of Joy and Celebration

The feminist principle of joy and celebration is at the heart of equality-seeking work. When we find ways to share joy and celebrate our collective action as women and organizations, we honour the generations of women who have worked for change throughout history. The feminist principle of joy and celebration can ignite passion in our work, strengthening our shared agenda for equality and inclusion.

The feminist principle of joy and celebration means that we honour each other and our work through sharing joy and celebrating our commitment to woman-centred, feminist principles, practices and processes.

The Feminist Principle of Leadership

The feminist principle of leadership is essential to our vision of healthy equality-seeking organizations. It is one of women and women's organizations sharing power, authority and decision-making in our common pursuit of social, legal, political, economic and cultural equality.

The feminist principle of leadership means embracing and sharing the skills and knowledge of individual women, and providing opportunities for all women to develop their leadership potential. As feminist organizations, we invest power and trust in our leaders with the expectation they will draw upon feminist practices and processes in our efforts toward equality and inclusion.

The Feminist Principle of Power Sharing

The feminist principle of power sharing is critical to feminist organizing. By sharing power with other members of our organization, we contribute to a healthy environment where all members feel engaged,

368

empowered, respected and validated. This distinguishes feminist equality-seeking organizations from mainstream organizational structures.

The feminist principle of power sharing means we are committed to creating balanced power relationships through democratic practices of shared leadership, decision-making, authority, and responsibility.

The Feminist Principle of Safety

The feminist principle of safety is essential to the development of healthy, inclusive organizations. As feminists, we work to create caring and supportive environments that promote our emotional and physical safety. The feminist principle of safety applies to all organizational practices and processes, and underlies much of what the women's equality movement is all about.

The feminist principle of safety means we are committed, as women and organizations, to creating environments where all women feel comfortable and safe to participate in our work toward equality. We build safety through healthy practices of inclusion, respect, self-care and confidentiality.

The kind of knowledge shared in *Feminism: Our Basis of Unity* is about feminist process, for that is how it was created. This is reflected in the years of ongoing consultations between the Provincial Advisory Council on the Status of Women and equality-seeking organizations that informed the book, as well as the process by which the book was actually written.

> This process has been most rewarding. Within these pages I see more than two decades of my experiences as a feminist activist, along with the hundreds of women who have informed and challenged these experiences. The style in which the book, *Feminism: Our Basis of Unity* has been crafted is a gift to the many women and women's organizations whose struggle for equality has given context and depth to the work. - Joyce Hancock

As feminists in equality-seeking organizations, our challenge is to build healthy feminist organizations where all women feel comfortable to voice their ideas and opinions, share stories and experiences, mentor and learn from each other, and seek information and assistance. The nature of our work presents many opportunities to discuss issues and strategies with members, and consult with other women on a regular basis. When we make the most of these opportunities, and demonstrate our commitment to feminist principles and practices, we advance our agenda for women's equality and inclusion.

Notes

[1] This is an excerpt from the book, *Feminism: Our Basis of Unity*, pro-

duced as a project of the Ad Hoc Committee of Equality Seeking Organizations coordinated by the Provincial Advisory Council on the Status of Women. The writing was completed in partnership with the Provincial Advisory Council on the Status of Women and the Women's Studies Program of Memorial University of Newfoundland. The book is intended for use as a mentoring tool for sparking discussions and facilitating workshops that are healthy, inclusive and participatory. Through discussion and dialogue, the book suggests how we may deepen our individual and common understanding of feminism as our basis of unity. Funding for this project was provided by the Women's Program, Status of Women Canada, and the Provincial Advisory Council on the Status of Women.

Her Mark

Michael Crummey

I, Ellen Rose of Western Bay in the Dominion of Newfoundland. Married woman, mother, stranger to my grandchildren. In consideration of natural love and affection, hereby give and make over unto my daughter Minnie Jane Crummey of Western Bay, a meadow garden situated at Riverhead, bounded to the north and east by Loveys Estate, to the south by John Lynch's land, to the west by the local road leading countrywards. Bounded above by the sky, by the blue song of angels and God's stars. Below by the bones of those who made me.

I leave nothing else. Every word I have spoken the wind has taken, as it will take me. As it will take my grandchildren's children, their heads full of fragments and my face not among those. The day will come when we are not remembered, I have wasted no part of my life in trying to make it otherwise.

In witness thereof I have set my hand and seal this thirteenth day of December, One thousand Nine hundred and Thirty Three.

Her
Ellen X Rose
Mark

REFERENCES

Adams-Roy, J. E. (1999). *Harassment in the Canadian Forces: Results of the 1998 Survey*. (Sponsor Research Report 99-11). Ottawa: Director of Human Resources Research and Evaluation.

Adkins, L. (1995). *Gendered Work: Sexuality, Family and the Labor Market*. UK: Open University Press.

Alexander, D. (1980). Newfoundland's Traditional Economy and Development. In J. Hiller and P. Neary (eds) *Newfoundland in the Nineteenth and Twentieth Centuries: essays in interpretation*. Toronto: University of Toronto Press: 17-30.

Alvesson, M. and S. Deetz. (1996). Critical Theory and Postmodernism Approaches to Organizational Studies. In S. R. Clegg, C. Hardy, W. R. Nord (eds.) *Handbook of Organization Studies*. UK: Sage Publications: 191-217.

Andersen, M. L. (1993). *Thinking About Women: Sociological Perspectives on Sex and Gender*. New York: Macmillan Publishing Company.

Andersen, M. L. (2003). *Thinking About Women: Sociological Perspectives on Sex and Gender*. Boston and Toronto:Allyn and Bacon.

Anspach, Rev. L. A. (1819). *A History of the Island of Newfoundland*. London: Anspach.

Antler, E. (1981). Fisherman, fisherwoman, rural proletariat: capitalist commodity production in the Newfoundland fishery. Doctoral Thesis. University of Connecticut.

Ashcraft, K. L. and D. K. Mumby. (2004). *Reworking Gender: A Feminist Communicology of Organization*. USA: Sage Publications.

Bailey, M. E. (1993). Foucauldian Feminism: Contesting Bodies, Sexuality and Identity. In C. Ramazanoglu (ed.) *Up Against Foucault: Explorations of Some Tensions Between Foucault and Feminism*. UK: Routledge: 19-122.

Bannister, J. (1999). The Custom of the Country: Justice and the Colonial State in Eighteenth Century Newfoundland. Doctoral Thesis. University of Toronto.

Barber, E.W. (1994). *Women's work: The first 20,000 years*. New York: W.W. Norton and Company.

Bauman, Z. (2000). *Liquid Modernity*. Cambridge: Polity Press.

Bay St. Lawrence Women's FishNet. (1996). Letter to the Nova Scotia Department of Human Resources. In *Nova Scotia Women's FishNet News* 2 (1): 2-3.

Beck, U. (1999). *World Risk Society*. Cambridge: Polity.

Becker, H. (1963). *Outsiders*. New York: Free Press.

Bellows, Brother G. R. (1975). The Foundations of Memorial University College: 1919-1925. *The Newfoundland Quarterly* 71 (4), Summer: 5-9.

Benoit, C. (1995). Urbanizing Women Military Fashion: The Case of Stephenville Women. In C. McGrath, B. Neis and M. Porter (eds.) *Their Lives and Times, Women in Newfoundland and Labrador: A Collage*. St. John's: Killick Press: 113-127.

Beynon, J. (2002). *Issues in Culture and Media Studies: Masculinities and Culture*. Buckingham: Open University Press.

Binkley, M. (1995). Lost Moorings: Offshore Fishing Families Coping with the Fisheries Crisis. In *Dalhousie Law Journal* 18 (1): 84-95.

Bissett-Johnson, A. and D. C. Day. (1986). *The New Divorce Law: A Commentary on the Divorce Act, 1985*. Toronto: Carswell.

Blackall, W.W. (1932). Adult Education in Newfoundland. In *The Newfoundland Quarterly* 32: 11-12.

Blackwood, G. (1996). Past and Future Goals and Objectives in the Allocation of the Northern Cod Resources. Masters Thesis. Memorial University.

Blades, T. (1996). *Three Years in the Woodshed*. Sunday Morning, December 1. Toronto: CBC Radio.

Boase, L. (ed.) (1961/1962). *Catholic Book of Knowledge*. Volume 3. London: Virtue and Company; reprint, Chicago: Catholic Home Press.

Bordo, S. (1993a). *Unbearable Weight: Feminism, Western Culture and the Body*. USA: University of California Press.

Bordo, S. (1993b). Feminism, Foucault and the Politics of the Body. In C. Ramazanoglu (ed.) *Up Against Foucault: Explorations of Some Tensions Between Foucault and Feminism*. UK: Routledge: 179-202.

Botting, I. (2002). Health restructuring and privatization from women's perspective in Newfoundland and Labrador. In P. Armstrong , C. Amaratunga, J. Bernier, K. Grant, A. Pederson, & K. Willson. (eds.) *Exposing Privatization: Women and health care reform in Canada*. Aurora: Garamond Press.

Bourke, A. (1988). The Irish Traditional Lament and the Grieving Process. In *Women's Studies International Forum* 11 (4): 287-91.

Boyce, J. K. (1995). Equity and the Environment: Social Justice Today as a Prerequisite for Sustainability in the Future. In *Alternatives* 21 (1): 12-17.

Brewis, J., M. P. Hampton and S. Linstead. (1997). Unpacking Priscilla: Subjectivity and Identity in the Organization of Gendered Appearance. In *Human Relations* 50 (10): 1275-1304.

Briskin, L. (1990). *Feminist Pedagogy: Teaching and Learning Liberation*. Feminist Perspectives Paper No. 19. Ottawa: CRIAW/ICREF.

Brookes, C. (1993). *On the Package: A Moratorium Diary*. Radio Documentary, CBC Fisheries Broadcast, October 18. St. John's: CBC Radio.

Burke, V. (1930). The Carnegie Corporation add to their Generosity. In *The Evening Telegram* 21 March 1930: 7.

Burke, V. (1937). Education in Newfoundland. In *The Book of Newfoundland* Vol. 1. St. John's: Newfoundland Book Publishers, 1937: 287-298.

Butler, J. (1990). *Gender Trouble: Feminism and the Subversion of Identity*. USA: Routledge.

Cadigan, S. (1991). Economic and Social Relations of Production on the Northwest Coast of Newfoundland, with specific reference to Conception Bay, 1785-1855. Doctoral Thesis. Memorial University.

Cahill, A. J. (2001). *Rethinking Rape*. Ithaca and London: Cornell University Press.

Campbell, C. (1998). Why action is needed in Sociology: A personal view. *Sociologia* 35 (2): 81-91.

Canadian Association of Elizabeth Fry Societies. (2004). Facts Sheets. Ottawa: CAEFS.

Canadian Council on Social Development. (2004). Poverty Lines. Retrieved 2004 from http://www.ccsd.ca/factsheets/fs_lico03_at.htm

Canadian Association of University Teachers (CAUT). (2004). *CAUT Almanac of Post-Secondary Education in Canada, 2004*. Ottawa: CAUT.

Canning, S. (1996). *A strategic plan for organizing and conducting community-based coastal resource inventories in Newfoundland and Labrador*. Consultation paper prepared for the Department of Fisheries and Oceans. Canning and Pitt Associates.

Canning, S. (1997). *Community coastal resources inventory handbook*. Prepared for the Department of Fisheries and Oceans. Canning and Pitt Associates.

Carlen, P. (ed.). (2002). *Women and Punishment: The Struggle for Justice*. Devon, UK: Willian Publishing.

Carlen, P. (1988). *Women, Crime and Poverty*. Milton Keynes: Open University Press.

Carr, D. (1996). Two Paths to Self-Employment? Women's and Men's Self-Employment in the United States, 1980. In *Work and Occupations* 23 (1), February: 26-53.

Carter, B. A. (1993). Employment in the Newfoundland and Labrador Fishery. In K. Storey (ed.) *The Newfoundland Groundfish Fisheries: Defining the Reality, Conference Proceedings*. St. John's: ISER, Memorial University.

Chamberlain, K. (1997). Socio-economic health differentials: from structure to experience. In *Journal of Health Psychology* 2: 399-411.

Changes in Rape Law Introduced. (1975). *Canadian Welfare* 51 (6): 23-24.

Church, J. T. (1999). Labouring in the Dream Factory, Part II. In *International Journal of Qualitative Studies in Education* (12) 3, May – June: 251-269.

Clark, L. (1977). Rape – Position Paper. In *Status of Women News* 4, (November): 11-15.

Clarke, J.N. (2000). *Health, Illness, and Medicine in Canada.* 3rd edition. Toronto, ON: Oxford University Press.

Clarkson, L. A. (1993). Love, Labour and Life: Women in Carrick-on-Suir in the Late Eighteenth Century. In *Irish Economic and Social History* 20: 18-34.

Cohen, A. (1982). *Belonging: Identity and Social Organisation in British Rural Cultures.* Social and Economic Papers No. 11. St. John's: ISER, Memorial University.

Cohen, A. (1986). *Symbolising Boundaries: Identity and Diversity in British Cultures.* Manchester: Manchester University Press.

Cohen, M. G. (1991). Women and Economic Structure. Paper presented to the National Association of Women and the Law Conference on the Feminization of Poverty. Toronto, February.

Cole, S. (1991). *Women of the Praia.* Princeton: Princeton University Press.

Collins, P. (1990). *Black Feminist Thought: Knowledge, Consciousness, and the Politics of Empowerment.* London: Harper Collins.

Comack, E. (1996). *Women in Trouble: Connecting Women's Law Violations to their Histories of Abuse.* Halifax: Fernwood.

Connelly, M. P. and M. MacDonald. (1995). State Policy: The Household and Women's Work in the Atlantic Fishery. In D. Frank and G. Kealey (eds.) *Labour and Working-Class History in Atlantic Canada: A Reader.* St. John's: ISER, Memorial University.

Connolly, S. J. (1982). *Priests and People in Pre-Famine Ireland, 1780-1845.* Dublin: Gill and Macmillan.

Cook, D. T. (1995). The Mother as Consumer: Insights from the Children's Wear Industry, 1917-1929. In *Sociological Quarterly* 36 (3): 505-522.

Cornfield, D. B., K. E. Campbell, and H. J. McCammon. (2001). Working in Restructured Workplaces: An Introduction. In D. B. Cornfield, K. E. Campbell, and H. J. McCammon (eds) *Working in Restructured Workplaces: Challenges and New Directions for the Sociology of Work.* Thousand Oaks, CA: Sage: xi – xxii.

Coveney, L., M. Jackson, S. Jeffreys, L. Kaye, and P. Mahoney. (1984). *Explorations in Feminism: the Sexuality Papers: Male Sexuality and the Social Control of Women.* London: Hutchinson and Company Ltd.

CRIAW. (2002). Violence Fact Sheet. Retrieved 17/05/05 from: http://www.criaw-icref.ca/factSheets/Violence_fact_sheet_e.htm.

Crill, R.C. (2003). *Parenting in the beginning years: Priorities for investment.* Invest in Kids Foundation, Toronto, Canada.

Cullum, L. K. (2003). *Narratives at Work: Women, Men, Unionization and the Fashioning of Identities.* St. John's: ISER, Memorial University.

Daly, M. (1981). Women in the Irish Workforce from Pre-industrial to Modern Times. *Saothar* 7: 74-82.

Davis, A. (1991). *Dire Straits: The Dilemmas of a Fishery: The Case of Digby Neck and the Islands.* St. John's: ISER, Memorial University.

Davis, D. (1995). Women in an Uncertain Age: Crisis and Change in a Newfoundland Community. In C. McGrath, B. Neis, M. Porter (eds.) *Their Lives and Times: Women in Newfoundland and Labrador, a Collage.* St. John's: Creative Publishing: 279-295.

DeKeseredy, W., S. Alvi, M. Schwartz, and A. Tomaszewski. (2003). *Under Siege: Poverty and Crime in a Canadian Public Housing Community.* Lanham, MD: Lexington Press.

Dellinger, K. and C. L. Williams. (1997). Makeup at Work: Negotiating Appearance Rules in the Workplace. In *Gender & Society* 11 (2): 151-177.

Dellinger, K. (2002). Wearing Gender and Sexuality 'On Your Sleeve': Dress Norms and the Importance of Occupational and Organizational Culture at Work. In *Gender Issues* 20 (1): 3-25.

DesRoches, M. and S. Lord. (1996). U.I. Problems: The Appeals and Frustrations. In *Nova Scotia Women's FishNet News* 2 (1): 11.

Deverell, K. (2001). *Sex, Work and Professionalism: Working in HIV/AIDS*. UK: Routledge.

Diner, H. R. (1983). *Erin's Daughters in America: Irish Immigrant Women in the Nineteenth Century.* Baltimore: Johns Hopkins University Press.

Donovan, C. and D. L. Gustafson. (2005). *Birth to five parenting guide*. Unpublished manuscript. Memorial University.

Drolet, M. (2001). The Persistent Gap: New Evidence on the Canadian Gender Wage Gap. Ottawa: Statistics Canada. Retrieved 20/07/04 from http://www.statcan.ca/english/research/11F0019MIE/11F0019MIE2001157.pdf

Drolet, M. (2002). The "Who, What, When and Where" of Gender Pay Differentials. Ottawa: Statistics Canada, Catalogue no.: 71-584-MIE2002004. Retrieved on 20/0704 from: http://www.statcan.ca/english/freepub/71-584-MIE/71-584-MIE02004.pdf

Drolet, Marie. (2003). Motherhood and Paycheques. In *Canadian Social Trends* (Spring) (68) Retrieved 07/04 from: http://estat.statcan.ca/content/english/articles/cst/cst-fin3.pdf

Duley, M. I. (1993). 'The radius of her influence for good': The rise and triumph of the women's suffrage movement in Newfoundland, 1909-1925. In L. Kealey (ed.) *Pursuing equality: Historical perspectives on women in Newfoundland and Labrador.* St. John's: ISER, Memorial University: 14-65.

Duley, M. I. (1993). *Where Once Our Mothers Stood We Stand: Women's Suffrage in Newfoundland, 1890-1925.* Charlottetown, PEI: Gynergy Books.

Dunfield, B. (1997). *Newfoundland Law Reports, 1947-1949.* St. John's: Law Society of Newfoundland.

Duxbury, L. and C. Higgins. (2003). Work-Life Conflict in the New Millennium: Status Report (Final Report: Executive Summary). Ottawa: Health Canada. Retrieved 01/02/04 from: http://www.hc-sc.gc.ca/pphb-dgspsp/publicat/work-travail/report2/index.html

McCurdy, E. (1996). *CBC Fisheries Broadcast.* December.

Eighty-year old Kansas native has had an interesting life. (1985). In *The Humber Log*, 6 March 1985: 5.

Educational Planning and Design Associates. (1994). *Women of the Fishery: Interviews with 87 Women Across Newfoundland and Labrador.* St. John's: Educational Planning and Design Associates.

E.I. E.I. Oh...Ottawa Picks Worker's Pockets. (1996). In *Union Advocate* 4 (2): 8-9, Spring/Summer. St. John's: Fish, Food and Allied Workers.

Ellis, P. B. (1995). *Celtic Women: Women in Celtic Society and Literature.* London: Constable.

English, C. (1990). The Development of the Newfoundland Legal System to 1815. In *Acadiensis* 20 (1): 89-119.

Enke, J. L. (1999). An Adjunct by Choice. In *Sociological Imagination* 36 (1): 13-17.

Enloe, C. (1983). *Does Khaki Become You? The Militarization of Women's Lives.* London: Pandora Press.

Entwistle, J. (2000). *The Fashioned Body: Fashion, Dress and Modern Social Theory.* UK: Polity Press.

Entwistle, J. (2002). The Dressed Body. In M. Evans and E. Lee (eds.) *Real Bodies: A Sociological Introduction.* USA: Palgrave.

Ewen, S. (1976). *Captains of Consciousness: Advertising and the Social Roots of the*

Consumer Culture. New York. McGraw-Hill Book Co.

Ewer, Rev. T. to Archbishop Troy. 30 November 1789 and 20 September 1796. (1984) In Cyril Byrne (ed.) *Gentlemen-Bishops and Faction Fighters: The Letters of Bishops O'Donel, Lambert, Scallan and Other Irish Missionaries*. St. John's: Jesperson Press: 77-9; 140-2.

Fairlie, S., M. Hagler, B. O'Riordan. (1995). The Politics of Overfishing. In *The Ecologist* 25 (2,3): 46-73.

FFAW/CAW Women's Committee. (1994). *Consultations with Women in the Newfoundland Fishery: A Report by the Women's Committee of Fishermen, Food and Allied Workers Union*. St. John's: Fish, Food and Allied Workers/Canadian Auto Workers.

Felt, L., B. Neis, B. McCay. (1998). Comanagement. In J. Boreman, B. S. Nakashima, J. A. Wilson and R. L. Kendall (eds.) *Northwest Atlantic Groundfish: Management Alternatives for Sustainable Fisheries*. Bethesda: American Fisheries Society: 185-195.

Fifty Years Ago at Muddy Bay. (1977). In *Among the Deep Sea Fishers* 74 (2) 1977:17-19.

Finlayson, C. A. (1994). *Fishing for Truth: A Sociological Analysis of Northern Cod Stock Assessments from 1977-1990*. St. John's: ISER, Memorial University.

Firestone, M. (1967). *Brothers and Rivals: Patrilocality in Savage Cove*. St. John's: ISER, Memorial University.

Fisheries Council of Canada. (1994). *Building a Fishery That Works: A Vision for the Atlantic Fisheries*. Ottawa: Fisheries Council of Canada.

Fiske, J. (1993). *Power Plays, Power Works*. UK: Verso.

FitzGerald, J. (1997). Conflict and Culture in Irish-Newfoundland Roman Catholicism, 1829-1850. Doctoral Thesis. University of Ottawa.

Fitzpatrick, D. (1987). The Modernisation of the Irish Female. In P. O'Flanagan, P. Ferguson, and K. Whelan (eds.) *Rural Ireland: Modernisation v. Change, 1600-1900*. Cork: Cork University Press: 162-80.

Flyvbjerg, B. (2001). *Making Social Science Matter: Why Social Inquiry Fails and How it Can Succeed Again*. Cambridge, UK.: Cambridge University Press.

Forestell, N. and J. Chisholm. (1988). Working Class Women as Wage Earners in St. John's, Newfoundland, 1890-1921. In P. Tancred-Sheriff (ed.) *Feminist Research: Prospect and Retrospect*. Kingston and Montreal: McGill-Queens Press: 141-155.

Forestell, N. M. (1987). *Women's Paid Labour in St. John's Between the Two World Wars*. Masters Thesis. St. John's: Memorial University.

Forestell, N. M. (1995). Times Were Hard: the Pattern of Women's Paid Labour in St. John's between the Two World Wars. In C. McGrath, B. Neis, & M. Porter (eds.) *Lives and Times: Women in Newfoundland and Labrador: A Collage*. St. John's: Killick Press: 76-92.

Fox, B. (2001). The Formative Years: How Parenthood Creates Gender. In *Canadian Review of Sociology and Anthropology* 38 (4), November: 373-390.

Frankish, C. J., L, W. Green, P. A. Ratner, T. Chomik, and C. Larsen. (1996). *Health Impact Assessment as a Tool for Population Health Promotion and Public Policy*. Vancouver, BC: Institute of Health Promotion Research, University of British Columbia.

Frazer, E. and N. Lacey. (1993). *The Politics of Community: A Feminist Critique of Liberal Communication Debate*. Toronto: University of Toronto Press.

Freeman, C. (1993). *Designing Women: Corporate Discipline and Barbados's Off- Shore Pink-Collar Sector*. In Cultural Anthropology 8 (2): 169-186.

Freidson, E. (1994). *Professionalism Reborn: Theory, Prophecy, and Policy*. UK: Polity Press.

Friel, J. K., M. Frecker, and F. C. Fraser (1995). Nutritional patterns of mothers of children with neural tube defects in Newfoundland. In *American Journal of Human Genetics* 55: 195-199.

Gadbois, S. (2002). Sickness, Health and Contract Employment. In E. Hannah, L. Paul, S. Vethamanay-Globus (eds) *Women in the Canadian Academic Tundra: Challenging the Chill.* Montreal: McGill-Queen's University Press: 63-66.

Gagan, D. and R. Gagan. (2002). *For Patients of Moderate Means: A Social History of the Voluntary Public Hospital in Canada, 1890-1950.* Montreal and Kingston: McGill Queen's University Press.

Giddens, A. (1994). Living in a Post-Traditional Society. In U. Beck, A. Giddens, and S. Lash (eds.) *Reflexive Modernization: Politics, Tradition and Aesthetics in the Modern Social Order.* Cambridge: Polity Press: 56-109.

Goodall Jr., H. L. (2003). What is Interpretive Ethnography? An Eclectic's Tale. In R. P. Clair (ed) *Expressions of Ethnography: Novel Approaches to Qualitative Methods.* Albany, NY: State University of New York Press: 49-61.

Goyder, J. (1992). Gender Inequalities in Academic Rank. In *Canadian Journal of Sociology* (17) 3: 333-343.

Green, E. (2001). Suiting Ourselves: Women Professors Using Clothes to Signal Authority, Belonging and Personal Style. In A. Guy, E. Green, M. Banim (eds.) *Through the Wardrobe: Women's Relationship with Their Clothes.* UK: Berg: 97-116.

Greenhill, P. and D. Tye. (1993). Women and Traditional Culture. In S. Burt, L. Code and L. Dorney (eds.) *Changing Patterns: Women in Canada.* 2nd edition. Toronto: McCelland and Stewart Inc: 309-329.

Grzetic, B. (2002). Between Life and Death: Women Fish Harvesters in Newfoundland and Labrador. Masters Thesis. St. John's: Memorial University.

Grzetic, B. (2004). *Women Fishes These Days.* Black Point, Nova Scotia: Fernwood Press.

Gustafson, D.L. (2005). Understanding Women and Health. In N. Mandell (ed.) *Feminist Issues: Race,Class and Sexuality.* 4th edition. Toronto: Pearson Prentice-Hall: 266-286.

Harling Stalker, L. L. (2000). Wool and needles in my casket: Knitting as habit among rural Newfoundland women. Masters thesis. St. John's: Memorial University.

Harman, L. D. and P. Remy. (2002). When Life Gets in the Way of Life: Work / Family Conflicts Among Academic Women and Men. In E. Hannah, L. Paul, S. Vethamanay - Globus (eds) *Women in the Canadian Academic Tundra: Challenging the Chill.* Montreal: McGill-Queen's University Press: 104-111.

Health Canada. (2003). *Women's Health Surveillance Report: A Multi-dimensional Look at the Health of Canadian Women.* Ottawa: Canadian Institute for Health Information.

Health Care Corporation of St. John's. (n.d.) The Waterford Hospital. Retrieved 14/12/04 from: http://www.hccsj.nl.ca/about/facilities/waterford.html

Hebert, C. (1998). *Guidelines for Gender Inclusive Analysis.* St. John's: Women's Policy Office, Government of Newfoundland and Labrador.

Heney, J., and C. Kristiansen. (1998). An Analysis of the Impact of Prison on Women Survivors of Childhood Sexual Abuse. In J. Harden and A. Hill (eds.) *Breaking the Rules: Women in Prison and Feminist Therapy.* New York: Haworth Press: 29-45.

Hertz, R. (1997). *Reflexivity and Voice.* Thousand Oaks, CA: Sage.

Hester, M. (1992). *Lewd Women and Wicked Witches: a Study of the Dynamics of Male Domination.* London and New York: Routledge.

Hills, M. (2002). *Fan Cultures.* London: Routledge.

Hochschild, A. R. (1997). *The Time Bind: When Work Becomes Home and Home Becomes Work.* New York: Metropolitan.

Holcombe, L. (1983). *Reform of Married Women's Property Law in Nineteenth-Century*

England. Toronto: University of Toronto Press.

hooks, b. (1988). *Talking Back: Thinking Feminist, Thinking Black.* Boston: South End Press.

hooks, b. (1990). *Yearning: Race, Gender and Cultural Politics.* Toronto: Between the Lines.

Horii, G. (2000). Processing Humans. In K. Hannah-Moffat and M. Shaw (eds.) *An Ideal Prison?: Critical Essays on Women's Imprisonment in Canada.* Halifax: Fernwood: 104-116.

House, J. D. (1985). *The Challenge of Oil: Newfoundland's Quest for Controlled Development.* St. John's: ISER, Memorial University.

Howley, M.F. (1888). *Ecclesiastical History of Newfoundland.* Boston: Doyle and Whittle.

Human Resources Development Canada. (2001). Employment Insurance (Fishing) Regulations: Part 1—Interpretation. Retrieved 05/02 from: http://www.hrdc-drhc.gc.ca/ae-ei/loi-law/ei_fish_regs_1.shtml/#interpretation_

Human Resources and Development (HRDC). (1994). *Agenda: Jobs and Growth Improving Social Security in Canada, A Discussion Paper.* Ottawa: Minister of Supply and Services.

Hutch, W. D. (1875). *Nano Nagle: Her Life, Her Labour and Their Fruits.* Dublin: McGlashen & Gill.

Hutchings, J. A. and R. A. Myers. (1995). The biological collapse of Atlantic cod off Newfoundland and Labrador: an exploration of historical changes in exploitation, harvesting technology, and management. In R. Arnason and L. Felt (eds.) *The North Atlantic Fisheries: Successes, Failures & Challenges.* Charlottetown, P.E.I.: Institute of Island Studies: 37-93.

Janzen v. Platy Enterprises Ltd. (1989) 10 C.H.R.R. D/6205 (S.C.C.)

Johnson, T. D. (1999). Matrimonial Property Law in Newfoundland to the end of the Nineteenth Century. Doctoral Thesis. Memorial University.

Johnson, Z. (1967-8). Calendar Customs and Rites of Passage at Renews. Memorial University of Newfoundland Folklore Archive [MUNFLA] ms. 68-011D. Unpublished research paper.

Jurik, N. C. (1998). Getting Away and Getting By: The Experiences of Self-Employed Homeworkers. In *Work and Occupations* 25 (1), February: 7 - 35.

Kaiser, S. B. (1997). *The Social Psychology of Clothing: Symbolic Appearances in Context.* 2nd edition revised. USA: Fairchild Publications.

Kasinsky, R. G. (1978). The Rise and Institutionalization of the Rape Crisis Movement in Canada. In M.A.B. Gammon (ed.) *Violence in Canada.* Toronto: Methuen: 151-167.

Kealey, L. (ed.). (1993). *Pursuing Equality: Historical Perspectives on Women in Newfoundland and Labrador.* St. John's: ISER, Memorial University.

Keough, W. G. (2001). The Slender Thread: Irish Women on the Southeastern Avalon, 1750-1860. Doctoral Thesis. Memorial University.

Keough, W. (2002). The Riddle of Peggy Mountain: The Regulation of Irish Women's Sexuality on the Southern Avalon, 1750-1860. In *Acadiensis* 31 (2), Spring: 36-70.

Keough, W. (2005). *The Slender Thread: Irish Women on the Southern Avalon Peninsula of Newfoundland, 1750-1860.* New York: Columbia University Press. Available at: http://www.gutenberg-e.org.

Keresztesi, G., J. Aucoin and D. L. Gustafson, with the Board of the Food Security Network. (2004). Submission to the Provincial Review of the Minimum Wage Rate: The case for a living wage. Food Security Network of Newfoundland and Labrador, St. John's, Newfoundland and Labrador. Retrieved 06/05 from: http://www.foodse-curitynews.com/

Knowles, M. (1964). The Field of Operations in Adult Education. In G. Jensen, A. A. Liveright, and W. Hallenbeck (eds.) *Adult Education: Outlines of an Emerging Field of University Study.* New York: Adult Education Association of the U.S.: 41-67.

Kosny, A. (2005). Women working in small workplaces. In *Envisioning Healthy Living For Women* 4 (2): 6-9.

Larkin, E. (1976). *The Historical Dimensions of Irish Catholicism.* New York: Arno Press.

Larkin, J. (1994). Walking through Walls: the sexual harassment of high school girls. In *Gender & Education* 6 (3): 263-80.

Larkin, M. (1990). Our Way of Living: Survival Strategies in Lobster Fishing Households in Prince Edward Island. Masters Thesis. Memorial University.

Leonard, M. (1994). Women's paid and unpaid handwork in a Belfast estate. In *Journal of Gender Studies* 3 (2): 187-195.

Litner, B. (2002). Teaching Doesn't Count. In E. Hannah, L. Paul, S. Vethamanay-Globus (eds) *Women in the Canadian Academic Tundra: Challenging the Chill.* Montreal: McGill-Queen's University Press: 129-132.

Livingstone, D. (2001). Public Education at the Crossroads: Confronting Underemployment in a Knowledge Society. In D. Glenday and A. Duffy (eds.) *Canadian Society: Meeting the Challenges of the Twenty-first Century.* Toronto: Oxford University Press: 143-167.

Lowe, G. S. (2000). *The Quality of Work: A People-Centered Agenda.* Don Mills: Oxford University Press.

Luxton, M. (ed) (1997). *Feminism and Families: Critical Policies and Changing Practices.* Halifax: Fernwood Publishing.

MacKinnon, C. (1982). Feminism, Marxism, Method, and the State: An Agenda for Theory. In *Signs* 7: 515-544.

Macleod, M. (1990). *A Bridge Built Halfway: a History of Memorial University College.* Montreal: McGill-Queen's University Press.

MacInnes, D. and A. Davis. (1996). Representational Management or Management of Representation?: The Place of Fishers in Atlantic Canadian Fisheries Management. In R. M. Meyer, C. Zang, M. L. Windsor, B. McCay, L. Hushak, and R. Muth (eds.) *Fisheries Utilization and Policy: Proceedings of the World Fisheries Congress, May 1992.* Theme 2 Volume. New Delhi: Oxford and IBH Publishing Co. Pvt. Inc: 317-332.

Mageean, D. (1997). To Be Matched or to Move: Irish Women's Prospects in Munster. In C. Harzig (ed.) *Peasant Maids — City Women: From the European Countryside to Urban America.* Ithaca: Cornell University Press: 57-97.

Maidment, M. (2002). Toward a Woman-Centered Approach to Community-Based Corrections: A Gendered Analysis of Women and Electronic Monitoring. In *Women & Criminal Justice* 13 (4): 47-68.

Marshall, B. (2000). *Configuring Gender: Explorations in Theory and Politics.* Peterborough: Broadview Press.

Mathews, M. and A. C. Edwards. (2004). Having a regular doctor: rural, semi-urban and urban differences in Newfoundland. In *Canadian Journal of Rural Medicine* 9 (3): 166-172.

Mauthner, N. S. and A. Doucet. (1998). Reflections on a Voice-Centred Relational Method of Data Analysis: Analysing Maternal and Domestic Voices. In J. Ribbens and R. Edwards (eds.) *Feminist Dilemmas in Qualitative Research: Private Lives and Public Texts.* London: Sage: 119-144.

Mauthner, N. S. (1999). Women and depression: Qualitative research approaches. In *Canadian Psychology* 40 (2): 143-61.

May, D. and A. Hollett. (1995). *The Rock in a Hard Place: Atlantic Canada and the UI Trap.* Ottawa: C.D. Howe Institute.

McCann, P. (1989). Class, Gender and Religion in Newfoundland Education, 1836-1901. In *Historical Studies in Education* 1 (2) Fall: 179-200.

McCann, P. (1994). *Schooling in a Fishing Society: Education and Economic Conditions in Newfoundland and Labrador 1836-1986*. St. John's: ISER, Memorial University.

McCay, B. (1988). Fish Guts, Hair Nets and Unemployment Stamps: Women and Work in Co-operative Fish Plants. In P. R. Sinclair (ed.) *A Question of Survival: The Fisheries in Newfoundland Society*. St. John's: ISER, Memorial University: 105-132.

McDowell, L. (1995). Body Work: Heterosexual Gender Performances in City Workplaces. In D. Bell and G. Valentine (eds.) *Mapping Desire: Geographies of Sexualities*. UK: Routledge.

McPherson, K. (1996). *Bedside Matters: The Transformation of Canadian Nursing, 1900-1990*. Toronto: Oxford University Press.

McRobbie, A. (1994). *Postmodernism and Popular Culture*. London: Routledge.

Messerschmidt, J. (1986). *Capitalism, Patriarchy, and Crime: Toward a Socialist Feminist Criminology*. Totowa, N.J.: Rowman & Littlefield.

Miller, R. (1990). Selling Mrs. Consumer: Advertising and the Creation of Suburban Socio-Spatial Relations, 1910-1930. In *Antipode* 23 (3): 263-306.

Mills, C. W. (1959). *The Sociological Imagination*. New York: Oxford University Press.

Mirchandani, K. (2000). The 'Best of Both Worlds' and 'Cutting My Own Throat': Contradictory Images of Home-Based Work. In *Qualitative Sociology* 23 (2): 159-182.

Moore, H. (1994). *A Passion for Difference: Essays in Anthropology and Gender*. Bloomington: Indiana University Press.

Morash, M. and P. Schram. (2002). *The Prison Experience: Special Issues of Women in Prison*. Prospect Hills, Illinois: Waveland Press.

Morris, M. (2001). *Women, health and action: A fact sheet. Canadian Research Institute on the Advancement of Women*. Retrieved 05/05 from: http://www.criaw-icref.ca

Moser, C. O. N. and F. C. Clark. (eds.) (2001). *Victims, Perpetrators or Actors? Gender, Armed Conflict and Political Violence*. London and New York: Zed Books.

Mosher, J., P. Evans, M. Little, Ontario Association of Interval Houses, and Ontario Social Safety Network. (2004). *Walking on Eggshells: Abused Women's Experiences of Ontario's Welfare System*. Final Report of Research Findings from the Woman and Abuse Research Project, Ontario.

Muddy Bay Sketches. (1929). In *Among the Deep Sea Fishers* 26 (4): 147-150.

Muggleton, D. (2000). *Inside Subculture: The Postmodern Meaning of Style*. Oxford: New York.

Munk-Madsen, E. (1996). *From Common Property to All-Male Property. Proceedings of the Workshop: Social Implications of Quota Systems*. Westman Islands, Iceland.

Murdoch, M., D. L. Gustafson and Independent Living Resource Centre [ILRC]. (2005). *Women with disabilities and adaptive technology: Summary report*. St. John's, NL: Independent Living Resource Centre.

Murray, C. L., L. Gien and S. M. Solberg. (2003). A comparison of the mental health of employed and unemployed women in the context of a massive layoff. In *Nurse Educator* 37 (2): 5-72.

Murray, H. C. (1979). *More Than 50%: A Woman's Life in a Newfoundland Outport*. St. John's: Breakwater Books.

Murray, H. C. (2002). *Cows Don't Know it's Sunday: Agricultural life in St. John's*. St. John's: ISER, Memorial University.

Nadel-Klein, J., and D. L. Davis. (eds.) (1988). *To Work and To Weep*. St. John's: ISER, Memorial University.

Neary, P. (1988). *Newfoundland in the North Atlantic World: 1929-1949*. Kingston and Montreal: McGill-Queen's University Press.

Neary, P. (1992). 'Wry Comment': Rhoda Dawson's Cartoon of Newfoundland Society, 1936. In *Newfoundland Studies* 8 (1), Spring: 1-14.

Neis, B. (1993). From "Shipped Girls" to "Brides of the State": The Transition from

Familial to Social Patriarchy in the Newfoundland Fishing Industry. In *Canadian Journal of Regional Science* 16 (2): 185-211.

Neis, B. (1998). The New Right Gender and Fisheries Crisis: Local and Global Dimensions. *Atlantis* 21 (2). Special Issue on Feminism and s: Strategies, Analysis and Praxis: 47-62.

Neis, B., L. Felt, D. C. Schneider, R. Haedrich, J. Hutchings and J. Fischer. (1999). Northern Cod Stock Assessment: What Can Be Learned From Interviewing Resource Users? In *Canadian Journal of Fisheries Aquatic Science* 56: 1949-1963.

Nevitt, J. (1978). *White Caps and Black Bands: Nursing in Newfoundland to 1934*. St. John's: Jesperson Press.

Newfoundland and Labrador Department of Health. (May 2004). *Oxycontin Task Force: Final Report*. St. John's, NL.: Queen's Printer.

Newfoundland and Labrador Sexual Assault Crisis and Prevention Centre Pamphlet. (n.d). St. John's: Newfoundland and Labrador Sexual Assault Crisis and Prevention Centre.

Newfoundland Population Returns. (1845). St. John's: Ryan and Withers.

Newton, R. (1951). *Memorial University of Newfoundland: A Survey*. Report to the Board of Regents, Memorial University.

Ng, R., G. Walker, and J. Muller. (1990). *Community Organization and the Canadian State*. Toronto, Ontario: Garamond Press.

Nolan, J. A. (1989). *Ourselves Alone: Women's Emigration from Ireland, 1885-1920*. Lexington: University Press of Kentucky.

Noreau, N. (2000). *Longitudinal Aspect of Involuntary Part-time Employment*. Ottawa: Statistics Canada. Retrieved July 17, 2004 from: http://www.statcan.ca/english/research/75F0002MIE/75F0002MIE2000003.pdf

O' Flaherty, P. (1999). *Old Newfoundland: A History to 1843*. St. John's: Long Beach Press.

O'Brien, A. (1967-8). Wake, Funeral and Burial Customs in Cape Broyle. Unpublished research paper. MUNFLA manuscript 68-016C.

O'Brien, D. (1991). *Suffer Little Children: An Autobiography of a Foster Child*. St. John's: Breakwater Books.

O'Neill, F. (1944). A Plan for the Development of an Adult Education Program for Rural Newfoundland. Doctoral Thesis. Columbia University.

Ocean Resources 19 (10), 2002.

Ommer, R. E. and P. R. Sinclair. (1999). Systemic crisis in rural Newfoundland: can the outports survive? In A. Dale and J. Pierce (eds.) *Communities, Development and Sustainability Across Canada*. Vancouver: University of British Columbia Press: 49-68.

Osberg, L. (1995). Is Unemployment or Unemployment Insurance the Problem in Atlantic Canada? In D. May and A. Hollett (eds.) *The Rock in a Hard Place: Atlantic Canada and the UI Trap*. Ottawa: C. D. Howe Institute: 215-228.

Otterstat, O. and D. Symes. (eds.) (1996). Sustainable Fisheries? Special issue of *Sociologia Ruralis* 36 (2).

Overton, J. (1996). Review of Doug May and Alton Hollett, The Rock in a Hard Place: Atlantic Canada and the UI Trap. Unpublished manuscript. Memorial University.

Palmer, Craig T. (1992). *The Northwest Newfoundland Fishery Crisis: Formal and Informal Management Options in the Wake of the Northern Cod Moratorium*. St. John's: ISER, Memorial University.

Parker, R. (1984). *The Subversive Stitch: Embroidery and the making of the feminine*. London: The Women's Press.

Parsons, M. (2002). McTeaching. In E. Hannah, L. Paul, S. Vethamanay-Globus (eds) *Women in the Canadian Academic Tundra: Challenging the Chill*. Montreal: McGill-Queen's University Press: 189-192.

Pate, K. (2003). A Tribute to Gayle Horii. In *Journal of Prisoners on Prisons* 12: 163-

169.

Pavalko, E. and B. Smith. (1999). The Rhythm of Work: Health Effects of Women's Work Dynamics. In *Social Forces* 77 (3): 1141-62.

Penney, Sr. M. P. (1980). A Study of the Contributions of Three Religious Congregations to the Growth of Education in the Province of Newfoundland. Doctoral Thesis. Boston: Boston College.

Pocius, G. (1979). *Textile Traditions of Eastern Newfoundland.* In National Museum of Man Mercury Series No. 29. Ottawa: National Museums of Canada.

Pope, S. G. and J. Burnham. (1993). Change Within and Without: The Modern Women's Movement in Newfoundland and Labrador . In L. Kealey (ed.) *Pursuing Equality: Historical Perspectives on Women in Newfoundland and Labrador.* St. John's: ISER, Memorial University: 163-221.

Porter, M., with B. Brown, E. Dettmer and C. McGrath. (1990). *Women and Economic Life in Newfoundland: Three Case Studies.* Report to the Social Sciences and Humanities Research Council of Canada.

Porter, M. (1993). *Place and Persistence in the Lives of Newfoundland Women.* Aldershot: Avebury.

Power-Kean, K.M. (2001). A stitch in time: Women and heart health quilt project. In *Canadian Nurse* 976: 30-32.

Pringle, R. (1988). *Secretaries Talk: Sexuality, Power & Work.* Australia: Allen & Unwin Pty. Ltd.

Pringle, R. (1989). Bureaucracy, Rationality and Sexuality: The Case of Secretaries. In J. Hearn, D. Sheppard, P. Tancred-Sheriff, G. Burrell (eds.) *The Sexuality of Organization.* UK: Sage Publications: 158-277.

Prowse, D.W. (1895). *A History of Newfoundland.* London: Macmillan and Co. Public Health Agency of Canada [PHAC]. (2003). Population health [website]. Retrieved 06/05 from: http://www.phacaspc.gc.ca/ph-sp/phdd/determinants/index.html#determinants

Quinton, D. (1962). Dr. Florence O'Neill. In *The Newfoundland Quarterly.* Fall 1962: 9-10.

Rail, G & Beausoleil, N. (2003). Introduction to 'Health panic and women's health.' In *Atlantis,* 27 (2): 1-5.

Rape Crisis Centre. (n.d.). How We Work Together. Rape Crisis Centre File. Centre for Newfoundland Studies, Queen Elizabeth II Library, Memorial University.

Rhoades, G. (1996). Reorganizing the Faculty Workforce for Flexibility: Part-time Professional Labor. In *Journal of Higher Education* (67) 6, December: 626-659.

Rhoda Dawson Obituary: A Missionary Zeal for Rag Rugs and Ruskin. (1992). In *The Guardian,* 31 March 1992.

Rinehart, J. W. (2001). *The Tyranny of Work: Alienation and the Labour Process.* 4th edition. Toronto: Harcourt Canada.

Robbins, N. (1995). *Gathering Our Voices: Women of Fishing Communities Speak.* Proceedings of workshops, West St. Modeste, Labrador June 9-10, 1995, Quirpon, Newfoundland, June 12-13, 1995. St. John's: ISER, Memorial University.

Robbins, N. (1997). *Images and realities: women's experiences in a Newfoundland and Labrador fishery crisis.* Masters Thesis. Memorial University.

Robinson, J. (1995). Women, Cultural Work and the Cod Moratorium. In *Parallelogramme* 20 (4): 21-29.

Rosenblum, G. and B. R. Rosenblum. (1990). Segmented Labor Markets in Institutions of Higher Learning. In *Sociology of Education* (63) 3, July: 151-164.

Ross, C. P. and M. P. Wright. (1998). Women's Work, Men's Work, and the Sense of Control. In *Work and Occupations* 25 (3), August: 333-355.

Rowe, A., Consulting Economists. (1991). *Effect of the Crisis in the Newfoundland Fishery on Women Who Work in the Industry.* St. John's: Women's Policy Office,

Government of Newfoundland and Labrador.

Rubinstein, R. P. (2001). *Dress Codes: Meaning and Messages in American Culture*. 2nd edition. USA: Westview Press.

Schur, E. (1984). *Labeling Women Deviant: Gender, Stigma, and Social Control*. New York: Random House.

Selman, G. and P. Dampier. (1991). *The Foundations of Adult Education in Canada*. Toronto: Thompson Educational Publishers.

Sennett, R. (1998). *The Corrosion of Character: The Personal Consequences of Work in the New Capitalism*. New York: W.W. Norton.

Shah, C. (2003). *Public health and preventative medicine in Canada*. 5th edition. Toronto: Elsevier.

Shanley, M. L. (1989). *Feminism, Marriage and the Family in Victorian England, 1850-1895*. Princeton: Princeton University Press.

Sheppard, D. (1989). Organizations, Power and Sexuality: The Image and Self-Image of Shore Pink-Collar Sector. In *Cultural Anthropology* 8 (2): 169-186.

Simon, R. (1995). Gender, Multiple Roles, Role Meaning, and Mental Health. In *Journal of Health and Social Behaviour* (36) 2, June: 182-194.

Sinclair, P. R. (1987). *State Intervention and the Newfoundland Fisheries*. Aldershot: Gower Avebury.

Sinclair, L., T. H. Downton, and H. Squires. (1999). Leaving and staying: Bonavista residents adjust to the moratorium. Occasional Paper Eco-Research Project, ISER, Memorial University.

Sketches of Labrador Life. (1979). In *Them Days* 5 (1): 28-31.

Skipwith, P. (1992). Rhoda Dawson. In *The Independent*, 2 April.

Smith, D. E. (1987). *The Everyday World as Problematic: A Feminist Sociology*. Boston: Northeastern University Press.

Smith, D. E. (1990). *The Conceptual Practices of Power: A Feminist Sociology of Knowledge*. Toronto: University of Toronto Press.

Solberg, S. (1997). The effect of the fishery closure on the health of the community. Paper presented at the *Summit of the Sea Conferences*, St. John's, Newfoundland.

Sparkes, A. C. (2002). Autoethnography: Self Indulgence or Something More? In A. P. Bochner and C. Ellis (eds.). *Ethnographically Speaking: Autoethnography, Literature and Aesthetics*. Walnut Creek: Altamira Press: 209 - 232.

St. John's Status of Women Council. (2003). *Something's Got to Change - Research Report: Gender Inclusive Analysis and Housing Policy Development in Newfoundland and Labrador*. St. John's: SJSWC.

Statistics Canada. (1993). The Violence Against Women Survey. In The Daily, November 18, 1993. Ottawa: Statistics Canada. Retrieved 17/05/05 from: http://www.swc-cfc.gc.ca/dates/dec6/facts_e.html#a.

Statistics Canada. (1996). Census of Canada. Retrieved 2004 from: http://www.statscan.estat2.ca

Statistics Canada. (2000). *Women in Canada 2000: A gender-based statistical report*. Ottawa, ON: Ministry of Industry.

Statistics Canada, Labor Force Characteristics. (2001). Experienced labor force 15 years and over by occupation and sex, by provinces and territories. Retrieved 2004 from: http://www.statcan.ca/english/Pgdb/labor45a.htm

Statistics Canada. (2002a). Gender Pay Differentials: Impact of the Workplace, 1999. Ottawa: Statistics Canada. Retrieved 19/06/2002 from: http://www.statcan.ca/Daily/English/020619/d020619b.htm

Statistics Canada. (2002b). Wives, Mothers and Wages: Does Timing Matter? Ottawa: Statistics Canada. Retrieved 1/05/2002 from: http://www.statcan.ca/Daily/English/020501/d020501a.htm

Statistics Canada. (2003). Reasons for Part-Time Work, Men and Women, 2002. Ottawa:

Statistics Canada # 89F0133XIE. Retrieved 11/10/03 from: http://www.statcan.ca/english/Pgdb/labor63c.htm

Statistics Canada. (2004). Average time spent on activities by sex, 1998. Ottawa: Statistics Canada, CANSIM, table 113-0001. Retrieved 18/08/04 from: http://www.statcan.ca/english/Pgdb/famil36a.htm

Statistics Canada. (2004). Labour Force Survey. Ottawa: Statistics Canada.

Statistics Canada. (2005). Study: the rising profile of women academics. In The Daily, February 24, 2005. Retrieved 24/02/05 from: http://www.statcan.ca/Daily/English/050224/d050224c.htm

Stetson, D. M. (1982). *A Woman's Issue: The Politics of Family Law Reform in England.* London: Greenwood Press.

Strategic Social Plan (SSP). (2003). *From the Ground Up.* St. John's: Government of Newfoundland and Labrador.

Strategic Social Plan. (2004). Community Accounts Profile. Government of Newfoundland and Labrador. Retrieved 2004 from: http://www.communityaccounts.ca

Strong-Boag, V. (1986). Ever a crusader: Nellie McClung, first-wave feminism. In V. Strong-Boag and A. S. Fellman (eds.) *Rethinking Canada: The Promise of Women's History.* Toronto: Copp Clark Pitman: 178-190.

Strong-Boag, V. (1988). *The New Day Recalled: Lives of Girls and Women in English Canada, 1919-1939.* Toronto: Copp Clark Pitman, Ltd.

The Cost of Eating in Newfoundland and Labrador. (2003). St. John's, Newfoundland and Labrador: Dietitians of Newfoundland and Labrador. Retrieved 06/05 from: http://n/asw.ca/news

Task Force on Federally Sentenced Women. (1990). *Creating Choices: Report of the Task Force on Federally Sentenced Women.* Ottawa: Ministry of the Solicitor General.

Task Force on Incomes and Adjustment in the Atlantic Fishery. (1993). *Charting a New Course: Towards the Fishery of the Future.* Ottawa: Minister of Supply and Services, Government of Canada.

Taylor, S. (2001). Living on the other side of nowhere: unravelling meanings of community in the context of the TAGS era. Doctoral Thesis. Memorial University of Newfoundland.

Theophano, J. (2002). *Eat my words: Reading women's lives through the cookbooks they wrote.* New York: Palgrave Macmillan.

Tirelli, V. (1997). Adjuncts and More Adjuncts: Labor Segmentation and the Transformation of Higher Education. In *Social Text* (51) Summer: 75.

Toril Pettersen, L. (1996). Crisis Management and Household Strategies in Lofoten: A Question of Sustainable Development. In *Sociologia Ruralis* 36 (2): 236-248.

Toulson, S. (1996). *The Celtic Year: A Month-by-Month Celebration of Celtic Christian Festivals and Sites.* Shaftesbury: Element.

Tremblay, S. (1999). Canadian Crime Statistics in Canada, 1998. In *Juristat* 19 (9). Ottawa: Canadian Centre for Justice Statistics (CCJS), Statistics Canada.

Trethewey, A. (1999). Disciplined Bodies: Women's Embodied Identities at Work. In *Organization Studies* 20 (3): 423-450.

United Nations. (1995). Report of the 4th World Conference on Women. Paper presented at the United Nations platform for action on women's equality, Beijing.

Vosko, L. (2003). Precarious employment in Canada: Taking stock, taking action. *Just Labour: A Canadian Journal of Work and Society* (3), Fall. Retrieved 10/04 from: http://www.yorku.ca/julabour/volume3

Waquant, L. (2003). America's New "Peculiar Institution": On the Prison as Surrogate Ghetto. In T. Blomberg and S. Cohen (eds.) *Punishment and Social Control.* New York: Aline de Gruyter: 471-482.

Waring, M. (1988). *If Women Counted: A New Feminist Economics*. San Francisco: Harper and Row.

Waring, M. (1995). *Who's counting?: Marilyn Waring on Sex, Lies & Global Economics*. Videorecording directed and edited by Terre Nash. Montreal: National Film Board of Canada.

Welch, M. (1997). Regulating the Reproduction and Morality of Women: The Social Control of Body and Soul. In *Women and Criminal Justice* 9 (1): 17-38.

Whelan, K. (1995). The Catholic Church in County Tipperary 1700-1900. In William Nolan (ed.) *Tipperary: History and Society Interdisciplinary Essays on the History of an Irish County*. Dublin: Geography Publications: 215-255.

White, L. (1992). The General Hospital School of Nursing, St. John's, Newfoundland. Master's Thesis. Memorial University.

Williams, K. (1980). From Sarah Gamp to Florence Nightingale: a Critical Study of Hospital Nursing Systems from 1840 to 1897. In C. Davies (ed.) *Rewriting Nursing History*. London: Croom Helm: 41-75.

Williams, S. (1996). *Our Lives are at Stake: Women and the Fishery Crisis in Newfoundland and Labrador*. ISER report no. 11. St. John's: ISER, Memorial University.

Williams, S. (1998*). What's Happening with Youth: The Impact of Economic Change on Young People in Newfoundland and Labrador*. A Report prepared for Health Canada by the Canadian Mental Health Association, Newfoundland and Labrador Division.

Willis, P. (1977/81). *Learning to Labor: How Working Class Kids Get Working Class Jobs*. New York: Columbia University Press.

Woodrow, M. (1996). Resistance to regulatory changes in the fishery: a study of selected Communities in Bonavista, Newfoundland. Doctoral Thesis. Université Laval.

Women's Centre Opens. *Evening Telegram* [St. John's] 26 June 1978: 2

Wright, M. (2001). *A Fishery For Modern Times: The State and the Industrialization of the Newfoundland Fishery, 1934-1968*. Toronto: Oxford University Press.

LINDA CULLUM is a teacher, researcher and writer working in Sociology and Women's Studies at Memorial University. She has written and presented most recently on women and fish plant work in the 1940s, and is active in community work with equality-seeking groups.

CARMELITA MCGRATH has written seven books of poetry, fiction and children's literature. She has also edited many books including *Their Lives and Times, Women in Newfoundland and Labrador, a collage* (Killick, 1995).

MARILYN PORTER is a University Research Professor, teacher and researcher in Sociology and Women's Studies at Memorial University. She has authored and edited several books and her articles have appeared internationally. Originally from the UK, she has called Newfoundland home since 1980.

CONTRIBUTORS

LOUISE BELBIN was born in 1897 in Jacques Fontaine, and worked for fourteen years as a "beach woman" at Grand Bank, making salt fish.

TERRY BISHOP-STIRLING teaches the History of Women in Newfoundland and Labrador and other courses at Memorial University. Her articles and presentations focus on Newfoundland social and political history, with emphasis on health and welfare policy, women's history and volunteerism.

MOIRA BOWRING, born in 1916, was the daughter of David and Emma Baird. She married Derrick Bowring in 1940, thus joining two prominent St. John's families. She raised four children and corresponded regularly with relatives in England and elsewhere about family life in St. John's.

NYMPHA BYRNE is an activist fighting for Innu land rights and self-determination. She worked for over ten years with Social Services, is trained in addictions counseling and has been active in the healing movement in her community of Utshimassits.

ROBERTA BUCHANAN is a writer and Memorial University Professor Emerita. Her books include *I Moved All My Women Upstairs* (poetry, Breakwater Books) and *The Woman Who Mapped Labrador: the Life and Expedition Diary of Mina Hubbard*; diary edited by Roberta Buchanan and Bryan Greene, biography by Anne Hart, recently short-listed for a Winterset award.

FRANCES CLUETT was born in Belleoram, Fortune Bay in 1883. She taught school there and in 1916 joined the Volunteer Aid Detachment of St. John Ambulance, becoming a nurse in France during World War I.

MICHAEL CRUMMEY is the author of three books of poetry, a collection of short stories and two novels. His most recent novel, *The Wreckage,* (Doubleday) was nominated for the 2005 Roger's Trust Fiction Prize.

MARY DALTON is the author of three books of poetry, *The Time of Icicles*, *Allowing the Light* and *Merrybegot* , winner of the 2005 E. J. Pratt Poetry Award. *Merrybegot* was released as an audiobook by Rattling Books in 2005. A new volume, *Red Ledger*, is coming out from Véhicule Press in 2006.

RHODA DAWSON, an artist and designer, was born in 1897 in Chiswick, England. She worked in Newfoundland and Labrador with Sir Wilfred Grenfell, teaching crafts and designing hooked mat patterns. In 1931-32, she traveled on the coast of Labrador, painting and exploring the communities.

FANNY FIANDER was a prolific writer of poems, stories and letters. She was born in Harbour Grace in 1889 and settled in Trinity with her husband George and their four children. During the late 1940s, she campaigned for Responsible Government, making radio broadcasts and public speeches around Conception Bay.

SARA FLAHERTY studied History at Memorial University of Newfoundland, completing a BA (Honours) in 1999 and MA 2002. She lives in Halifax, Nova Scotia where she works as an historical researcher for the Department of Justice.

LOUISA FLOWERS was born in Quebec but moved with her family to Hebron, northern Labrador soon after. In 1959, she moved to Nain and married there. For many years, Louisa returned north in the summer, living off the land with her family, following traditional ways.

DIANA GUSTAFSON'S keen interest in health-related social justice issues infuses her life as a researcher, educator, nurse, mother, and active community member. She is an assistant professor of social sciences and health in Community Health and Humanities, Faculty of Medicine at Memorial University.

BRENDA GRZETIC worked as an electronics technologist and an advocate of women in trades and technology before completing her MA in Women's Studies at Memorial University. She is pursuing her PhD at Dalhousie University. Her research focuses on women's changing lives in rural Newfoundland and Labrador.

L. LYNDA HARLING STALKER comes from a long line of knitters. When not knitting, she is completing her PhD in Sociology at Carleton University, focusing on self-employed Newfoundland craftspeople and the place of craft in contemporary society, or spending time with her family: Andrew, Asta Merie, and Adam.

LYNN HARTERY graduated from the Memorial University Master's of Women's Studies Program in 2002. She continues to work in research, particularly in the areas of anti-violence and social justice.

CAROL HOBBS grew up in Springdale, NL and lives in Massachusetts. Her writing has appeared in journals in the United States, Canada and Ireland. Her poetry manuscript *New Founde Lande* was awarded a PEN New England Discovery Award in 2004.
Marie Pokue is from Natuashish, the daughter of Shimun and Shaet (Simon and Janet Poker). She is married to Simon Pokue, Chief of Natuashish and has four children living, Dorothy, Donna, Damien and Desiree, and four grandchildren. Her son Darren died in 2003. Marie trained as an addictions counselor and has worked with the Mushuau Innu First Nation since 2003.

ANNETTE JOHNS is a registered social worker and former Executive Director of the Newfoundland and Labrador Sexual Health Centre. She was one of the principal investigators for and co-author of *Adolescent Sexual Decision-Making in Newfoundland and Labrador.*

WILLEEN KEOUGH is an assistant professor of history at Simon Fraser University, with research interests in gender, ethnicity and class in eighteenth and nineteenth-century Newfoundland communities.

BRENDA L. KITCHEN was born in Robinson's, NL. She holds BA and MA degrees in Sociology fom Memorial University. She is the Executive Director of the Newfoundland and Labrador Sexual Health Centre. She strongly identifies as a feminist and is proud to be a contributor to this book.

MADONNA MAIDMENT is assistant professor in Sociology and Anthropology, University of Guelph. Her most recent work, *Doing Time on the Outside: Deconstructing the Benevolent Community*, will be published by University of Toronto Press in 2006.

DONNA MALONE was the first Coordinator of the Regional Coordinating Coalition Against Violence, 2000-2002. She is interested in gender and anti-racism issues, and is completing a Master of Adult Education degree on anti-racist and whiteness education by white people.

MELANIE MARTIN was born in Stephenville, NL and raised in Manitoba. In 1998, she returned, completed an undergraduate degree in History and Newfoundland Studies and then an MA in History in 2003. She lives in St. John's with her husband, and continues to research and write.

BERNICE MORGAN is the author of the novels *Random Passage* and the award-winning *Waiting for Time* and the short story collection, *The Topography of Love*, all published by Breakwater Books.

LISA MOORE is the author of two collections of short stories, *Degrees of Nakedness* and the Giller Prize nominated *Open*. Her first novel, *Alligator*, (Anansi, 2005) was shortlisted for the Giller Prize and won the Commonwealth Prize for the Canadian/Carribean Region.

ROBIN MCGRATH is the author of nine books of poetry, fiction, children's literature and non-fiction. Her most recent book is the poetry collection *Covenant of Salt* (Killick Press, 2005).

KATHERINE MCMANUS is an adult educator, instructional designer for online distance education programs, and textile artist. She works at the Centre for Online and Distance Education at Simon Fraser University in British Columbia.

BARBARA NEIS is co-director of SafetyNet, A Research Alliance in Workplace Health and Safety in Marine and Coastal Work, and professor of Sociology at Memorial University. Her areas of research include occupational asthma to snow crab and fishing vessel safety, the health impacts of restructuring in the Newfoundland and Labrador fisheries, and local ecological knowledge and science.

LINDA PARSONS has been a contract teacher in Sociology for too many years to count and is currently working on her doctorate in Sociology at Memorial University. She hopes to finish that degree before she retires.

CHRISTINE (KISITINIS) POKER was born in North West River and lives in Natuashish. She uses her writing, filmmaking and video art to explore issues such as sobriety, self-government, leadership and traditional healing.

HELEN FOGWILL PORTER is the author of four books, including *A Long and Lonely Ride* (Breakwater Books, 1991) and the award-winning *January, February, June or July* (Breakwater Books, 1988). She is working on a novel.

FRANCES PYE was born in Kansas, USA in 1904. During the mid-1920s, she worked as a teacher in Labrador, serving at Muddy Bay, North West River and St. Mary's for the International Grenfell Association.

SUSAN RENDELL wasn't born in Newfoundland but it couldn't be helped. She is a free-lance writer and editor in St. John's. Her first fiction collection, *In the Chambers of the Sea* (Killick, 2003), won the 2004 Newfoundland and Labrador/Bennington Gate Book Award.

JANE ROBINSON worked on gender, diversity and housing issues for the St. John's Status of Women Council. She is President of CRIAW and sits on the National Working Group on Women and Housing. She works for the Canadian Coalition for Women in Engineering, Science, Trades and Technology, and teaches in Women's Studies at Memorial University.

BETH RYAN is a St. John's writer and editor. Her first book of short fiction, *What Is Invisible*, (Killick, 2003), won the Margaret and John Savage First Book Award and was shortlisted for the Newfoundland and Labrador Book Award for Fiction and Best Atlantic Published Book prize. She is working on a new book.

PETER R. SINCLAIR is University Research Professor in Sociology at Memorial University. His current research interests are global commodity networks and local restructuring; power relations. He is the author of *From Traps to Draggers*, *When the Fish Are Gone*, six other books and over 100 refereed articles, chapters and reviews.

JOANNE SOPER-COOK is the author of five books of fiction, including *Waterborne* (Goose Lane Editions), *The Opium Lady* (Goose Lane Editions) and the debut of her Inspector Devlin period mystery series, *A Cold-Blooded Scoundrel* (Brazen Books/Flanker Press).

SUE SINCLAIR grew up in Newfoundland and lives in Toronto. She is the author of three books of poetry, *Secrets of Weather & Hope* (Brick Books, 2001), *Mortal Arguments* (Brick Books, 2004) and *The Drunken Lovely Bird* (Goose Lane Editions, 2004).

MICHELLE SMITH is a feminist advocate working in women's equality-seeking organizations. She pioneered the first community-based internship Master's in Women's Studies at Memorial University, developing *Feminism: Our Basis of Unity*, a guidebook for women on the front lines of feminist work.

SHARON TAYLOR participates in provincial, national and international initiatives to improve social justice through health and education. An associate professor of Social Work at Memorial University, she is co-director of a project to develop the first School of Social Work in Vietnam.

KARENE TWEEDIE is a Nurse Educator at the Centre for Nursing Studies in St. John's. She studied Social Sciences, then midwifery, in the UK and worked as a midwife in northern Newfoundland before entering nursing education. She is Vice-President of the Newfoundland and Labrador Sexual Health Centre.

ONAR USAR has a BSc. in Business Management. She is completing her Master's in Women's Studies at Memorial University and plans to complete her doctorate as well.

AGNES WALSH is the first Poet Laureate of St. John's. She has worked in professional theatre for 25 years and is artistic director of Tramore Theatre on the Cape Shore. Her first collection of poetry was *In the Old Country of My Heart*; her second will be published by Brick Books in 2007.

KATHY WATKINS is a Nurse Educator at the Centre for Nursing Studies in St. John's and teaches at Memorial University. Prior to teaching, she was a staff nurse at the Grace General Hospital in Women's Health. She is President of the Newfoundland and Labrador Sexual Health Centre.

CARLA WHEATON completed a Ph.D. in Newfoundland history at Memorial University of Newfoundland in 2002 and now works with the national historic sites section of Parks Canada.

MARIAN FRANCES WHITE'S published works include two books of poetry, ten editions of *A Woman's Almanac*; *Voices of Atlantic Canadian Women*; *The Finest Kind, a Compendium of Almanac stories; Not A Still Life, the art and writings of artist Rae Perlin* and a *History of Newfoundland and Labrador* (Grolier Ltd.)

SUSAN WILLIAMS is a researcher in St. John's who has worked on gender and fisheries, occupational health in fish plants and housing needs of low-income women. She is the author of *Our Lives are at Stake: Women and the Fishery Crisis in Newfoundland and Labrador* (ISER, Memorial University).

LORI YETMAN has worked as Memorial University's Sexual Harassment Advisor since 2000. In addition to handling complaints and educating the campus about issues pertaining to gender and sexual harassment, she teaches an introductory Women's Studies course.

ACKNOWLEDGEMENTS
The editors and publishers wish to thank the copyright holders, including individual authors and the following publishers and publications, for permission to use the works in this volume.

Atlantis: A Women's Studies Journal 21.2 for "The New Right, Gender and the Fisheries Crisis: Local and Global Dimensions by Barbara Neis and Susan Williams, an earlier version of which was published in this journal;
Atlantis: A Women's Studies Journal 26.2 for "Narrowing the Gap" by Peter Sinclair, an earlier version of which was published in this journal;
Breakwater Books for "Unfinished Houses" from *The Topography of Love* by Bernice Morgan, 2000;
Brick Books for "Green Pepper" and "The Pitcher" from *Secrets of Weather & Hope* by Sue Sinclair, 2001;
Brick Books for "Her Mark" from *Hard Light* by Michael Crummey, 1998;
Educational Planning and Design Associates for Life Stories of Louise Belbin and Violet Green & Louisa Flowers from *Strong as the Ocean: Women's Work in the Newfoundland and Labrador Fisheries* by Frances Ennis and Helen Woodrow (eds.), 1996;
Goose Lane Editions for "A Suitable Woman" and "Effie's Landwash" from *The Opium Lady* by Joanne Soper-Cook, 2003;
House of Anansi for "The Stylist" from *Open* by Lisa Moore, 2002;
Vehicule Press for "Mat" and "Rosella and Bride" by Mary Dalton from *Merrybegot*, 2003.